Complexity Perspectives on Researching Language Learner and Teacher Psychology

FSC
www.fsc.org
MIX
Paper from
responsible sources
FSC® C014540

PSYCHOLOGY OF LANGUAGE LEARNING AND TEACHING

Series Editors: Sarah Mercer, *Universität Graz, Austria* and Stephen Ryan, *Waseda University, Japan*

This international, interdisciplinary book series explores the exciting, emerging field of Psychology of Language Learning and Teaching. It is a series that aims to bring together works which address a diverse range of psychological constructs from a multitude of empirical and theoretical perspectives, but always with a clear focus on their applications within the domain of language learning and teaching. The field is one that integrates various areas of research that have been traditionally discussed as distinct entities, such as motivation, identity, beliefs, strategies and self-regulation, and it also explores other less familiar concepts for a language education audience, such as emotions, the self and positive psychology approaches. In theoretical terms, the new field represents a dynamic interface between psychology and foreign language education and books in the series draw on work from diverse branches of psychology, while remaining determinedly focused on their pedagogic value. In methodological terms, sociocultural and complexity perspectives have drawn attention to the relationships between individuals and their social worlds, leading to a field now marked by methodological pluralism. In view of this, books encompassing quantitative, qualitative and mixed methods studies are all welcomed.

All books in this series are externally peer-reviewed.

Full details of all the books in this series and of all our other publications can be found on http://www.multilingual-matters.com, or by writing to Multilingual Matters, St Nicholas House, 31–34 High Street, Bristol BS1 2AW, UK.

PSYCHOLOGY OF LANGUAGE LEARNING AND TEACHING: 10

Complexity Perspectives on Researching Language Learner and Teacher Psychology

Edited by
Richard J. Sampson and Richard S. Pinner

MULTILINGUAL MATTERS
Bristol • Blue Ridge Summit

DOI https://doi.org/10.21832/SAMPSO3552
Library of Congress Cataloging in Publication Data
A catalog record for this book is available from the Library of Congress.
Names: Sampson, Richard J., editor. | Pinner, Richard S., editor.
Title: Complexity Perspectives on Researching Language Learner and Teacher Psychology/Edited by Richard J. Sampson and Richard S. Pinner.
Description: Bristol, UK; Blue Ridge Summit, PA: Multilingual Matters, 2021. | Series: Psychology of Language Learning and Teaching: 10 | Includes bibliographical references and index. | Summary: "This book showcases the experiences of researchers conducting complexity research in situated educational contexts. The chapters present practical examples of how complexity research can be done, with convincing evidence of why a complexity perspective is useful for investigating and conceptualizing the psychology of language learners and teachers"—Provided by publisher.
Identifiers: LCCN 2020024911 (print) | LCCN 2020024912 (ebook) | ISBN 9781788923545 (paperback) | ISBN 9781788923552 (hardback) | ISBN 9781788923569 (pdf) | ISBN 9781788923576 (epub) | ISBN 9781788923583 (kindle edition)
Subjects: LCSH: Languages, Modern—Study and teaching—Psychological aspects. | Second language acquisition—Psychological aspects. | Classroom environment. | Motivation in education.
Classification: LCC PB36 .C56 2021 (print) | LCC PB36 (ebook) | DDC 418.0071—dc23 LC record available at https://lccn.loc.gov/2020024911
LC ebook record available at https://lccn.loc.gov/2020024912

British Library Cataloguing in Publication Data
A catalogue entry for this book is available from the British Library.

ISBN-13: 978-1-78892-355-2 (hbk)
ISBN-13: 978-1-78892-354-5 (pbk)

Multilingual Matters
UK: St Nicholas House, 31–34 High Street, Bristol BS1 2AW, UK.
USA: NBN, Blue Ridge Summit, PA, USA.

Website: www.multilingual-matters.com
Twitter: Multi_Ling_Mat
Facebook: https://www.facebook.com/multilingualmatters
Blog: www.channelviewpublications.wordpress.com

Typeset by Nova Techset Private Limited, Bengaluru and Chennai, India.
Printed and bound in the UK by Short Run Press Ltd.
Printed and bound in the US by NBN.

Contents

Contributors

Takumi Aoyama is an Assistant Professor of English language education at Shinshu University, Japan. He received his MA in English Language Teaching from the University of Warwick in 2016, where he is currently pursuing his PhD in English Language Teaching and Applied Linguistics. His current research interests include Japanese EFL learners' motivation, language learning experience and research methods for second language research. Also, he is presently co-organizing the Forum on Language Learning Motivation (FOLLM) with Sal Consoli.

Sal Consoli is a lecturer in Applied Linguistics and TESOL at Newcastle University. Before joining Newcastle, he taught on the BA and MA in TESOL & Applied Linguistics at the University of Warwick. His research interests are concerned with EAP practice and policy, internationalization of higher education, motivational psychology for teaching and learning, and research ethics. His work sits within the epistemological and method-ological traditions of narrative inquiry and practitioner research (i.e. Action Research and Exploratory Practice). Sal is co-founder of the Forum on Language Learning Motivation (FOLLM) and serves on the Executive Committee of the British Association of Applied Linguistics (BAAL).

Joseph Falout authored or co-authored over 50 papers and book chapters about language learning psychology. He received awards for publications and presentations from the Japan Association for Language Teaching (JALT). He edits for JALT's *OnCUE Journal* and *Asian EFL Journal*. Collaborations include creating theoretical and applied foundations of critical participatory looping, present communities of imagining and ideal classmates. An associate professor at Nihon University (Japan), Joseph teaches EAP and ESP to graduate and undergraduate students, and he conducts workshops for teachers at all educational levels. He has taught rhetoric and composition, public speaking and ESL at colleges in the USA.

Anne Feryok is a Senior Lecturer in the Department of English and Linguistics at the University of Otago, New Zealand. Her research area is language teacher cognition and development. Most of it uses Vygotskian sociocultural theory, which has influenced her occasional cautious forays into complex dynamic systems theory. Her work has been published in international journals such as *Modern Language Journal, Language Teaching Research, System* and *Teachers and Teaching: Theory and Practice.*

Christina Gkonou is Associate Professor of TESOL and MA TESOL Programme Leader in the Department of Language and Linguistics at the University of Essex, UK. She convenes postgraduate modules on teacher education and development, and on psychological aspects surrounding the foreign language learning and teaching experience. She is the co-editor of *New Directions in Language Learning Psychology* (with Sarah Mercer and Dietmar Tatzl) and *New Insights into Language Anxiety: Theory, Research and Educational Implications* (with Jean-Marc Dewaele and Mark Daubney), and co-author of *MYE: Managing Your Emotions Questionnaire* (with Rebecca L. Oxford). Her new book, entitled *The Emotional Rollercoaster of Language Teaching* (co-edited with Jean-Marc Dewaele and Jim King) was published in May 2020.

Tammy Gregersen, a Professor of TESOL at the American University of Sharjah in the United Arab Emirates, received her MA in Education and PhD in Linguistics in Chile, where she began her academic career. She is co-author, with Peter MacIntyre, of *Capitalizing on Language Learners' Individuality* and *Optimizing Language Learners' Nonverbal Behavior.* She is also a co-editor with Peter and Sarah Mercer of *Positive Psychology in SLA* and *Innovations in Language Teacher Education.* She has published extensively in peer reviewed journals and contributed several chapters in applied linguistics anthologies on individual differences, teacher education, language teaching methodology and nonverbal communication in language classrooms.

Alastair Henry is Professor of Language Education at University West, Sweden. He has carried out a number of studies using CDST methodologies. In addition to teacher identity development, this research has focused on L2 motivation and, most recently, willingness to communicate. With Zoltán Dörnyei and Peter MacIntyre he is the co-editor of *Motivational Dynamics in Language Learning* (2015, Multilingual Matters).

Jim King is based at the University of Leicester where he directs the institution's campus-based postgraduate courses in applied linguistics and teaching English as a second language. His books include the monograph *Silence in the Second Language Classroom* (Palgrave Macmillan, 2013) and the edited volumes *The Dynamic Interplay between Context and the Language Learner* (Palgrave Macmillan, 2015), *The Emotional Rollercoaster of Language Teaching* (with Christina Gkonou and Jean-Marc Dewaele, Multilingual Matters, 2020) and *East Asian Perspectives* *on Silence in English Language Education* (with Seiko Harumi, Multilingual Matters, 2020).

Peter D. MacIntyre is Professor of Psychology at Cape Breton University. He earned his PhD from the University of Western Ontario and completed a post-doctoral fellowship at the University of Ottawa. His research focuses on the psychology of language learning and communication. Peter has published over 100 articles and chapters on language anxiety, willingness to communicate, motivation and other topics. He has co-authored or co-edited books on topics including research-driven pedagogy, contemporary motivation research, positive psychology in second-language acquisition, motivational dynamics, nonverbal communication, teaching innovations and capitalizing on language learner individuality. Peter has received awards for teaching excellence (Atlantic Association of Universities), the Gardner Award (International Association for Language and Social Psychology), the Mildenberger Prize (Modern Language Association) for contributions to the study of language, and awards for service to students and the community.

Sarah Mercer is Professor of Foreign Language Teaching at the University of Graz, Austria, where she is Head of ELT methodology. Her research interests include all aspects of the psychology surrounding the foreign language learning experience. She is the author, co-author and co-editor of several books in this area. She has been Principal Investigator on various funded research projects. She is currently vice-president of the International Association for the Psychology of Language Learning (IAPLL). In 2018, she was awarded the Robert C Gardner Award for excellence in second language research by the International Association of Language and Social Psychology (IALSP).

Christine Muir is an Assistant Professor in Second Language Acquisition in the School of English, University of Nottingham. She has published on varied topics relating to the psychology of language learning and teaching, particularly in the area of individual and group-level motivation in language education. Recent publications include *Directed Motivational Currents and Language Education: Exploring Implications for Pedagogy* (2020, Multilingual Matters) and 'Role models in language learning: Results of a large scale international survey' (2019, *Applied Linguistics*, with Zoltán Dörnyei & Svenja Adolphs).

Yoshiyuki Nakata is a Professor of English Language Education in the Faculty of Global Communications at Doshisha University, Kyoto, Japan. He has been involved mainly in in-service (as well as pre-service) language teacher education in Japan for more than 20 years. His research interests include self-regulated language learning, language learning motivation, learner/teacher autonomy in the school context and language teacher education. Relevant publications have appeared in journals such as *Teaching and Teacher Education, International Journal of Educational Research, International Journal of Applied Linguistics, EuroSLA Yearbook, TESL Canada Journal, Innovation in Language Learning and Teaching, System* and *Contemporary Educational Psychology.*

Ryo Nitta is a Professor and Dean of the Center for Foreign Language Education and Research, Rikkyo University, Japan. He completed his PhD at the University of Warwick, UK. His research interests are language learning motivation, task-based language teaching and second language writing from the perspective of CDST.

Rebecca L. Oxford (PhD, University of North Carolina) is Professor Emerita and Distinguished Scholar-Teacher, University of Maryland. She is interested in emotional (affective) complexity, self-regulation and peace. Among her 15 books are three on peace, including *Peacebuilding in Language Education* (2020), and several on language learning strategies, involving affective self-regulation. She co-edits two book series: Spirituality, Religion and Education (Palgrave) and Transforming Education for the Future (Information Age). She edited the Tapestry ESL/EFL book series, with North American, Middle Eastern, Chinese and Japanese editions. A Lifetime Achievement Award states, 'Rebecca Oxford's work has changed the way the world teaches languages.'

Richard S. Pinner is an Associate Professor in the Department of English Literature at Sophia University. He holds an MA in Applied Linguistics and ELT from King's College London and a PhD from The University of Warwick. He is the author of three books, as well as several articles which have appeared in international journals such as *Language Teaching Research* and *Applied Linguistics Review.* His research focuses on the dynamic relationship between authenticity and motivation in language teaching and learning.

Heath Rose is Associate Professor of Applied Linguistics at the University of Oxford. His research covers self-regulation, language learner strategies, Global Englishes and English Medium Instruction. Publications include a number of authored and edited books on topics associated with language teaching and research methods in applied linguistics, including the *Routledge Handbook of Research Methods in Applied Linguistics.* His research on the psychological aspects of language learning has appeared in such journals as *Applied Linguistics, Modern Language Journal, TESOL Quarterly* and *Applied Linguistics Review.*

Richard J. Sampson began working in the Japanese educational context in 1999, and is currently an Associate Professor at Rikkyo University. He holds a Master of Applied Linguistics from the University of Southern Queensland (Australia) and a PhD from Griffith University (Australia). He is the author of one research monograph and numerous research articles published in international journals such as *System*, *Studies in Second Language Learning and Teaching*, *Innovation in Language Learning and Teaching* and *Language Teaching Research*. He uses action research approaches to give voice to the complex, situated experience of language learner psychology.

Kedi Simpson is a part-time doctoral student at the University of Oxford, as well as a part-time teacher of French, German and Spanish in an English comprehensive school. She is interested in how second language listening (particularly French among English learners) develops in the complex and messy environment of the English L2 classroom, and the chapter in this volume describes the methodology of her doctoral research. She has a particular interest in methodology and ontology within applied linguistics and second language listening in particular.

Lesley Smith is a third-year PhD candidate in Linguistics at the University of South Carolina. She previously worked as an English language instructor at the University of Notre Dame and Richland County, South Carolina. She is particularly interested in instructed language acquisition, and her research interests include group dynamics in second and foreign language contexts and the effects of instruction on second language processing.

Ema Ushioda is a Professor and Head of Applied Linguistics, University of Warwick, where she has been based since 2002. Ema is known for her work on motivation and autonomy in language learning, particularly for promoting qualitative approaches to researching motivation, and she has published widely in these areas. Her books include *International Perspectives on Motivation: Language Learning and Professional Challenges* (2013), *Teaching and Researching Motivation* (co-authored with Dörnyei, 2011), *Motivation, Language Identity and the L2 Self* (co-edited with Dörnyei, 2009), and the forthcoming title *Language Learning Motivation: An Ethical Agenda for Research* (2020).

Takenori Yamamoto is an Associate Professor at Kobe City College of Technology, Japan. His research interest focuses on the collaboration of second language education and engineering education. He is currently working on a project which focuses on English vocabulary learning in a course of engineering education in Japan. He finished his MA degree at

Chiba University. He is a member of The Council of College English Teachers (COCET) and Japan Society of English Language Education (JASELE).

Tomoko Yashima is a Professor of Applied Linguistics and Intercultural Communication at Kansai University, Japan. Her research interests include L2 learning motivation, affect and language identity. Her research has been published in journals such as *Modern Language Journal*, *Language Learning*, *System* and *International Journal of Intercultural Relations*. She has authored book chapters such as those in *Motivational Dynamics in Language Learning* (edited by Dörnyei, MacIntyre & Henry, 2015, Multilingual Matters) and *Psychology for Language Learning* (edited by Mercer, Ryan & Williams, 2012; Palgrave MacMillan) as well as books published in Japanese, including *Intercultural Communication: Global Mind and Local Affect* (2012, Shohakusha).

Introduction: [simple and complex?]

Richard S. Pinner and Richard J. Sampson

This edited volume brings together both established and emerging researcher voices from around the world to illustrate how complexity perspectives might contribute to new ways of researching and understanding the psychology of language learners and teachers in situated educational contexts. We have encouraged contributors to very much include themselves in their discussions of the research of which they are a part. At this juncture, we are reminded of a pertinent thought from Miyahara (2015: 177):

> It is somewhat surprising that not many researchers make transparent their journeys as learners, teachers or researchers. Rarely do we find information about them in their writings, yet we are expected to read, contemplate and discuss their research.

We hope that the voices and stories of our contributors are 'visible' in the chapters that follow. We also would like to make ourselves as editors more transparent by including here two short vignettes detailing our own roads into appreciating what complexity might offer.

Our (abridged) Journeys into Complexity

Richard P

My interest in complexity comes initially from a single chapter which I read about chaos theory and complexity by Menezes (2013) in an edited volume by Benson and Cooker (2013) called *The Applied Linguistic Individual*. I was reading up on autonomy and identity as part of my work on authenticity, which shows that I was already looking at other concepts in order to understand connections between abstract phenomena. Until reading this paper by Menezes, my only encounter with chaos theory was on my bachelor's degree in Fine Art; we'd had a rather funny young teacher, who I will call Mr Lick, who we felt wasn't all that bright. He was using 'chaos theory' by putting maggots on a canvas and letting them squirm around in paint, which of course we had all made fun of behind his back. However, this chapter was my first real introduction to the theory, and completely drove bad art from my mind. It did not just speak to me as a teacher, but more generally to the way I think about the universe. It mainly dealt with chaos theory, which is of course connected with and indeed part of what we refer to as *complexity perspectives* in this book. One thing I particularly liked was the discussion of fractals, which are patterns or shapes that are self-similar at all levels, so that, like the universe, they are 'no simpler or more complicated whether examined through microscope or telescope' (Davis & Sumara, 2006: 43–44). These shapes appear in nature all the time, from snowflakes to coastlines. Going back to my art school days, I actually experimented with such drawings when I was working on a project about infinity (see Figure 1.1 for an example of a fractal I drew), although I don't think Mr Lick thought much of my drawings back then, which perhaps explains why I ended my artistic career and found myself doing a PhD in applied linguistics. Nevertheless, I wound up using complexity as a unifying lens for my hybrid of methodologies in my doctoral thesis.

Menezes posits that language learning identities are fractals of our whole identity. As we develop a voice in the target language and learn to express more and more of ourselves, the fractal set expands, and with it so does our identity. Fractals seemed very apt as a way of thinking about the smaller and bigger connections between the classroom and the

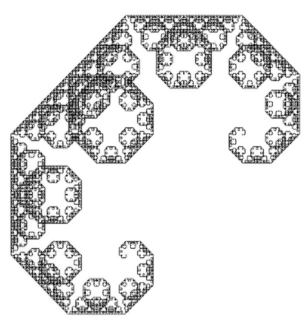

Figure 1.1 A fractal known as the Levy Curve drawn by hand using a computer mouse, started from three interconnected pixels

external contexts that people bring to it, too. This did not just pique my interest and capture my attention as a teacher researcher, but more broadly it was a theory which could easily map onto my own philosophical understanding of being. Further reading, such as Kramsch (2002), Dörnyei *et al.* (2015) and especially Sampson (2016a), confirmed that complexity thinking would also be useful for me professionally, in terms of the metaphors it uses to describe lived experience, as well as the connections and drives (motivations) behind them. I briefly mentioned complexity in my first book, and as I already pointed out, I employed a complexity paradigm in my doctoral research to investigate the complex relationships between authenticity and motivation.

In my PhD viva I came up against some resistance to complexity by both of my examiners. They seemed to be under the impression that as I was doing practitioner research (which would be of primary interest to fellow practitioners) complexity would not be useful or accessible to this intended audience. I disagreed strongly, and managed to pass the defence, but I was still asked to remove some of the data and analysis which the examiners felt was too 'complex', by which I think they really meant technical. I will be presenting these data in my chapter later in this volume. I still believe that this paradigm helped me make sense of how I see the classroom, and what unites both Richard S and I is our shared and passionate belief that complexity is not an elite-only and inaccessible research paradigm that further alienates research from practice (Horn, 2008), but on the contrary it is something that could unite these two professional strands in applied linguists and language teaching.

Richard S

My mother was a home-economics teacher. From a young age (and during my secondary education also), I learnt the joys of combining various ingredients in sometimes radically different ways, via which exquisite wonders of taste, smell and vision would emerge that seemed to have very little to do with their components. Naturally, at times I was also successful in concocting what could only be seen as an affront to the term 'cuisine', despite my understanding that the ingredients ought to have combined well. My father was a geography and history teacher. He used to ask me interesting questions whenever we went anywhere 'historical', like 'What was going on in the world at the time these people were living such that they decided to build like this?'. And we would together make an image of a diverse range of historical currents in the context of which some phenomenon occurred. Perhaps also influenced by his thoughts on geography, in my secondary school days I was fascinated by the interactions between earth systems and the way that everything seemed connected. However, it was not until my postgraduate studies that I re-encountered similar ideas in the form of complexity (even at one point prompting me to ponder the possibility of changing my entire research focus and occupation to something related to earth systems). I connected with complexity at a number of levels. As a classroom teacher, it just made sense, a lot more sense than much research that I was reading, of what I experienced day-in day-out of being part of language learning class groups. Experiences from my ongoing identity projects as a person other than a language teacher/researcher also connected with complexity: the non-linearity of my own Japanese language learning motivation and identity development; the co-adaptive nature of my attempts at bilingual childrearing with my Japanese–Australian children in Japan; and, more recently, the attrition of my first language. Even further back, growing up in countryside Australia had already allowed me to experience the interactions between 'the whole and the parts' of the beautiful natural ecosystems around me, such that complexity was not an earth-shatteringly novel idea.

The more that I read and thought about complexity, the more I came to believe that one of the main benefits of drawing on complexity theories is the philosophical aspect. Complexity thinking cautions against simplism, and asks us to consider experience and perception in deeper, more relational terms. And this is not such an overwhelming ask: We already live our lives in complex webs of dynamic interaction with both material and ideological artefacts (including other humans) across different timescales. In our existence and interactions and interpretations the world becomes a different place, and we become different at the same time. As Kuhn (2007: 173) remarks, in a complexity philosophy 'not only are the knower and the known dynamic, self-organizing and emerging, the relationship of the knower to the known is likewise dynamic, self-organizing and emerging'. Complexity offers a fundamentally different way of approaching and thinking about life to that offered by much of our education into simplistic ideas (Morin, 2008).

Our Reasons for Bringing these Chapters Together

Complexity theory has been taken up with vigour in both theoretical and empirical psychology due to recognition of a longstanding tension between the inherent dynamism in everyday life and psychology's quest to understand stability and coherence in phenomenal experience (Vallacher & Nowak, 2009). Prompted by Larsen-Freeman's (1997) seminal paper, complexity research has also spread throughout the field of second language acquisition (SLA), not least in the investigation of various aspects of language learner and teacher psychology. A small sample of the diverse dimensions explored to date includes:

- learner agency (Mercer, 2011a);
- learner motivation (Dörnyei *et al.*, 2015a, 2015b; Muir & Dörnyei, 2013; Nitta, 2013; Sampson, 2015, 2016a);

- learner self and identity (Menezes, 2013; Mercer, 2011b, 2011c; Sade, 2011; Sampson, 2016a);
- learner images of ideal classmates (Murphey *et al.*, 2014; Sampson, 2018);
- learner emotions (Gkonou, 2017; Sampson, 2020a, 2019);
- critical incidents in learning (Finch, 2010; Pinner, 2016a, 2018);
- learner reticence and silence in the classroom (King, 2015; Yashima *et al.*, 2016);
- learner willingness to communicate (Yashima *et al.*, 2018);
- learner demotivation (Kikuchi, 2017);
- language learner group dynamics (Poupore, 2018);
- synergy between teacher and student motivation (Pinner, 2019);
- teacher identity (Henry, 2016; Pinner, 2019);
- teacher immunity (Hiver, 2015);
- teacher motivation (Kimura, 2014; Sampson, 2016b; Pinner, 2016b, 2019);
- teacher cognition (Feryok, 2010, 2018).

As a paradigm, complexity seems to offer intriguing new avenues to investigate and describe the interrelated, co-adapting and emergent nature of the social psychodynamics among the actors in learning. Yet, the drive to incorporate complexity perspectives into education research has been met with caution by some (Hardman, 2010; Richardson & Cilliers, 2001). Fears remain that a rush to apply novel metaphors or advance neoteric models may hinder the development of deeper understandings rendered by research and analysis built on the philosophical underpinnings of complexity. While many valuable contributions to our understandings have been forthcoming, at times there is also a tendency towards systems theories (such as dynamic systems theory), many of which 'started as a branch of theoretical mathematics' (de Bot & Larsen-Freeman, 2011: 9). Ushioda (this volume) asserts that 'such discussions of human behaviour can create, as Larsen-Freeman and Cameron (2008: 74) openly admit, something of a "distancing" effect, where individual intentionality, reflexivity and decision-making become transmuted into mathematical models representing abstract systems above the level of the individual person'. Moreover, approaches from a complexity perspective may pose challenges for researching the psychology of self-aware agents in language learning and teaching (Al-Hoorie, 2015; MacIntyre *et al.*, 2015). This volume aims to dispel such fears through looking at concrete examples of how researchers are doing research into the field of language learner and teacher psychology with complexity.

When we wrote the proposal for this edited volume, we originally said that this book would be for language teachers, students and scholars of applied linguistics, and researchers in the field of SLA. The publishers, to their credit, asked for a more focused audience rather than trying to please everyone, which actually aligned with our initial intentions. We united under the motto *complexity should be simple*. Our aim was to make complexity paradigms and research more accessible to people like ourselves, that is, practitioning language teachers who also engage in research. Our reasons for feeling this volume was necessary were based on various observations and discussions we had had with colleagues in which at times people had expressed fear or confusion about the concept of complexity in language research. An example from Richard S: For better or worse, recently his proposal for a presentation on using complexity thinking to explore the psychology of L2 learners was accepted for a conference in Taiwan, at which the majority of sessions would revolve around technology and language teaching. Apprehensive as to whether anyone would indeed turn up for his session, he was astonished when he found himself with a packed room. So much so, that he joked at the start of his presentation, 'I presume you're all here because of the word "psychology" in my title, rather than the word "complexity"?' To which there was a resounding nod of assent from the assembled participants. Some even appeared to grimace at the mention of 'complexity'. Nevertheless, as the session concluded, the room seemed to emit a collective energy in the realization that in complexity, there was something that does justice to understanding the real learners in our real classrooms. When Richard S organized a symposium at the 3rd Psychology of Language Learning (PLL3) conference in Tokyo entitled *Simply Researching Complexity* (Sampson *et al.*, 2018), we were both able to feel a similar wave of enthusiasm for the topic, and this book was born out of that enthusiasm.

Yet, various experiences led us to the working theory that complexity was seen from the perspective of practitioning teachers as either a mere buzz-word, or (worse) an intimidating and elitist direction for SLA research which could possibly exclude classroom research from the future research agenda. Both of us were particularly worried about this as, from our reading, much of the literature on complexity was actually very loudly and clearly saying that we needed more insights from the classroom and more involvement with practitioners themselves. Considering the strongly relational approach in a complexity worldview, in a recent commentary on links between complexity and the study of the psychology of language learners, Larsen-Freeman (2019: 75) urges: 'Clearly, more attention needs to be given to the relationship between the researcher and research participants'. Practitioners-as-researchers are uniquely placed to add more contextualized understandings of the complexity of the psychologies of learners in their class groups, whilst also recognizing their positions as part of the observed.

Even more importantly, the complexity paradigm seemed to us to offer an approach to understanding knowledge which could really help us make sense of the lived realities of our classrooms. The metaphors used in complexity perspectives give us a set of tools to describe things we have been observing in our practice for a long time, they help us to explore why things don't always go as planned, and why research that isolates single factors or attempts to control experiments in laboratory conditions has little relevance for those of us who interact with *real* people in a *real* classroom environment.

Complexity in Bringing the Chapters Together

In order to show how all this might work in practice, we have collected some sample data from our experiences of preparing this manuscript. This book is the product of around 713 emails, over 300 hours of editing and writing, with approximately 1000 comments on 25 different drafts of chapters, with an uncountable number of Skype comments and calls between the two of us (uncountable literally, as many of these chats descend into banter and then come back to professional work as our friendship developed, making it almost impossible to tell which ones to include in this quantifying exercise).

These data help us to illustrate an important point about complexity. These data on their own tell us nothing about the process of editing this book. They need to be situated within the context of the narrative and framed from a human perspective in order to be meaningful. For example, these numbers tell us nothing about how long each of the authors spent preparing their chapters, or the banter and professional work that went on between the co-authors of individual chapters. The numbers show that a lot of work went into the book, but they speak nothing of the difficult human aspects that came up with missed deadlines and negotiations over content, with authors having personal events interrupt their professional lives (changing jobs, moving house, car crashes and other serious family events) which then had a knock-on effect on this book. It has certainly been an eye-opening experience for the two of us, and we shall never pick up an edited book and flippantly look through the pages now without wondering at what a huge labour is involved in putting together such a volume. At the same time, the narrative and the context have little impact without the data to show that we are not making surface-level assumptions. There were undoubtedly a multitude of other happenings that impacted authors and us as editors as we strove to bring this volume together, yet without data – in this case, an email record and an estimate of the number of hours we put in – we can say very little. It is also important that we stress this is our experience, and by no means is this generalizable to other contexts. There may be some books that have been through an even more tangled journey, and others that seem to slide effortlessly down a water chute. All we can say is, this was our experience and we both feel it was worth every moment.

Returning now, as we do in our daily work, to the classroom, complexity paradigms allow us to think about classroom experiences and contexts in ways which help us make sense of their various realities. The tools and the methods of complexity approaches allow us to tell our stories in convincing ways. They support us in efforts to turn classroom research and practice into a valid and robust category of research which we believe should allow teachers' voices to find their way into even the most prestigious and selective of journals and publications. In other words, by understanding complexity as it can apply to our work, we hope to empower other practitioners and encourage them to share their rich understandings about the realities of classroom teaching and learning. We feel that this is a crucial step, in order that our field can benefit and move forward, without falling back into reductionist, isolating, statistic-heavy and yet reality-evading research practices which do little to further our understanding of the vital psychological aspects to foreign language learning and teaching.

What the Chapters Offer

In the chapters that follow, authors discuss their own perspectives on researching within a complexity paradigm, exemplified by concrete and original examples from their research histories. Moreover, as the title of the volume suggests, chapters explore research approaches to a variety of learner and teacher psychological foci of interest in SLA. Each chapter draws on concrete examples of research conducted by the author(s) with a meta-discussion to expound their take on complexity and researching from a complexity perspective. How do complexity understandings underlie the phenomena or processes that are being researched? How does complexity inform the research approach? How do researchers conduct empirical investigation from a complexity perspective, for example, looking at dynamics, timescales, co-adaptation, emergence? What data collection tools and analysis methods are appropriate? How can we represent findings in ways that sufficiently express the complexity of lived experience, while ensuring representations are conceptually accessible to more than just a few complexity enthusiasts? And, importantly, how does all of this complexity perspective-taking add anything new and useful to our understandings of language learner and teacher psychology? Through contributors detailing and discussing their experiences of conducting complexity research, chapters present practical illustrations of how complexity research can be done, with convincing evidence of why a complexity perspective is useful to investigating and conceptualizing the psychology of language learners and teachers.

In Chapter 2, Peter MacIntyre, Sarah Mercer and Tammy Gregersen offer us their reflections on researching dynamics in language learning psychology. We as editors were very grateful for this contribution, not least because it includes a very handy glossary of terms associated with complexity research, which makes it essential reading for those wishing to learn more about the complexity theory itself. They discuss some useful terms which will appear again and again in the volume, such as time-scales, attractor states, self-organization and fractals. What is more, they do so in accessible language and provide a blueprint really for those seeking to apply the complexity lens to their own enquiries.

For Chapter 3, Richard Sampson shares his research on emotions, using timescales to understand how emotions change and develop, and how they possibly influence learning and teaching at various levels. His presentation of *multiple threading* for learners' feelings offers not only a fascinating way to understand the myriad of emotions that students reported feeling in the classroom, but it is also a lovely vision of complexity in its own right (according to Richard P).

In Chapter 4, Rebecca Oxford and Christina Gkonou continue the discussion of emotions, and tell us how they developed the *Managing Your Emotions* survey tool. While a survey might not seem overly complex, they argue that this new, scenario-based method which encourages narrative responses can take into account the ecologies of learning and teaching and focus the complexity lens on affective strategies.

Chapter 5 by Tomoko Yashima is an extended report of her work with Willingness to Communicate (WTC). As Tomoko was one of the original symposiasts at the PLL3 conference, we were delighted that she accepted our invitation to contribute this chapter, especially as her work so artfully demonstrates the use of both qualitative and quantitative data for gaining situated and nuanced understandings from the classroom.

We could not resist following up Tomoko's paper on WTC with a wonderful paper by Lesley Smith and Jim King, which focuses on the complex issue of silence in the classroom. We thought this juxtaposition was very interesting as it shows the range of complexity research. Their thorough examination of silence also skilfully utilizes both qualitative and quantitative data to gain a more holistic picture of why students do not contribute to foreign language classes in Japanese universities.

We are very happy to feature the fourth and final member of our original symposium, Joe Falout, in Chapter 7. Joe brings the concept of motivational resonance to learner self-concepts, and applies a complexity perspective from outside of SLA. What is intriguing about Joe's chapter is the way that he provides a narrative of his researching lifetime, rather than homing in on any one particular study. Although not explicitly doing so at the times specific research was carried out, his experiences all speak to complexity.

For Chapter 8, Sal Consoli provides us with an up-close and personal account of his own teaching and research with pre-sessional courses in a UK university, working from an ecological perspective that employs Exploratory Practice to gain contextually situated insights into learner motivation. He draws on Bordieuan sociological ideas to situate his learners' personal motivations, following Ushioda's (2009) person-in-context relational view of motivation, and shares some samples of Potentially Exploitable Pedagogic Activities, which give us an insight into his classroom and his learners' lives and experiences.

In Chapter 9, Kedi Simpson and Heath Rose argue that a complexity approach offers a more 'ecologically rich' foundation for research. In rejecting the reductionist approaches which attempt to compartmentalize the 'messy' complex nature of real-world classroom research, they invite a complexity perspective which draws on a wonderful horticultural metaphor to help situate aspects of learner psychology in a listening class with children learning French. As such this is an invaluable chapter as it brings another contextual dimension to the volume and helps broaden the discussion.

Chapter 10 sees Takumi Aoyama and Takenori Yamamoto demonstrating the Trajectory Equifinality Approach. This is an approach that can be used to retrospectively explore the psychology of L2 learners and teachers, and delve into both the redundancy and diversity of life experiences evolving to similar points of interest. We are delighted that these authors were able to join us, as it allows a methodology which has been chiefly developed in Japan (and hence written about in Japanese) to be brought to an English-speaking audience.

Ryo Nitta and Yoshiyuki Nakata then share their use of a retrodictive research approach to understanding class climate in Chapter 11. Once again exemplifying the skilled combination of quantitative and qualitative tools, they highlight differences between the English class climates that developed in two separate groups at a Japanese senior-high school. A key insight from their study is the value of collaboration between the local teacher and the researchers, through which they were able to understand their data in a more contextualized fashion.

Chapter 12 by Christine Muir again demonstrates the utility of collaboration between teachers-as-co-researchers and academics. Drawing on recent research into directed motivational currents (DMCs), she extends this construct by investigating the emergence of group-level DMCs during project work in an Australian setting. Her chapter aims to demonstrate to practitioner-researchers the suitability of formative experiments as one situated way of exploring the emergence and management of group-level motivation.

In Chapter 13, Richard Pinner shows how he used autoethnography and social network analysis to question assumptions about his learners, providing us with a short narrative of two very different students with surprising characteristics in common. There are unfortunately those who believe research done by teachers ought to simply focus on teaching 'tips and tricks' (see Sampson, in preparation). Richard P's chapter is a fine (according to Richard S) example of the valuable, deeper understandings of practitioners, their learners and their contexts of practice that can emerge through looking back at a 'completed' teacher-researcher study.

Alastair Henry brings together a collection of contradictory selves in Chapter 14. Drawing on the theory of the dialogical self, under-researched in L2 settings, he presents research from Sweden looking at teacher identity. His studies uncovered the ways in which student-teacher understandings of teacher identity evolved through a teaching practicum, impacted in large part by the presence or not of their mentor-teacher in the classroom with them. His fascinating demonstration of the use of both introspective and dialogical data suggests a constructive approach to exploring mediated and less-mediated psychological processes.

In Chapter 15, Anne Feryok provides a refreshingly clear account of the non-linearity of the research process. She describes how she picked up on a particular utterance in data from a study with one of her doctoral students. Conducting microgenetic analysis prompted by this seemingly trivial starting point led to a further application of frame analysis to understand the situated emergence of a language teacher's cognition.

To conclude this volume, we are honoured to feature Ema Ushioda's chapter which rounds everything off better than we possibly could...

Finally...

In closing this introductory chapter, we would like to thank the contributors for their amazing work with us in seeing this project through to this stage. From the very outset, various people expressed their hopes for this volume, with the feeling that it was high time such a work be undertaken. Yet, to be completely honest, when we put out the initial call for proposals, and then gave authors the guidelines for construction of their chapters, little did we know how much we were asking. It was only when it came time for us to also write our individual chapters that it finally sank in. Naturally, it is quite a skill in itself to see a research project through to completion, and write about it as an empirical article or chapter. We then pushed our contributors to expound on their take on complexity theory, and the actual practice of researching from a complexity perspective. We asked them not simply what, but also *how* they do what they do. At the time of putting together the call for proposals, we often used the metaphor of a magician revealing their tricks. The trouble is, researchers are not magicians, and the research we do is not a trick or an illusion. And, so, we now realize that writing up a previous study with this reveal-all approach is extremely hard. The balance of narrative, data and methods all need to come together in order to help the reader retrace the steps of the researcher through what was no-doubt a very windy and uphill path. That being said, we hope that this book helps pave the way as one smoother path for complexity research into the psychology and practice of language teaching and learning.

References

Al-Hoorie, A.H. (2015) Human agency: Does the beach ball have free will? In Z. Dörnyei, P.D. MacIntyre and A. Henry (eds) *Motivational Dynamics in Language Learning* (pp. 55–72). Bristol: Multilingual Matters.

Benson, P. and Cooker, L. (eds) (2013) *The Applied Linguistic Individual*. Bristol: Equinox.

Davis, A.B. and Sumara, D.J. (2006) *Complexity and Education: Inquiries into Learning, Teaching and Research*. London: Routledge.

de Bot, K. and Larsen-Freeman, D. (2011) Researching second language development from a dynamic systems theory perspective. In M. Verspoor, K. de Bot and W. Lowie (eds) *A Dynamic Approach to Second Language Development* (pp. 5–23). Amsterdam: John Benjamins.

Dörnyei, Z., Ibrahim, Z. and Muir, C. (2015a) 'Directed motivational currents': Regulating complex dynamic systems through motivational surges. In Z. Dörnyei, P.D. MacIntyre and A. Henry (eds) *Motivational Dynamics in Language Learning* (pp. 95–105). Bristol: Multilingual Matters.

Dörnyei, Z., MacIntyre, P. and Henry, A. (eds) (2015b) *Motivational Dynamics in Language Learning*. Bristol: Multilingual Matters.

Feryok, A. (2010) Language teacher cognitions: Complex dynamic systems? *System* 38, 272–279.

Feryok, A. (2018) Language teacher cognition: An emergent phenomenon in an emergent field. In S. Mercer and A. Kostoulas (eds) *Language Teacher Psychology* (pp. 105–121). Bristol, UK: Multilingual Matters.

Finch, A. (2010) Critical incidents and language learning: Sensitivity to initial conditions. *System* 38 (3), 422–431.

Gkonou, C. (2017) Towards an ecological understanding of language anxiety. In C. Gkonou, M. Daubney and J. Dewaele (eds) *New Insights into Language Anxiety: Theory, Research and Educational Implications*. Bristol: Multilingual Matters.

Hardman, M. (2010) Is complexity theory useful in describing classroom learning? *The European Conference on Educational Research*. Helsinki.

Henry, A. (2016) Conceptualizing teacher identity as a complex dynamic system: The inner dynamics of transformations during a practicum. *Journal of Teacher Education* 67 (4), 291–305.

Hiver, P. (2015) Once burned, twice shy: The dynamic development of system immunity in teachers. In Z. Dörnyei, P.D. MacIntyre and A. Henry (eds) *Motivational Dynamics in Language Learning* (pp. 214–237). Bristol: Multilingual Matters.

Horn, J. (2008) Human research and complexity theory. In M. Mason (ed.) *Complexity Theory and the Philosophy of Education* (Vol. 40, pp. 124–136). London: Wiley-Blackwell.

Kikuchi, K. (2017) Reexamining demotivators and motivators: A longitudinal study of Japanese freshmen's dynamic system in an EFL context. *Innovation in Language Learning and Teaching* 11 (2), 128–145.

Kimura, Y. (2014) ELT motivation from a complex dynamic systems theory perspective: A longitudinal case study of L2 teacher motivation in Beijing. In K. Csizér and M. Magid (eds) *The Impact of Self-Concept on Language Learning* (pp. 310–329). Bristol: Multilingual Matters.

King, J. (2015) Classroom silence and the dynamic interplay between context and the language learner: A stimulated recall study. In J. King (ed.) *The Dynamic Interplay between Context and the Language Learner* (pp. 127–150). Basingstoke: Palgrave Macmillan.

Kramsch, C. (ed.) (2002) *Language Acquisition and Language Socialization: Ecological Perspectives*. London: Continuum.

Kuhn, L. (2007) Why utilize complexity principles in social inquiry? *World Futures* 63, 156–175.

Larsen-Freeman, D. (1997) Chaos/complexity science and second language acquisition. *Applied Linguistics* 18 (2), 141–165.

Larsen-Freeman, D. (2019) Thoughts on the launching of a new journal: A complex dynamic systems perspective. *Journal for the Psychology of Language Learning* (1), 67–82.

Larsen-Freeman, D. and Cameron, L. (2008) *Complex Systems and Applied Linguistics*. Oxford: Oxford University Press.

MacIntyre, P.D., Dörnyei, Z. and Henry, A. (2015) Conclusion: Hot enough to be cool: The promise of synamic systems research. In Z. Dörnyei, P.D. MacIntyre and A. Henry (eds) *Motivational Dynamics in Language Learning* (pp. 419–429). Bristol: Multilingual Matters.

Menezes, V. (2013) Chaos and the complexity of second language acquisition. In P. Benson and L. Cooker (eds) *The Applied Linguistic Individual* (pp. 59–74). Bristol: Equinox.

Mercer, S. (2011a) Understanding learner agency as a complex dynamic system. *System* 39, 427–436.

Mercer, S. (2011b) Language learner self-concept: Complexity, continuity and change. *System* 39, 335–346.

Mercer, S. (2011c) *Towards an Understanding of Language Learner Self-concept*. Heidelberg: Springer.

Miyahara, M. (2015) *Emerging Self-identities and Emotion in Foreign Language Learning: A Narrative-oriented Approach*. Bristol: Multilingual Matters.

Morin, E. (2008) *On Complexity*. Cresskill, N.J.: Hampton Press.

Muir, C. and Dörnyei, Z. (2013) Directed motivational currents: Using vision to create effective motivational pathways. *Studies in Second Language Learning and Teaching* 3 (3), 357–375.

Murphey, T., Falout, J., Fukuda, T. and Fukada, Y. (2014) Socio-dynamic motivating through idealizing classmates. *System* 45, 242–253.

Nitta, R. (2013) Understanding motivational evolution in the EFL classroom: A longitudinal study from a dynamic systems perspective. In M.T. Apple, D. Da Silva and T. Fellner (eds) *Language Learning Motivation in Japan* (pp. 268–290). Bristol: Multilingual Matters.

Pinner, R.S. (2016a) Trouble in paradise: Self-assessment and the Tao. *Language Teaching Research* 20 (2), 181–195.

Pinner, R.S. (2016b) Using self-assessment to maintain motivation in a dynamic classroom environment: An exploratory practice inquiry of one Japanese university speaking course. *Asian Journal of Applied Linguistics* 3 (1), 27–40.

Pinner, R.S. (2018) Re-learning from experience: Using autoethnography for teacher development. *Educational Action Research* 26 (1), 91–105.

Pinner, R.S. (2019) *Social Authentication and Teacher-Student Motivational Synergy: A Narrative of Language Teaching*. London: Routledge.

Poupore, G. (2018) A complex systems investigation of group work dynamics in L2 interactive tasks. *Modern Language Journal* 102 (2), 350–370.

Richardson, K. and Cilliers, P. (2001) Special editors' introduction: What is complexity science? A view from different directions. *Emergence* 3 (1), 5–23.

Sade, L.A. (2011) Emerging selves, language learning and motivation through the lens of chaos. In G. Murray, X. Gao and M. Lamb (eds) *Identity, Motivation and Autonomy in Language Learning* (pp. 42–56). Bristol: Multilingual Matters.

Sampson, R.J. (2015) Tracing motivational emergence in a classroom language learning project. *System* 50, 10–20.

Sampson, R.J. (2016a) *Complexity in Classroom Foreign Language Learning Motivation: A Practitioner Perspective from Japan*. Bristol: Multilingual Matters.

Sampson, R.J. (2016b) EFL teacher motivation in-situ: Co-adaptive processes, openness and relational motivation over interacting timescales. *Studies in Second Language Learning and Teaching* 6 (2), 293–318.

Sampson, R.J. (2018) Complexity in acting on images of ideal classmates in the L2 classroom. *Konin Language Studies* 6 (4), 387–410.

Sampson, R.J. (2019) Real people with real experiences: The emergence of classroom L2 study feelings over interacting timescales. *System* 84, 14–23.

Sampson, R.J. (2020a) The feeling classroom: Diversity of feelings in instructed L2 learning. *Innovation in Language Learning and Teaching* 14 (3), 203–217.

Sampson, R.J. (2020b) Evolving understandings of practitioner action research from the inside. Manuscript in review.

Sampson, R.J., Pinner, R.S., Falout, J. and Yashima, T. (2018) Simply researching complexity in language learning and teaching. In J. Mynard and I.K. Brady (eds) *Stretching Boundaries: Papers from the Third International Psychology of Language Learning Conference, Tokyo* (pp. 13–24). Tokyo: International Association for the Psychology of Language Learning.

Ushioda, E. (2009) A person-in-context relational view of emergent motivation, self and identity. In E. Ushioda and Z. Dörnyei (eds) *Motivation, Language Identity and the L2 Self* (pp. 215–228). Bristol: Multilingual Matters.

Vallacher, R.R. and Nowak, A. (2009) The dynamics of human experience: Fundamentals of dynamic social psychology. In S.J. Guastello, M. Koopmans and D. Pincus (eds) *Chaos and Complexity in Psychology* (pp. 370–401). New York: Cambridge University Press.

Yashima, T., Ikeda, M. and Nakahira, S. (2016) Talk and silence in an EFL classroom: Interplay of learners and context. In J. King (ed.) *The Dynamic Interplay between Context and the Learner* (pp. 104–126.) Basingstoke: Palgrave Macmillan.

Yashima, T., MacIntyre, P. and Ikeda, M. (2018) Situated willingness to communicate in an L2: Interplay of individual characteristics and context. *Language Teaching Research* 22, 115–137.

2 Reflections on Researching Dynamics in Language Learning Psychology

Peter D. MacIntyre, Sarah Mercer and
Tammy Gregersen

Introduction

Humans are highly complex beings. Language and communication are complex systems. Combining psychology and language learning with the multifaceted communication process increases the complexity substantially. Add then to the mix the idea that all of these things are constantly changing over time and with even small differences in context, the challenge facing researchers in this field rounds into form. How does a research project capture such complexity and dynamism in a meaningful way without oversimplifying the lived reality? All three authors of this chapter have found taking a complexity-informed approach to research to be a most satisfying way of tackling this problem, but one that creates its share of challenges. In this chapter, we will reflect on our own experiences of grappling with the issues created by adopting a complexity perspective, focusing on timescales and dynamism. We will conclude this chapter with a series of recommendations, emerging from our experience, that we hope will assist other scholars wanting to research the dynamics of learner and/ or teacher psychologies.

A Gap between Theorizing and Empirical Research

Within applied linguistics, theorizing complexity is well ahead of its empirical investigations (MacIntyre *et al.*, 2017). Perhaps the reason for the imbalance between describing complex dynamic systems theory (CDST) and using it for empirical research is that CDST is itself meta-theoretical in nature, meaning that it is not a theory of language learning *per se* but an approach to creating theory (Larsen-Freeman, 2017); research does not test CDST directly. The ideas underlying CDST have been developed in several of the natural sciences, and now the social sciences and humanities including developmental psychology (Thelen & Smith, 1994) and communication (Fogel, 2006) have followed suit. In second language acquisition (SLA), CDST has attracted a collection of researchers interested in testing its applicability to various processes, many of whom are writing chapters in this volume and who have used it both as a theoretical lens as well as a basis for empirical design and analysis.

SLA provides a rich context for understanding dynamics with its focus on language development, change and stability. However, it is not just language competences that are in a state of flux, but a range of related factors during these processes that are constantly interacting with learner and teacher psychologies. This makes the psychology of language learning an especially fertile ground for dynamic studies to take root. To date, research has tested the question of the applicability of CDST to familiar topics in this field such as willingness to communicate, motivation, the self, agency, anxiety, enjoyment, teacher efficacy and strategies; we discuss specific research examples. The studies we describe below unanimously conclude that the approach is well suited and the phenomena under study meet the key conditions for CDST. The work so far has indicated how a CDST perspective can lead to novel developments in conceptualization, methodology and data analysis/presentation; the possibilities for future research excite the imagination. The question now is how to proceed with research that will further our appreciation of the scope and potential of this theoretical framework to extend our understandings of the field of language learning and teaching.

Benefits of a CDST Perspective on the Psychology of Language Learning

Our interest in CDST is based in large part on what it offers as a way of thinking about the psychology of language learning (PLL) and communication and how CDST can contribute to new ways of studying the processes involved. The continuous interactions among the myriad of inter-personal and intra-personal processes are intricate, nuanced, contextualized and ever-changing. The focus on complex interactions requires a new set of tools for building theory and research.

Before we consider the conceptual devices in the CDST toolbox that create the context for the approach, we must first establish what is being specified as a system. Defining a system is a matter of perspective; a lens that the researcher puts on a complex reality so that a system comes into focus as a functioning whole. The system remains open but its boundaries can be described. Discussions of CDST sometimes can become difficult to interpret if the system is not specified and this is an essential first step. Defining a system for study is a matter of emphasis, focussing on the most relevant processes. Not everything functions as a complex dynamic system and certain criteria must be fulfilled before a system can be defined (Mercer, 2016). To set the stage for the rest of the chapter and illustrate some of those characteristics, we highlight attributes of CDST that differ from other research approaches and make it especially relevant to PLL.

Timescales

Perhaps the most fundamental contribution of CDST is thinking explicitly about time and how it affects the processes under study. CDST forces a researcher to consider how a process unfolds over a chosen period of time. For example, in prior research, anxiety has typically been conceptualized as a long-term, trait-like quality of a learner, but in recent research it has been studied as rapidly changing from moment-to-moment, interacting with many of the features of communication events (MacIntyre, 2017). Both shorter and longer timescales have been used in prior research but they require very different approaches and answer different types of research questions. The novel contribution of CDST is to explicitly consider multiple, interacting processes occurring within the selected timescale. For example, the trend toward increasingly communicative forms of language teaching has been taking place over many years (Canale & Swain, 1980; Savignon, 2000); nested within such a broad trend will be patterns of talking within specific classrooms (King, 2013), and nested within a specific day in the classroom will be fluctuations in communication for teachers and learners as various activities take place (Mystkowska-Wiertelak & Pawlak, 2017). To probe further the conceptual context, de Bot (2014) recommends thinking about processes one timescale level up and one timescale level down in addition to the timescale of the process under study. For example, in one of the studies described below, we studied anxiety changes over the course of a 20-minute presentation. We found it helpful to think about the sub-processes (cognitive, emotional, physiological) that affect anxiety on a per-second timescale as well as how anxiety arousal during a classroom presentation is itself part of longer-term processes, such as learning during a semester-long course and how anxiety changes in the process of becoming a language teacher. Timescales are nested within each other, as seconds are nested in minutes, minutes within hours, hours within days, and so on. It may be that different dynamics are visible on different timescales, or possibly that patterns repeat across different timescales (see the discussion of *fractals* below).

Openness

The openness of a system refers to the notion that the system is subject to sources of influence that perhaps were not contemplated when planning a research design. Essentially, openness to unexpected influences increases substantially the difficulty of predicting the most relevant processes or systems to study, especially if considered at the individual level where personal psychological idiosyncrasies abound. In the research examples below, we note that allowing for unexpected influences on a system can help to bring clarity to the dynamics involved, highlighting what is typical and what might be unusual. To provide specific examples, we will highlight how density of measurement and including a qualitative component to research designs allows for the description of unexpected factors.

Predictability, stability and variability

A particular strength of CDST is the focus on variability and change over time. Each state of the system under study is taken to be a modification of the system's previous state, and the trajectory of change in a system can be highly sensitive to its initial conditions. Given that we cannot know everything about a system and the interactions within it, there will always be some level of unpredictability about the kinds of potential changes that may occur. However, unpredictable does not mean 'anything goes' because there is not an infinite number of possible outcomes or states of the system. Some states are more likely to arise than others (see *attractor states* below). It is important to note the range of outcomes is influenced by initial conditions and the system dynamics meaning that the potential states of a system cannot be absolutely anything at all, but also cannot be precisely defined or predicted exactly in advance. The concept of dynamic stability reflects the potential for a system to remain in a relatively steady state for some period of time. It means there can be minor changes, fluctuations and variations but the overall state of the system remains relatively stable, but not fixed or static. In the research examples below, we show the importance of defining the timescale to focus on variability or stability, as processes may be volatile over short periods of time but relatively stable over longer ones.

Attractor and repeller states

The terms attractor and repeller states come from chemistry where they are not loaded with the connotations that occur when they are applied to human beings. In the vernacular, the term attractor connotes valuable and desirable; the term repeller connotes pushing something away. However, this is *not* the definition of those terms in CDST and their misuse will be problematic unless researchers are clear that attractor states are those to which a system tends to be drawn whether or not the state is thought to be pleasant and welcome – a long-running feud between rival teachers is an attractor state because it is relatively stable, even if it is also a nasty experience. Similarly, a repeller state may be pleasant or unpleasant, but by definition a system will not remain in that state for very long. The terms merely refer to the preferred state of the system, not whether that preferred state is positive or negative in valence. In the research examples below we take individual difference factors that have been studied using other methods, such as willingness to communicate and language anxiety, to be instances of attractor or repeller states of a system.

Emergence, self-organization and soft assembly

The idea of emergence suggests the state of the system can be considered more than the sum of its multiple, continuously interacting parts. Self-organization suggests that systems are not operating according to a predefined blueprint and do not reflect the inevitable unfolding of a plan. Rather, systems organize themselves and have an intrinsic tendency to display coherent patterns. Soft assembly refers to the idea that the interacting parts of a system can be shared and re-configured into coherent patterns, as systems organize themselves. A learner might describe 'feeling motivated' or 'feeling anxious,' two emergent states that often share features such as engagement with the learning process, involvement of the self, relationships with other people, a role for the teacher, emotional arousal, salience of learning goals and so on. Yet motivation and anxiety are experienced by individuals as qualitatively different states; generally speaking, motivation is pleasant and anxiety is not, motivation favours approach but anxiety suggests avoidance. The concept of emergence has been influential in connecting the dynamics of process to established research on familiar topics previously studied from other perspectives. In the examples below, we offer suggestions about how emergent states (being willing to communicate, experiencing anxiety, feeling motivation) make sense when considered as coherent, organized states dynamically assembled through the interactions of associated systems.

Fractals

Fractalization refers to the characteristic of systems to display self-similar patterns across levels. This means that the behaviour of a system on one timescale or level can potentially predict similar behaviour on different levels. Similarly, if patterns are found across timescales or levels, this can serve as evidence for a complex dynamic system. This means similar attractor/repeller states and similar types of dynamics can be manifested across system levels. For example, Mercer (2015) found that the self system of her learners exhibited comparable kinds of dynamics across different timescales of minutes, hours, weeks and months. The findings implied patterning in the types of system dynamics and system states when examined on different timescales. Fractals reveal that there can be surprising patterns and regularities in what may at first appear as random, chaotic systems, which, of course, can have important implications for research. In the research examples below, we are starting to see that some of the processes that occur on longer timescales also appear on shorter ones (see in particular descriptions of research into *willingness to communicate* and *the self*).

Research Questions from Standard and Complexity Approaches

Understanding these characteristics of a complex dynamic system has implications for how we formulate research questions, and even what is the focus of research. To illustrate the nature of research from a CDST perspective, we will outline typical characteristics and forms of quantitative and qualitative studies and show how they can be reconfigured and reconceptualized to better reflect CDST characteristics.

Quantitative compared with CDST approaches

The difference between a CDST approach to research and a traditional quantitative approach is substantial. CDST approaches can use quantitative data, and a number of data analytic techniques have been initiated (see Hiver & Al-Hoorie, 2020). But quantitative data analysis must be guided by research questions. Not only do the research questions themselves change, but the nature of the answers change as well. To clarify, Table 2.1 offers three examples of research questions that have been studied from a quantitative perspective, and a dynamic re-phrasing of questions in the same domain.

Within a particular study, questions such as those in the left-hand column of Table 2.1 will have a definite answer. Using statistical tests, we can say that the correlation between anxiety and course grades is −0.36 (Teimouri *et al.*, 2019), extraversion correlates with willingness to communicate (WTC) at $r = 0.39$ (MacIntyre & Charos, 1996) and the correlation between the Ideal L2 Self (motivation) and intended effort is 0.61 (Al-Hoorie, 2018). Across quantitative studies, different values will emerge. It is understood that correlations will vary from one study to another, as will group means and so on, but often the statistical results are similar and discrepancies accounted for by differences in sampling or methods used from one study to the next. The answers produced most often are phrased in concrete terms, using statistical values to create a sense of confidence, and when theory is added to the mix, a sense of genuine research progress can arise. Many researchers and research consumers find this approach satisfying.

The CDST toolbox produces a different approach by starting with a process-oriented account of the phenomena. Instead of finding *the* value of a correlation between motivation and intended effort or language course grades for example, the CDST account might describe what

Table 2.1 Quantitatively-oriented research questions compared with CDST variations

Standard questions	CDST re-phrasing
Does language anxiety correlate with course grades?	What happens as anxiety rises and falls during a test?
On average, are extraverts more willing to communicate than introverts?	How does introversion/extraversion combine with other factors to contribute to creating a learner's willingness to communicate?
Does motivation predict effort invested in learning?	What happens to effort as avoidance motivation rises?

learners who feel motivated are thinking and feeling, what is changing in their cognitive and emotion systems, what they are doing behaviourally, what is happening with their language production and nonverbal communication, and so on. In this case, the motivation system is under scrutiny as an emergent, self-organizing state that is soft assembled from a learner's cognition, emotions, behaviours, social context, interactions with peers, teachers, culture, other interlocutors and more. The specific details of the motivation process will differ from one person to the next – perhaps one person clearly imagines a desired future of smooth L2 communication getting closer and closer, but another ties their motivation directly to enjoying the present classroom context and the relationships therein. The research focus shifts from discovering generalizable patterns and estimating group averages to a focus on the specific perspectives of individual experiences and processes.

An additional implication of changing the phrasing of research questions is that it alters the types of analytic techniques that can be applied. Questions such as those in Table 2.1 often are answered with statistical analysis such as correlation, regression, structural equation modelling and analysis of variance, among others. Broadly speaking, there are two ways of constructing research questions - group comparisons and correlation. In group comparisons, we might ask whether differences between the means (averages) for two or more groups have arisen by chance or whether a difference between group means is statistically significant and meaningful. In studies based on correlation the objective is to describe the strength of a tendency for scores to rise and fall together; stronger correlation leads to better prediction. In both cases, variability or deviations (from the mean or from the predicted values in the case of correlations) usually cannot be explained and are used for statistical purposes as estimates of random error. Large sample sizes are valued because they provide more stable estimates of means, correlations and random error, allowing for more confidence in the results.

A dynamic focus follows different rules. Methods to answer CDST questions are not yet commonplace and there is need to further develop and disseminate methodology. In writing CDST projects for publication, we are learning that a focus on dynamics upends many of the accepted criteria for the evaluation of research. Quantitative research projects in the psychology of language learning are most often done with a cross sectional design where a researcher uses a pre-determined set of instruments to measure the concepts being studied while collecting data in as large a sample as possible. In a cross-sectional research design, each person is tested once. The kind of data relevant to a dynamic approach are different. van Dijk *et al.* (2011: 62) proposed three key criteria for research methods to address CDST questions:

> ...if we really want to know how an individual (or group) develops over time we need data that is dense (i.e. collected at many regular measurement points), longitudinal (i.e. collected over a longer period of time), and individual (i.e. for one person at a time and not averaged out).

The differences between approaches can upset the expectations of readers. One of the implications of shifting the focus so radically is that the gatekeepers in the field – the reviewers and editors of grant applications, journal articles, dissertation committees and so on – may be accustomed to applying a set of principles drawn from one methodological approach that are inappropriate in the other. For example, in a typical statistical approach, a large sample size is highly valued but in a dynamic approach, a large sample size may be overwhelming because of the density of data at the individual level.

The comparison of quantitative research methods with dynamic ones shows that the perspectives are quite different – not irreconcilable – but different. To provide a more complete picture, the next section contrasts qualitative and dynamic methods.

Qualitative compared with CDST approaches

Qualitative studies are often designed to describe the phenomena under study and to explain what is happening from the participants' perspective, and sometimes in their voice. Compared to quantitative studies, qualitative studies usually make fewer *a priori* assumptions about the data and instead carefully interpret the information from interviews, focus groups, textual analysis and other multimodal sources. Qualitative investigations typically allow for the openness of the systems discussed above, are often narrative in style, tend to be closely tied to context, and are often concerned with specificity and uniqueness by examining smaller samples in depth. In terms of describing the dynamics and openness of a given situation, qualitative methods have distinct advantages and require generally less substantial adjustments than a quantitative approach from a CDST perspective.

However, qualitative data are not inherently complex or dynamic. Unless a researcher is careful to include it in the design of the study, identifying the timescale under discussion can sometimes be difficult. The type of data utilized will depend on the specific research projects and questions. Many tools can be designed to focus on stability or variability such as narratives, journals or interviews. Typically, qualitative data is based on self-report data and this implies a host of methodological concerns such as impression management, memory problems, degree of awareness about the issues under investigation and ability to articulate responses. To capture the dynamics created by interacting systems, data can be collected in an ongoing fashion or retrospectively. However, in both cases, the processes that contribute to the dynamics of change may or may not be known by the respondents who typically are asked to account for events as they understand them. Ongoing approaches to data collection are possibly the most promising for investigating dynamics, enabling a research perspective on before, during and after the process under investigation. Capturing the ongoing dynamics as close to the moment they happen allows for a high density of data collection points as well as a reduction in the problems associated with memory and distance to the actual events in action. In contrast, retrospective research risks gaps in relevant data as well as a lower degree of data density.

One of the advantages of qualitative data is that it enables a holistic perspective on phenomena and processes and can potentially reveal more of the complexity of the system than an approach which reduces or fragments variables and processes. However, there is a danger that researchers might use the conceptual framework of CDST as a meta-theory to seek to explain data without the appropriate design to support it. As CDST becomes more widely known as a research approach, there is a risk that it becomes merely a nod to the methodological fashion of the moment. We should caution against dressing a traditional study in CDST clothing because it is something new or different. A gratuitous mention of CDST is not appropriate or even relevant unless a CDST perspective has been applied throughout the design of the study, data collection and analysis process.

Research Examples of CDST in Language Learning

To research dynamics from a CDST perspective, the central concern is not whether the data are quantitative versus qualitative in nature, but rather how the data are collected and analysed. Many cross-sectional and longitudinal designs to date can claim to have looked at change over time but typically they are not examining the dynamics in action and the actual processes of change which is the focus of a CDST perspective. Note also that longitudinal data in the form of test-retest designs where data collection occurs on only two occasions would not usually lead to the density of data required to assess dynamic changes as they happen. Furthermore, qualitative data do not automatically meet van Dijk *et al.*'s (2011) criteria for CDST data unless that data explicitly targets interacting processes. Data that best address the concerns of CDST are dense, longitudinal and individual. Here the term 'longitudinal' implies specifying a timescale for study which might be a long time period (measured by change over the years, the typical sense of 'longitudinal') or the timescale can be relatively brief measured by change over a few minutes which also can be considered longitudinal, especially if change is rapidly occurring.

The types of data required for dynamic studies are best obtained from methods designed to be dynamic from the outset rather than retro-fitting a study that used one-time measurement or pre-post designs. We have undertaken several such studies and found them to be quite challenging. We made our share of mistakes along the way. In doing so, we learned some lessons that can be shared in the hopes of allowing future researchers a smoother experience. In this final section, we will share some of those challenges, problematize them and describe the solutions we have worked out. The topics below include some of the most widely studied topics in the psychology of language learning, reinforcing the notion that the goal is to look at familiar processes in a different way to create new understandings and challenge existent conceptualizations.

Willingness to communicate

WTC was originally defined and studied in the native language communication literature, reflecting a stable predisposition to approach or avoid communication. The original WTC scale presented a set of 12 situations where a person might choose to initiate conversation with friends, acquaintances or strangers in a public speaking situation, large meeting, small group, or a dyad. In the L2 literature, additional measures of WTC were developed to focus also on tendencies to communicate inside versus outside classrooms, different skill areas and in different educational contexts (MacIntyre & Ayers-Glassey, in press).

The shift to a more dynamic perspective began most notably with MacIntyre and Legatto (2011) who examined WTC from a dynamic perspective using what has become known as the idiodynamic method. The challenge of adopting the dynamic approach was to measure WTC on a near continuous basis, in real time. Given that it is not possible to have research participants both speak and rate their WTC simultaneously, the solution was to record the speech on video for immediate playback. A second challenge was to provide numerical ratings of WTC that showed meaningful fluctuations over time. To capture those ratings required new software which could play back the participants' video and synchronize it with the WTC ratings made by the participant every second. The video serves to stimulate recall and immediate playback mitigates memory biases that affect reporting of previous affective states. This procedure allows researchers to gather a series of numerical ratings, linked in time with the video playback and to capture fluctuations in WTC longitudinally but over a short period of time (less than 5 minutes). The method also requires an interview with the person making the ratings to explain their rationale for increases and decreases in WTC scores, and allows for interviews with interlocutors and other observers. The interviews help to account for the unseen thought and emotion processes that contribute to communication.

Data analysis in this study examined both tendencies at the group level and analysis within persons, and what the authors called analysis in both horizontal and vertical directions. Results at the group (horizontal, across persons) level showed, unsurprisingly, that some tasks produced more WTC and longer speaking times than others. Results of the vertical analysis (within an individual) showed that there were meaningful exceptions to those trends. Further, results emphasized the intricate, continuous interactions among WTC, anxiety, vocabulary retrieval from memory, prior experience, self-presentation and nonverbal communication. In presenting the pattern of WTC fluctuations the authors emphasized that WTC was an attractor state built in part as an evolution from the previous state of the system; once a task was initiated, the respondent tended to continue even if there was some difficulty encountered and anxiety was aroused.

Motivation

Much of the literature on motivation has been studied from the theoretical standpoint of either the integrative motive (Gardner, 2010) or the L2 self system (Dörnyei, 2005). In both cases, motivation is considered over a long timescale of months and years. The integrative motive refers to a long-term process of taking on valued characteristics of another group. Similarly, the L2 self system reflects relatively long term processes including accumulated L2 experience, a sense of obligation (ought-to self), and the ideal future self. The most common research methods involve questionnaire-based measures of motivation.

MacIntyre and Serroul (2015) studied motivation from a dynamic perspective, over a short time period. The first challenge in doing so was to define the specific dimensions of motivation on which to focus. The problem in practical terms was to define a quality of motivation that changes on a per-second basis. The solution was to go outside the language arena, back to motivational basics, and look at approach and avoidance motives because they are defined as changing from moment-to-moment (see Epstein & Fenz, 1965). The experimental task featured a structured set of eight questions, administered orally by a research assistant, to be answered in the L2, similar in format to an oral quiz. Results showed fluctuations in approach-avoidance motives that were tied closely to interactions among attributes of the specific tasks, ongoing vocabulary retrieval, emotion processes, self-related cognition and other processes. There was no evidence of influence from integrative motivation or the L2 self. This pattern was somewhat surprising given the relative lack of emphasis on tasks as the driver of motivation in the L2 literature, but in retrospect the results make sense given the nature of the situation and timescale under study. The issues raised by central concepts in both integrative motivation and the L2 self system seem to refer to processes occurring over longer timescales or which might not be applicable in the specific experimental situation created by the study. In this study, the change in methods and timescales precipitated revisiting theory to find a perspective that better suited a CDST study on a per-second timescale. This suggests not only practical changes and fresh insights when researching from this perspective but also potential benefits offered by revisiting theories through a new lens.

Anxiety

As is the case for WTC and motivation, language anxiety has been studied widely in SLA. The theoretical approach to anxiety research was originally a mix of concepts adapted from other areas (including trait anxiety and test anxiety) with uncertain applicability to language learning contexts. In the mid 1980s, however, a specialized approach created scales to measure typical levels of anxiety in language-related contexts including classrooms (Horwitz et al., 1986), language use in the community (Gardner, 1985) and anxiety tied to specific skills such as reading and writing (Horwitz, 2017).

Gregersen et al. (2014) studied anxiety from a dynamic perspective linking anxiety arousal with physiological changes (heart rate) in the context of delivering a classroom presentation by L2 learners. One challenge of this study was to coordinate the measurement of anxiety and heart rate in real time. Physiological measures such as heart rate are tied to specific measurement timescales (e.g. beats-per-minute). The recording equipment used, similar to the heart rate tracking band that a runner might wear around the chest, also produces missing data when the sensor briefly loses contact with the skin as a person moves around. One significant problem was that the per-second timescale of measurement produced fine-grained information but with many missing data points. The solution was to define segments of a much longer communication event, averaged over longer time periods, which could be graphed together. By averaging ratings within a segment of communication stable measures of both anxiety and heart rate were generated, removing some of the noise that affects data collection under real world conditions (i.e. outside a controlled laboratory setting).

A second challenge presented by this study was the process of data summary and interpretation. In addition to analysing the connection between heart rate and anxiety ratings, the upward and downward trends or slopes in the line graph of participants' reactions were assessed to track the periods in which anxiety was rising and falling. The inspiration for this approach was Newton's famous laws of motion which were taken as analogous to the 'motion of emotion.' In essence, the tendency to experience anxiety was taken to be subject to external influences that provide impetus to change the emotional trajectory of the participant, either upward toward more anxiety or downward toward lower anxiety. The slope of the resulting line of anxiety ratings reflects the strength of the resulting force of change. Connecting multiple sources of data gathered in real time allowed the researchers to address the challenge of coordinating different data sets on multiple timescales.

This study showed how dynamic perspectives can challenge assumptions from more traditional studies, such as the correlation studies that are prevalent in the literature. Certainly there is value in taking long term stability into consideration, as typically less anxious speakers prepared and performed differently than the typically anxious ones. However, the anxiety reaction of a usually less anxious speaker seemed to be different from those more accustomed to the experience. Traditional quantitative methods would have glossed over this unusual case, treating its variability from the norm as error.

Anxiety + enjoyment

Although anxiety has been well studied in SLA, other emotions have not been widely investigated. There is a recent series of studies on language enjoyment that provide a positive emotional counterpart to the large number of anxiety studies that exist. Many of the enjoyment studies use the Dewaele and MacIntyre (2014) Foreign Language Enjoyment scale (Dewaele & MacIntyre, 2016; Dewaele et al., 2016; Dewaele et al., 2017).

Boudreau et al. (2018) studied the dynamics of not one but two emotions, anxiety and enjoyment. The idiodynamic approach allows for studies of the coordinated actions of different emotions. The challenge was to conceptualize how the emotions might jointly operate. Although prior questionnaire-style research showed a significant negative correlation between them ranging between −0.24 and −0.34, the size of the correlation suggests anxiety and enjoyment are not mutually exclusive or opposite ends of the same continuum. From a CDST perspective, the challenge was to measure the emotions with two separate ratings. The solution was to employ the idiodynamic software twice, once to get ratings of anxiety and a second time to get ratings for enjoyment, in counter-balanced order. A second challenge was to show the relationship between anxiety and enjoyment during free-flowing communication. The solution was to create meaningful segments of time wherein a communicative event occurred, such as during a complete, fluent utterance on a single topic, and then examine the coordinated trends for anxiety and enjoyment. Doing so allowed a description, within segments, of the periods in time where anxiety rises and enjoyment falls (indicative of negative correlation), and the reverse tendency of falling anxiety and rising enjoyment (also indicative of a negative correlation). Further, there were occasions where anxiety and enjoyment both were increasing at the same time, a pattern not predicted by the negative correlation found in questionnaire research. Furthermore, results showed that the various correlational patterns were found even within the same person, suggesting that the relationship between anxiety and enjoyment can change from negative to positive based on what is happening in the communication context. The results of this study show the value of CDST concepts such as emergence, dynamic stability and soft assembly.

Teacher stress

The teacher has been a somewhat neglected topic in the psychology of language learning, with much more of the focus placed on learner psychology. Prior research suggests that language teaching can be a stressful occupation (Hiver & Dörnyei, 2015).

A study currently underway is examining teacher stress using the experience sampling method (Talbot *et al.*, 2019). Experience sampling has been a preferred method of studying flow experiences in daily life (Csikszentmihalyi, 2014). The method provides research participants with a device (e.g. a pager or smartphone) that beeps at various points in time during the day. After receiving the beep, respondents answer questions about the activity they were performing at the moment. The method allows researchers to collect data in real time, as immediately as possible. Our study examined sources of teacher stress and uplifts, which are moments of positivity. We sought a diverse sample of teachers who were willing to install a new app on their phone. The app administered established, multi-item questionnaires on topics such as personality, wellbeing and stress (assessed on one occasion, not dynamically) along with multiple daily notifications (8 per day) to assess current stress levels dynamically through a series of structured responses that quickly described the context in which the beep arrived (e.g. I am in school, I am at home, etc.) as well as self-ratings of stress or uplifts.

The study examined 47 teachers, producing data points numbering in the tens of thousands. Summarizing that data is a challenge. On the one hand, individual level data analysis allows tracking of stress ratings over the time frame of the study. We can contextualize those fluctuations using information from questionnaires (teacher personality, wellbeing, life stressors) and demographic information. Yet this is not (yet) a description of a complex dynamic system. We have identified three teachers who scored high and three who scored low in wellbeing for case study analysis that triangulates information about the teacher and changes in stress over time. The challenge we face as researchers is to integrate the data to show the interactions among factors that contribute to teachers' stress as part of the system of teachers' emotional reactions to events, and not simply that there are highs and lows in the dynamics in stress ratings over time. We will look closely at the changes in stress ratings over time, asking questions such as 'how quickly do those ratings change?', 'what is the teacher doing when she/he is making the ratings?' and 'how might additional information such as employment status or family context be factored into the changes in stress reaction?' Preliminary results show the complex patterns of stress reactions in which a teacher's home life, relationships, obligations, leadership activities and so on are interacting with both teaching and non-teaching activities to create stress on some occasions and uplifts on other occasions. Our plan is to identify the signature dynamics related to stress for the teachers who have high wellbeing scores and those with low wellbeing scores to see if there are discernible differences between the teachers. After the case studies are complete, the rest of the data set can be interrogated using the case study information to focus analysis. The data present challenges because a large number of data points need to be summarized without losing the complex interactions they show.

Self

The self in its various guises has been an increasing focus of research in SLA (Mercer & Williams, 2014). As a notion, it has been fragmented into various constructs designed to capture various aspects of self and typically reflecting different research perspectives. For example, self-efficacy is very tightly defined and typically measured through questionnaires, whereas identity is more broadly defined and connected to specific social roles and contexts, and is typically the focus of qualitative work.

Mercer (2015) has defined the self as a complex dynamic system. She has studied how the self functions on different levels of perception and across different timescales. The focus has been on how the different facets and aspects of self interact to create an overall emergent sense of self. In her 2015 study, Mercer focused on the dynamics of the self on different timescales. To do this, she collected data with four volunteer students on the timeframe of seconds/minutes using idiodynamic software, across minutes/hours within class using a survey, across days/weeks using journals and across weeks/months using interviews. The data were analysed on each level for dynamics and these were compared. She found that there were similar patterns of dynamics and 'if… then' signature dynamics (Mischel, 2004) across timescales. This refers to patterns where *IF* this happens, *THEN* this is likely to happen. These findings raise interesting questions about the role of fractalization in the dynamics of systems and thus the possibility of predicting dynamic patterns across timescales. The challenge for researchers is how to best integrate dynamic research across different timescales.

In summary, this brief overview of specific research reveals how studies designed and implemented from a CDST perspective are beginning to show some of the possibilities afforded by the approach. WTC, motivation, anxiety, enjoyment, stress and the self have been studied extensively from traditional quantitative and qualitative perspectives. Yet, there is something new about the CDST account that foregrounds interactions among concepts and provides novel insights into the processes underlying familiar concepts.

Insights for Researching Language Learning Psychology from a CDST Perspective

The above illustrative studies and their research methods have presented a number of challenges. Real time data are messy, dense and can be difficult to summarize without losing the nature of the dynamics. Issues that arose were addressed sometimes by blending data sets and forms of analysis at both the group and individual level, with emphasis on the latter. We have also experienced challenges when writing about CDST and the need to use language that can be conceived as jargonistic to those unfamiliar with the notions and concepts underlying CDST as well as the need to explain extensively the theory before getting to the study itself.

Yet, despite the challenges, the benefit of a CDST perspective in the above studies was that it allowed us to offer a different interpretation of what was happening than traditional methods would allow. We feel there are five main types of insights such work can afford:

(1) Exploring different timescales/levels of granularity: In a complex dynamic system, there are many ways of defining a system and it depends where a researcher chooses to set the boundaries and focus. A guiding principle for deciding what is being defined as a system is to consider what functions as a whole (Larsen-Freeman & Cameron, 2008). This can then be considered in terms of levels of granularity and the related timescales of dynamism. By starting with the explicit recognition of the timescale under study, we are able to set limits on the processes under consideration, providing focus for the studies. The idiodynamic studies reported above specified a brief timescale measured in seconds and minutes, the ESM study deals with a timescale of days in a week. But as the notion of fractals suggests, these specific timescales are nested within other timescales, as the study of the self demonstrates. Patterns observed on one timescale can sometimes be found at others. The challenge becomes how to combine research examining systems at various levels of granularity and across timescales.

(2) Investigating various forms of dynamism and stability: The focus of this chapter has been on how systems change or remain stable over time. Dynamism does not have to mean change from one state to

another; it can mean fluctuations within a relatively stable state. Dynamic stability can be observed as changes in processes on lower timescales may not have noticeable effects on higher levels of granularity and across longer timescales. Systems may show homeostasis. The challenge is how to view different degrees and types of dynamism and stability and how these may interact across levels and timescales.

(3) Focusing on ongoing processes: When examining dynamics, we have stressed that single data collection points may establish a snapshot of the state of a system for the participants in the research, but the research design does not necessarily reveal processes in action. Research must be designed from the start to examine the actual processes of change as they happen and this necessitates specific research designs with dense data collected at appropriate points in time.

(4) Examining uniqueness AND commonalities: A CDST perspective does not imply that scholars ignore patterns across systems or parts of systems, there is much to be learned from examining how findings may be similar across individuals and units of analysis. However, CDST does foreground strongly the benefits to be gained from looking at outliers, the unusual, the unique and the unexpected. These reflect the core characteristics of a complex dynamic system.

(5) Taking holistic perspectives and conceiving of open systems: The psychology of language learning has defined, differentiated and measured a number of specific concepts such as motivation, anxiety and WTC. However, as we observe them in operation in real time, many theoretical distinctions melt away. A CDST approach requires putting concepts such as motivation, anxiety and WTC in motion, describing how they move together, and what constitutes a meaningful system. The notion of open systems provides a lesson in contrasting the group level of data analysis with individual level. Traditional quantitative methods require defining the concept in the study in advance and measuring them with appropriate instruments. This has the effect of closing the potential influences on the system to only those defined in advance. By allowing for open systems, and gathering qualitative data repeatedly to assess how the processes interact over time, we are able to identify influences from the perspective of a language speaker or teacher that would have been missed otherwise. This allows for a richer description than otherwise would be possible.

Conclusion

In this chapter, we have reflected on our understandings of what researching language learning psychology from a CDST perspective implies. We have considered how the kinds of questions, use of theoretical frameworks and constructs as well as methodologies and forms of analysis must adjust to accommodate the specific characteristics of a complex dynamic system and its commensurate meta-theory. We have focused in particular on the dynamics of such systems and looked at several illustrations of research focused on dynamics, how such studies need to be conducted, the challenges posed by such work and the fresh insights they can generate. We hope to have inspired others who may wish to research from this perspective and examine dynamics specifically. We have shown how challenges can be creatively met and how the insights gained from such work can push forward our understandings to challenge our established and conventional views of constructs and their interrelationships. A CDST perspective is still in its relative infancy in the field and its merit for language learning psychology will be tested out over time. As a theory, it must offer something new and worthwhile, making a substantial contribution of growth to the field; otherwise, it becomes merely another short-lived academic fashion or fad. We feel this perspective offers rich potential, especially for the field of language learning psychology. As we have argued in this chapter and as we believe our work to date has shown, CDST is an innovative lens through which to reflect on the complex and dynamic nature of human psychology and its collective as well as individual characteristics. We feel exciting research times lie ahead and the challenges inherent in such work will be met when scholars work together with a spirit of innovation, criticality and openness to new ways of thinking and researching.

References

Al-Hoorie, A. (2018) The L2 motivational self system: A meta analysis. *Studies in Second Language Learning and Teaching* 8, 721–754.

Boudreau, C., MacIntyre, P.D. and Dewaele, J.-M. (2018) Enjoyment and anxiety in second language communication: An idiodynamic approach. *Studies in Second Language Learning and Teaching* 8 (1), 149–170.

Canale, M. and Swain, M. (1980) Theoretical bases of communicative approaches to second language teaching and testing. *Applied Linguistics* 1, 1–47. doi:10.1093/applin/1.1.1

Csikszentmihalyi, M. (2014) *Validity and Reliability of the Experience-Sampling Method.* New York: Springer.

de Bot, K. (2014) Rates of change: Timescales in second language development. In Z. Dörnyei, P.D. MacIntyre and A. Henry (eds) *Motivational Dynamics in Language Learning* (pp. 29–37). Bristol: Multilingual Matters.

Dewaele, J-M. and MacIntyre, P.D. (2014) The two faces of Janus? Anxiety and enjoyment in the foreign language classroom. *Studies in Second Language Learning and Teaching* 4 (2), 237–274.

Dewaele, J.-M. and MacIntyre, P.D. (2016) The predictive power of multicultural personality traits, learner and teacher variables on Foreign Language Enjoyment and Anxiety in classrooms. Presented at the International Association for Language and Social Psychology, Bangkok, Thailand.

Dewaele, J.-M., MacIntyre, P., Boudreau, C. and Dewaele, L. (2016) Do girls have all the fun? Anxiety and enjoyment in the foreign language classroom. *Theory and Practice of Second Language Acquisition* 2, 41–63.

Dewaele, J.-M., Witney, J., Saito, K. and Dewaele, L. (2017) Foreign language enjoyment and anxiety: The effect of teacher and learner variables. *Language Teaching Research,* 1–22.

Dörnyei, Z. (2005) *The Psychology of the Language Learner: Individual Differences in Second Language Acquisition*. London: Routledge.

Epstein, S. and Fenz, W.D. (1965) Steepness of approach and avoidance gradient in humans as a function of experience: Theory and experiment. *Journal of Experimental Psychology* 70 (1), 1–12.

Fogel, A. (2006) Dynamic systems research on interindividual communication: The transformation of meaning-making. *Journal of Developmental Processes* 1, 7–30. See http://www.psych.utah.edu/people/people/fogel/publications/Fogel-Dynamic%20Systems%20Research.pdf

Gardner, R.C. (1985) *Social Psychology and Second Language Learning: The Role of Attitudes and Motivation*. London: Edward Arnold Publishers.

Gardner, R.C. (2010) *Motivation and Second Language Acquisition: The Socio-educational Model*. New York: Peter Lang.

Gregersen, T., MacIntyre, P.D. and Meza, M.D. (2014) The motion of emotion: Idiodynamic case studies of learners' foreign language anxiety. *Modern Language Journal* 98 (2), 574–588.

Hiver, P. and Al-Hoorie, A.H. (2020) *Research Methods for Complexity Theory in Applied Linguistics*. Bristol: Multilingual Matters.

Hiver, P. and Dörnyei, Z. (2015) Language teacher immunity: A double-edged sword. *Applied Linguistics*, 1–20. https://doi.org/10.1093/applin/amv034

Horwitz, E.K. (2017) On the misreading of Horwitz, Horwitz, and Cope (1986) and the need to balance anxiety research and the experiences of anxious language learners. In C. Gkonou, M. Daubney and J.-M. Dewaele (eds) *New Insights into Language Anxiety: Theory, Research and Educational Implications* (pp. 31–47). Bristol: Multilingual Matters.

Horwitz, E.K., Horwitz, M. and Cope, J. (1986) Foreign language classroom anxiety. *Modern Language Journal* 70, 125–132. doi: https://doi.org/10.1111/j.1540-4781. 1986.tb05256.x

King, J. (2013) Silence in the second language classrooms of Japanese universities. *Applied Linguistics* 34, 325–343.

Larsen-Freeman, D. and Cameron, L. (2008) Complex systems and applied linguistics. *The Modern Language Journal* 92 (4), 644–645.

Larsen-Freeman, D. (2017) Complexity theory: The lessons continue. In L. Ortega and Z. Han (eds) *Complexity Theory and Language Development: In Celebration of Diane Larsen-Freeman*. Amsterdam: John Benjamins.

MacIntyre, P.D. (2017) An overview of language anxiety research and trends in its development. In C. Gkonou, M. Daubney and J.-M. Dewaele (eds) *New Insights into Language Anxiety: Theory, Research and Educational Implications* (pp. 11–30). Bristol: Multilingual Matters.

MacIntyre, P.D. and Ayers-Glassey, S. (in press) Measuring willingness to communicate. In P. Winke and T. Brunfaut (eds) *The Routledge Handbook of Second Language Acquisition and Language Testing*. Abingdon: Routledge.

MacIntyre, P.D. and Charos, C. (1996) Personality, attitudes, and affect as predictors of second language communication. *Journal of Language and Social Psychology* 15, 3–26.

MacIntyre, P.D. and Legatto, J.J. (2011) A dynamic system approach to willingness to communicate: Developing an idiodynamic method to capture rapidly changing affect. *Applied Linguistics* 32, 149–171.

MacIntyre, P.D., MacKay, E., Ross, J. and Abel, E. (2017) The emerging need for methods appropriate to study dynamic systems. In L. Ortega and Z. Han (eds) *Complexity Theory and Language Development: In Celebration of Diane Larsen-Freeman* (pp. 97–122). Amsterdam: John Benjamins.

MacIntyre, P.D. and Serroul, A. (2015) Motivation on a per-second timescale: Examining approach-avoidance motivation during L2 task performance. In Z. Dörnyei, P.D.

MacIntyre and A. Henry (eds) *Motivational Dynamics in Language Learning* (pp. 95–108). Bristol: Multilingual Matters.

Mercer, S. (2015) The dynamics of the self in SLA: A multilevel approach. In Z. Dörnyei, P. MacIntyre and A. Henry (eds) *Motivational Dynamics in Language Learning* (pp. 139–163). Bristol: Multilingual Matters.

Mercer, S. (2016) Complexity and language teaching. In G. Hall (ed.) *The Routledge Handbook of English Language Teaching* (pp. 473–485). Abingdon: Routledge.

Mercer, S. and Williams, M. (2014) *Multiple Perspectives on the Self in SLA*. Bristol: Multilingual Matters.

Mischel, W. (2004) Toward an integrative science of the person. *Annual Review of Psychology 55* (1), 1–22.

Mystkowska-Wiertelak, A. and Pawlak, M. (2017) *Willingness to Communicate in Instructed Second Language Acquisition. Combining a Macro and Micro-Perspective*. Bristol: Multilingual Matters.

Savignon, Sandra J. (2000) Communicative language teaching. In M. Byram (ed.) *Routledge Encyclopedia of Language Teaching and Learning* (pp. 125–129). London: Routledge.

Talbot, K., MacIntyre, P., Gregersen, T., Mercer, S., Ross, J. and Banga C.A. (2019) Language teacher stressors and uplifts, wellbeing, and personality Traits: An International ESM study. Presented at the annual conference of the American Association of Applied Linguistics, Atlanta GA, 2019.

Teimouri, Y., Goetze, J. and Plonsky, L. (2019) Second language anxiety and achievement: a meta-analysis. *Studies in Second Language Acquisition*, 1–25. doi:10.1017/S0272263118000311

Thelen, E. and Smith, L.B. (1994) *A Dynamic Systems Approach to the Development of Cognition and Action*. Cambridge, MA: MIT Press.

van Dijk, M., Verspoor, M. and Lowie, W. (2011) Variability and DST. In M. Verspoor, K. de Bot and W. Lowie (eds) *A Dynamic Approach to Second Language Development: Methods and Techniques* (pp. 55–84). Amsterdam: John Benjamins Publishers.

3 Interacting Levels and Timescales in the Emergence of Feelings in the L2 Classroom

Richard J. Sampson

> Weaving my way between desks, the students seemed oblivious to my passage. As I watched them in activity, I had been drawn in by the expressions on their faces. Smiles seemed to be amplified as they rippled to the surface in many pairs. Yet, at other times and in other individuals, there were looks of consternation met by empathetic understanding; outbursts of laughter and flourishes of voices raised in excitement. Moving again to one side of the room, I stood back and tried to take it all in, this feeling classroom.

I work in Japan with undergraduates studying English as a Foreign Language (EFL) and language learning psychology. At the same time, I am a researcher of my own classrooms. My interest in researching second language (L2) emotions has emerged naturally through my teaching career, across daily experiences like that in the vignette. Learning involves a complex interplay with our feelings, so much so that 'it is literally neurobiologically impossible to build memories, engage complex thoughts, or make meaningful decisions without emotion' (Immordino-Yang, 2016: 18). Yet, in terms of additional language learning, there is still clearly room for empirical work, as Boudreau *et al.* (2018: 149) remark with dismay: 'Prior research in SLA has either ignored emotions, underestimated their relevance, or has studied them as a relatively stable individual difference variable'.

In this chapter, therefore, I wish to lay out some of the ways in which I have recently been working to gain situated understandings of the L2 feelings of learners in my classrooms. I commence by briefly reviewing a key selection of literature concerning emotions in general and L2 education settings. The chapter then turns to a narrative exposition of my own developing interest in researching feelings. I touch upon two different angles from which I examined the same introspective data collected from undergraduate EFL students in my classes. In particular, I present tools founded on complexity thinking through which to consider L2 emotions in terms of individual learners and a class group (multiple threading), as well as in terms of different interacting timescales (timescales analysis). Ultimately, the chapter argues implicitly that complexity perspectives furnish reminders to maintain a focus on describing situated phenomena rather than prescribing to rules.

Emotions and L2 Learning

Emotions are believed to have evolved as an adaptive tool in response to the necessities of the environment (e.g. Plutchik, 2001). They are considered to be psychological and physiological episodes emergent from interactions with the world around us (Cahour, 2013; Lemke, 2013). They comprise bodily reactions, expressive behaviour, as well as a subjective feeling – conscious aspects of our interactions with/in context (Cahour, 2013; Damasio, 2003). The trigger for an emotion is known as its object or event focus (Shuman & Scherer, 2014 – although see later in the chapter for my revised conceptualization). Emotions are also said to involve an action-tendency element (Shuman & Scherer, 2014). They channel our behaviour, through processes of 'appraisal of the situation by the persons, as a function of the meaning that they attribute to it, as well as their interests and goals … including beliefs, values, and aspects of previous experience that are mobilized in the situation' (Cahour, 2013: 58). Finally, while there are undoubtedly problems with dichotomizing emotions, they have traditionally been grouped into negative and positive valences based on whether the feeling is pleasant or unpleasant. On the one hand, negative emotions are said to prompt 'fight or flight' actions, such as anger engendering attacking tendencies or fear calling forth the urge to run away; on the other hand, positive emotions elicit broader tendencies to build resources, such as curiosity to seek information (e.g. Fredrickson, 1998; Plutchik, 2001; Shuman & Scherer, 2014).

Concerning L2 learning, researchers have tended to focus on distinct emotions. One of the most researched, language anxiety, is a situation-specific worry or nervousness about using an L2 (Horwitz et al., 1986). In many cases, it concerns perceived negative evaluation by others and threats to self-image due to difficulties in presenting ideas to the same degree as in one's native language (e.g. Dewaele & Alfawzan, 2018; MacIntyre & Gregersen, 2012). A good deal of recent empirical work has also begun to investigate the relationships between anxiety and enjoyment (Boudreau et al., 2018; Dewaele & Alfawzan, 2018; Dewaele & Dewaele, 2018; Dewaele & MacIntyre, 2014, 2016). Such a focus would seem overdue, as positive L2 emotions have been correlated with greater willingness to communicate (Dewaele & Dewaele, 2018), motivation (MacIntyre & Vincze, 2017) and performance in L2 classes (Dewaele & Alfawzan, 2018). This line of research has revealed that L2 anxiety and enjoyment function independently rather than proportionally (Dewaele & MacIntyre, 2016: 230; see also Dewaele & MacIntyre, 2014). Dewaele and MacIntyre (2016) moreover illuminated two different dimensions of L2 enjoyment – a social dimension from supportive peers and teachers, and a private dimension involving an internal sense of pride through succeeding in the face of challenges.

Situated and dynamic research into L2 study emotions is much more limited in extent yet has provided alluring insights. For instance, research by Garrett and Young (2009) has found the profound impact of understandings of identity on L2 feelings. In their study, the participant's identity as a proficient speaker of other additional languages lead to negative emotions connected with her comparisons between abilities in languages; her social identity as a student initially fostered negative emotions as she made erroneous social comparisons between her own ability and that of her peers, yet transformed into positive emotions as she revised her appraisal of peers and developed relatedness with them; and her identity as an L2 French teacher connected with positive emotional evaluations of the teaching styles of her instructors and materials. In another study, Méndez López and Peña Aguilar (2013) unearthed some fascinating relationships between classroom emotions and action tendencies. Intriguingly, while positive emotions at times spurred greater self-efficacy and motivation to take risks, at other times such feelings engendered a kind of coasting wherein students sat back and just enjoyed the pleasant feeling; conversely, negative emotions such as anxiety about assessment tasks led some participants to stop trying in class and consider giving up entirely, while a sense of difficulty such as when learners realized a mistake elicited motivation to improve that particular skill. Their study reveals that, while teachers may prefer students to always experience pleasant feelings, in fact, both pleasant and unpleasant feelings can prompt helpful and detrimental action tendencies. As Pinner (2016: 182) similarly articulates based on his experiences with classroom research, 'not all learning experiences have to be *good*. In fact, some of the best learning experiences come from *bad* experiences and these have an important contribution to make in both education and learning.' Lastly, Imai (2010) followed a group of three Japanese university EFL students as they participated in a series of lesson-external meetings in order to prepare for a group presentation in English. Imai collected data from multiple perspectives, through video recording discussions (in Japanese), asking participants to fill out emotion logs and questionnaires and using stimulated recall to gain participants' own interpretations. Imai uncovered that while participants brought their own understandings of the task and course to the discussions, these understandings were adapted via verbally manifested 'emotional intersubjectivities.' Intriguingly, these co-formed, emotional understandings had a large, non-linear impact on the learning task, as group members collectively changed their goal for the presentation in rejection of the teacher-intended pedagogical outcome. As such, Imai (2010: 288) argues that there is a need to consider 'emotions as socially and discursively constructed acts of communication that mediate learning and development'.

My Path to Studying L2 Feelings

As a classroom teacher, I have always been keenly interested in the emotional experiences of learners in my classes. However, my entry to exploring L2 feelings as a *research* focus involves a somewhat more meandering path. A couple of years ago, I received funding to study the social nature of L2 learning motivation. I implemented action research together with undergraduates in two of my compulsory EFL classes ($n = 47$), introducing change-action through classroom activities that encouraged learners to think about and discuss the meaning of their EFL studies. My interest was in the ways in which motivation and action emerged through social processes connected to students' hopes for the actions of their peers in the classroom (Sampson, 2018), as well as their felt expectations from significant others and society (Sampson, 2017, 2019a). Data were collected via action research activity worksheets, classroom seating charts with observational notes (students were randomly assigned new partners every lesson), introspective learner journals and an open-ended semester-final questionnaire. It is the journals that inform discussion in this chapter.

As a form of introspective data collection, journals in classroom research have the potential to 'take us to a place that no other data collection method can reach – into the mind of the learner or teacher' (Nunan & Bailey, 2009: 307). They offer a feasible tool that does not overburden participants nor interrupt the natural processes of classroom action, yet has the ability to provide contextualized, dynamic, personal and candid perceptions of learning experiences (Gilmore, 2016; Nunan & Bailey, 2009; Sampson, 2016a). In arguing for the aptitude of journals for classroom research, Phelps (2005: 40) remarks that:

> No-one knows the complex interplay of factors that impact on an individual, or the significance of any one factor, greater than the individual themselves. This is not to assume for a moment that the individual learner is fully aware of all these factors, but rather that they are in a better position to understand them than anyone else.

Based on past experiences using journals in classroom research (e.g. Sampson, 2012, 2016a, 2016b), I worked to ensure such benefits, whilst trying to alleviate possible drawbacks sometimes found in this method of data collection. In order to reduce concerns about low compliance rates and large variations in the length of entries (Gilmore, 2016), the journal was introduced as a reflective pedagogical task. Students were assessed by how many weekly entries they submitted, and whether entries were over a minimum of 70 words. As part of facilitating the journaling process, as well as trying to head off problems of recall (Hall, 2008; Nunan & Bailey, 2009; Porto, 2007), participants wrote the journals as an email to me directly following each lesson. The prompt was simply:

> Please write about your experiences in lessons. However, do not merely list the activities we did in the lesson. Try to write your perceptions and reflections about your actions and those of other class members doing the various activities.

Hall (2008) warns of utilizing data collected in the L2 of participants, as their capacity to write what they truly think is determined by their level of L2 capability. However, the English level of learners in this context was reasonable (Test of English for International Communication (TOEIC) scores ranged from mid-400 to 800). Being part of pedagogical practice, it was also my wish as a teacher to show my respect for participants' developing L2 identities (Sampson, 2016a). Learners were therefore encouraged and wrote these journals in English, although occasionally using some Japanese phrases. Entries were collected for 13 of 15 lessons across a semester.

As I was reading and replying to students' email journals every week, what struck me was their consistently emotional tone. This was certainly not dry data. It was literally bursting with feelings. As I have argued elsewhere (Sampson, 2016a; see also Radford, 2007), I find that action research offers the possibility of looking back historically after the collection of data in order to explore new directions in the researcher's understandings. It was an interest in investigating the situated, emotional nature of my own EFL classrooms that prompted me to re-analyse participant journals from the perspective of L2 study feelings.

Looking at Levels: Describing the Whole and the Parts

I started with a seemingly straightforward quest to look at the collected data and describe the feelings and connected object foci to which writing in the participant journals pointed. I will not dwell in too much detail on this initial re-analysis, but instead refer readers to Sampson (2020). Suffice to say, I carried out routine thematic content analysis, without predetermined categories, of different feelings and object foci using the qualitative data management application NVivo. Entries were additionally coded to 'week' codes in order to facilitate an examination of the ebb and flow of feelings across the semester. This first stage of analysis involved a process of quantifying the qualitative data to gain a sense of the kinds of emotions and the extent of their experience by my students (Onwuegbuzie & Daniel, 2003).

Analysis revealed a kaleidoscope of feelings. Confirming my initial intuition of the emotional tone to the journals, an incredible 94% of collected responses touched upon feelings in some way. A total of 10 feelings frequently emerged across the entries of learners in the two classes: seven pleasant (or 'positive') feelings – a sense of achievement, enjoyment, gratitude, interest, admiration, excitement, surprise – and three unpleasant (or 'negative') feelings – disappointment, a sense of difficulty and anxiety. In congruence with past research (Garrett & Young, 2009; MacIntyre & Vincze, 2017), and supporting Pavlenko's (2013) call for an expansion of research away from an obsession with L2 anxiety, there was a far greater incidence of pleasant feelings. As the most prevalent, a sense of achievement was apparent in a remarkable 44% of entries. Moreover, the greatest spread of students (45 of 47) wrote about enjoyment. In terms of unpleasant emotions, disappointment (31% of entries) and a sense of difficulty (27% of entries) were more prominent than anxiety (18%). All in all, suggesting the range of feelings experienced in the L2 classroom, over 30 different students mentioned eight of the feelings at least once. Even the remaining two feelings were mentioned by around 20 different students.

However, complexity thinking fosters an understanding that in looking only at the averaged, generalized whole, we may lose sight of the experience of any one learner. As Morin (2006: 6) describes, 'knowledge of the parts is not enough, the knowledge of the whole as a whole is not enough' but we must attempt 'to comprehend the relations between the whole and the parts'. Teaching, even more so than other 'helping' professions like nursing and social work, requires a focus at one and the same time upon individuals as well as a group as a whole (Urdan, 2014). In order to more adequately represent the whole (class group, whole semester) and the parts (individual participants, specific lessons), I employed a tool known as multiple threading (Davis & Sumara, 2006). In their original exposition, these researchers used this tool to illustrate how often and to what extent individual voices or ideas contribute to an overall text, such as a research paper or dramatic performance. Multiple threading 'involves the presentation of several narrative strands' in which 'some may be only brief phrases or single images that punctuate the text, and strands may overlap or interlink at times' (Davis & Sumara, 2006: 162). I adapted this tool to visually represent not only how often, but also in what ways individual students joined the overall 'feeling narrative' of their class group on any specific day, and over the semester. The multiple threading used weeks across a horizontal axis and individual learners along a vertical axis. As such, I allocated a 'square' to each learner for each week of data collected. Emergent from analysis of the qualitative data, I then counted the number of different feelings experienced by a learner for a particular week. The square at the intersection of learner-week was then divided as evenly as possible based on this count, and different shading or hatching applied to represent these feelings (see Figure 3.1 – names are pseudonyms). (One word of caution here is that squares with a larger area devoted to a specific feeling do not imply that this feeling is stronger.)

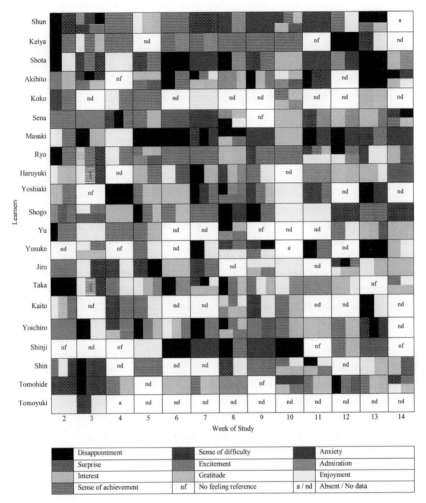

Figure 3.1 Multiple threading of learners' reference to feelings by lesson

The multiple threading representation is somewhat of a visual over-load which requires more effort – or allows more freedom of insight – on the part of the observer. Nevertheless, using multiple threading from a complexity perspective reminds us to maintain our understanding of the ways in which *individual* students all contribute to the *whole* of the feeling narrative of their class.

I recognize that multiple threading is partial, as proponents of complexity understand all representations of data and 'knowing' to be (Davis & Sumara, 2006). I do, however, find it offers potential as one tool to preserve a sense of the whole and the parts, in terms of learner-class and lesson-semester. It allows us to zoom in on the feelings of an individual student in one particular lesson, or trace their emotional trajectory across the semester; concurrently, we can contrast the feelings of multiple students in the same class during a lesson or across time. By examining any week in Figure 3.1, we can gain a sense of the ambivalent nature of feelings perceived by individual students and across students in any given lesson. That is, the multiple threading aligns with Boudreau *et al.* (2018) in hinting that there is a great deal of interpersonal variation in how feelings evolve over the course of classroom experiences. Multiple threading moreover allows us to maintain sight of the longer timescale of the semester: Some learners tended to mention positively-valenced feelings more consistently across the semester, other students more negatively-valenced feelings, while still others revealed a relatively even mix. In line with Garrett and Young (2009: 221), it suggests a focus on how feelings were 'modified by new experiences ... over time' and emerged in different ways within and across lessons. Finally, we can also use the multiple threading matrix to gain a sense of the general emotional orientation of the class as a whole. By assigning contrasting colours or hatching for more pleasant or unpleasant feelings, we can make a rudimentary analysis of the emotional valence dynamics of the whole. This said, we must remain cognizant that more pleasant feelings across the class group does not necessarily equate with constructive action tendencies or motivation, with the reverse also being true (Méndez López & Peña Aguilar, 2013; Pinner, 2016). Notwithstanding, I feel that a multiple threading does a reasonable job of representing the kinds of implicit understandings that teachers develop of the general emotional climate dynamics of a class group.

Describing the Emergence of Feelings over Interacting Timescales

My take on complexity as a philosophical and research position aligns with Kuhn (2007: 299 – emphasis mine) in understanding that 'it is more useful to have evocative rather than prescriptive descriptions,' such that research based on complexity thinking 'is utilized for *exploring possibilities* rather than *prescribing* relationships and processes'. Ushioda's (2009: 217) argument that much research to date has intended to 'uncover rule-governed psychological laws that explain' instead of 'explor[ing] the dynamic complexity of personal meaning-making in social context' sums up well a fundamental difference in perspective. Complexity thinking runs in opposition to 'the principle of simplicity [which] either separates that which is linked (disjunction), or unifies that which is diverse (reduction)' (Morin, 2008: 39). As Morin (2008: 5) also proposes:

> Complexity is a fabric (complexus: that which is woven together) of heterogeneous constituents that are inseparably associated: complexity poses the paradox of the one and the many. ... Complexity is in fact the fabric

of events, actions, interactions, retroactions, determinations, and chance that constitute our phenomenal world.

I therefore wanted to further explore dynamics in the situated emergence of feelings from the perspectives of individual learners. The initial re-analysis presented in Sampson (2020) revealed a variety of object foci. However, as I was conducting this analysis, I found my categories to be too static, and that there were usually multiple object foci in the context of a learner's experience of emotion. While object foci are commonly considered as 'triggers' for an emotion, I began to recognize that 'which emotion surfaces is neither determined solely by the context nor by an individual's psychological tendencies, but by the organismic interplay of the two' (Boiger & Mesquita, 2015: 383). I was moreover reminded that a recurrent quality mentioned in studies is the 'momentary' or 'instantaneous' nature of emotions. Yet my understandings instead seemed to suggest that the feelings of my participants were not in most cases a fleeting and linear response to a currently present event.

Complexity thinking reminds us that the L2 classroom is open and interacting with other systems, rather than being a completely 'bounded' entity (van Lier, 2004). Multiple agents with past experiences, evolving identities and projections about the future come together to focus on this domain of study. These open psychological systems interact with learners' moment-to-moment experiences of materials and activities, even as learners also socially interact with their classmates. One key aspect of such dynamicity is the ways in which complex systems interact over different timescales. A timescale appertains to the granularity of a developmental process (de Bot, 2015). As de Bot (2015: 36) reminds us, 'we cannot undo the interaction between timescales and study phenomena on one timescale without taking into account other timescales'. I therefore wondered how coding and representing object foci based on interacting timescales might provide a more detailed picture of the emergence of L2 study feelings of my learners (Sampson, 2019b).

I approached what I term rather unimaginatively the 'timescales analysis' over several recursive stages:

(1) I coded object foci *across participants* by timescales ranging from seemingly short perceptions during an activity, to a lesson or series of lessons, to months or years of continuing (past, present and future) L2 study experiences and still longer life timescales of personality, multiple identities and beliefs. In this sense, the timescales appear similar to Yashima and Arano's (2015) use of sociocultural domains or Aoyama and Yamamoto's (this volume) levels in Trajectory Equifinality Modelling; however, I used timescales which made sense to me as someone working in and dealing with data from an educational context.

(2) I next homed in on coding for *individual* participants. I employed the matrix coding function of NVivo, a kind of Boolean search tool, in two ways: To glimpse intersections between object foci and different timescales for each learner, and to obtain a picture of data coded to object foci and timescales at each week.

(3) I examined such coded data for each participant, and organized brief summaries and excerpts into an egocentric coding comparison table. These tables were designed with timescales running across as rows, and week of study as columns. The process of representing analysis in this fashion raised my awareness of a need to revisit some coding to explore dynamics across weeks of the study. I moreover reviewed the weekly seating charts to reconfirm students' partners during any given lesson, and investigate related data concerning shared events and object foci. Relevant partner-perspectives were incorporated into the egocentric coding comparison tables. Figure 3.2 displays a truncated example of one such table for a period of two weeks of the semester.

(4) Finally, Dörnyei (2014) contends that, in conducting complexity research, one must look for salient patterns or signature dynamics associated with system outcomes. He continues: 'even though we cannot generalise such signature dynamics from one situation to another … the identified patterns are fundamental enough to be useful in understanding the dynamics of a range of other situations' (Dörnyei, 2014: 10). In my analysis, the 'system outcomes' of interest were the feelings that students experienced. I therefore looked across the coding comparison tables of individuals to describe patterns in the emergence of these classroom L2 study feelings.

Timescale		Week of study 2	Week of study 3
	Months / Years	• Personality / life experience: 'Unusually talk with girl'	• Reinforcement of belief in 'Showing Enjoyment': 'Smiles make us happy naturally'
	Lesson Series		• Continued to choose 'Show Enjoyment': Felt progress • Motivation to try again next lesson: Not be nervous
	Lesson	• Motivation to 'Show Enjoyment' → Couldn't achieve? • 'It was so fun' ('and she's cute')	• Motivation to 'Show Enjoyment' → 'Probably achieved although with embarrassed smiles'
	Activity	• Nervous: 'Hardly made my words to say' • Couldn't keep remembering to smile	• Being embarrassed too much • Supported by Nanami: 'He looked nerves, so I asked him many questions'

Figure 3.2 Timescales coding comparison table example (egocentric for one student, Kanata, revealing the emergence of his classroom feelings focused on cooperation with different female students over a two-week period)

Towards a Situated, Dynamic View of L2 Feelings

My interpretation through the timescales analysis revealed the feelings that students experienced in the classroom to *not* be a linear, instantaneous reaction to something currently present. Advocates of complexity perspectives view development as *non-linear* (parallel, inconsistent and disproportionate cause–effect), that is, as not occurring in ordered stages with proportional effects linearly attributable to specific, proportional causes. Up to the point in time at which we observe it, a present phenomenon (such as a feeling) instead *emerges* through the accumulation of dynamics in numerous interrelated, nested systems (de Wolf & Holvoet, 2005; Witherington, 2011). The novel, emergent qualities at the level of the system we are observing are a representation of the non-linear interactions making up its history (Larsen-Freeman & Cameron, 2008). The L2 study feelings of participants were a complex and emergent outcome of various psychological timescales interacting with a particular situation, with these psychological timescales themselves also often involving traces of feeling (Sampson, 2019b). Minami's extract is illustrative:

> My weak point is talking with others aggressively. Also, I'm shyness. So I want to improve it. In today's class, it was easy to speak because my partner was friendly. Also, I could ask and react aggressively through Lego. Unfortunately, we didn't finished making Lego. However, I could enjoyed and act positively! (Minami, W3)

From the extract, we can understand Minami's long-term sense of disappointment in what she perceives as an aspect of her core personality, whereby she does not 'talk[] with others aggressively' and has 'shyness' (life timescale – personality). Interactions between this overall personality and her L2 identity are evident as she writes about bringing these perceptions into the classroom, with motivation to 'improve it' (L2 study experiences – L2 identity – to lesson timescale). In the context of these ongoing, unpleasant understandings of identity she reflects upon two occurrences that hold significance for her (Phelps, 2005): First, the co-constructed nature of feelings is apparent as she expresses gratitude for the actions of her partner in the lesson (lesson timescale), in that it was 'easy to speak because my partner was friendly'. The second event occurred while learners worked in pairs with simple Lego kits; one learner had the manual, the other the Lego blocks, and they needed to negotiate in English in order to construct a model. While Minami notes disappointment that she was not able to complete the Lego model (activity timescale), in the context of this activity she remarks upon what, for her, seems a breakthrough: 'I could ask and react aggressively'. Minami's use of an exclamation mark gives a sense of the impact her present experiences have on her understandings of personality, and the strongly positive feelings emergent: 'I could enjoyed and act positively!'

In considering emergence, we might be inclined to understand purely the interaction of local processes giving rise to a global phenomenon. However, complexity exponents contend that emergence involves circular causality, or bottom-up and top-down processes (Juarrero, 2002; Witherington, 2011). As Witherington (2011: 67) describes, 'a system's patterning is not merely an end product of more fundamental system process dynamics', but instead 'such patterning itself contributes, by means of constraint, to the very processes that give rise to it'. Such features are clearly evident in the emergence of feelings described by Minami. What the timescales analysis encourages us to bear in mind is that her excitement and sense of achievement in the present are contextually situated in understandings of personality, interpreted through the lens of feeling (Immordino-Yang & Fischer, 2016). Ongoing disappointment with her personality provides a salient through which her sense of achievement is strongly channelled (Kauffman, 2008), yet these new feelings also feed back to impact longer timescale understandings of personality (Lemke, 2000, 2013).

Noticeable also in Minami's reflection, the timescales analysis provided me with insight into the complex, socially formed nature of my students' feelings in the classroom. A two-lesson series of extracts focused on one participant, Kouhei, is illuminative of such processes:

> Help others understand. I always talk quitely even when I speak Japanese. In addition to this, I can't speak English well. So when I don't speak English loudly, you can't hear and understand what I want to say. It is not good. That is the reason I chose this one. I could teach the English word meaning to my pair. And I speak clearly in that, and my pair look like he understand. ... I tried to speak loudly and clearly in today's class. I can almost do, but sometimes I can't. I thought I should keep trying. (Kouhei, W4)

To provide some background: As part of the wider action research, I had encouraged students to choose and try to act on a behavioural hope each lesson (Sampson, 2018). In the extract, Kouhei hoped to 'help others understand' (lesson timescale – motivation). Long timescale processes of personality and past experiences form the psychological context for this intention. It seems that Kouhei feels disappointment with his personality – 'I talk quitely even when I speak Japanese' alongside conflict between understandings of his L2 identity as somebody who 'can't speak English well' and a belief that 'it is not good' when others 'can't hear and understand what I want to say' (L2 study experiences – life timescale). Interactions with these understandings strongly channel his actions at the activity timescale (Witherington, 2011), whereby he notes that he 'could teach the English word meaning to my pair'. He attributes a partial sense of achievement of his behavioural hope to his perception that he could 'speak clearly in that, and my pair look like he understand', feeding forward to additional motivation to 'keep trying' similar actions (activity, lesson and lesson-series timescales). That is, Kouhei's sense-making is heavily dependent on his perceptions of his own actions and the re-actions from his partner, in the ongoing context of his psychology.

Although Ushioda (2011: 21–22) does not refer to feelings explicitly, she argues that 'it is through social participation in opportunities, nego-tiations and activities that people's motivations and identities develop and emerge as dynamically co-constructed processes'. Individuals co-form social context, which iteratively forms the playing field for behaviour and understandings – including feelings – of individuals making up the social context (Sampson, 2016a). These feelings and perceptions are carried for-ward to form the context for future interactions (Juarrero, 2002; Kauffman, 2008). By tracing reflections of participants over time and com-paring with those of their partners, I could understand not only interact-ing timescales but moreover the dynamic co-construction of feelings in the classroom from different perspectives. Moving to extracts from the entries of Kouhei and his new partner for the following lesson:

> I chose 'Praise each other' in today's class. I could encourage my pair at today's activity. I remembered what I tried to do last week lesson, so I told my pair that she can speaking English clearly. I could understand well what she wanted to say. I understand clearly because of my partner, so I think it important to speak clearly. ... I also could speak more actively and clearly, so I think it was good to improve our English each other. (Kouhei, W5)

> I choose 'help each other understand' because I have been returned to listen some times. I tried to speak clearly. Today, I wasn't said 'one more time', so I might speak clearly than usual. ... I seemed that I could have a conversation in English this lesson. So I would like to keep trying to use English. (Moe, W5)

From Kouhei's perspective, he chooses an ideal for action different from that of the previous week, with motivation to 'praise each other' (lesson timescale). While this is a new intention, it is clearly positioned in the midst of his experiences from the previous week (lesson series timescale): Kouhei recalls his own efforts and reflections on his beliefs such that he 'could encourage my pair' by telling Moe that 'she can speaking English clearly' (activity timescale – sense of achievement). He also experiences a kind of gratitude towards Moe in that he 'could understand well what she wanted to say'. Interestingly, it is also possible to see how Kouhei's percep-tions are afforded, perhaps serendipitously, by investigating the journal entry of his new partner: Moe had chosen to act on the hope 'help each other understand' (lesson timescale – motivation) through disappoint-ment in her experiences that she had 'been returned to listen some times' (life timescale). She acts on this hope to change by trying to speak more clearly. Although she does not mention Kouhei's praise, she does note a sense of achievement in that 'I wasn't said "one more time"' (lesson time-scale). That is, while Moe's feelings are afforded by both her own and Kouhei's actions, Kouhei's belief that 'I think it important to speak clear-ly' (lesson-series to life timescale) is reinforced through the interaction of his own ongoing psychology with his noticing that 'I understand clearly because of my partner' (lesson timescale). Moreover, we can also under-stand that both Kouhei and Moe's sense of progress, related positive affect and motivation in the development of an L2 identity emerge through the interplay of their ongoing psychologies with the context that they co-formed for the lesson.

Conclusion

The data discussed in this chapter were drawn from a research project which did not initially set out to investigate L2 study feelings. Instead, it was my developing interest in the feelings of my learners emergent from my interactions with the data that prompted me to look at one tool in more detail. To this end, questions may undoubtedly be raised about the reliability of making claims based on only this one form of data (partici-pant journals). Nevertheless, the journals did provide situated insights into the psychologies and perceptions of experience of learners in my classes, suggesting a useful direction for research explicitly focusing on L2 study feelings. In general, employing complexity thinking encouraged me to attempt to interpret the frequently ambivalent ebb and flow of my learners' feelings through interactions across different timescales with other aspects of their psychologies and the social context. The two meth-ods of data analysis described in this chapter do take considerable time to conduct. However, I also believe that multiple threading and timescales analysis does a reasonable job of furnishing visual representations of the emotional context that any teacher encounters and co-forms together with learners in a classroom (Sampson, 2016b). And, considering that recent work in neurobiology (Immordino-Yang, 2016; Immordino-Yang & Fischer, 2016) and the sociodynamic construction of emotions (Boiger & Mesquita, 2015) reveals the constant, dynamic interplay between emo-tions, cognition and the environment, our students' feelings matter for their learning. Future research might usefully mix data collection tools to gain multiple perspectives and explicitly gather data on different times-cales, adding to learner and teacher journals by employing classroom observations, video-recording of classroom activity or analysis of (verbal) interactions. It is my hope that the current chapter provides at least some suggestions for how complexity perspectives can further assist in working towards describing more situated and nuanced landscapes of the emer-gence of L2 study feelings.

References

Boiger, M. and Mesquita, B. (2015) A sociodynamic perspective on the construction of emotion. In L. Feldman Barrett and J.A. Russell (eds) *The Psychological Construction of Emotion* (pp. 377–398). New York, NY: Guilford Press.

Boudreau, C., MacIntyre, P.D. and Dewaele, J.-M. (2018) Enjoyment and anxiety in second language communication: An idiodynamic approach. *Studies in Second Language Learning and Teaching* 8 (1), 149–170.

Cahour, B. (2013) Emotions: Characteristics, emergence and circulation in interactional learning. In M. Baker, J. Andriessen and S. Jarvela (eds) *Affective Learning Together: Social and Emotional Dimensions of Collaborative Learning* (pp. 52–70). Abingdon: Routledge.

Damasio, A. (2003) *Looking for Spinoza: Joy, Sorrow and the Feeling Brain*. London: Vintage.

Davis, B. and Sumara, D. (2006) *Complexity and Education: Inquiries into Learning, Teaching, and Research*. Mahwah, NJ: Lawrence Erlbaum Associates.

de Bot, K. (2015) Rates of change: Timescales in second language development. In Z. Dörnyei, P.D. MacIntyre and A. Henry (eds) *Motivational Dynamics in Language Learning* (pp. 29–37). Bristol: Multilingual Matters.

de Wolf, T. and Holvoet, T. (2005) Emergence versus self-organization: Different concepts but promising when combined. In S.A. Brueckner, G. Di Marzo Serugendo, A. Karageorgos and R. Nagpal (eds) *Engineering Self-Organising Systems: Methodologies and Applications* (pp. 1–15). Berlin: Springer.

Dewaele, J.-M. and Alfawzan, M. (2018) Does the effect of enjoyment outweigh that of anxiety in foreign language performance? *Studies in Second Language Learning and Teaching* 8 (1), 21. https://doi.org/10.14746/ssllt.2018.8.1.2

Dewaele, J.-M. and Dewaele, L. (2018) Learner-internal and learner-external predictors of willingness to communicate in the FL classroom. *Journal of the European Second Language Association* 2, 24–37.

Dewaele, J.-M. and MacIntyre, P.D. (2014) The two faces of Janus? Anxiety and enjoyment in the foreign language classroom. *Studies in Second Language Learning and Teaching* 4, 237–274.

Dewaele, J.-M. and MacIntyre, P.D. (2016) Foreign language enjoyment and foreign language classroom anxiety: The right and left feet of the language learner. In P.D. MacIntyre, T. Gregersen and S. Mercer (eds) *Positive Psychology in SLA* (pp. 215–236). Bristol: Multilingual Matters.

Dörnyei, Z. (2014) Researching complex dynamic systems: 'Retrodictive qualitative modelling' in the language classroom. *Language Teaching* 47 (1), 80–91.

Fredrickson, B.L. (1998) What good are positive emotions? *Review of General Psychology* 2, 300–319.

Garrett, P. and Young, R.F. (2009) Theorizing affect in foreign language learning: An analysis of one learner's responses to a communicative Portuguese course. *The Modern Language Journal* 93 (2), 209–226.

Gilmore, A. (2016) Language learning in context: Complex dynamic systems and the role of mixed methods research. In J. King (ed.) *The Dynamic Interplay Between Context and the Language Learner* (pp. 194–224). Basingstoke: Palgrave Macmillan.

Hall, G. (2008) An ethnographic diary study. *ELT Journal* 62 (2), 113–122.

Horwitz, E.K., Horwitz, M.B. and Cope, J. (1986) Foreign language classroom anxiety. *The Modern Language Journal* 70, 125–132.

Imai, Y. (2010) Emotions in SLA: New insights from collaborative learning for an EFL classroom. *The Modern Language Journal* 94, 278–292.

Immordino-Yang, M.H. (2016) Introduction: Why emotions are integral to learning. In M.H. Immordino-Yang (ed.) *Emotions, Learning, and the Brain: Exploring the Educational Implications of Affective Neuroscience* (pp. 17–24). New York: Norton.

Immordino-Yang, M.H. and Fischer, K.W. (2016) Neuroscience bases of learning. In M.H. Immordino-Yang (ed.) *Emotions, Learning, and the Brain: Exploring the Educational Implications of Affective Neuroscience* (pp. 79–92). New York: Norton.

Juarrero, A. (2002) *Dynamics in Action: Intentional Behavior as a Complex System* (1st MIT Pr). Cambridge, MA: MIT Press.

Kauffman, S. (2008) *Reinventing the Sacred*. New York: Basic Books.

Kuhn, L. (2007) Denouement. *World Futures* 63, 298–299.

Larsen-Freeman, D. and Cameron, L. (2008) *Complex Systems and Applied Linguistics*. Oxford: Oxford University Press.

Lemke, J. (2013) Feeling and meaning in the social ecology of learning: Lessons from play and games. In M. Baker, J. Andriessen and S. Jarvela (eds) *Affective Learning Together: Social and Emotional Dimensions of Collaborative Learning* (pp. 71–94). Abingdon: Routledge.

Lemke, J.L. (2000) Across the scales of time: artifacts, activities, and meanings in ecosocial systems. *Mind, Culture, and Activity* 7 (4), 273–290. https://doi.org/10.1207/S15327884MCA0704_03

MacIntyre, P.D. and Gregersen, T. (2012) Affect: The role of language anxiety and other emotions in language learning. In S. Mercer, S. Ryan and M. Williams (eds) *Psychology for Language Learning: Insights from Research, Theory and Practice* (pp. 103–118). Basingstoke: Palgrave Macmillan.

MacIntyre, P.D. and Vincze, L. (2017) Positive and negative emotions underlie motivation for L2 learning. *Studies in Second Language Learning and Teaching* 7 (1), 61. https://doi.org/10.14746/ssllt.2017.7.1.4

Méndez López, M.G. and Peña Aguilar, A. (2013) Emotions as learning enhancers of foreign language learning motivation. *Profile: Issues in Teachers' Professional Development* 15 (1), 109–124. See http://dialnet.unirioja.es/servlet/articulo?codigo=4858457&info=resumen&idioma=SPA

Morin, E. (2006) Restricted complexity, general complexity. See http://cogprints.org/5217/1/Morin.pdf

Morin, E. (2008) *On Complexity*. Cresskill, N.J.: Hampton Press.

Nunan, D. and Bailey, K.M. (2009) *Exploring Second Language Classroom Research: A Comprehensive Guide*. Boston: Heinle.

Onwuegbuzie, A.J. and Daniel, L.G. (2003) Typology of analytical and interpretational errors in quantitative and qualitative educational research. *Current Issues in Education*. See http://cie.ed.asu.edu/volume6/number2/

Pavlenko, A. (2013) The affective turn in SLA: From 'affective factors' to 'language desire' and 'commodification of affect.' In D. Gabryś-Barker and J. Bielska (eds) *The Affective Dimension in Second Language Acquisition* (pp. 3–28). Bristol: Multilingual Matters.

Phelps, R. (2005) The potential of reflective journals in studying complexity 'in action.' *Complicity: An International Journal of Complexity and Education* 2 (1), 37–54.

Pinner, R. (2016) Trouble in paradise: Self-assessment and the Tao. *Language Teaching Research* 20 (2), 181–195.

Plutchik, R. (2001) The nature of emotions: Human emotions have deep evolutionary roots, a fact that may explain their complexity and provide tools for clinical practice. *American Scientist* 89 (4), 344–350.

Porto, M. (2007) Learning diaries in the English as a Foreign Language classroom: A tool for accessing learners' perceptions of lessons and developing learner autonomy and reflection. *Foreign Language Annals* 40 (4), 672–696.

Radford, M. (2007) Action research and the challenge of complexity. *Cambridge Journal of Education* 37 (2), 263–278.

Sampson, R.J. (2012) The language-learning self, self-enhancement activities, and self perceptual change. *Language Teaching Research* 16 (3), 313–331.

Sampson, R.J. (2016a) *Complexity in Classroom Foreign Language Learning Motivation: A Practitioner Perspective from Japan*. Bristol: Multilingual Matters.

Sampson, R.J. (2016b) EFL teacher motivation in-situ: Co-adaptive processes, openness and relational motivation over interacting timescales. *Studies in Second Language Learning and Teaching* 6 (2), 293–318. https://doi.org/10.14746/ssllt.2016.6.2.6

Sampson, R.J. (2017) Expectations and dreams: Industry and student ideas about future English use. *OnCUE Journal* 10 (1), 21–38. https://doi.org/10.1002/ana.23528/pdf

Sampson, R.J. (2018) Complexity in acting on images of ideal classmates in the L2 classroom. *Konin Language Studies* 6 (4), 387–410.

Sampson, R.J. (2019a) Openness to messages about English as a foreign language: Working with learners to uncover purpose to study. *Language Teaching Research* 23 (1), 126–142. https://doi.org/10.1177/1362168817712074

Sampson, R.J. (2019b) Real people with real experiences: The emergence of classroom L2 study feelings over interacting timescales. *System* 84, 14–23. https://doi.org/10.1016/j.system.2019.05.001

Sampson, R.J. (2020) The feeling classroom: Diversity of feelings in instructed L2 learning. *Innovation in Language Learning and Teaching* 14 (3), 203–217.

Shuman, V. and Scherer, K.R. (2014) Concepts and structures of emotions. In *International Handbook of Emotions in Education* (pp. 13–35). New York: Routledge.

Urdan, T. (2014) Understanding teacher motivation: What is known and what more there is to learn. In P.W. Richardson, S.A. Karabenick and H.M.G. Watt (eds) *Teacher Motivation: Theory and Practice* (pp. 227–246). New York: Routledge.

Ushioda, E. (2009) A person-in-context relational view of emergent motivation, self and identity. In Z. Dörnyei and E. Ushioda (eds) *Motivation, Language Identity and the L2 Self* (pp. 215–228). Bristol: Multilingual Matters.

Ushioda, E. (2011) Motivating learners to speak as themselves. In G. Murray, X. Gao and T. Lamb (eds) *Identity, Motivation and Autonomy in Language Learning* (pp. 11–24). Bristol: Multilingual Matters.

van Lier, L. (2004) *The Ecology and Semiotics of Language Learning: A Sociocultural Perspective*. Boston: Kluwer Academic Publishers.

Witherington, D.C. (2011) Taking emergence seriously: The centrality of circular causality for dynamic systems approaches to development. *Human Development* 54 (2), 66–92. https://doi.org/10.1159/000326814

Yashima, T. and Arano, K. (2015) Understanding EFL learners' motivational dynamics: A three-level model from a dynamic systems and sociocultural perspective. In Z. Dörnyei, P.D. MacIntyre and A. Henry (eds) *Motivational Dynamics in Language Learning* (pp. 285–314). Bristol: Multilingual Matters.

4 Working with the Complexity of Language Learners' Emotions and Emotion Regulation Strategies

Rebecca L. Oxford and Christina Gkonou

Although simplicity is often considered a great virtue, complexity is at the heart of most aspects of human life. Second and foreign language (L2) learning is a complex process. The nature of L2 learning has been frequently described and explained in terms of complexity theory (see, e.g. Dörnyei *et al.*, 2015; Kostoulas *et al.*, 2018; Larsen-Freeman & Cameron, 2008). This theory considers components of complex systems in terms of fluctuating, mutually influential connections, not unidirectional causal relationships.

L2 learners bring into the classroom their own complex experiences, backgrounds, beliefs and emotions, all of which influence the L2 learning strategies used and hence the academic outcomes achieved. Unfortunately, L2 researchers have notoriously neglected affective (emotion regulation) learning strategies, hereafter called affective strategies, despite the crucial importance of such strategies in L2 learning. This chapter explains that affective strategies are necessary. Such strategies are also necessarily complex because of the complexity and highly subjective nature of emotions and the fact that individuals often must abide by culturally-influenced, complex 'feeling rules' (Benesch, 2017; Hochschild, 1983; Zembylas, 2005).

We begin this chapter by linking features of complex systems to emotions in L2 learning. Next we describe emotional intelligence and emotion regulation in relation to complex systems theory in the context of L2 learning. We subsequently explain several kinds of affective strategies for emotion regulation, followed by a description of an innovative data collection tool, the *Managing Your Emotions* (MYE) questionnaire (Gkonou & Oxford, 2016, 2019). Ultimately, our chapter is a call to fellow researchers to revive interest in affective strategies and to view them through a complexity lens, which takes into account a range of ecologies of learning and teaching.

Complex Systems and Emotions

The concept of complexity, specifically complex systems,[1] is, not surprisingly, flooded with meaning. A complex system is a system that emerges – spontaneously occurs – from the interaction of its multiple components or subsystems (Larsen-Freeman, 2015; Larsen-Freeman & Cameron, 2008). Dörnyei (2009) noted three interactive subsystems in the human mind: affect (emotion), cognition and motivation. Emotion and cognition are intertwined and inseparable and naturally interact with motivation. As Buck (2005: 198) stated, 'In their fully articulated forms, emotions imply cognitions imply motives imply emotions, and so on'. Each of the subsystems in the mind can also be viewed as a complex system with its own interactive elements.

By definition, a complex system has a set of important features, such as situatedness, nestedness and dynamism. Unlike components of merely 'complicated' ideas, every element in a complex system affects all other elements in intricate ways. Table 4.1 lists and summarizes the most salient features of a complex system (Oxford, 2017, 2018), with linkages to emotions in the right column.

In a given person, aspects of emotion have multiple durations, from instantaneous, rapid emotions to longer moods and finally to long-standing emotional traits. We live our lives on multiple, constantly interacting timescales, of which time differences among emotion, mood and trait are an example. Diverse levels of emotional intensity also occur, with certain individuals being influenced by emotion (or specific emotions) more strongly than others.

Emotion research, not just within second language acquisition (SLA) but also in other disciplines, has primarily centered on the emotion-cognition dilemma (though complexity theory would suggest that there is no dilemma, since emotion and cognition are constantly intertwined and interactive). Emotion research has also aimed to distinguish emotions in terms of their valence, that is, positive versus negative (Frederickson, 2004; Prior, 2020; Seligman, 2011), but valence is oversimplified/reified if specific emotions are described as inherently positive or negative, ignoring outcomes for particular people in a range of real contexts. For specific contexts and people, 'positive' or 'negative' emotions might create unexpected results (e.g. contentedness might lower motivated effort, leading to failure and low self-esteem, while anger might increase motivated effort, resulting in focused courage and high self-esteem); this certainly accords with complexity theory, which could not embrace a simplistic concept of valence. Given such problems, certain researchers (Ahmed, 2004; Benesch,

Table 4.1 Features of complex systems in relation to emotions

Feature	Linkage with emotions
Contextualization (situatedness): This refers to being situated in a given context, which has particular affordances and challenges at a given time. Learners are both influenced by their contexts and influence those contexts. Contexts often shed light on cultural and individual values. Ushioda (2009), King (2015) and Oxford and Amerstorfer (2018) strongly stress the importance of contexts.	L2 learners are situated in external contexts (e.g. a classroom, a refugee tent, a store, a living room, a mosque, a church, or a detention center), all of which are culture-bound. Of course, a learner's valuing of a certain external context depends partly on that context's affordances and challenges, such as sufficiency or insufficiency of the following: (a) material resources; (b) supportive, caring and knowledgeable people; (c) a welcoming, accepting cultural, social and emotional atmosphere. In some external contexts named above, contextual affordances and challenges might also include presence or absence of encouragement given to the individual to interact with and contribute to others in the context, learn and develop, and become more self-regulated. Each learner also has an interior context in which emotion plays one of the main interacting roles, along with motivation and cognition, and all these are linked with biological and behavioural factors that go beyond the interior context. With guidance, individuals can learn to regulate emotion, motivation, and cognition to a significant degree, thus influencing learning. Of course, causality also runs in the other direction, with learning in turn influencing all other aspects of the interior context (and some aspects of the external context).
Interconnectedness: This feature is the interactivity among various components at multiple levels within a complex system. No part of the system is independent; all parts are interdependent.	Many researchers focus mainly on one emotional aspect of a learner, such as learner anxiety, and fail to consider the interactions of multiple components of a complex system that are interacting at any given time within and beyond the learner. Anxiety operates within contexts interior to the learner and within outer situational and cultural contexts. Anxiety also interacts with other emotions within the larger complex system of learner emotions. Not considering interconnectedness (interactivity) provides a very partial and often inaccurate understanding.
Dynamism: This means changeability or fluctuation within the complex system. However, dynamic internal states (thoughts, emotions and motivations) can become stable over time by converging on a narrow range of 'preferred' states (a fixed-point attractor, Hiver, 2015). The attractor can develop in two ways: (a) Internal states can synchronize through social interaction, or (b) internal states can self-organize with reference to a higher-order property (e.g. self-concept, goal) (Nowak et al., 2005).	Dynamism of emotions is captured in the image of the 'emotional rollercoaster' (Gkonou et al., 2020). Dynamism apparent in learners' quickly fluctuating emotional states and in shifts in longer-term mood. Even long-lasting emotional traits can seemingly shift, especially in certain situations and contexts. For instance, an L2 learner who has dispositional or trait anxiety can become calmer in a given setting by means of emotional and social support and instruction in emotion regulation. This L2 learner's lowering of anxiety can, over time, become relatively stable through a convergence on a small range of preferred, calm states. However, complexity theory does not promise a rose garden; stability of emotion, even of a comforting emotion, is not permanent. Therefore, the learner might have moments or periods of anxiety even after experiencing greater calmness through emotion regulation.

Multiplicity: This feature refers to the diversity of constructs or the different versions of the same construct within the complex system.	Multiplicity can relate to the diversity of emotions simultaneously occurring within a classroom or within a learner. For instance, a learner might be happy to see a friend in German class but simultaneously upset at having to give a talk during the class because he forgot his notes. Another reflection of multiplicity is the diverse contexts in which this learner experiences emotions on a given day.
Multiple simultaneous causes: This feature involves a range of influences, such as main causes, secondary causes and hidden or distant causes. Complexity theory takes a socially grounded perspective whereby neither the context nor the person's internal development is considered the major or only cause.	Emotions and emotion regulation arise from multiple simultaneous causes (Gkonou et al., 2017). Self-regulation theory suggests that L2 learners have a role in managing their emotions, motivations and thoughts – the interior context (Oxford, 2017). Interacting roles are also played by external contextual factors (see contextualization above) and individual factors that are more than just internal (gender, educational background, life experiences, personality and many more). Willpower alone cannot cause emotion regulation strategies to be developed and used.
Nestedness: Complex systems are nested in a hierarchical structure of levels. A learner can be considered a complex system containing many nested subsystems. However, any subsystem or sub-subsystem can be viewed as a complex system, depending on the investigator's, teacher's or learner's focus.	If the L2 classroom is the complex system of concern, then the teacher and each learner is a nested subsystem within the classroom, and the teacher's and each learner's nested mental sub-subsystems include emotion, cognition and motivation, intertwined within and across individuals. Additional nested subsystems could include resources, classroom atmosphere, instructional mode and numerous others. If the L2 learner is the complex system of interest, mental subsystems include emotion, cognition and motivation, all of which are tightly interwoven with each other, with biological and behavioural aspects of the learner, and with the external context. Nested sub-subsystems could be named and described for each of these subsystems. If emotion is the complex system we are most interested in, nested subsystems might include the learner's particular emotional states (anxiety, contentment and others), moods and emotional traits; the learner's cultural rules for emotion expression; and the learner's current emotion regulation strategies. Nested sub-subsystems of each subsystem could be identified.
Openness: Any given system, such as a learner as a whole, or a set of the learner's emotions, opens to a larger web of complex systems, creating growth and change through exchanging information or matter.	The learner as a complex system, including the learner's emotions, opens to a larger web of complex systems within the educational institution, the community, the politically or militarily demarcated city/province/state/county, the culture, the human race and all other sentient beings on earth. Information is exchanged within and among all these levels. It is sometimes easier to conceptualize openness to a larger web of complex systems, rather than looking at smaller and smaller components (see nestedness).
Emergence: Emergence means that patterns (based on a fluid, self-organizing capacity in the complex system) spontaneously arise from the interconnections among the system's components, without any external direction or control.	Oxford's (2016, 2017, 2018) EMPATHICS system of the L2 learner's interactive components (e.g. emotions, empathy, meaning, hope and self-efficacy) would allow new, fluid, self-organizing patterns to emerge.

(Continued)

Table 4.1 (Continued)

Feature	Linkage with emotions
Self-modification: Complex systems are self-modifying (*autopoietic*), meaning that a given complex system becomes a resource for its own further development. Complex systems keep on developing. However, complex systems have no foresight, goals, or endpoints (Larsen-Freeman, 2015).	A learner's emotions self-modify, becoming resources for their ongoing development. For instance, anxiety can shift into anger at one's anxiety, which can shift into a desire to take responsibility to change to a different, more positive emotional state.
Adaptiveness: This feature means that the complex system adapts by learning from experience and changes in response to new contextual changes. Within a complex system, adaptiveness-enhancing features might include nestedness, interconnection of components, openness, multiple causes, etc.	A learner's emotion regulation is adaptive and depends on (a) willingness to take in, understand and use new ideas from experience (the learner's educational and other experiences and other peoples' experiences) about the need to manage emotions and possible ways to do so; (b) multiple interactions with others who practice emotion regulation and are willing to share their strategies; and (c) consideration of multiple causes of emotion regulation, as well as the learner's influence over any of those causes.
Nonlinearity: This feature refers to unpredictable, disproportionate outcomes, which are important and observable in L2 learning. Nonlinearity is apparent when a given event or experience has notably different outcomes for diverse people at the same time, or for one person at different times.	A *small* amount of meaningful, emotional guidance given by the teacher to a particular L2 learner might lead to an unexpectedly *large* benefit in that learner's L2 progress and achievement. On the other hand, without any evident reason, a *large* amount of equally meaningful emotional guidance given to the very same learner at another time, or to a different learner at the same time, might result in an unpredictably *small* result.
Sensitive dependence on initial conditions: This feature, related to but not the same as nonlinearity, means that relatively small differences in the *initial condition* influence the complex system in general (Lorenz, 1969). The butterfly's wing flapping can create a massive weather change somewhere on the other side of the earth. Nevertheless, such dependence on initial conditions does not always happen. A complex system can have major 'perturbations' without much change at all (Dörnyei, 2009).	This story illustrates sensitive dependence on initial conditions. The university president's emotional state (nervous, on-edge and angry) arises when he worries about a range of problems in the faculty. He therefore experiences a sleepless night. The president's seemingly inconsequential emotional state grows in importance when he goes to work and has a combative, morning meeting with the faculty council. Faculty council members become upset, and they immediately share their feelings by texting and emailing other faculty members on campus. The spreading emotions affect L2 classes taught by any faculty member who has been caught up in the disturbing emotions of the morning. This is an example of the 'butterfly effect', starting with the university president's worried, sleepless night. By afternoon, the exhausted university president's anger from earlier in the day is now stronger than ever, and it seeps into his other communications. He engages in an argumentative email exchange with a peer, a university president many kilometers away. That university president reacts in kind. The tired-out university professor succeeds in spreading anger far beyond his own campus. The good news is that such ballooning emotional difficulties do not have to happen. For instance, the sleepless university president's emotional state could have dramatically changed if, before launching into the day's duties, he had enjoyed a cup of coffee and a good laugh with his assistant, had received supportive phone call from his favourite sister, or, best of all, had used emotion regulation strategies.

2017; Oxford, 2016, 2018; Pavlenko, 2013) have suggested that instead of focusing on what emotions are or seem to be, we need to turn to what emotions do and the impact they have on people's lives.

Complexity in Emotional Intelligence and Emotion Regulation

Emotional intelligence, often known as EI, is the cognitive capability to use reason to comprehend and deal effectively with emotions. In particular, emotional intelligence is 'the ability to understand feelings in the self and others and to use these feelings as informational guides for thinking and action' (Salovey *et al.*, 2011: 238). Emotional intelligence (EI) is often viewed as having four aspects of ability: (a) perceiving emotions in self and others, (b) using emotions to facilitate cognition, (c) understanding emotions and (d) managing emotions in self and others (Salovey *et al.*, 2011). A five-part formulation of EI is given by Goleman (2005): (a) self-awareness; (b) self-regulation (emotion regulation), discussed after EI; (c) motivation; (d) social skills; and (e) empathy.

EI can reduce anxiety and conflict; increase harmony, achievement, stability, self-motivation and social awareness; and improve relationships (Goleman, 2005). In an applied linguistics study, adult multilinguals with higher EI perceived themselves as more self-confident, more capable of controlling stress and better able to understand others' emotions (Dewaele *et al.*, 2008). Mayer *et al.* (2016) described EI as a 'hot' intelligence, i.e. an intelligence that combines reasoning with personally significant information. This contrasts with cool intelligences, which relate to less personal knowledge (e.g. math, visual-spatial).

Complexity is evident in interactions between emotion and cognition, or emotion and memory, especially in EI. For example, Dewaele *et al.* (2008) found that trait EI contributes toward lower levels of communicative anxiety and foreign language anxiety among adult multilinguals. They also showed that trait EI is linked to participants' age of onset of acquisition, number of languages known, frequency of use and self-perceived proficiency, thus highlighting the complexity of EI and its interconnectedness with a range of other learner variables. Additionally, research with English language teachers has shown that EI develops over time, is not stable but dynamic, and that even those teachers who are naturally less emotionally intelligent than others still develop their emotional self-awareness, self-regulation and empathy toward students and colleagues (Gkonou & Mercer, 2017). L2 teachers can help students to develop EI and to use it when in contact with other people or when dealing with their own inner issues.

Emotion regulation, like EI, uses reason and logic. According to Gross (2014), the core features of emotion regulation are: (a) activating a *goal*, either intrinsic (regulating one's own emotions), or extrinsic (regulating someone else's emotions); (b) choosing and employing relevant *strategies*, or processes, from explicit to unconscious/automatic, that can alter the emotion trajectory and thus fulfill the goal (regulation of one's or someone else's emotions); and (c) identifying the *outcome* (the emotion dynamics, as well as the emotion modulation or change caused by activating the goal and using the strategies). Gross noted that emotion regulation is only part of affective regulation, which also includes mood regulation and coping. However, it is very difficult to separate emotion from mood; they are almost the same, except that mood is longer in duration. Therefore, in our work we do not find any value in differentiating between emotion regulation and affective regulation. Complexity does, of course, involve interacting timescales, as mentioned earlier, although precisely dividing those timescales can be difficult.

Miller and Gkonou (2018) also demonstrated that English teachers' emotion regulation skills develop over time and are not one-off, momentary reactions to what is happening in class. Specifically, teachers were found to have developed strong emotion regulation skills after a number of years of teaching experience and as a response to numerous moments of hardship and emotional challenges, also called 'critical incidents' in their careers (Gkonou & Miller, 2020; Tripp, 2012). These examples are indicative of emotions sharing many of the characteristics of complex systems listed above.

On the other hand, complexity theory, with its emphasis on dynamism or change, multiple simultaneous causes, unpredictability, openness to larger complex systems and adaptiveness might call into question some strong forms of strategic self-regulation in L2 learning – forms that might suggest too emphatically (and incorrectly) that the learner can always be in charge of his or her emotions while learning. Strategy use is *not* always equal to or fully commensurate with self-regulation; in fact, strategy use could be a function of 'other-regulation', that is, following the directions of the teacher, who wants learners to use strategies (Thomas & Rose, 2019). The possibility that self-regulation might not occur, but that the individual could successfully use strategies anyway, seems to fit with what we know about self-regulation from Vygotsky (1978, 1981). Vygotsky explained how the learner depends on the 'more capable other' (e.g. teacher, parent, peer, book, or film) to guide him or her through the Zone of Proximal Development (ZPD) before the learner reaches a state of inner regulation (inner speech). Some learners go all the way through the ZPD to inner speech, while others go only part-way. This might also relate to the concept of 'social autonomy', which is based on cooperative relationships (Esch, 2004), particularly in collectivist cultures such as those in Asia. In our view, Asian respect for teachers and others in authority makes it difficult for individual autonomy to root itself in such settings (see Thomas & Rose, 2019). Thinking from another angle, respect for others might mean that emotion regulation is socially valuable and necessary to learn, either through overt guidance or through motivated imitation.

We have raised some issues to consider about complexity theory in relation to emotions, EI and emotion regulation. Now we turn to affective strategies for L2 learners' emotion regulation.

Practical Affective Strategies for L2 Learners' Emotion Regulation

For simplicity, in this section we show a given strategy in only one category (or 'master strategy') of L2 affective strategies for emotion regulation, although a given L2 affective strategy could easily be placed into more than one affective strategy category. Speaking in terms of complexity, a strategy can often serve multiple strategic functions, not just one (Oxford, 2017), but it is very difficult to express the functions of a given strategy while keeping the number of words down. The first four categories (also called master strategies) below are similar to those proposed by Gross (2014), but with two major differences: Our category names are more user-friendly, and the affective strategies come from the L2 learning field (see Gkonou, 2018; Oxford, 2017). Following the first four categories, we discuss the contributions and attitude of Viktor Frankl (1984) and present three more categories (master strategies) flowing from his work.

Naturally, enacting a given strategy requires making a prior decision (a metacognitive strategy), either slowly or almost instantaneously.[2] We do not include the decision-making function here. For the strategies below, we use the first person (I, me, my) to indicate the idiosyncratic, personal nature of affective strategies and to show that a given strategy is not necessarily helpful to every learner.

- **Category (or master strategy): Selecting or modifying the situation** – Strategies in this category involve (a) strategies for selecting a situation associated with pleasant rather than unpleasant emotions, or (b) strategies for modifying the emotional impact of a situation. Such strategies include: Avoiding an unpleasant student in my class. Selecting my L2 class because the teacher is known for his fair grading. Going to the library to increase my confidence. Seeking peer support (e.g. working with a capable student, going to a session with my study group). Straightening up the study location. Enhancing my interest by listening to L2 songs or watching L2 films. Using automatic study reminders to increase my confidence.
- **Category (or master strategy): Focusing attention** – Strategies in this category require directing or redirecting attention to control emotions. Such strategies include: Using a distraction to reduce my L2 anxiety. Focusing on a television show so I can be more relaxed. Thinking of something interesting from my L2 class. Thinking about something funny to relax and increase my confidence.

- **Category (or master strategy): Reframing cognitive appraisals** – Strategies in this category involve modifying or 'reframing' a cognitive appraisal of an external or internal situation to change its emotional significance. Such strategies include: Telling myself that the upcoming presentation is a learning experience, not a threat to my confidence. Saying to myself that learning the language is easier than my past difficulties as a refugee. Recognizing that though my exam mark was not my best, I will be better prepared when I retake it. Telling myself that though my pronunciation is not great, it is better than it used to be. Telling myself that although time is short, there is still enough time to practice.
- **Category (or master strategy): Influencing the response** – Strategies in this category influence experiential, behavioural, or physiological aspects of emotional responding. Such strategies include: Using meditation, deep breathing, or mild exercise to reduce anxiety. Telling myself to take it easy. Going out with friends. Relaxing with music. Taking a short break if I am feeling overly tense.

The next three categories or master strategies are based on the work of psychiatrist Viktor Frankl, whose influence, amazingly enough, has hardly been recognized in discussions of L2 affective strategies. Frankl's entire family was killed in the Holocaust, but he survived by helping himself and others to find meaning even in dire circumstances. 'Meaning' is personal significance and relevance that gives purpose to life. Frankl believed that even if a person might be killed tomorrow, he or she could create meaningful, beautiful moments today – a fine example of emotion regulation. We have expressed his suggestions for meaning-making in our own words and have included our recommendations of possible affective strategies for L2 learners.

- **Category (or master strategy): Helping someone by means of a deed or a creation** – Strategies in this category involve aiding others by action or creativity, and thus fostering better feelings in both people. Such strategies include: L2-captioning a picture or photo for someone else. Making a card for someone in the L2. Inviting someone to watch an L2 video. Finishing my L2 assignment on time so the teacher will not worry.
- **Category (or master strategy): Encountering another human being, loving that person and doing something for him or her** – This group of strategies again involves helping someone else, but specifically for reasons of love and the desire to make that person happier. Such strategies include: Taking a very good friend to a foreign language film she would enjoy. Expressing thanks to an L2 speaker with whom I am very close and who has helped me for several years. Doing something good for my dear language teacher and his family. Tutoring someone I especially like.
- **Category (or master strategy): Experiencing something special (good, beautiful or kind) and valuing it** – This category encompasses

strategies for finding something special and appreciating it, no matter what the circumstances. Frankl taught others to experience a memory of a loved one, a piece of grass, a flower, or anything else that could be felt as good, beautiful or kind. Such strategies include: Seeing a lovely flower, rock or pebble that lightens my heart. Looking online for fascinating cultural information in the L2 and appreciating it. Finding a wonderful website where the L2 is written and spoken and where interesting practice activities are found.

The *MYE*: Exploring the Complexity of Emotions and L2 Emotion Regulation Strategies

All sets of strategies in this section refer to complex processes involved in L2 learning; not only do learners need strategies to manage the actual learning of the language, but they also need to regulate their emotions in some fashion (self-regulation, other-regulation or a combination) throughout the different stages of learning. Over our years of teaching and advising learners regarding emotions and affective strategies for emotion regulation, we have come to realize the complexity of emotion, emotion regulation and strategies. We therefore wanted to create a research tool that could potentially capture to some degree that complexity and to concentrate on the situated nature of emotion generation and emotion regulation. In this section, we present an innovative data collection tool called *Managing Your Emotions* (MYE, Gkonou & Oxford, 2016) for language learning.

The purposes of the *MYE* are (a) to assess language learners' affective strategies for emotion regulation, (b) to uncover learners' experiences and interpretations of their emotions and strategies, (c) to discover whether learners' emotion regulation strategies are generated by the learners themselves or taught by others and (d) to reveal the complexity of emotions and L2 emotion regulation strategies. The *MYE* is a scenario-based questionnaire, in which the scenarios represent hypothetical but realistic and recognizable situations.

The *MYE* is imbued with complexity. It is designed to assess L2 learners' complex emotions and complex emotion regulation as situated in social contexts, which are complex. The complex system of emotions and emotion regulation contains multiple, interactive, dynamic features (see Table 4.1). If large differences appear within or across scenarios for emotions or emotion regulation strategies reported by a given learner, this probably reflects complexity features, especially dynamism, in the learner and differences in situations (contexts). The *MYE* uses nontechnical language that makes multiple-choice items easy to answer. The simple language also encourages respondents to be open, free and candid in narrative responses to qualitative items and thus helps them to provide complex data, even though responses are necessarily kept short.

The *MYE* asks for background information about gender, age, home language, L2 being learned, motivation to learn the L2, other foreign languages known and perceptions about the importance of L2 learning. However, no personal information is asked that would compromise the anonymity of the individual. The *MYE* includes 20 scenarios (see an example of one scenario in the Appendix), which we have divided into two sets of 10 to facilitate their completion by L2 learners, maintain high interest and ensure attrition rates are kept as low as possible. In writing the scenarios, we reflected on emotion-laden experiences that we had noticed among our L2 learners from the past and on our own experiences as L2 learners.

Each scenario is presented briefly but clearly, followed by nine items, 56% of which (#2, 3, 5, 7 and 9) require short, narrative, write-in responses and 44% of which (#1, 4, 6 and 8) are multiple-choice items that require selecting the most relevant option from a short list. All items concern emotions or emotion regulation in a given situation. Some of the items refer specifically to the situation in the scenario, while others refer to the participant's experience with the same situation as in the scenario or a similar situation. As an example, the appendix includes scenario 1 (out of the 20 potential scenarios).

Written guidelines for teachers, researchers or others who administer the *MYE* explain the following: how to schedule *MYE* administration realistically, given that 10 scenarios generally take 25 to 30 minutes to administer, or longer if participants do not know the language in which the questionnaire is written or translated; how to administer both sets of 10 scenarios (definitely at different times to ensure participants' interest and their dedication to finishing); how to analyse quantitative data (find the frequencies for each multiple-choice response option for a given item, tabulate percentages, and perhaps go further)[3]; how to analyse and interpret narrative data; how to link background data (e.g. gender, L2 experience, motivation) with narrative data on emotions and emotion regulation; and how to write up results. Of course, the guidelines are not prescriptions, because they also encourage investigators' own research creativity.

Research using the *MYE* is still in its infancy, though several *MYE* pilot studies from different countries have been completed. Thus far the early *MYE* researchers (excellent scholars from Greece, Poland and the UK) have employed the questionnaire in ways that generally followed our guidelines. Due to space restrictions, we will look at just the Greek study, 'Affective Dimensions of L2 Learning' (Kantaridou & Psaltou-Joycey, submitted 2018). This study involved a total of 106 first-semester students from two northern Greek universities. This investigation focused on four common scenarios as reported by the students: *writing in class, teacher correction, coming to class unprepared* and *grammar rule repetition*. In response to these four situations, extremely negative emotions arose, and the authors said later in their report that follow-up interviews with selected students could have provided insight about why the emotions were so severe. (We believe this is a helpful idea even for studies that did not find very difficult emotions.) Participants in the Greek study highlighted the teacher's role in helping them manage such extreme emotions. Self-confidence was one of the most frequent 'positive' emotions, and self-talk was the most frequently used affective strategy.[4] Differences occurred for gender and academic specialization. The researchers cited the need for research on emotion regulation in diverse groups (e.g. immigrants, professionals) and in people with different educational backgrounds. Kantaridou and Psaltou-Joycey stated that they administered the MYE online, and this could have been a limitation. The researchers emphasized that people in general are not overly willing or able to talk about emotions precisely, so practice is needed for completing questionnaires in the affective domain. We believe that use of the online MYE, as well as any other form of the MYE, would work especially well if participants had an earlier workshop on how to understand and talk about emotions.

We hope to raise other colleagues' awareness of the MYE, encourage them to consider using it, and develop international research teams for cross-validation studies. To date the research teams that have used the MYE have not been specifically trained in complexity theory or features of complex systems (see Table 4.1). However, when such training is accomplished, doors will start opening for deeper understandings of emotion regulation in L2 learning.

Conclusion

In this chapter, we explained key features of complex systems and gave examples of those features in relation to L2 learners' emotions and emotion regulation. We looked at EI and emotion regulation through the complexity lens and then presented affective learning strategies useful to L2 learners. We also described the purposes and characteristics of the MYE, a questionnaire that enables learners to provide short narratives about their responses to common L2 learning scenarios that might be experienced as emotionally charged. The MYE, an excerpt of which is included in this chapter, is a potentially valuable emotion regulation assessment tool. It also raises learners' awareness about emotions in L2 learning and could become a bridge to affective strategy instruction. We explained how the MYE reflects a complexity viewpoint and why such a viewpoint is important. We enthusiastically encourage readers to contact us indicating an interest in collaborative, international research using the MYE.

Notes

(1) Because of dynamism, which is an intrinsic part of a complex system, such a system is sometimes called a 'complex dynamic system' (Oxford, 2017, 2018).
(2) An automatic, frequently used, helpful learning behaviour is a 'habit' because it is no longer strategic, which involves intentional use (Oxford, 2017).

(3) Some researchers wish to go further by using statistics. Nonparametric statistics are generally preferred because they are distribution-free. This means nonparametric statistics do not require meeting the distributional assumption (e.g. normally distributed data) and other assumptions demanded by parametric statistics. However, we have found that the use of nonparametric statistics can often produce similar p-values to those produced by parametric statistics (Oxford, 2011), and this applies for self-regulation strategies (Gunning & Oxford, 2014).

(4) Though we prefer not to call emotions 'positive' or 'negative,' the MYE has done so, and that is why 'positive' and 'negative' are used in the Kantaridou and Psaltou-Joycey study to describe emotions. See also note 5 (in the appendix).

(5) As noted earlier, the terms 'positive' and 'negative' are still used in the slightly revised MYE to refer to emotions, because these terms, although problematic, continue to be employed in ordinary parlance. However, we added more descriptive terms to Items #1 and #3 to create these concepts: 'positive (pleasant, comfortable) emotions' and 'negative (unpleasant, uncomfortable) emotions.' This is a small step toward solving the valence problem (see earlier), and we are considering other options as well.

References

Ahmed, S. (2004) *The Cultural Politics of Emotion.* Edinburgh: Edinburgh University Press.

Barkhuizen, G. (2013) *Narrative Inquiry in Language Teaching and Learning Research.* New York: Routledge.

Benesch, S. (2017) *Emotions and English Language Teaching: Exploring Teachers' Emotion Labor.* New York, NY: Routledge.

Buck, R. (2005) Adding ingredients to the self-organising dynamic system stew: Motivation, communication, and higher-level emotions – and don't forget the genes! *Behavioral and Brain Science* 28 (2), 197–198.

Dewaele, J.-M., Petrides, K.V. and Furnham, A. (2008) The effects of trait emotional intelligence and sociobiographical variables on communicative anxiety and foreign language anxiety among adult multilinguals: A review and empirical investigation. *Language Learning* 58, 911–960.

Dörnyei, Z. (2009) *The Psychology of Second Language Acquisition.* New York, NY: Oxford University Press.

Dörnyei, Z., MacIntyre, P.D. and Henry, A. (eds) (2015) *Motivational Dynamics in Language Learning.* Bristol: Multilingual Matters.

Esch, E. (2004) Clash or crash? Autonomy ten years on. Paper presented at the Conference on Autonomy in Language Learning – Maintaining Control, Hong Kong University of Science and Technology. See http??lc.ust.hk/~centre/conf2004/esch.html

Frankl, V.E. (1984) *Man's Search for Meaning: An Introduction to Logotherapy.* Trans. I. Lasch. Boston: Beacon.

Frederickson, B.L. (2004) The broaden-and-build theory of positive emotions. *Philosophical Transactions of the Royal Society of London (Biological Sciences)* 359, 1367–1377.

Gkonou, C. (2018) Listening to highly anxious EFL learners through the use of narrative: Metacognitive and affective strategies for learner self-regulation. In R.L. Oxford and C.M. Amerstorfer (eds) *Language Learning Strategies and Individual Learner Characteristics: Situating Strategy use in Diverse Contexts* (pp. 79–97). London: Bloomsbury.

Gkonou, C. and Oxford, R.L. (2016) *Managing Your Emotions (MYE) Questionnaire.* University of Essex, UK: Department of Language and Linguistics.

Gkonou, C. and Mercer, S. (2017) *Understanding Emotional and Social Intelligence Among English Language Teachers.* London: British Council.

Gkonou, C. and Miller, E.R. (2020) Critical incidents in language teachers' narratives of emotional experience. In C. Gkonou, J.-M. Dewaele and J. King (eds) *The Emotional Rollercoaster of Language Teaching* (pp. 131–149). Bristol: Multilingual Matters.

Gkonou, C. and Oxford, R.L. (2019) Revised Scenario 1 from the *Managing Your Emotions (MYE) Questionnaire*. University of Essex, UK: Department of Language and Linguistics.

Gkonou, C., Daubney, M. and Dewaele, J.-M. (eds) (2017) *New Insights into Language Anxiety: Theory, Research and Educational Implications*. Bristol: Multilingual Matters.

Gkonou, C., Dewaele, J.-M. and King, J. (eds.) (2020) *The Emotional Rollercoaster of Language Teaching*. Bristol: Multilingual Matters.

Goleman, D. (2005) *Emotional Intelligence: Why it Can Matter More Than IQ*. (2nd edn). New York: Bantam.

Gross, J.J. (ed.) (2014) *Handbook of Emotion Regulation*. (2nd edn). New York: Guilford Press.

Gunning, P. and Oxford, R.L. (2014) Children's learning strategy use and the effects of strategy instruction on success in learning ESL in Canada. In R.L. Oxford and C. Griffiths (eds) *Language Learning Strategy Research in the Twenty-First Century*. Special issue, *System 43*, 82–100.

Hiver, P. (2015) Attractor states. In Z. Dörnyei, P.D. MacIntyre and A. Henry (eds) *Motivational Dynamics in Language Learning* (pp. 20–28). Bristol: Multilingual Matters.

Hoschchild, A. (1983) *The Managed Heart: Commercialization of Human Feelings*. Berkeley: University of California Press.

Kantaridou, Z. and Psaltou-Joycey, A. (submitted 2018) Affective dimensions of L2 learning. [Article]

King, J. (ed.) (2015) *The Dynamic Interplay between Context and the Language Learner*. Basingstoke: Palgrave Macmillan.

Kostoulas, A., Stelma, J., Mercer, S., Cameron, L. and Dawson, S. (2018) Complex systems theory as a shared discourse space for TESOL. *TESOL Journal 9* (2), 246–260.

Larsen-Freeman, D. (2015) Ten 'lessons' from complex dynamic systems theory: What is on offer. In Z. Dörnyei, P.D. MacIntyre and A. Henry (eds) *Motivational Dynamics in Language Learning* (pp. 24–43). Bristol: Multilingual Matters.

Larsen-Freeman, D. and Cameron, L. (2008) *Complex Systems and Applied Linguistics*. Oxford: Oxford University Press.

Lorenz, E.N. (1969) Atmospheric predictability as revealed by naturally occurring analogues. *Journal of the Atmospheric Sciences 26* (4), 536–646.

Mayer, J.D., Caruso, D.R. and Salovey, P. (2016) The ability model of emotional intelligence: Principles and updates. *Emotion Review 8*, 290–300.

Miller, E.R. and Gkonou, C. (2018) Language teacher agency, emotion labor and emotional rewards in tertiary-level English language classes. *System 79*, 49–59.

Nowak, A., Vallacher, R.R. and Zochowski, M. (2005) The emergence of personality: Dynamic foundations of individual variation. *Developmental Review 25* (3-4), 351–385. doi: 10.1016/j.dr.2005.10.004

Oxford, R.L. (2011) *Teaching and Researching Language Learning Strategies* (1st edn). Harlow, Essex: Pearson Longman.

Oxford, R.L. (2016) Toward a psychology of well-being for language learners: The 'EMPATHICS' vision. In P.D. MacIntyre, T. Gregersen and S. Mercer (eds) *Positive Psychology in Second Language Acquisition* (pp. 10–87). Bristol: Multilingual Matters.

Oxford, R.L. (2017) *Teaching and Researching Language Learning Strategies: Self-regulation in Context* (2nd edn). New York: Routledge.

Oxford, R.L. (2018) EMPATHICS: A Complex Dynamic Systems (CDS) vision of language learner well-being. In J.I. Liontas (ed.) *The TESOL Encyclopedia of English Language Teaching*. Hoboken, NJ: Wiley. doi: 10.1002/9781118784235.eelt0953

Oxford, R.L. and Amerstorfer, C.M. (eds) (2018) *Language Learning Strategies and Individual Learner Characteristics: Situating Strategy Use in Diverse Contexts*. London: Bloomsbury.

Oxford, R.L. and Gkonou, C. (2018) Interwoven: Culture, language, and learning strategies. In R.L. Oxford and M. Pawlak (guest eds) *Language Learning Strategies: Linking with the Past, Shaping the Future*. Special Issue. *Studies in Second Language Learning and Teaching* 8 (2), 403–426. doi: 10.14746/ssllt.2018.8.2.10

Pavlenko, A. (2013) Language desire and commodification of affect. In D. Gabryś-Barker and J. Bielska (eds) *The Affective Dimension in Second Language Acquisition* (pp. 3–28). Bristol: Multilingual Matters.

Prior, M. (in press) Elephants in the room: An 'affective turn,' or just feeling our way? *The Modern Language Journal* 103 (2), 516–527.

Salovey, P., Mayer, J.D., Caruso, D.E. and Yoo, S.H. (2011) The positive psychology of emotional intelligence. In S.J. Lopez and C. R. Snyder (eds) *The Oxford Handbook of Positive Psychology* (pp. 237–248). New York: Oxford University Press.

Seligman, M.E.P. (2011) *Flourish: A Visionary New Understanding of Happiness and Well-being*. New York: Atria/Simon & Schuster.

Thomas, N. and Rose, H. (2019) Do language learning strategies need to be self-directed? Disentangling strategies from self-regulated learning. *TESOL Quarterly* 53 (1), 248–257. doi: 10.1002/tesq.473

Tripp, D. (2012) *Critical Incidents in Teaching: Developing Professional Judgment*. Abingdon: Routledge.

Ushioda, E. (2009) A person-in-context relational view of emergent motivation and identity. In Z. Dörnyei and E. Ushioda (eds) *Motivation, Language Identity, and the L2 Self* (pp. 215–228). Bristol: Multilingual Matters.

Vygotsky, L.V. (1978) *Mind in Society*. Cambridge, MA: Harvard University Press.

Vygotsky, L.V. (1981) The genesis of higher mental functions. In J. Wertsch (ed.) *The Concept of Activity in Soviet Psychology*. Armonk, NY: Sharpe.

Zembylas, M. (2005) *Teaching with Emotion: A Postmodern Enactment*. Greenwich, CT: Information Age Publishing.

Appendix

Scenario 1 from the *MYE,* revised version (Gkonou & Oxford, 2019)[5]

Scenario 1: *The teacher assigns an essay writing task in class and allows 60 minutes for completion of the task. After a couple of minutes, you notice that your classmates have already started writing while you are still working on the outline of your essay.*

1. What kind of emotions would you experience in this situation? (Please circle the appropriate letter.)
   a. Positive (pleasant, comfortable)
   b. Negative (unpleasant, uncomfortable)
   c. Both types of emotions

2. Please name the emotions (one or more) you would feel in this situation. (maximum 10 words)

3. What would you do in order to manage these emotions in this situation? (maximum 50 words)

a. What would you do to *increase any positive (pleasant, comfortable) emotions* in this situation?	b. What would you to do *handle any negative (unpleasant, uncomfortable) emotions* in this situation?

4. Have you ever encountered this situation or something like it? (Please circle the appropriate letter.)
   a. Yes
   b. No

Important: If the answer to #4 is yes (that is, _you encountered this situation or something like it before_), please respond to each of the following items (#5–9).

5. Please describe the situation, if any, that you encountered before. (maximum 30 words)

6. If your *teacher or someone else* tried to teach you how to manage your emotions in the situation, please circle the appropriate letter below.
   a. My teacher (current or past) or someone else tried to teach me how to manage my emotions in this situation, and it was successful.
   b. My teacher or someone else tried to teach me how to manage my emotions in this situation, but it was *not* successful.

7. If your teacher or someone else tried to teach you how to manage your emotions in the situation, please explain *how* he or she tried to teach you this (maximum 30 words).

8. If *nobody* tried to teach you how to manage your emotions in the situation, please circle the appropriate letter below.
   a. I *consciously* tried to manage my emotions without help in this situation, and it was successful.
   b. I *consciously* tried to manage my emotions without help in this situation, but it was *not* successful.
   c. I *consciously* tried to manage my emotions without help in this situation, and it was partly successful and partly unsuccessful. (Please explain: _____
   _____)
   d. I was *not conscious enough* of my emotions in the situation and therefore could not manage my emotions.

9. If you tried to manage your emotions without help in the situation, please explain *how* you did this. (maximum 30 words)

5 Nested Systems and their Interactions: Dynamic WTC in the Classroom

Tomoko Yashima

Introduction

While a complex systemic perspective contributes new insights to research, to capture all aspects or characteristics of a complex system in one study is impossible. Since the language acquisition process is highly complex and dynamic, involving various linguistic, psychological, social and environmental factors, taking a complexity viewpoint makes much intuitive sense; yet the question is how we can go about actually conducting research with this process as the focus. Larsen-Freeman and Cameron (2008: 41) suggest that we employ 'concepts and ideas from complexity theory as a perspective from which to approach particular problems in applied linguistics'. They recommend that we approach these problems by engaging in 'complexity thought modeling', and suggest how we can do this:

(1) identify different components of a system;
(2) for each component identify timescales and levels of social organization on which it operates;
(3) describe the relations between components;
(4) describe how system and context interact with each other and;
(5) describe the dynamics of the system.

I regard this procedure as a set of guidelines we can apply in our research. We can start with a problem we face in our field and see if any concepts or ideas from Complexity Theory are helpful in understanding the phenomena better. Hereafter, I use the term Complex Dynamic Systems Theory (CDST) following Dörnyei *et al.* (2015).

A problem that has long concerned me in Japanese English as a Foreign Language (EFL) learning is student silence or reticence in classrooms, which is what originally motivated my research into willingness to communicate (WTC) in a second language (e.g. Yashima, 2002). To understand WTC phenomena better, what I focused on within CDST is interconnectedness between components and their dynamics. According to Larsen-Freeman and Cameron (2008: 198), 'a complexity perspective on the language classroom highlights connections across levels of human and social organization, from individual minds up to the social-political context of language learning, and across timescales from the minute-by-minute of classroom activity to teaching and learning lifetimes'. Drawing on these ideas, this chapter discusses how I went about attempting to capture as nested systems the communication behaviour and WTC exhibited by individual learners as well as the group (i.e. the class) that learners constitute, while also capturing situated and enduring aspects of learner affect on different timescales.

Willingness to Communicate in an L2

WTC is defined as readiness to initiate communication at a particular time and with a specific person or persons in an L2 (MacIntyre *et al.*, 1998). MacIntyre and colleagues' pyramid-shaped WTC model integrates psychological, linguistic, educational and communicative approaches to L2 research in an attempt to graphically represent factors assumed to influence a learner's decision to communicate at a given point in time. The stratified model shows how both trait and state variables influence momentary L2 WTC. At the base of the pyramid are relatively stable, trait-like variables, including intergroup climate and personality, which are hypothesized to have an indirect influence on L2 WTC. In the layers above are enduring variables that have somewhat more direct influence on WTC, including attitude toward different groups, communicative competence and intergroup motivation, self-confidence, and so on. In the upper layer of the pyramid are two immediate precursors of WTC: a desire to communicate with a specific person at a specific moment, and the situated (or state) self-confidence that partly reflects more enduring self-confidence in using the L2. According to MacIntyre *et al.* (1998), self-confidence is a combination of reduced anxiety and perceived L2 competence.

This model foreshadows approaches informed by CDST (Dörnyei *et al.*, 2015). It presents a systemic view of how both enduring and situated variables interact in a complex manner and converge as L2 WTC at specific moments. When WTC reaches a certain threshold, language use is triggered, resulting in communication (e.g. asking a question). A slight change in one element in the model, such as intergroup motivation, affects the whole system's dynamics.

The research that is the basis for this chapter (Yashima *et al.*, 2016, 2018) extends the original model by showing how CDST perspectives can reveal connections between individuals' WTC and group-level WTC as nested systems as they co-adapt to each other. In addition, from a CDST perspective, learner characteristics such as anxiety and WTC can be conceptualized as phenomena operating on different timescales. In this sense, trait WTC as originally postulated by McCroskey (1992) as a personality trait, should be regarded as more enduring, or placed on 'the ontogenetic timescale', while situated WTC should be seen as on 'the microgenetic timescale' (Larsen-Freeman & Cameron, 2008: 169). It is, therefore, possible that state WTC in the L2 classroom be studied as the result of interactions between trait-like learner characteristics developed throughout an individual's learning history and contextual contingent factors emerging in the classroom.

History of WTC research

While empirical research inspired by MacIntyre *et al.*'s (1998) model has been conducted in various parts of the world, earlier studies mainly addressed how enduring variables affect trait-like L2 WTC, using psychometric scales (e.g. Clément *et al.*, 2003; Denies *et al.*, 2015; MacIntyre & Charos, 1996; MacIntyre & Clément, 1996; Peng & Woodrow, 2010; Yashima, 2002; Yashima *et al.*, 2004). These studies confirmed that many of the enduring factors shown in the model, including intergroup attitudes, communicative competence, anxiety and L2 self-confidence influence trait-like L2 WTC. In contrast, recent studies have captured the situated nature of WTC (e.g. Cao, 2011; Kang, 2005; Peng, 2012). Taking WTC as an emerging state indicating readiness to speak, qualitative and mixed-methods research has revealed a number of factors influencing state WTC (for a review see, for example, Pawlak *et al.*, 2015).

MacIntyre and Legatto's (2011) CDST-based study brought about a new turn in research with its focus on the dynamic moment-to-moment state of WTC. Using an idiodynamic method, their laboratory study demonstrated that WTC fluctuated dramatically over the few minutes during which the participants talked about eight pre-selected topics. While each participant exhibited unique reactions to the task, consistent patterns were also observed, including a decline in WTC while discussing supposedly less familiar topics compared to others. This study stimulated a number of recent studies on the dynamic nature of WTC conducted in language classrooms (e.g. Bernales, 2016; Pawlak & Mystkowska-Wiertelak, 2015; Pawlak *et al.*, 2015).

As shown above, research had identified various antecedents of WTC by focusing on either trait-like or situated, contextually emerging aspects of the phenomenon. However, researchers had yet to integrate situated and trait-like WTC as individual characteristics in order to come to a fuller understanding of WTC as originally conceptualized in the WTC model (MacIntyre *et al.*, 1998). To reach this goal, we need to investigate why learners choose (or avoid) communication in L2 classrooms at specific moments and how a combination of learner-internal and learner-external factors result in communication. In other words, we need to pay attention to 'the interplay of learner characteristics and the learning environment'

(Dörnyei, 2009: 179) by approaching WTC as a complex dynamic system. With this goal in mind, my colleagues and I used a CDST perspective to grasp the dynamic and complex characteristics of individual and group WTC in two previous studies (Yashima *et al.*, 2016, 2018). In this chapter, I summarize the findings of this research in order to present one way of conducting research using CDST and to illustrate some of the benefits of drawing on a complexity perspective in applied linguistics research.

The Research

Objectives

Our objective was to capture WTC and communication behaviour at both individual and group levels from a CDST perspective by focusing on individual EFL learners as well as the whole class these learners constitute. A second objective was to capture situated and enduring aspects of learner affect on different timescales.

From a pedagogical perspective, ours was also an interventional study in response to King (2013), who reported that following 48 hours of classroom observation in a Japanese EFL context, students' self-initiated communication amounted to only seven minutes, or 0.24% of the total 48 hours. This, King (2013: 12) claims, constitutes empirical evidence of 'a robust trend, with minimal variation, toward silence', or an attractor state, in Japanese university foreign language classrooms.

To reverse this trend, we planned 'a design-based study', which as Barab (2006: 155) explains, 'deals with complexity by iteratively changing the learning environment over time–collecting evidence of the effect of these variations and feeding it recursively into future design'. This is particularly effective when the focus of investigation is not the outcome of learning but learning processes. A design-based study shares the same features as action research, where practitioner researchers 'deliberately introduce "noise" into the system' and see how the system responds (Larsen-Freeman & Cameron, 2008: 244). In other words, by changing the teaching procedures or teacher reactions or adding slight perturbation to the classroom environment, it becomes possible to investigate how learners adapt to such change, which contributes to a deeper understanding of learners and learning.

Method

Participants

Participants were 21 Japanese first-year university students (15 females and six males) learning EFL in Japan and planning to study abroad for one academic year as a requirement of the curriculum. Our research team (see Yashima *et al.*, 2016) selected this group of students, whom the second author was teaching, because we knew that they were highly motivated, though somewhat quiet students, and we believed that the intervention to stimulate their WTC should be helpful to their upcoming study abroad experience. These students had received six years of EFL instruction in secondary school as a prerequisite for matriculation to the university. Of the 21 participants, 16 had overseas experience of more than two weeks, and five had spent more than six months abroad.

Teaching intervention

Before implementing the intervention, we had frequent team meetings to decide on the details of the design. We wanted to introduce informed, focused change to the system, which, as Mason (2008) suggests, takes effort as the teacher-researchers ponder what may or may not work to bring about positive changes. As mentioned above, we knew that these students were highly motivated and eager to improve their English, but not quite ready to move away from routine activities in which their roles were rather passive. To create a situation where learners could take the initiative to communicate or exhibit their WTC in a public sphere, we created 20-minute discussion sessions at the end of regular 90-minute classes to replace existing teacher-controlled activities. In the intervention, which lasted for 12 weeks within a 15-week semester, all 21 participants took part in the discussions as one group. During this whole-class discussion, the instructor's control of interactions was kept to a minimum by eliminating I–R–F (initiation–response–feedback) sequences and refraining from appointing a student as the next speaker, as typically occurred in ordinary class interactions. Instead, any one of the participants could take the initiative to speak at any time.

To prepare for each whole-class discussion, which was considered a challenge, participants were given a chance to discuss the topic in question first in pairs, then in smaller groups (of three to six) prior to the whole-class discussion. Discussion topics (e.g. What should you do to make a restaurant business successful? Do you have a phobia? If so, how do you try to overcome this phobia?) were based on the content of the textbook and given to the participants beforehand so that they could prepare for the discussion if they wished. Finally, the instructor gave participants autonomy to switch topics during the discussion if they found the topic uninteresting or difficult.

Data collection

This was a mixed-methods study in which both quantitative and qualitative data were collected in multiple ways to address two timescales (enduring and situated). For enduring or trait individual characteristics, prior to the intervention, (a) a questionnaire was administered to elicit the participants' trait L2 anxiety level, L2 self-confidence trait L1WTC and L2WTC, and motivation (intended effort),[1] following Yashima (2009) and Ryan (2009). Also included in the questionnaire was the Personal Report of Communication Anxiety (PRCA-24, see Pribyl *et al.*, 1998), used to assess trait communication apprehension levels.

To collect situated data during the intervention, (b) audio-recordings of each of the 12 sessions were made and subsequently transcribed, with the students' permission and (c) observation notes were taken by a research assistant (RA). Transcribed classroom interactions along the timeline combined with the observation notes enabled the measurement of speech or silence duration. These data were also used to count the number of (self-initiated) utterances made by each student, which we regarded as a manifestation of state L2 WTC.

To triangulate data from the students' perspectives, (d) state WTC was self-assessed by the students at the beginning of each class period, while state anxiety level was self-assessed at the end of each discussion session, both on a 10-point scale. If these had been assessed during the ongoing discussion, it would have been a reflection of truly situated affect, though we did not choose this option because it would have stopped the dynamic flow of the discussion. Besides, students wrote (e) reflections on their performance each time, which were found useful in understanding their psychological processes leading to speech or silence.

Following the intervention, (f) a semester-end questionnaire asked students to state their overall reactions to the intervention as well as how much they prepared for the discussion each time. Finally, (g) stimulated recall interviews [using learners' reflections from (d) and (f) as stimuli] were conducted in Japanese with three students who agreed to share their experiences. (See the Results section for an explanation of why these specific students were selected.)

Analysis

Discussion sessions were transcribed for numerical and discourse analysis. To analyse the data, we measured the amount of silence between turns, amount of talk by the instructor, and amount of talk by students. We counted the number of utterances by each student based on the research assistant's observation note, which were confirmed on the transcripts. Utterances were defined as turn-taking switches following Fujie (2000). Interviews were transcribed, open-coded and analysed for salient differences between the three interviewees. For analysis of the quantitative data, SPSS was used to calculate descriptive statistics as well as correlational analyses.

Results

Group-level phenomena

Group-level performance (with proportion of student talk versus silence and teacher talk) is shown in Figure 5.1. This reveals that the

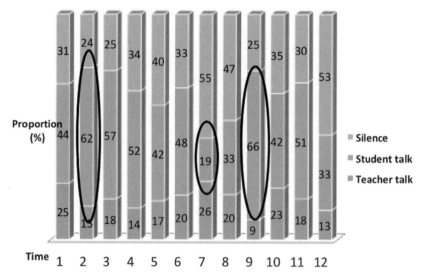

Figure 5.1 Proportion of student talk, teacher talk and silence (Adapted from Yashima *et al.*, 2018)

amount of student talk varied somewhat widely over the semester. To understand what created so much variation, we examined three sessions that differed greatly in this respect: Times 2, 7 and 9, when the proportion was 62%, 19% and 66%, respectively. Table 5.1 shows the students' communication behaviours and reactions during the three focal sessions as a group. The table compares the number of students who participated in discussions in these three sessions, total number of students' utterances during each session, average length of their utterances (in words) and mean level of state anxiety assessed on a scale of 1 to 10 in the reflection sheet the students completed at the end of each class as well as the self-assessment of state WTC level.

Based on these findings, we derived a number of insights into how group-level communication patterns were created by drawing on the different perspectives gained with different data collection tools.

Firstly, we examined students' average word counts and reflective comments regarding the sessions under focus. It emerged that topic was vitally important in determining discourse flow. The Time 2 topic (*How first names are chosen*) elicited average length of students' utterances of 20.21 words, the Time 9 topic (*Multiple intelligence*) an average of 17.09 words and that of Time 7 (*Factors in owning a successful restaurant*) only 6.24 words. Evidently, students found the latter topic harder to deal with, which was confirmed in their explanation of why they could not contribute opinions in that session.

Secondly, we found that attendance dramatically changed group dynamics. The data we collected through discourse analysis of transcribed

Table 5.1 Summary of students' communication behaviours and affective reactions in three sessions as a group

Session	Proportion of student talk	No. of students who took part in the discussion	Total No. of student utterances	Average word counts in students' utterances	Anxiety (state)	WTC (state)
2	62%	15	39	20.2	5.05	6.83
7	19%	13	31	6.2	3.14	6.78
9	66%	19	31	17.1	3.52	6.93

Note: State anxiety and WTC were self-rated on a 10-point scale.

data yielded critical insights. At Time 2, leadership by one student, Masa (all names are pseudonyms), was conspicuous, as he expressed his views frequently and distributed turns among students or broke the silence by saying 'Who's going to speak?' (or something similar) when silence filled the room. At Time 7, however, Masa was exceptionally quiet, and this was one reason why the discussion was rather stagnant that day. In his reflection sheet, he wrote: 'My mind was not working well'. My co-researchers present in the classroom as instructor and RA had the impression that he was not as fit as in other sessions. When they talked to him after class, he revealed that he had not had enough sleep the previous night.

At Time 9, Masa was absent. Interestingly, this was when the student talk ratio was highest of the 12 sessions. Again, our team members witnessed what happened, and we later confirmed through discourse analysis that it was partly attributable to Taki, another constant contributor to discussions, who triggered a Question-and-Answer chain. After expressing ideas about her own multiple intelligence (MI) type, the topic of the discussion, Taki then asked her neighbour, Kumi, to talk about her own MI profile. Kumi hesitated for a while but started to explain that she was not good at reading maps because she was not a spatial type. Then Taki quickly whispered to Kumi that she should ask the question to the next person, to which Kumi reacted by asking Otoka the question. This chain reaction continued until 13 students talked about their MI type and offered rationales for their views. This took up 15 minutes, during which time the students talked continuously. We regard this as a good example of co-adaptation of individuals as systems in CDST terms (see Yashima *et al.*, 2016, for discourse analyses of classroom interactions).

Thirdly, we sensed that the timing of each session within the semester mattered. At Time 2, immediately after the start of university life in April, students were motivated to try something new and challenging. At Time 7 in June, however, students showed signs of tiredness following two months of excitement and high motivation to learn. From our experience, and as many teachers note, this is the period in Japanese universities when students generally show signs of fatigue. In addition, by that time, student roles in the class (those who talked and those who did not) had become somewhat fixed.

Individual communication behaviours

As any class is made up of individuals, we were also vitally interested in individual-level phenomena and perspectives. Integrating different data sources allowed us to form a picture of individual learners' stories, in turn yielding insights into what creates individual differences in communication frequency. A specific individual's decision to communicate (or not) at a specific time is affected by momentary self-confidence, topic familiarity and a sense of responsibility as well as other students' reactions and class ambience (among others). This in turn affects the talk/silence pattern for the whole class, which then becomes the context for ongoing communication. As a result, individuals as well as the group formed by individuals interact and co-adapt as nested systems, thus creating specific communication behaviour in both individuals and the group.

To learn more about the emergence of these communication patterns, we selected three participants for in-depth interviews. These interviewees were selected on the basis of the frequency and style of their participation (high, moderate and low). One interviewee participated frequently, a second participated regularly but not extensively and a third was mostly quiet and might be considered rather passive. Table 5.2 presents individual learner characteristics for the three participants, including attendance, English proficiency (Test of English as a Foreign Language – Institutional Testing Paper (TOEFL-ITP)), frequency of self-selected turns we regard as an indication of situated WTC, trait WTC in the L1 and L2 and anxiety as assessed by the questionnaire. Class means and comparable data from other studies with Japanese university students are shown for comparison.

Qualitative analysis of the stimulated recall interviews revealed how individuals' communication behaviours emerged and evolved during the discussion sessions and led to the differences in amount of talk. Next, I present data for each of the three individuals, integrating multiple data sources in order to better understand how the learners' communication behaviours emerged. I report trait WTC as an enduring characteristic as well as state WTC resulting from the interaction of trait WTC and emergent contextual influences.

Taki

Trait (enduring) WTC

Taki scored higher-than-average trait WTC in both the L1 and the L2. In the interview, she stated that she was ready to speak English at any time. Her strong L2 WTC may be rooted in her ample experience of communicating in English. In senior-high school, she took a number of

Table 5.2 Summary of three participants' communication behaviour, proficiency, trait anxiety and trait WTC

Student	TOEFL-ITP	Total No.s of turns (self-selected)	L2 anxiety	WTC (L1)	WTC (L2)
Taki	487	40 (33)	2.33	4.75	4.75
Nachi	487	12 (9)	4.67	5.75	2.75
Oto	490	1 (0)	5.67	3.50	3.50
Class mean (SD)	469.06 (24.48)	21.9 (15.43) (25.4 (20.41))	4.23 (1.32)	4.24 (0.65)	3.72 (1.02)
Norm 1 (SD)			4.36 (1.02)	4.42 (0.85)	2.88 (1.11)
Norm 2 (SD)			4.09 (0.82)	4.04 (0.99)	1.89 (1.07)

Note: N = 244 for Norm 1, based on Yashima (2014), and N = 1896 for Norm 2, based on Ryan (2008).

The wordings of items in the WTC scales used in the present study are slightly different from those used by Ryan (2008).

communication-focused English classes. She also experienced one year of study-abroad as part of her senior-high school curriculum and stated that as a result, she found herself speaking quite naturally. Her higher than average trait WTC in the L2 likely results from a combination of her personality traits (high L1 WTC) interacting over time with readiness for L2 communication acquired through her learning history, in particular her overseas experience.

State (situational) WTC

Taki stated in the interview that although she was nervous in the whole-group discussion, she had no difficulty in expressing herself in English. She was genuinely concerned about the difficulties her classmates appeared to be experiencing in participating in the discussions, and earnestly wanted them to participate equally. She said that she hated to see herself monopolizing the discussion. Although other students' quietness gave her many chances to participate in discussions, she refrained from doing so as often as she could. Examination of the transcripts of the classroom discussions revealed that she often related her comments to what other students said, using expressions of agreement such as 'I can understand both sides, but I agree with Yaya and Masa's opinion, because...' (Time 3). When she expressed her own opinion, she showed willingness to relate her contribution to other students' statements, such as 'I also have a phobia about darkness, same as Shiki' (Time 5). Her comments in the reflection sheets indicated that she often felt compelled to say something to make the discussion more active, for example by trying to engage others and get the discussion to flow by involving them. At Time 7, she started a

Q&A chain by asking a question and whispering an instruction to pass it around. Her comments indicate a sense of responsibility about collective performance as well as a reluctance to monopolize the floor (possibly a culturally constructed tendency) that might have occasionally acted to put the brakes on her initiative to talk.

Overall, the interplay between her stable tendency to initiate communication in both the L1 and the L2 along with a sense that she could exercise responsibility to engage with her classmates in this context led to a strong tendency to initiate communication, especially during periods of silence, and then to facilitate extended conversation with her peers.

Nachi
Trait WTC

Nachi showed higher-than-average anxiety about speaking English and lower L2 WTC. In contrast, she reported high L1 WTC. Her prior experience with communication in English was limited. She attended a public senior-high school where English language teaching focused on grammar and preparation for college entrance examinations, and where no oral English classes were offered. Unlike Taki, she had no overseas experience. Despite her anxiety and lack of experience with communication in English, Nachi said that she found her university EFL classes 'new and refreshing'.

State WTC

Nachi did not take any turns in the first session and remained quiet throughout. Commenting on this, she wrote in the reflection sheet: 'I was frightened to participate in the discussion, though I wanted to say something'. At Time 2, however, she successfully contributed her opinion, giving a fairly lengthy explanation about how her name was chosen. On the day, she wrote in the reflection sheet: 'People talked actively today, which encouraged me to speak too'. This was the day when student talk occupied 62% of the total time, with 15 of 21 students participating (see Table 5.2 and Figure 5.1), thus illustrating the part played by contextual factors, including a relatively accessible topic and a conducive class atmosphere. In the interview based on the final questionnaire, it also became apparent that this stretch of English communication was the result of her efforts and willingness to participate, as I explain below.

In the questionnaire we administered at the end of the semester, we asked how students prepared for discussions. Nachi reported that she 'thought about what to say in Japanese and then in English,…looked up words to be used in the discussion in the dictionary,…and rehearsed in her mind what to say', performing these actions more frequently than the other two interviewees. In the interview, she said: 'I simulated the interaction, imagining myself responding to what other students said'. In effect, she tried to visualize her L2 self as vivid and elaborate (Dörnyei, 2005, 2009), saying: 'I prepared for the discussion because I wanted to participate. Without preparation, I cannot speak…because I don't have the ability to say what comes to my mind yet'. She also listened to the tape recording when preparing at home, which she believed gave her confidence. Preparation thus helped boost her state self-confidence, enabling her to contribute one turn on average at each time.

Nachi admitted that it was very hard to be the first to speak or to be the one to break the silence. In fact, seeing her good friend expressing her opinion made it easier for her to follow suit. In addition, as time went by, classmates came to know each other, and this 'helped soften the atmosphere', reducing her anxiety. It was also revealed in the interview that she was sensitive to who was speaking and what was being said moment-to-moment. When she was quiet, she 'was following the flow of the discussion, trying to analyse how good speakers organize ideas when they take turns'. This was reflected in her observed communication performance, where she managed to contribute to the discussion approximately once during each class meeting. In this sense, she tried to fill the gap between her natural inclination to communicate and her perceived inability to communicate in English by preparing herself in a particular way that was sensitive to the conditions around her.

Oto
Trait WTC

Oto kept mostly silent during the group discussion sessions over the 12 weeks and spoke on only one occasion when a question was directed to her. Compared to Taki and Nachi, Oto showed higher trait anxiety and lower trait WTC in both L1 and L2. Her history shows that she had had more exposure to communication in English than Nachi, having attended a school where she sometimes experienced an 'easier version of the discussions in English' and had made a short trip to Australia when she was in her first year of junior-high school. In fact, her proficiency based on her TOEFL score was not particularly low compared to the others; yet, it would appear that prior learning experiences in English did not help raise her L2 WTC much.

State WTC

Illustrating the observation that trait-level characteristics interact with contextual factors, Oto felt that her classmates were 'very fluent and overwhelming', and the discussion topics were 'difficult', claiming that she 'had no opinions' about those topics. However, it was revealed in the interview that her high anxiety arose partly from self-awareness of her quiet voice, a feature that could have affected her state self-confidence and led her to remain silent. As she stated, 'When people react to what I say with "Pardon?" I feel frightened'. She appreciated the Q&A chain started by Taki, which gave her the only opportunity to talk in response to a question directed to her. The anticipation of a question gave her time to think and give a response.

Oto's personality combined with relatively high L2 anxiety contributed to her quietness. Her momentary self-consciousness and ongoing comparison with classmates she felt were better than her seemed to reduce both her state self-confidence and desire to communicate. Once quietness becomes habitual, it can be difficult to change. In the interview, she stated: 'At the beginning, my attitude was, like, I'll just watch others having a discussion, but eventually I felt it's important to say something'. She noticed that many of her peers contributed their opinions while making grammatical errors, speaking only in short phrases or stumbling: 'Still, others listened to them and asked questions if they didn't understand. I realized that it was OK to speak like that'. These comments suggest that she initially believed that she should produce grammatically correct full sentences, which may have placed extra pressure on her and reduced her state desire to communicate. However, she was somewhat awakened to how people communicate in real life. As she also said, 'I learned that trying to say something is important, because if I say something, people will listen'.

Discussion

Interaction of group and individuals as nested systems

WTC has long been studied as an individual psychological characteristic, yet communication is a supra-individual phenomenon. To reconcile this contradiction, we turned to CDST in analysing group-level communication behaviours as well as individuals as complex nested systems. Specifically, CDST was used to understand how individual WTC amounts to group-level communication behaviour that, in turn, becomes the context of individuals' communication behaviour. Beyond the perception that individuals are influenced by the environment external to them, this helps clarify 'how humans shape their own context' and how 'the individual and context is coupled' such that 'the context itself can change in a process of co-adaptation between the individual and the environment' (Larsen-Freeman & Cameron, 2008: 7).

Considering the communication activity in the classroom, at the group level, it was revealed that the amount of student talk and number of student-initiated turns was far greater than observed by King (2013) or the stereotype of a Japanese classroom might suggest. Our results show that student communication fluctuated dynamically over the semester, even as anxiety within the group gradually fell over time and stabilized (see Figure 5.2). The group-level tendencies were echoed in students' own comments in the reflection sheets. Although many expressed anxiety as a reason for

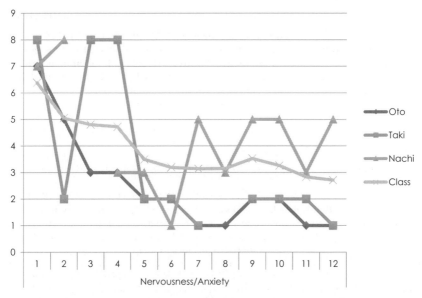

Figure 5.2 Individual and group-level (class mean) situated anxiety levels in 12 discussion sessions

non-participation in the early stages, their reported anxiety fell substantially during the second half of the semester. This group-level tendency thus became part of the context for individual participation as nested systems, as Nachi mentioned in the interview, thus softening the class atmosphere and helping reduce her anxiety. She also stated that when many classmates talked actively, she found it easier to participate.

The three profiles outlined above show that each student experienced many thoughts and emotions emergent in context as a reaction to other students' behaviours. A student such as Oto, who demonstrated a high level of trait anxiety and low trait WTC, may be more sensitive to contextual factors. When her classmates were perceived to be overwhelmingly fluent and active, Oto felt frightened and fell into chronic silence. By contrast, even though she was very nervous, Nachi had a strong desire to contribute an opinion in class, and on several occasions she 'crossed the Rubicon' (Dörnyei, 2001: 88) from silence to speech. She prepared thoroughly in order to overcome her lack of self-confidence and had heightened willingness to communicate when an appropriate opportunity arose. On the other hand, with her high WTC, Taki was more concerned with the group-level performance and often tried to fill the silence in order to move the discussion along. Nevertheless, her state WTC fell somewhat as she was hesitant to dominate the discussion.

From a CDST nested systems perspective, students' momentary psychological reactions to contextual factors both facilitated and constrained their participation in the discussions, thus revealing interesting situational dynamics. At the same time, individual reactions created a group-level pattern. This group-level talk–silence pattern becomes a key part of the social context, inviting (or inhibiting) individual participation. For example, a long silence with a solemn atmosphere discouraged many students from talking but also stimulated an individual such as Taki to say something in order to reverse the trend.

Connections between different timescales

A CDST conceptualization of timescales was helpful in exploring the connection between trait-like learner characteristics assessed with a questionnaire and situated learner characteristics emerging in classroom contexts. By applying this idea, learner psychology, including motivation, anxiety and WTC, can be understood along different timescales, with, for example, the microgenetic level focusing on momentary changes as well as the ontogenetic level seeing them as long-term phenomena (for details, see Yashima & Arano, 2015). In this sense a complexity lens sheds different light on the phenomenon and helps us understand it better.

We depicted L2 WTC for each of the three focal participants using two timescales: trait-level enduring patterns and state-level emergent variability. We saw how the interplay of trait WTC and emerging contextual influences created situated emotional responses, leading to state WTC and self-initiated turns (or lack thereof). With respect to individuals' trait-level WTC, each of the three learners showed classroom patterns generally consistent with the traits being reported: Taki was high in both L1 and L2 WTC and she spoke often; Nachi was lower than average in L2 WTC but had above average L1 WTC, and her willingness to communicate was contingent on a suitable opportunity arising; finally, Oto had rather low L1 and L2 WTC and remained quiet most of the time. Yet their state WTC emerged at a particular moment, offsetting the enduring influence. Context, including topic, group-level affective state, ambience, other students' reactions and exquisitely contingent processes interact to trigger fleeting, momentary psychological reactions at a particular moment.

Figure 5.2 shows the state anxiety level reported by each of the three interviewees over the 12 sessions as well as the class mean at each point. The class mean gradually declines, indicating that the class as a whole became gradually more relaxed, even though this did not necessarily lead to a higher amount of communication. Notably, Oto's reaction contradicts what her trait L2 anxiety predicts and what she herself reported in the interview. Overall, students' reflections showed that they felt anxious when they tried to participate in the discussion without full confidence. In other words, when the desire to contribute an opinion is high, they become nervous as they struggle to find words to express their thoughts while searching for opportunities to do so within this type of open discussion.

On the other hand, once a participant decides to be a listener and learn from others rather than contribute, there is less cause to be nervous, which might explain Oto 's declining anxiety level in her chronic state of silence. A CDST perspective thus suggests that a relationship between anxiety and silence is not necessarily explicable by linear causality.

Using a traditional correlational approach, we calculated the average of situated anxiety (assessed 12 times) for individuals and found that they correlated moderately with individuals' trait-like language anxiety ($r = 0.54$) and highly with communication anxiety assessed using PRCA-24 ($r = 0.70$). This means that this trait-like characteristic accounted for part of the individual's situated performance. Conversely, when repeated over time, what is experienced in each classroom amounts to what is described as a trait-like feature. Here, we are looking at anxiety on different times-cales: situated and momentary on the one hand, and trait and enduring on the other, and, importantly, interacting with each other.

In past research, trait-like L2 WTC regarded as an enduring learner characteristic was discussed separately from situated WTC, with a grow-ing interest in the latter as a characteristic more relevant to the classroom language learning context. However, our study shows – and the case of anxiety reported above implies – that trait-like L2 WTC is connected to situated performance. This in turn suggests that enhancing situated L2 WTC through repeated practice may lead to higher long-term trait-like L2 WTC, a pedagogically encouraging insight.

Reflecting on the research approach

The design-based study reported here shed light on processes of learn-ers' behavioural transformation and the psychology behind it, when a tra-ditional experimental design employing a control group could have only verified a change in the outcome. The study helped yield valuable educa-tional insights into learners as well as communities of learners by focusing on their emotions throughout the intervention. Moreover, the study dem-onstrated how quantitative and qualitative data could be combined to capture the complexity of learner behaviour in context.

Conclusion

L2 learning is a complex process, and so is human communication. In a sense, a complexity perspective offers what teachers and researchers intuitively know already. While traditional research helps us view phe-nomena clearly by simplifying them, a complexity perspective helps us capture complexity by closely examining it, but without necessarily sim-plifying it. To achieve this aim, as Larsen-Freeman and Cameron (2008) suggest, a good place to start is an issue we face in our practices but that we struggle to understand. Complexity theory offers a toolkit of concepts from which researchers can select instruments with which to grasp a problem they face here and now in all its complexity and dynamicity.

Note

(1) In the tradition of psychological research on motivation and affect, four variables often investigated to have significant correlations are motivation, anxiety, perceived competence and WTC. This was validated in recent meta-analysis of quantitative WTC research by Elahi Shirvan *et al.* (2019), in which strong high-evidence correlates of WTC and these three variables are reported. Based on the past research, we assessed these variables (here self-confidence instead of perceived competence) in this study.

References

Barab, S. (2006) Design-based research: A methodological toolkit for the learning scientist. In R. Sawyer (ed.) *The Cambridge Handbook of the Learning Sciences.* Cambridge: Cambridge University Press.

Bernales, C. (2016) Towards a comprehensive concept of willingness to communicate: Learners' predicted and self-reported participation in the foreign language classroom. *System* 56, 1–12.

Cao, Y. (2011) Investigating situational willingness to communicate within second language classrooms from an ecological perspective. *System* 39, 468–479.

Clément, R., Baker, S.C. and MacIntyre, P.D. (2003) Willingness to communicate in a second language: The effects of context, norms, and vitality. *Journal of Language and Social Psychology* 22, 190–209.

Denies, K., Yashima, T. and Janssen, R. (2015) Classroom versus societal willingness to communicate: Investigating French as a second language in Flanders. *Modern Language Journal* 99, 718–739.

Dörnyei, Z. (2001) *Teaching and Researching Motivation.* Harlow: Longman.

Dörnyei, Z. (2005) *The Psychology of the Language Learner: Individual Differences in Second Language Acquisition.* Mahwah, NJ: Lawrence Erlbaum.

Dörnyei, Z. (2009) *The Psychology of Second Language Acquisition.* Oxford: Oxford University Press.

Dörnyei, Z., MacIntyre, P.D. and Henry, A. (eds) (2015) *Motivational Dynamics in Language Learning.* Bristol: Multilingual Matters.

Elahi Shirvan, M., Khajavy, G.H., MacIntyre, P.D. and Taherian, T. (2019) A meta-analysis of L2 willingness to communicate and its three high-evidence correlates. *Journal of Psycholinguistic Research* 48, 1241–1267.

Fujie, Y. (2000) Isseijugyou no hanashiai ni okeru kodomo no ryougiteki na hatsuwa no kinou: Shougakkou gonensei no shakaijugyou ni okeru kyoushitudanwa no bunseki [Children's in-class participation mixing academic and personal materials: Teachers' instructional response]. *[Kyouikushinrigaku Kenkyu]* 48, 21–31.

Kang, S.J. (2005) Dynamic emergence of situational willingness to communicate in a second language. *System* 33, 277–292.

King, J. (2013) Silence in the second language classrooms of Japanese universities. *Applied Linguistics* 34, 325–343.

Larsen-Freeman, D. and Cameron, L. (2008) *Complex Systems and Applied Linguistics.* New York: Oxford University Press.

MacIntyre, P.D. and Charos, C. (1996) Personality, attitudes, and affect as predictors of second language communication. *Journal of Language and Social Psychology* 15, 3–26.

MacIntyre, P.D. and Clément, R. (1996) A model of willingness to communicate in a second language: The concept, its antecedents, and implications. Paper presented at the 11th World Congress of Applied Linguistics, Jyväskylä, Finland (August).

MacIntyre, P.D., Clément, R., Dörnyei, Z. and Noels, K. (1998) Conceptualizing willingness to communicate in an L2: A situated model of confidence and affiliation. *Modern Language Journal* 82, 545–562.

MacIntyre, P.D. and Legatto, J.J. (2011) A dynamic system approach to willingness to communicate: Developing an idiodynamic method to capture rapidly changing affect. *Applied Linguistics* 32, 149–171.

Mason, M. (2008) What is complexity theory and what are its implications for educational change? *Educational Philosophy and Theory* 40, 35–49.

McCroskey, J.C. (1992) Reliability and validity of the willingness to communicate scale. *Communication Quarterly* 40, 16–25.

Pawlak, M. and Mystkowska-Wiertelak, A. (2015) Investigating the dynamic nature of classroom willingness to communicate. *System* 50, 1–9.

Pawlak, M., Mystkowska-Wiertelak, A. and Bielak, J. (2015) Investigating the nature of L2 willingness to communicate (WTC): A micro-perspective. *Language Teaching Research* 20, 1–19.

Peng, J. (2012) Towards an ecological understanding of willingness to communicate in EFL classrooms in China. *System* 40, 203–213.

Peng, J. and Woodrow, L. (2010) Willingness to communicate in English: A model in the Chinese EFL classroom context. *Language Learning* 60, 834–876.

Pribyl, C.B., Keaten, J.A., Sakamoto, M. and Koshikawa, F. (1998) Assessing the cross-cultural content validity of the Personal Report of Communication Apprehension scale (PRCA-24). *Japanese Psychological Research* 40, 47–53.

Ryan, S. (2008) The ideal L2 selves of Japanese learners of English. Unpublished doctoral dissertation, University of Nottingham.

Ryan, S. (2009) Self and identity in L2 motivation in Japan: The ideal L2 self and Japanese learners of English. In Z. Dörnyei and E. Ushioda (eds) *Motivation, Language Identity and the L2 Self* (pp. 120–143). Bristol: Multilingual Matters.

Yashima, T. (2002) Willingness to communicate in a second language: The Japanese EFL context. *Modern Language Journal* 86, 54–66.

Yashima, T. (2009) International posture and the ideal self in the Japanese EFL context. In Z. Dörnyei and E. Ushioda (eds) *Motivation, Language Identity and the L2 Self* (pp. 144–163). Bristol: Multilingual Matters.

Yashima, T. (2014) Japanese university students' attitudes toward and affect about learning English. Unpublished raw data.

Yashima, T. and Arano, K. (2015) Understanding EFL learners' motivational dynamics: A three-level model from a dynamic systems and sociocultural perspective. In Z. Dörnyei, P.D. MacIntyre and A. Henry (eds) *Motivational Dynamics in Language Learning* (pp. 285–314). Bristol: Multilingual Matters.

Yashima, T., Ikeda, M. and Nakahira, S. (2016) Talk and silence in an EFL classroom: Interplay of learners and context. In J. King (ed.) *The Dynamic Interplay Between Context and The Learner* (pp. 104–126). Basingstoke: Palgrave Macmillan.

Yashima, T., MacIntyre, P. and Ikeda, M. (2018) Situated willingness to communicate in an L2: Interplay of individual characteristics and context. *Language Teaching Research* 22, 115–137.

Yashima, T., Zenuk-Nishide, L. and Shimizu, K. (2004) The influence of attitudes and affect on willingness to communicate and second language communication. *Language Learning* 54, 119–152.

6 Researching the Complexity of Silence in Second-language Classrooms

Lesley Smith and Jim King

Introduction: Research into Silence

Many language educators perceive silence characterized by non-participation and avoidance of interactional tasks in the classroom as a serious issue. The issue of silence is particularly poignant in language-learning environments, as a large body of research has shown the importance of classroom interaction and oral production for language development (e.g. Ellis, 1999; Gass, 1997; Long, 1996; Swain, 2005). Context is key for researchers investigating silence, who seek to understand the causes and meanings of individual silent episodes. Context is an often-used and multifaceted term within the field of applied linguistics, but it can simply refer to 'the field of action within which an event is embedded' (Duranti & Goodwin, 1992: 3). More specifically, educational contexts include everything from individual narratives and relationships, to the social and physical features of classroom environment, to the larger sociocultural and national context (King, 2015: 2). In language learning environments, context includes all individual, social and environmental aspects of the classroom. Moreover, because silence and other forms of non-verbal communication are necessarily more dependent on context for interpretation than speech (e.g. Saville-Troike, 1985), investigating how individuals and their environment interact is crucial to understanding the mechanisms behind silent behaviours. Educational researchers have used a variety of frameworks to investigate silence, including interpretive (e.g. Jaworski, 1993), psycho-analytic (Granger, 2004) and ethnographic approaches (Gilmore, 1985), through which they attempt to unravel the many factors which contribute to silence. Empirical classroom research has found various motivations for learner silence. For example, silence can be a conscious decision by the student to negotiate power relationships in the classroom (e.g. Gilmore, 1985), or to provide themselves more time to process input when the cognitive burden is particularly high (Jaworski &

Sachdev, 1998). Investigating silence is additionally complicated by the unpredictability and ambiguity in communication. Those who are silent and those observing the behaviour often interpret silence differently, due to social and cultural differences between the interlocutors (Jaworski & Sachdev, 2004; Nakane, 2007). Where learners commonly see their silence as facilitative or reflective of their perceived lack of proficiency in the L2, others interpret their silence as rude or as indicative of defiance or academic failure. Such examples highlight the need for an approach to educational research that allows for the complexity inherent in social interaction. To this end, the current chapter presents research which investigates learner silence through approaches informed by Dynamic Systems Theory (DST), and more broadly, notions of complexity in communication. The chapter also provides examples of research methods and means of visually presenting data which complement DST-informed approaches.

Dynamic Systems Theory (DST) and the Idea of 'Open-complexity' in Language Education Research

An increasing number of researchers in the field of applied linguistics have turned to DST and the closely related field of complexity theory for a more-nuanced view of language learning and communication. Complexity-informed approaches maintain that the behaviour of complex systems is not the result of static, causal relationships; rather, it evolves from the dynamic interaction between individuals and their environment (de Bot *et al.*, 2007; Larsen-Freeman & Cameron, 2008). Here, dynamic means that the social environment and the actors in it are always changing and being changed by the context in which they reside. Accordingly, research that incorporates notions of complexity attempts to account for the constant flux and evolution inherent in classroom environments and for the complexity in human interaction and behaviour. DST has been a theoretical pillar in many fields of language learning research, including motivation (Dörnyei, 2014), willingness to communicate (WTC) (MacIntyre & Legatto, 2011) and grammatical accuracy (Larsen-Freeman, 2006). Recently, the approach has also provided a useful lens through which researchers can view the silences of language learners (see King, 2013a, 2013b; King *et al.*, 2020; Yashima *et al.*, 2015).

Using complexity theory, we can conceptualize classroom discourse as a dynamic system, responding to feedback within and outside of the learning environment. Changing a feature of the system, or *parameter* in DST terminology, can affect the system in unpredictable ways because interactions between parameters and actors in a complex system evolve over time, meaning they are non-linear (Larsen-Freeman & Cameron, 2008). For example, instructors lengthening the duration of wait time, the amount of time between a teacher elicitation and student response, may expect students to give longer responses because they are given more time to think. However, research has shown that wait time interacts with other parameters of the classroom system, such as how much discourse is controlled by the instructor, and does not always predict longer and more complex responses from students (Smith & King, 2017). Additionally, changes in the system can result in particular patterns of behaviour which the system prefers called *attractors* (Thelen & Smith, 1994: 56). Attractors can interact with each other and other parts of the system to guide the system into an *attractor state*, i.e. a period of relative stability within the system. Larsen-Freeman and Cameron (2008) note that a common attractor state across classrooms is the 'initiation–response–feedback' (IRF) pattern of discourse (Coulthard, 1992), which consists of teacher initiation, student response and teacher feedback. Influenced by various factors, such as larger sociocultural ideas about the 'ideal' learning environment and teacher-controlled classroom activities, discourse in most classrooms often moves into an IRF attractor state which discourages naturally flowing student communication. Smith and King (2017) found that when classroom discourse became entrenched in an IRF attractor state, longer wait time did not always result in longer student responses, in part due to the highly structured nature of the classroom systems they investigated. Attractor states occur as a result of the interaction of multiple, dynamic aspects of the systems, often without a direct causal relationship between the agents and the system outcome. The concept of attractor states is crucial to studies of classroom discourse, as they are, by definition, difficult to overcome and can become problematic if the attractor state does not foster a collaborative and communicative classroom environment.

Importantly, we do not believe that the construct of complexity on its own can provide convincing holistic explanations of how language learners behave and how classroom environments work. Rather than a rigid model for research, the construct of complexity works best as a flexible, overarching paradigm that allows different theories to flourish within it (cf. Davis & Sumara, 2006.) A so-called 'open-complexity' approach acknowledges the importance of complexity in researching the behaviour of complex systems, while allowing other ideas to complement analyses. For example, in Jim's study of silence in Japanese university language classrooms he used DST to explain key features of the classroom and learner discourse systems within this context, while at the same time drawing on various psychological and socioculturally based theories to better understand the many individual silent episodes he encountered. This flexibility with theory proved vital in helping to make sense of the ambiguous, complex phenomenon of silence. We believe that mixed-methods research designs are best suited to investigating complex phenomena like silence and so accordingly, our chapter outlines some key empirical methods for collecting both quantitative and qualitative data, which can be used in complexity-informed analyses of classroom silence.

A Quantitative Approach: COPS (Class Oral Participation Scheme)

Complexity research in applied linguistics has tended to focus on individual learners and hence adopt qualitative methodologies. Even so, empirical research within a complexity framework can use quantitative data to help identify overarching trends and patterns of behaviour within systems. The current section outlines a systematic approach to observation used to obtain reliable quantitative data about the extent of silence in the classroom. The COPS (Class Oral Participation Scheme) observation instrument was used by King (2013a, 2013b, 2014) to investigate silent behaviour in multiple and diverse university English language classes in Japan. The COPS was developed so that a minute-to-minute picture of classroom events could be recorded in real time, with an emphasis on oral participation throughout the lesson. The observation scheme consists of two sections, which are divided into 60 one-minute segments (later adapted in King *et al.*, 2020, to 30-second intervals for even greater accuracy). The first section focuses on the class's overall participation and organization of oral interaction. Using an *exclusive* focus approach to coding (see Spada & Fröhlich, 1995: 31–32), this section measures who is speaking during the lesson and how the interaction is organized. Through observing who is speaking and how the speech is arranged, much can be learned about those who remain silent as the lesson proceeds.

The COPS scheme differentiates who is speaking by coding separately for teachers and students. Additionally, teachers and students are coded into different categories based on whether they initiated or responded to an utterance. For the teacher, initiating can be in the form of asking questions, providing feedback, presenting information, and so on, while for the student it requires an unsolicited turn to which the majority of the class is exposed. COPS also codes separately for student speech in a single pair of students – usually modelling an exchange for the rest of the class – and multiple pairs, wherein the whole class is paired or grouped for speaking tasks, such as role plays, discussions, and so on. The last three coding categories include whole-class choral drills, off-task melee wherein the majority of the class is off-task and chatting/laughing in the L1, and of course, silence.

The second section of COPS aims to provide a more in-depth analysis by focusing on up to three individual students in each class. As with the first section, the second uses a one-minute time sampling method, which allows for students' modality (i.e. in terms of speaking, listening, reading and writing) to be tracked throughout the lesson. It should be noted here that shortening coding intervals below one minute makes it much more difficult for a single researcher to reliably track whole class oral participation *and* the activities of three individual learners at the same time. This can be mitigated by having multiple observers in the classroom but, of course, such a solution brings with it its own problems in terms of learner reactivity and inter-observer reliability. The coding in the second section of the instrument reflects how student speech is organized during the observation and thus, *talk* is divided into four categories which correspond to those in the first section. The categories code whether talk is initiated by the student or a response; whether talk occurs in a pair or group; or whether talk is part of a whole-class choral exercise. Additionally, to include data about the input, COPS separates listening into three categories: listening to the teacher, listening to a student; or listening to audio equipment. The COPS also includes coding for *reading*, which comprises two modes: silent reading or reading aloud. The final categories are *writing* and *off-task*, the latter of which includes such popular student activities as sleeping, playing with mobile phones, throwing paper aeroplanes, and so on.

At first, structured observation seems counterintuitive to research which incorporates notions of complexity. One could argue that the use of predetermined categories would preclude the observer from detailing the rich variety of events which can occur in the classroom. However, it fits quite nicely into a complexity-informed framework because it allows researchers to identify overall patterns of classroom discourse, while providing the individual perspective that is crucial in complexity research. Moreover, to account for the drawbacks of using predetermined coding categories, the COPS includes a section in which the observer can take free-hand notes in tandem to the time-sampling data. Although the notes must be brief, they give the observer the ability to record emergent data outside of the pre-selected categories. From our experience, chronologically-ordered data produced by the COPS aligns well with complexity-informed analyses, as tracking change and development over time is another important feature of complex systems. Using the COPS over a period of classes allows the researcher to track dynamic changes in whole-class and individual students' silences and discourse patterns more generally. This is illustrated by a recent longitudinal intervention study (King *et al.,* 2020) which sought to tackle non-participatory silence among students in three first-year undergraduate EFL classrooms over the course of an academic semester. The COPS enabled the second author and his colleagues to track in detail learners' oral participation levels before and after the implementation of intervention activities which were designed to encourage improved group and interpersonal dynamics and promote target language production within classes. To complement this quantitative data focusing on changes in student talk and silence over the course of the project, stimulated recall interviews combined with self-report reflection sheets allowed for a more nuanced individual-level analysis as to why learners refrained from target-language talk during lessons.

The data gathered with the COPS observation scheme during this recent intervention study and from Jim's earlier research, provide clear evidence of a robust trend toward learner silence in Japan's university L2 classrooms. In the original multi-site project (King, 2013a, 2013b) which looked at nearly a thousand learners studying English at nine different universities, results from the COPS's whole-class oral participation section revealed less than 0.25% of lesson time was taken up by student self-selected speech. In 48 hours of observation, only seven instances of student self-selection were found, compared to the 1,297 instances of teacher-initiated discourse. Additionally, Jim found that there was no oral participation by either staff or students during about 25% of class time. While silence within this category included periods during which oral participation was not required (e.g. listening tasks, silent reading), the frequency of such instances indicates a very narrow window of opportunity in which students were able to speak in the L2. Interpreting these findings through the lens of complexity, the COPS identified a semi-permanent attractor state of silence through highlighting frequent and prominent patterns of silent behaviour across different learning environments.

However, the quantitative data collected using the COPS does not provide insight into individual motivations and beliefs about silence. We believe that in complexity-informed research, the interactional context and the underlying motivations for certain behaviours are a necessary addition to quantitative data. For example, if a student is silent during an entire class period, a purely quantitative analysis would yield the length and frequency of the behaviour. Only qualitative data would show whether the student was intentionally silent, or if they had simply fallen asleep in class. Qualitative methods like semi-structured interviews can be useful in providing learners a voice to describe their experiences with silence in the classroom (King, 2013a). While interviews may yield information about the individual experiences and beliefs of specific learners, this approach does not uncover learners' thoughts and feelings about specific incidents of classroom silence. To better understand individual silence episodes, it is necessary to adopt introspective methodologies, like stimulated recall.

A Qualitative Approach: Naturalistic Stimulated Recall of Specific Silent Incidents

Stimulated recall is an introspective method that has been used extensively in educational research to gain insight into a learner's thoughts about their own cognitive and psychological processes during a specific past event (for an extensive over-view of stimulated recall in second-language education, see Gass & Mackey, 2000). Stimulated recall encourages individuals to comment on what was happening during a particular event, often using oral or visual prompts connected to the event in question. Researchers have employed stimulated recall in studies on a variety of language learning topics, including written composition (Bosher, 1998) and interlanguage pragmatics (Robinson, 1992). Importantly, stimulated recall has been used in research on L2 oral interaction under frameworks which stress the facilitative nature of interaction on second language acquisition (SLA) (e.g. Mackey *et al.*, 2000; Mackey, 2006). Mackey's (2002) investigation of conversational interactions in classroom and pair settings found that learners' perceptions about their interactions with other students aligned with researchers' claims about the benefits of interaction. Specifically, students noted that interacting with other learners provided them opportunities to negotiate meaning to make input more comprehensible when they need it for comprehension.

Because stimulated recall asks the participant to detail thoughts behind their own past behaviours, research using this method to probe silent behaviour is rare. Two notable, albeit very different studies of Japanese learners and intercultural communication are Nakane (2007) and Sato (2007). Nakane's (2007) conversation-analysis based study of three Japanese international students in Australia used a mixed methods approach that included a retrospective interview. Through triangulation of multiple data sources, Nakane found that there is a mismatch between how silence is used and perceived by students and staff in intercultural contexts. For example, some of the Japanese students she studied were silent to allow for more cognitive processing time during class discussions. However, this silence was often misinterpreted by the Australian lecturers as a lack of criticality, showing a mismatch between the expectations of the Australian lecturers for their students (engaging in irony, etc.) and how the Japanese students performed. Sato (2007) used stimulated recall to investigate how eight L1 Japanese L2 English university students modified output based on dyadic interaction with peers or native English speakers. Sato (2007) found that Japanese students would feign understanding and negotiate less for meaning with native English speakers than when talking to their peers. Such studies clearly show the importance of introspective methods in examining social interactions, as learner-internal and contextual factors affect the intentions and perceptions of silent behaviour.

Stimulated recall methods used under a complexity framework acknowledge that learner behaviour can be impacted by a number of individual and contextual factors whose influence can shift over time (Dörnyei, 2009; Larsen-Freeman & Cameron, 2008). MacIntyre and Legatto (2011) use a DST-framework in a stimulated recall study on the construct of WTC with six female Canadian learners of French. Participants were filmed while performing eight communicative tasks in the L2 and used special software to continuously rate their WTC while watching their performance of the tasks. They were then shown the video again along with a graph of their self-rating and were asked to describe why their WTC changed at certain points. MacIntyre and Legatto found that, in their participants, WTC was a dynamic phenomenon which interacted with other factors, like language anxiety and vocabulary retrieval. The researchers posit that WTC is produced and maintained by interconnected linguistic, social, cognitive and emotion processes, which was revealed through their complexity-informed methodology.

The stimulated recall methods used in Jim's research (King, 2013a, 2015) share a similar conceptual background to MacIntyre and Legatto (2011), in that they also use complexity approaches to research what learners are thinking in relation to whether they speak or not at a specific point in time. However, rather than MacIntyre and Legatto's (2011) more controlled, laboratory-based approach, Jim investigated learner silence using naturalistic classroom data from the COPS scheme. The purpose was to explore learners' perceptions about specific silent behaviours, either those that they produced or experienced in the classroom. Data were collected in a series of seven stimulated recalls at three sites to reflect the variety of tertiary institutions that exist in Japan: a small municipal university, a middle-ranking provincial university and a large urban university. The participants chosen for stimulated recall were those individuals who were tracked during whole observation using the COPS instrument. All of these students had remained silent during exchanges where speech was expected, for example, during whole class choral drill exercises, small group speaking activities, and so on. The stimuli used to prompt learners' recall took the form of the completed COPS sheets and audio recordings of the lesson.

Conducting stimulated recall presents unique challenges that quantitative data collection does not, particularly on the subject of silence. Most obviously, encouraging reticent students to talk about not talking is challenging in many respects. Participants had to be unaware of the specific topic of the recall because prior knowledge of the research topic, i.e. unresponsiveness in the classroom, may have resulted in unreliable accounts of their silences. Additionally, as Gass and Mackey (2000) indicate, learners with limited L2 proficiency may not only have difficulty responding to the interviewer, but only report what they can rather than give a full account of their cognitive processes. In light of these issues, the timing and the language of the stimulated recall sessions were key to mitigating the reticence of the interviewees. All sessions were conducted with Dörnyei's (2007) recommendation that there should be ideally less than 24 hours between the recall session and the event being recalled. To mitigate difficulties from L2 proficiency, all interviewees could use their L1, Japanese, during the sessions. While conducting interviews in the L1 does not override all limitations in this type of research – some students still struggled to articulate their silent behaviours – using the L1 certainly helped participants tap into implicit knowledge more easily. Other stimulated recall studies institute similar parameters to ensure the validity of the responses.

Results from the stimulated recall showed that learner silence manifested from an array of individual and social factors during lessons. We will illustrate this with examples from two students: Nao and Jiro. Nao, a first-year non-languages major, was observed to be consistently silent and unresponsive during three observations and was asked to recall her motivations when she failed to participate during whole class choral exercises. Although various concurrent factors, like teacher-controlled methodology, contributed to Nao's disengagement, her apathy toward the exercises and learning a foreign language, in general, was the most salient attractor in maintaining her silence. Jiro, a second-year sports science major, who also did not participate in the whole-class oral drill, expressed similar feelings of apathy to Nao. His class was similarly teacher-led, with no instances of student-led speech in either class, and both students used the phrase *mendokusai*, or 'I couldn't be bothered/It was too much trouble' when describing their experience in class. However, unlike Nao who had difficulty expressing herself in Japanese, Jiro was self-confident, and perfectly capable of expressing himself in Japanese. Additionally, he distinguished between speaking in and outside of class, noting that in English as a Foreign Language (EFL) class he often falls into silence or lets his mind wander for extended periods of time, but that he is talkative outside of class. Jiro's comments support the notion that silent behaviour is dynamic and highly dependent on contextual factors; for Jiro, the task and teacher-led classroom caused him to lapse into silence. From a complexity perspective, we could say that Jiro's silent behaviour had been 'softly-assembled' (Thelen & Smith, 1994), in that it was a non-permanent reaction to the task at hand and the various contextual influences at play. Nao and Jiro's retrospective interviews revealed how their silence is not a static phenomenon, but highly dependent on the here-and-now of context. The cognitive-related data with the concurrent interpretations of silent events proved useful for identifying the various types of phenomena that emerge in complex systems.

Summary of COPS and Stimulated Recall Findings: Silent Attractor State

Data from the COPS and stimulated recall allowed for a fine-grained analysis of students' silent episodes that yielded remarkable information regarding silence in the language classroom. Viewing classroom discourse as nested systems, i.e. multiple individual learners' talk subsystems within the larger classroom system, Jim found a fossilized and relatively predictable attractor state across observations (King, 2013a, 2013b). The COPS scheme was key in identifying these patterns in different classrooms, but because it was found across the board, it is likely that silence emerged through a number of different routes. Because attractor states are maintained by many individual and contextual attractors, similar attractor states can be sustained in different classrooms and by distinctive, but related, phenomena. Factors that contributed to the silent attractor state Jim observed included language processing difficulties, identity construction and environmental factors, like teacher-controlled classroom activities. For a more in-depth view of specific silent attractors, Jim used the stimulated recall to explore how learners perceived silent events. Two examples of how different attractors can contribute to the same silent state were found in the interviews of Nao and Jiro. Both students displayed apathy during the same whole class activity and were disengaged, in part, due to their status as non-language majors and the prominence of teacher-led classroom methods. However, while Nao appeared equally reticent in her L1, Jiro was confident and talkative outside of the classroom environment. Comparing Nao and Jiro shows how learner-internal (personality, proficiency) and external elements (teaching methods, tasks) act as attractors for different students to maintain the same silent attractor state. Both interviews also show how individual silent states can bleed into the overall classroom discourse system.

The mixed-methods approaches used in King (2013a, 2015) were crucial in identifying the attractor state of silence. The frequency data from COPS not only outlined holistic patterns across multiple, diverse classrooms, but also suggested participants – those who seemingly contributed to classroom silence – and provided prompts for the stimulated recall. The combination of methods allowed for emergent phenomena to become apparent and identification of the silent attractor state. Additionally, Jiro and Nao's stimulated recalls show that acoustically, silence is the same, but it has distinct implications for different people. One of the limitations of the COPS instrument was that because of the one-minute coding interval, it was only possible for one observer to monitor three individual students. Having multiple observers could increase the sample of individually monitored students. An alternative strategy could be to use multiple observers to reduce coding intervals. However, as we alluded to earlier, having a large number of nosy researchers in the classroom brings with it its own issues in terms of inter-observer agreement and how their presence might affect the naturalness of students' behaviours. Even so, using a series of lessons to train observers in the use of the COPS before actual data collection takes place would work well to habituate students to the presence of more than one researcher in their classroom (see also King, 2013a: 190–191, for further suggestions on how to reduce student reactivity during classroom observations).

Wait Time

The types of student silence analysed using the COPS and stimulated recall scheme in Jim's research (King, 2013) are a few of the many types of silent behaviour that can be found in the language classroom. A related, yet understudied, type of behaviour is wait time, defined as the duration between a teacher elicitation and student response, or second teacher utterance. Wait time can either manifest as a conscious effort to diminish classroom silence or a subconscious behaviour which occurs after asking a question (Swift & Gooding, 1983). Past research shows that classroom discourse can be improved (i.e. longer student utterances and a more relaxed classroom environment), by strategically lengthening wait time, as teachers in most disciplines pause for an average one second in L1 classrooms and just over two seconds in L2 classrooms (Shrum, 1985). However, contemporary studies with process-oriented approaches have mixed results regarding the benefits of longer wait time on classroom discourse. Ingram and Elliott (2014) investigated how wait time affected turn-taking behaviours and found that while longer wait time sometimes led to longer student responses, it produced a highly structured classroom discourse. Because wait time entails teacher control over pauses, even extended wait time often precluded student self-selection and hindered naturally flowing conversation (Ingram & Elliott, 2014). In short, the environment in which wait time is used can have unexpected, and perhaps unintended, impacts on classroom discourse and behaviour. To this end, we wanted to investigate how wait time evolves as classroom discourse develops over time.

The Complexity of Wait Time

In our recent study (Smith & King, 2017), we used a complexity framework to investigate how wait time varied with other features of classroom discourse. Using a mixed-methods approach, we collected data from a series of structured observations of a UK university postgraduate classroom. Quantitative data were collected on various discourse features, including length of pauses, frequency and type of teacher question, and turn-taking sequence. Field notes and discourse analysis of the observation transcripts provided a basis for qualitative analysis on the learners' interactions and the classroom discourse environment.

While the methods we used were different from the stimulated recall and COPS from Jim's study (King, 2013a, 2013b), they yielded similar findings regarding how aspects of the classroom environment interacted to produce and maintain silence. Importantly, in line with Jim's findings (King, 2013a, 2013b), we found a fairly stable attractor state, which was largely enabled and controlled by the teacher. Although the classroom setting we observed involved a great deal more student speech, the teacher-led environment often discouraged students from initiating talk and inhibited naturally flowing conversation. For example, classroom speech frequently moved into the same pattern of discourse: IRF. IRF discourse is common in classroom settings because it is an economical means of producing and interpreting language, which is the goal of most L2 classrooms (Seedhouse, 2015). Additionally, Larsen-Freeman and Cameron (2008: 11) note that through adaptation to common aspects of the language classroom, IRF has become an attractor state in classroom discourse. Such aspects include the type of questions asked and a power dynamic which holds instructors as the gatekeepers to knowledge and the moderators for discussions (Hale, 2011). While increased wait time could lengthen student responses to specific questions, because it is a part of turn-taking behaviour which is controlled by the instructor, it often resulted in fewer opportunities for student-selected speech. The results reveal wait time's multiple functions in the interpretive acts of the teacher and student, as just one of many factors within the 'local and sequential phenomenon' at play in complex systems (Markee, 2015: 10).

Applying Mixed-methods to Inform Complexity Research

Both Jim's studies (King, 2013a, 2013b) and our joint research (Smith & King, 2017) use mixed-methods to investigate the complexity of learners and their environments. The data collected through classroom observations and interviews allowed them to investigate both macro-level patterns of silent behaviour and micro-level silences. Collecting data on both whole class and individual behaviour provided evidence that many of the individual silent behaviours interacted to push classroom discourse toward a non-responsive attractor state, which discouraged spontaneous student speech. Collecting different types of data on frequency of behaviours in complex systems and on the individual actors in those systems allows researchers to capture emergent phenomena and to see how micro-level behaviours influence larger patterns within complex systems. For example, Kormos *et al.* (2014) used mixed methods in their longitudinal study on language learning motivation and international contexts. The researchers analysed variations in motivation and the frequency and type of contact the learners experienced at different points during their international study and interviewed 10 students at the end of their international study programme. Overall, language learning motivation decreased for students over the academic year, but interviews with individual students indicated that reasons for this decrease varied. Some students noted that their anxiety about communicating in the L2 fostered an avoidance of speaking, while some noted specific negative events with native speakers that affected their motivation. Here again, the notion that complex systems soft-assemble, guided by the emergence of individual and environmental influences can explain how different attractors can guide systems toward similar attractor states. These insights were gained, in large part, due to the use of mixed methods in our research (King, 2013; Smith & King, 2017) and it is doubtful that a mono-methodological approach would have produced the same richness of data.

Displays that Highlight Complexity: Min–max Graphs

While written descriptions of complexity are adequate for addressing the behavioural dynamics in qualitative analyses, the same dynamics in quantitative data can also be shown through visuals. Graphs not only provide a clean, easy-to-read means of analysing large amounts of numerical data, but can moreover highlight developing emergent behaviour over time. One such graph that is particularly useful for showing system development is a moving min–max graph. Rather than presenting data measurements as simple dots, min–max graphs show a score range for individual data points. This range of scores is presented as a bandwidth of values over a period of time, i.e. five minutes, ten minutes, and so on. Bandwidth values are determined using a moving window, i.e. a time-frame that moves up one measurement position each time (the size of the window, e.g. five consecutive data points, 1 month, etc.) (van Geert & van Dijk, 2002). Each window overlaps the previous window and uses the same measurements, minus the first measurement and plus the next (van Geert & van Dijk, 2002). For example, taking five consecutive measurements and calculating maximum and minimum values with the moving window technique would yield the following:

max(t1 . . . t5), max(t2 . . . t6), max(t3 . . . t7), etc.
min(t1 . . . t5), min(t2 . . . t6), min(t3 . . . t7), etc.

(adapted from van Geert & van Dijk, 2002)

Using this method, once the min and max values are graphed, the researcher is able to see not only fluctuations over time in the raw data, but in the changes in bandwidths between the minimum and maximum values.

From a complexity perspective, min–max graphs are able to show change over time because they display a system's development beside the raw data, visualizing moment-to-moment variability (for more on moment-to-moment approaches, see MacIntyre & Legatto, 2011). Figure 6.1, from Smith and King (2017), displays wait time pause length (in seconds) over a pre-determined period of 10 minutes in one classroom observation. The graph shows that the length of individual wait times during this time period was highly variable, lasting anywhere from 3.5 seconds to less than one second. Additionally, the bandwidth between the min- and max- values shows that the system displays the highest variability when the bandwidth is the largest, i.e. between the fifth and tenth instances of wait time and again towards the end of the measurement window, between the eighteenth and twenty-second instances of wait time.

High variability on min–max graphs is often used to show how the system moves in and outside of attractor states, as there is generally thought to be high variability (i.e. a wider bandwidth) around these shifts in dynamic systems (van Geert & van Dijk, 2002). Comparing the min–max graph with one of student response length and observation

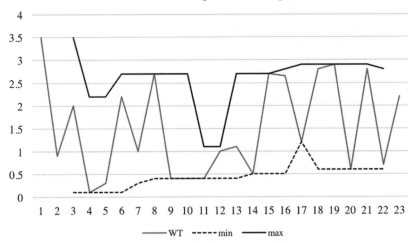

Figure 6.1 Example moving min–max graph, from Smith and King (2017)

transcripts in Smith and King (2017) revealed that low points in the graph corresponded to periods of highly teacher-controlled discourse, short student responses (less than two seconds) and no student-selected speech. Additionally, areas with the largest bandwidths, i.e. between the fifth and 10th instances and between the 18th and 20-second instances of wait time, exhibited shifts away from the IRF attractor state and into new patterns of student-guided behaviour. While min–max graphs are not the only means of showing moment-to-moment variability in complex systems, they allow researchers to take away general developmental trends and how the system's variability is related to these trends. In short, min–max graphs can provide researchers with a hint of where 'meaningful changes in variability' occur (van Geert & van Dijk, 2002: 358).

Conclusion

While we uncovered attractor states which can preclude spontaneous student output, our findings indicate that single cause–effect explanations for individual and classroom behaviours are not adequate for explaining complex phenomena like silence. Researching silence and other aspects of language learning requires methods that account for the evolution found in real classroom environments and for the complexity in human interaction and behaviour. By employing mixed-methods approaches, we were able to achieve a fine-grained analysis of individual learner behaviours, while keeping in view overarching trends within those individuals and their environments. Importantly, the pairing of empirical data with an open-complexity approach showed how multiple, interconnected variables emerge over time to influence both individual and classroom silence. We hope that the tools presented demonstrate how complexity perspectives to language research might be complemented by mixed-methodologies. Educators and educational researchers can use the tools and accompanying methodology found here to discover relationships between classroom aspects that may otherwise go unnoticed without an approach that encourages appreciation of context-driven differences and complexity.

References

Bosher, S. (1998) The composing processes of three Southeast Asian writers at post-secondary level: An exploratory study. *Journal of Second Language Writing* 7 (2), 117–128.

Coulthard, M. (ed.) (1992) *Advances in Spoken Discourse Analysis*. London: Routledge.

Davis, B. and Sumara, D. (2006) *Complexity and Education: Inquiries into Learning, Teaching and Research*. Mahwah, NJ: Lawrence Erlbaum.

de Bot K., Lowie, W. and Verspoor, M. (2007) A dynamic systems theory approach to second language acquisition. *Bilingualism: Language and Cognition* 10 (1), 7–21.

Dörnyei, Z. (2014) Researching complex dynamic systems: 'Retrodictive qualitative modelling' in the language classroom. *Language Teaching* 47 (1), 80–91.

Dörnyei, Z. (2007) *Research Methods in Applied Linguistics: Quantitative, Qualitative, and Mixed Methodologies*. Oxford University Press.

Dörnyei, Z. (2009) *The Psychology of Second Language Acquisition*. Oxford University Press.

Duranti, A. and Goodwin, C. (1992) *Rethinking Context: Language as an Interactive Phenomenon*. Cambridge, Cambridge University Press.

Ellis, R. (1999) *Learning A Second Language Through Interaction*. Amsterdam: John Benjamins.

Gass, S.M. (1997) *Input, Interaction, and the Second Language Learner*. Mahwah, NJ: Lawrence Erlbaum Associates.

Gass, S.M. and Mackey, A. (2000) *Stimulated Recall Methodology in Second Language Research*. Mahwah, NJ: Lawrence Erlbaum.

Gilmore, P. (1985) Silence and sulking: Emotional displays in the classroom. In D. Tannen and M. Saville-Troike (eds) *Perspectives on Silence* (pp. 139–162). New York: Ablex.

Granger, C.A. (2004) *Silence in Second Language Learning: A Psychoanalytic Reading*. Clevedon: Multilingual Matters.

Hale, C. (2011) Breaking with the IRF and EPA: Facilitating student-initiated talk. In A. Stewart (ed.) *JALT 2010 Conference Proceedings*. Tokyo: JALT.

Ingram, J. and Elliott, V. (2014) Turn taking and 'wait time' in classroom interactions. *Journal of Pragmatics* 62, 1–12.

Jaworski, A. (1993) *The Power of Silence: Social and Pragmatic Perspectives*. London: Sage.

Jaworski, A. and Sachdev. I. (1998) Beliefs about silence in the classroom. *Language and Education* 12 (4), 273–292.

Jaworski, A. and Sachdev, I. (2004) Teachers' beliefs about students' talk and silence: Constructing academic success and failure through metapragmatic comments. In A. Jaworski, N. Coupland and D. Galasinski (eds) *Metalanguage. Social and Ideological Perspectives* (pp. 227–244). Berlin, Boston: De Gruyter

King, J. (2013a) *Silence in the Second Language Classroom*. Basingstoke: Palgrave Macmillan.

King, J. (2013b) Silence in the second language classrooms of Japanese universities. *Applied Linguistics* 34 (3), 325–343.

King, J. (2014) Fear of the true self: Social anxiety and the silent behaviour of Japanese learners of English. In K. Csizér and M. Magid (eds) *The Impact of Self-Concept on Language Learning* (pp. 232–249). Bristol: Multilingual Matters.

King, J. (2015) *The Dynamic Interplay between Context and the Language Learner.* Basingstoke: Palgrave Macmillan.

King, J., Yashima, T., Humphries, S., Aubrey, S. and Ikeda, M. (2020) Silence and anxiety in the English-medium classroom of Japanese universities: A longitudinal intervention study. In J. King and S. Harumi (eds) *East Asian Perspectives on Silence in English Language Education* (pp. 60–79). Bristol: Multilingual Matters.

Kormos, J., Csizér, K. and Iwaniec, J. (2014) A mixed-method study of language-learning motivation and intercultural contact of international students. *Journal of Multilingual and Multicultural Development* 35 (2), 151–166.

Larsen-Freeman, D. (1997) Chaos/complexity science and second language acquisition. *Applied Linguistics* 18 (2), 141–165.

Larsen-Freeman, D. (2006) The emergence of complexity, fluency, and accuracy in the oral and written production of five Chinese learners of English. *Applied Linguistics* 27 (4), 590–619.

Larsen-Freeman, D. and Cameron, L. (2008) *Complex Systems and Applied Linguistics.* Oxford: Oxford University Press.

Long, M.H. (1996) The role of the linguistic environment in second language acquisition. In W.C. Ritchie and T.K. Bhatia (eds) *Handbook of Language Acquisition* (pp. 412–68). New York: Academic Press.

MacIntyre, P.D. and Legatto, J.J. (2011) A dynamic system approach to willingness to communicate: Developing an idiodynamic method to capture readily changing affect. *Applied Linguistics* 32 (2), 149–171.

Mackey, A. (2002) Beyond production: Learners' perceptions about interactional processes. *International Journal of Educational Research* 37 (3/4), 379–394.

Mackey, A. (2006) Feedback, noticing, and instructed second language learning. *Applied Linguistics* 27 (3), 405–430.

Mackey, A., Gass, S.M. and McDonough, K. (2000) How do learners perceive interactional feedback? *Studies in Second Language Acquisition* 22 (4), 471–497.

Markee, N. (ed.) (2015) *The Handbook of Classroom Discourse and Interaction.* Oxford: Wiley-Blackwell.

Nakane, I. (2007) *Silence in Intercultural Communication.* Amsterdam: John Benjamins.

Robinson, M.A. (1992) Introspective methodology in interlanguage pragmatics research. In G. Kasper (ed.) *Pragmatics of Japanese as a Native and Target Language* (pp. 27–82). University of Hawai'i Press.

Rowe, M.B. (1986) Wait time: Slowing down may be a way of speeding up. *Journal of Teacher Education* 37 (1), 43–50.

Sato, M. (2007) Social relationships in conversational interaction: Comparison of learner-learner and learner-NS dyads. *JALT Journal* 29 (2), 183–208.

Saville-Troike, M. (1985) The place of silence in an integrated theory of communication. In D. Tannen and M. Saville-Troike (eds) *Perspectives on Silence* (pp. 3–18). Norwood: Ablex.

Seedhouse, P. (2015) L2 classroom interaction as a complex adaptive system. In N. Markee (ed.) *The Handbook of Classroom Discourse and Interaction* (pp. 373–389). Oxford: Wiley-Blackwell.

Shrum, J.L. (1985) Wait-time and the use of target or native languages. *Foreign Language Annals* 18 (4), 305–314.

Smith, L. and King, J. (2017) A dynamics systems approach to wait time in the L2 classroom. *System* 68, 1–14.

Spada, N. and Fröhlich, M. (1995) *COLT Communicative Orientation of Language Teaching Observation Scheme: Coding Conventions and Applications.* Sydney: Macquarie University, National Centre for English Language Teaching and Research.

Swain, M. (2005) The output hypothesis: Theory and research. In E. Hinkel (ed.) *Handbook of Research in Second Language Teaching and Learning* (pp. 471–483). Lawrence Erlbaum

Swift, J.N. and Gooding, C.T. (1983) Interaction of wait time feedback and questioning instruction on middle school science teaching. *Journal of Research in Science Teaching* 20 (8), 721–730.

Thelen, E. and Smith, L.B. (1994) *A Dynamic Systems Approach to the Development of Cognition and Action*. Cambridge: MA, MIT Press.

van Geert, P. and van Dijk, M. (2002) Focus on variability: New tools to study intra-individual variability in developmental data. *Infant Behavior and Development* 25, 340–374.

Yashima, T., Ikeda, M. and Nakahira, S. (2015) Talk and silence in an EFL classroom: Interplay of learners and context. In J. King (ed.) *The Dynamic Interplay between Context and the Language Learner* (pp. 127–150). Basingstoke: Palgrave Macmillan.

7 Researching Motivational Resonance Hands-on: Learner Self-concepts, Learning Groups and Educational Cultures

Joseph Falout

> For reasons we don't yet understand, the tendency to synchronize is
> one of the most pervasive drives in the universe, extending from
> atoms to animals, from people to planets.
> (Strogatz, 2003: 14)

Connected Complex Systems of Students, Classrooms and Cultures

I work as a teacher-researcher in the Japanese tertiary educational system in which student silence, resistance and disengagement have been observed as systemic (King, 2013). The roots of these problems have been found within various nested systems, including constructions of individual identities, interpersonal dynamics of small groups in the classroom and of whole-classes as a group, and effects of society-wide cultures (King, 2016). The educational culture, it seems, is not working for many students. However, possibilities for systemic change are linked between students and teacher-researchers such as Pinner (2019) and Sampson (2016), who are courageously opening up their classrooms and teaching practices by publishing their action research. Conducted through complexity perspectives, their research details the dynamic and socially constructed connections of motivations among those in their classrooms and within their own particular nested systems. Larsen-Freeman and Cameron (2008) explain that nested complex systems of the classroom are interrelated and can be viewed upward and downward, or inward and outward, by scale. Starting on the low end of the scale, learning motivation might move upward in this fashion: Neuron, neural network, brain, body, person, group, class and school.

Actually, I cannot say that I myself have delivered a cogent study strictly based in the complexity paradigm. But I have been researching motivated language learning within my classes and others across Japan over multiple investigations and from different angles. Interweaving narratives from my researching life, this chapter shares my hands-on approach to investigating the interrelated complex systems of learner self-concepts, learning groups and educational cultures, and it attempts to assemble from a complexity perspective the meaning of motivational resonance. The chapter begins with motivations for researching motivational resonance and related definitions thereof. The following parts portray an element of learner self-concept known as past selves, then relate past selves to the present and future selves of language learners. The next part traces intervention-based research, known as ideal classmates priming, which is aimed at influencing the whole-class group level of motivation. The last part depicts how collaborative research with my students, as well as other teachers and their students, has helped gain a bigger picture of the complex system of educational culture, which someday I and other teacher-researchers may try to further piece together.

Tangible Beginnings

In attempting to grasp the complex system of educational culture, an abstract mosaic cobbled from infinitesimally smaller abstractions, it is good to start with something I can actually put into my hands. On the inside flap of my plump, well-thumbed, repeatedly taped-and-glued-together pocket dictionary, a blue paper post-it note gradually oxidizes to brown, like rust, like the paper to which it still adheres. I recall Yvonne Pitts (a pseudonym), giggling, secretively lettering her message freshly onto that post-it note and sandwiching it into my dictionary. She requested that I not read it until I was home, whereupon I opened the front cover to see her gift, her little surprise:

12-10-92

Joe,

Guess What? I hate english. I have enjoyed talking with you! Thank-You for all of your help with my essays and my research paper! Your help means alot to me! I'll always remember the fun times in the hall. Call me sometime! Take care! Yvonne Pitts ☺

A glance at this note instantly transports me back to tutoring at the Writing Workshop, only a small table and two chairs in a back-corner hall, servicing students who came in and out of the nearby classrooms used for English composition courses. These were typical writing composition and rhetoric courses taught in freshman year in American colleges, designed to build the academic writing skills that students will need throughout their four years of college and beyond. I had been tutoring at this workshop station and teaching my own writing courses at this college, plus writing courses and public speaking courses at another. Both colleges attracted a mix of traditional and non-traditional students: first-generation college students, socioeconomic elites, immigrants, young parents, old parents, grandparents, farmers, nuns and budding young professionals of all types. Most of them feared writing and public speaking. Yet they came together for each other, and almost all ended up courageously sharing their first-hand stories of war, disease, poverty, prejudice, love, hope, community and spirituality. Helping these students get past struggles in expressing themselves, helping Yvonne, made me believe I could make a difference. But this was back then, back before I moved overseas to Japan and had to learn how to teach all over again.

Japan was where I first encountered college students who put their heads down on their desks to sleep, or pretend to; students who could not look at each other, going so far as to face away from their classmates, clam up, refusing to show anyone what I considered the basic courtesy of a gesture, a glance, an expression of friendly recognition; students who left class at any moment under false pretexts or by surreptitious exits; students who effortfully created fanciful paths of prevarication that would spin them away from lessons at hand, homework that followed and engagement in every succeeding class session the rest of the whole academic year. So many students did not seek help or respond to offers of assistance, nor acknowledged even a modicum of something redeemable from the experience, as Yvonne had discovered for herself. So many simply lacked motivation.

Extrications: Motivational Resonance, Harmony and Entropy

Consider just some of these elements that can push at, pull on and shape learner motivation regarding the complex nested systems connected to the classroom (Larsen-Freeman & Cameron, 2008). Learners have different personal histories, learning beliefs, aptitudes and preferences for learning and relating with others. Different mixtures of learners have their own unique tendencies and habits of group interaction, which can change depending on time of day and moments in individuals' lives. Similarly, different educational systems and social milieus differently influence the experiences and expectations of students – not to mention those of teachers, parents, caregivers and policymakers, which then carries back to students in explicit and implicit messages and educational structures that contribute to shaping student motivations to learn. This is why it can be quite trying if not impossible to nail down any one textbook, syllabus, or teaching approach for a given classroom that could aptly address each learner's motivational needs.

But there may be a way of making certain adjustments in educational policies and teaching practices so that the potential energies of motivational elements within students line up, respond off each other and reverberate in a pattern that magnifies their confluences upon motivations for learning languages. I call this *motivational resonance*.

Thinking motivational resonance is possible can bring hope to those of us teachers who are struggling with energy-drained classrooms. If we could bravely conduct and publish more action research about what makes learner motivation tick, we would have a better chance of making the larger rearrangements and the smaller fine-tuning it takes to get our students, classrooms and educational systems motivationally switched on.

Motivationally switched on or off goes beyond metaphorical meaning. Being switched on or off could represent, respectively, states of *harmony* or *entropy*. To help explain motivational resonance, I adopt Csikszentmihalyi's (1993) definitions of harmony and entropy for describing complex systems of organisms and their successful evolution.

When organisms develop in both *differentiation* and *integration*, they can attain greater harmony, or in other words, greater systemic complexity. Increased differentiation is denoted by a greater number of elements comprising a system with an expanded diversity between their respective functions. Increased integration happens by improved communications among these elements and greater coordination together toward their mutual goals. In contrast, communication breakdown, impotence and confusion mark entropy, which amounts to systemic breakdown, or a system befallen by sickness and sadness (Csikszentmihalyi, 1993).

Examples of interrelated systems for classrooms include a student's or teacher's psychology, small-group and whole-class group dynamics and the educational system's social milieu. The level of a student's differentiation can be gauged by the number of things in which the student is interested, can do at present and dreams of doing in the future. When all of these elements tie together well in the student's academic and extracurricular pursuits, it can be said the student's interests, skills and goals have reached integration. If these things are well integrated but the student lacks in differentiation, then the student may lead a happy but dull academic life in terms of productive value to classroom contributions. A student rich in differentiation but with poorly integrated elements will rarely experience boredom in class or alone, but may not find personal direction. To the classmates and teacher, this student will seem interesting but not necessarily purposeful or pleasant for class. A student who is both differentiated and integrated will have attained personal harmony and can potentially make many beneficial contributions to classroom group dynamics.

In a parallel way, a class would be differentiated insofar as there exists a diversity of interests, skills and dreams among its members. For a class experiencing differentiation but not integration, students would get to be themselves but fail to stay on target with the learning tasks. In a class that is well integrated but not much differentiated, students would toe the line – but overly so – and display low creativity in their learning achievements. A class both differentiated and integrated has the harmony it takes to be playful, spontaneous and innovative together while getting the job done. In schools full of classroom systems like these there are likely harmonic exchanges between comprising subsystems of learner and teacher self-concepts and encompassing systems of educational culture. Moreover, energy generated from these exchanges could reach across interrelated systems, such as households and community centres, feeding back and forth in motivational resonance. Nested systems would not have to be motivationally lit up throughout, though, for a classroom to experience motivational resonance. However, any classroom would have a better chance of being motivationally lit if its neighboring systems were too.

Researching the motivational resonance of learners, learner groups and educational cultures requires a complexity approach. Complexity in a system does not mean it is complicated; its elements are simply differentiated and integrated: 'A complex system is not confusing, because its parts, no matter how diverse, are organically related to one another' (Csikszentmihalyi, 1993: 157). Nor does researching within a complexity paradigm mean the methods need to be elaborate or that it necessarily has to be difficult. It does require, however, careful attention. As Ushioda once explained in my interview (Falout, 2011: 28) with her:

> If it's a complex system, to my mind it's got to be focused on a particular case—whether that case is an individual, class, teacher and student, or group. You need to have a fairly sharp focus if you're going to try to capture the complex system or systems around that focus, and so you try to define what your core unit of analysis is going to be. Then for that research to have significance beyond that case, you've got to engage in multiple case studies. Not necessarily you yourself, but in a way that's perhaps replicable.

Teacher-researchers need not cover everything they wish to research in one investigation. They can build up to it. Complexity experts Thelen and Smith (1994: 11), who made breakthroughs in understanding infant stepping stages through multiple investigations of the same phenomenon and from different angles, advise: 'forget about any single causation and look at the behavior itself and the context in which it is performed'. Rose (2015: 71) summarized this stance as the *analyse, then aggregate approach*.

Learner Self-concepts

Dynamics of learner past selves

The head professor of the department and his close colleague smiled as they handed me a stack of papers. These surveys on demotivation had been completed by freshmen who scored in the top third in their department on the college's English placement test. Upon hearing the purpose of my study, which was to explore if and how students had lost motivation to learn English before coming to university, the professors had offered to track down these students to distribute my survey. I had recently been employed as a research assistant, low on the totem pole, working in a different department at the college, and so I could not do all this by myself. Bowing in gratitude in Japanese style and returning to my office, I looked again at the stack of surveys in my hands. Now I had two sets of data to compare, one from lower-proficiency (LP) students and the other from higher-proficiency (HP) students.

The LP students were also freshmen from the same department, but who had scored in the bottom third of the placement test. They had been sent to take supplementary classes, non-credit-bearing courses designed to help students get caught up to speed with curricular expectations, which I taught during their lunch break. The following year I had one more supplementary course for another department's freshmen, similarly placed at the bottom third of proficiency in their department, and I collected their responses to the survey too.

The survey was solidly based on previous research into learner motivation and affect, but at that time little was known about the dynamics of learner demotivation. Setting forth in this exploratory study (Falout & Maruyama, 2004), Maruyama and I had not guessed we were about to stumble upon four seminal findings. All verified by later studies (e.g. Falout et al., 2009, 2013a), these discoveries would keep me exploring language learner motivations up to the present day.

The first finding simply came from tallying up the responses to two questions: *Have you ever been demotivated in your English studies?* and *Do you like studying English?* Although blank spaces were left for the students to write as they chose, most of their responses clearly indicated either an affirmation or negation. Upon compiling these answers, I noticed the LP students who had reported past demotivation also tended to answer they presently disliked English. In contrast, those HP students who did report past demotivation tended to affirm they presently liked English. But I did not know how to statistically prove that LP students' past demotivation could be linked to their present dislike for learning English, whereas the HP students' demotivational experiences were not likewise tied to their present affect toward English.

Then I thumbed back through a book for beginning researchers (Brown, 1988), and found how to make the necessary calculation by conducting a *chi-square test.* It was so easy I could do most of it by paper and pencil, although a calculator helped with the last part. What I found was a connection, known as a *probability dependence*, between LP learners' demotivating experiences and present negative affect, but no such connection for the HP set. Unfortunately, in this first research paper (Falout & Maruyama, 2004) I erroneously called it a correlation, which is also a kind of relationship but proven by different statistical means. In a later paper (Falout *et al.*, 2009), however, I was able to correctly label it as a probability dependence.

The second finding similarly came from tallying responses to the questions: *Do you like studying English? If you don't, when did you start hating it?* Again, blank spaces were left for students to write as they chose, and we were surprised to find many responses that pinpointed the very year in school that they began to dislike English. Most of the LP students began to dislike English in the first or second year of junior high school (JHS), whereas for the HP students it happened sometime later, often during high school (HS). With these data we could deduce that initial demotivating experiences seemed to have occurred, on average, earlier in formal schooling for LP learners than HP learners.

The final open-ended question on the survey was: *Were there any specific experiences or incidents which demotivated you?* Maruyama translated all of the responses into English, and keeping the LP and HP sets separate, I printed these onto plain white paper. Then with scissors, I cut each distinct concept into its own segment, converting the attributions of demotivation into single units and began sliding these slips of paper around on a big table, arranging and rearranging these concepts into like-themed groupings. As the groupings formed and reformed, distinguishing locutions caught my attention; sometimes the attributions were similar in concept but couched differently. For example, in a grouping with the working concept of a demotivator I called *vocabulary & grammar*, many students said that they did not like vocabulary or grammar (they blamed their demotivation on the *L2 itself*), or that there was too much of it to learn (blaming the *course contents & pace*), while others said they could not learn the vocabulary or grammar rules (blaming themselves about *disappointment in performance*).

I thought about recombining these concepts in a way to distinguish these attributions by internal and external loci, but was concerned about the accuracy in doing so. So I checked with Maruyama, who assured me the translations related the nuances of meaning that would make these distinctions possible, and reconfigured the slips of paper from *vocabulary & grammar* into newer groupings based on locus. This step gave the third finding, which was that LP learners more often attributed their demotivation internally, blaming themselves, while HP learners more often attributed externally, blaming the courses or teachers.

If the findings were presented only this way, however, the salient attributions of *vocabulary* and *grammar* would become lost. Recombining and calculating separately for these attributions, I was able to retain the fourth finding, that vocabulary was the most common specific attribution across both sets. Furthermore, regardless of attributional locus, LP students were much more likely to have become demotivated by vocabulary and grammar than HP students.

It is not the vocabulary and grammar themselves, exactly, but the difficulties students face in learning all the things expected of them. What happens after a few stumbles is they begin to doubt themselves. They see themselves as not the type who can learn English and they attribute their academic failures to their own personal uselessness. This is self-concept. It is about who you are and what good you are for. Students suffering from demotivation in learning English may believe they are worthwhile people capable at many things, just not English. Their self-concept has taken a hit in this area of their lives, and it can retard their ability to act and react in adaptive ways when the hits keep on coming. Self-concept is a powerful psychological system of each individual's making that can set up and trail their lives.

After publishing these findings (Falout & Maruyama, 2004), I started to use a statistical software package, which gave me a different look at the same data. From an exploratory factor analysis, a grouping of items (survey questions) were shown to fit together according to the way students had responded that depicted a potential psychological trait. Among other factors that resulted, this factor had the highest separations with statistical differences between the LP and HP groups of students. Looking carefully at its items, I had interpreted the factor to reflect the academic emotional baggage about learning English that students carry with them from their past and that sets up their expectations for their future learning.

The factor, which I named *antecedent conditions of the learner*, had too many items for practical use. So I aimed to whittle them down by looking at how students answered the same items in a study with a larger set of respondents (Falout *et al.*, 2009). To these data I applied a statistical procedure commonly used in developing questions for standardized tests called *item discrimination*. It helps test makers find which items (test questions) work best in being able to separate test-takers who achieve either higher or lower scorers on the test overall. This is another calculation that is relatively easy to do (Brown, 2005). Usually used for tests that measure knowledge or ability, I applied the procedure to a questionnaire designed to measure motivational elements. I selected questions that best separated proficiency according to how students had responded to those questions. What I ended up with was a short set of survey items that could become a handy index to determine the degree of positivity or negativity of a university student's academic emotional baggage about learning English in Japan (Falout, 2012, 2016).

The next discovery happened only because of a work-around to a problem met when designing an exploratory study (Falout *et al.*, 2013a).

Friends and I had formed a research team to investigate in our university classrooms the causes of fluctuations of language-learning motivations in our students' pasts. Initially we had hoped to use self-reported proficiency scores to separate the data into different sets of proficiency groups. But even though any individual student's proficiency score would be obscured through the analysis of averaging, one of the members of our research team was concerned because his university disallowed such personal data to be reported outside the university.

To get around this roadblock, I devised the index for academic emotional baggage because it would come with a special built-in feature; since the items for *antecedent conditions of the learner* performed well in separations of proficiency with statistical differences, they could also potentially discriminate the proficiencies of our survey-takers. This means we would get a rough idea of comparative proficiency levels – higher or lower – without directly asking for them.

Ready by the beginning of the academic year, we entered our classrooms and asked our students to individually answer the index questions and chart out along a motivational grid their motivational ups and downs over years past. Additionally, the students described the reasons why their motivations had gone up or down.

On the first level of analysis, we determined three separate groups for the study population according to level of academic emotional baggage, ranging in valences from high positive, to positive, to negative. Then we averaged the motivational ups and downs by group, year-by-year, through JHS into HS and university, and plotted the three sets of lines onto the same graph. We expected differences of some sort to show up. But what unfolded before our eyes, all glued to the computer screen at the same moment, was definitely unexpected. We saw an order emerging from the chaos and it did not look good for students carrying negative academic emotional baggage.

Unfurling from a common starting point in JHS, the three lines dovetailed outward (Figure 7.1). By slight variance of degree, they mirrored each other's gradual downturn to the middle of HS and upturn by the end of those years. They splayed into *fractal* (Strogatz, 2003) trajectories of remembered motivations aiming at future expectations. The fractal was emergent. It captured our fancies. But the meaningful part was the differences in the psychological adaptability of the students in this educational context.

Students who had negative academic emotional baggage looked back differently than those whose baggage was positive. Students carrying negative baggage experienced the greatest losses of motivation, or *demotivation*, starting at the earliest stages during their formal education and lasting over a longer period. Not only did their motivation drop the most, it happened by different psychological processes. Again, it was self-blame that turned out to be the biggest culprit. And in an

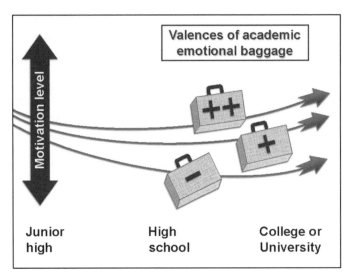

Figure 7.1 Fractal trajectories of remembered motivations aiming at future expectations

upward climb of regaining their motivation, called *remotivation*, these students needed to work harder to make the same degree of gains as the others. They also remotivated with different, and more often maladaptive, coping strategies, used adaptive coping strategies to less effect, and were more likely to falter and give up. Conversely, students carrying the most positive baggage seemed to cruise above the other's motivational pitfalls, requiring less remotivational efforts and acting with greater metacognitive sophistication to maintain their motivations (Falout *et al.*, 2013a).

From these results, we confirmed that academic emotional baggage, or what I now call *past selves* (Falout, 2016), matters to long-term motivational development and language acquisition. Thus, *past selves dynamics* alludes to the idea that for every new class students step into, they each carry their own unique set of expectations based on the meanings they make of previous learning experiences, which in turn affects the individual's psychological frames and social interactions in present and future learning situations. The upshot is that reactions to early academic experiences of demotivation seem particularly crucial to long-ranging influences on future learning, depending on how the demotivational experiences and effects of the reactions to them become incorporated into the ongoing construction of self-concept. Self-blame for failures can be most detrimental, triggering a *negative affective cycle* (Falout & Falout, 2005), whereas adaptive coping strategies can help perpetuate engagement in learning. But how do past selves relate to other elements within the self-concept system, namely present and future selves?

Differentiation and integration of past, present and future selves

I remember holding the tringle, which was one of the instruments I had played in band as a drummer, and getting a kick out of its dynamics. If you take the steel wand and knock on the triangle hard, or spin the wand around inside to make a triangle roll, a sound like a drum roll, you can hear the harmonic overtones ring out. From its vibrations, you can even see a fuzzy iron haze-image reshaping the triangle, puffing up the whole instrument.

'Resonance,' I said to my research team. We had gathered in a tiny rent-an-office in Tokyo, a space that could offer us a quieter atmosphere than our usual coffee shop hangout, to go over the preliminary data analysis of our latest research project. We were drawing triangular figures in upward and downward orientations, brainstorming how to visually represent and meaningfully interpret the numbers from the results of the motivational questionnaires our students had filled out and handed back to us. 'Resonance,' I repeated, failing to find any better words.

The model we eventually conceptualized (Falout *et al.*, 2013b; Fukada *et al.*, 2017) looks something like a downward-pointing triangle that fuzzes outward in both increased differentiation and integration (Figure 7.2). On the upper left angle rests a bulbous oval representing the averaged values of our students' images of their past selves as English learners. Compared with the pre-semester oval, the post-semester oval bulges further outward, representing an average increase in the positivity of our students' past selves. By sharing their past learning experiences with their classmates, and by gaining new past learning experiences by the

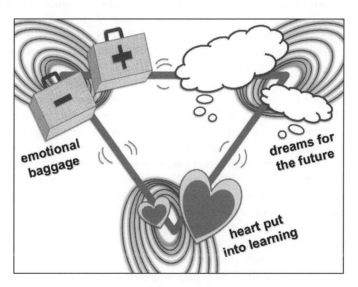

Figure 7.2 Motivational resonance among past, present and future selves

end of the semester in our communicative-based English classes, our students reported a broader understanding of their own and other's past selves, and in some cases had reframed how they looked at their own past learning experiences. Their past selves had become differentiated.

During the semester our students also shared their future expectations and dreams of using English, their *future selves* (Markus & Nurius, 1986). What resulted was an increase from pre-semester to post-semester measurements, with their future selves represented in the upper right angle of the triangle as another outward-bulging oval. With a broader understanding of the possible and with newer expectations and dreams, their future selves had also become differentiated.

Two more ovals show up at the bottom angle on the triangle. They represent the reported efforts, or *investments*, the students were currently making to learn English, their *present selves*. One oval each was given for in-class and out-of-class investments, and their measured increase over the semester also indicated an enhanced differentiation of their present selves, meaning greater variation of the students' interests and activities involving English language learning and use.

The resonance among past, present and future selves appeared when we ran a correlation check. This is a statistical calculation to show a two-way relationship between elements. Measurements taken at the beginning of the semester yielded moderately strong correlations for each pairing of all the self-concept elements. But by the end of the semester they had increased dramatically, with a particularly powerful relationship connecting past and future selves. The triangle in the model was blooming outward in thriving, resonating interconnectivity of its elements. Since the questionnaire was worded toward each individual's own motivational self-concepts, and the analysis involved an averaging of the numerical values students had given as answers, the increased correlations could be interpreted as increased integrations between past, present and future selves of most students.

Given greater differentiation and integration among self-concept elements, the self-concept systems within individual students became harmonized. The elements grew richer and their interrelationships more coherent. Envision each student holding up a triangle and playing it, each triangle representing the student's own self-concept, and each triangle expanding its shape from its own vibrations and ringing out in motivational tones. But were the tones reverberating from triangle to triangle and swelling in concert? Was it class-group level harmony or cacophony?

With such numerical data, or quantitative data, our research team could only theorize that the correlations were indirectly reflective of the students in our classrooms as acquiring a greater understanding, acceptance and appreciation – mutual reverberations – of each other's differences. Actually, these numbers represented self-congruency (intrapersonal integration) of self-concept elements within individuals only, rather than mutual reverberations (interpersonal integration) across each other's self-concepts. But we had also collected qualitative data, or open-ended answers, from our students. We showed them these research results and asked them to account for these motivational changes. The students attributed, to some extent, that the motivational improvements were brought about by positive interactions with their classmates (Falout *et al.*, 2013b). We ourselves attributed these improvements to a harmonizing effect through: synchronization of motivational inspirations and aspirations among and across small-group and class-group scales through feedback; fractalization of motivational elements among and across intrapersonal and interpersonal scales; and self-organization of goal-formation and purposeful learning (Fukada *et al.*, 2017).

Learning Groups

'We both like smiling when talking together!' two students gleefully exclaimed to each other in unison. They both raised two arms and slapped each other's hands overhead in a high ten – *slap!* They were celebrating a common connection between themselves, the high ten being a custom in my classes initiated at the start of the semester, which these two students had naturally carried over into mid semester. The common point this time was that they agreed smiling could promote classroom communications. They were participating in an ideal classmates activity (Murphey *et al.*, 2014) designed for helping students understand – from each other's perspectives directly – how they could learn better and more enjoyably together. Simultaneously they were participating in classroom-based research called critical participatory looping (CPL; Murphey & Falout, 2010).

CPL researches complexity with complexity (Falout *et al.*, 2016), a class-group researching about the group together with the group. CPL involves gathering data individually from students, compiling it anonymously, giving back the compilations with invitations to reflect on the data and respond further about it for the teacher-researcher, which adds another layer of data to a study. Looping data could potentially go beyond a single class-group to multiple class-groups, and even data from previous classes can be looped to subsequent generations of classes. CPL can be seen as a kind of group-level *biofeedback*, which helps the organism or organisms integrate their mind-body systems and gain the flexibility and power of choice to cope and adapt better to challenges posed to them (Francis, 1998).

Here is how ideal classmates activities work: The language teacher asks students to explain how their classmates can help them learn English better and more enjoyably than they could without their classmates' help. The teacher gathers all of the students' responses and anonymously shares them with the whole class. Common examples of what students want from each other include smiling when talking together, listening carefully and not laughing at each other's mistakes. After reading and reflecting on their classmates' ideas of how to help each other learn better and more enjoyably, students gain explicit understanding of how they can help their classmates learn the target language together. Students then start to become each other's ideal classmates in their behaviors toward each other, switching on motivated action, or engagement. Action research into replicating and expanding ideal classmates priming has already begun in the complexity paradigm (Sampson, 2018).

To stringently test the efficacy of ideal classmates activities, my research team randomly placed whole-class groups into either an ideal classmates priming or a future selves priming treatment (Fukuda *et al.*, in press). Classes in both treatments achieved roughly equal increases in their intrapersonal past, present and future selves motivations; made similar measurable gains in subjective self-reports of interpersonal prosocial peer learning engagement; and attained statistical correlations between intrapersonal motivations and interpersonal engagement. However, only in the ideal classmates priming did the degree of intrapersonal motivational change correlate with statistical significance to degree of interpersonal engagement. Thus, ideal classmates priming appears to line up intrapersonal psychological systems with interpersonal behavioral systems so that together they become *phase coherent*, meaning they are acting in unison and growing in lockstep fashion (Strogatz, 2003). For analogy, ideal classmates priming seems to help each student hold up one's own unique triangle, representing motivational self-concept, and play it until the triangles in the classroom resonate in sympathetic vibration.

Educational Cultures

My research into student perceptions of educational cultures began almost by accident, and only later did we formally name the research process as CPL. Recollecting to years back, I see myself waving goodbye to my students as they left the classroom, and holding in my hands several pages of data tables upon which they had scribbled their thoughts. Initially I was not expecting much, but I soon realized their voices for change in education deserved to be heard (Murphey *et al.*, 2009). Allow me to back up a bit and relate how this research got started.

One of our research team members was preparing to run a teaching workshop with JHS and HS English teachers and wanted to give them anonymous advice from our university students. We explained the plan to our students, who wrote open-endedly about their positive and negative experiences in their JHS and HS English classes, and also what they would have wanted done differently in their English learning. We coded their responses into three respective data tables of what they liked, disliked and wished they would have had in JHS and HS. The students had more often reported liking things in JHS than HS, and disliking things in

HS than JHS. As planned, these data tables were shared with teachers at the workshop.

Later in the year, our research team was preparing to show the same data tables for a conference presentation. Professing a student-voice perspective, we suddenly realized that their interpretations of their ideas would be obligatory. So, we looped the data tables back to them, explaining the latest plan to publicly share their views and inviting them to reflect and respond openly about what they thought of the research.

From their comments, we could tell that this opportunity to look at their own data and voice their opinions helped our students reach broader perspectives. They stepped outside themselves and looked back at what had happened as they transitioned across secondary education and into tertiary education. They stepped inside other students' shoes and empathized with what had happened to them; how formal educations had differed from their own, such as lacking in communicative-based classes or not having classes taught by expatriate teachers from English-speaking countries, and how some students had struggled in learning English while they themselves had not. The students were starting to understand educational cultures of English in Japan, and they responded with suggestions for change, suggestions which were intended to raise English-learning interest and motivation of future generations of students.

One common suggestion was to have a greater consistency in education. They felt they had undergone too many jolting changes in educational practices. For a while they were learning English at the beginning of JHS with games, then they were forced into curricula heavy on rote memorization and testing in the latter part of JHS through HS, only to wind up at university unprepared for the communication-based classes. Another suggestion was therefore less grammar instruction during secondary education and more opportunities for communicative interaction and enjoyment in learning. The last common suggestion was for the Japanese teachers of English to improve their teaching methods, attitudes towards students and their own English before going into the classroom.

English education in Japan has been changing. What would the suggestions be if current university students were given a chance to collaboratively reflect back on their educations and voice their opinions for future change? Whatever the suggestions, their potential value would be lost if the data looped back to teacher-researchers does not get *looped forward* to a wider audience of practitioners in the students' educational cultures. Looping forward means that teacher-researchers and even students are publishing, presenting, posting, or otherwise disseminating the information about what works in their local educational areas for the purposes of stimulating ecological adaptability on wider scales. Looping forward thus can nourish all organisms sharing interconnected ecosystems of education (Falout *et al.*, 2016).

Excitations: Instigating Motivational Resonance

This chapter presented some of my inspirations and innovations for researching and instigating motivational resonance *within* learner self-concepts, learner groups and educational cultures. What I have not done is create a theoretical framework that proposes to explain how motivational resonance can propagate *across* learner self-concepts, learner groups and educational cultures. Nor have I contextualized or integrated my own research findings with those of others. Without taking such steps, I am restrained from making any bolder claims other than to re-emphasize: If we teachers could bravely conduct and publish more action research about what makes learner motivation tick, we would have a better chance of making the larger rearrangements and the smaller fine-tuning it takes to get our students, classrooms and educational systems motivationally switched on.

Acknowledgements

Thanks to Mika Falout for instigating this research and to my research teams – Christopher Carpenter, Etsuko Shimo, Glen Hill, James Elwood, Maria Trovela, Matthew Apple, Michael Hood, Tetsuya Fukuda, Tim Murphey, Yoshifumi Fukada – for perpetuating it.

References

Csikszentmihalyi, M. (1993) *A Psychology for the Third Millennium*. New York, NY: Harper Collins.

Brown, J.D. (1988) *Understanding Research in Second Language Learning: A Teacher's Guide to Statistics and Research Design*. Cambridge: Cambridge University Press.

Brown, J.D. (2005) *Testing in Language Programs: A Comprehensive Guide to English Language Assessment*. New York, NY: McGraw-Hill.

Falout, J. (2011) Pedagogical implications of motivation research: An interview with Ema Ushioda. *The Language Teacher* 35 (2), 25–28.

Falout, J. (2012) Coping with demotivation: EFL learners' remotivation processes. *TESL-EJ* 16 (3), 1–29.

Falout, J. (2016) Past selves: Emerging motivational guides across temporal contexts. In J. King (ed.) *The Dynamic Interplay Between Context and the Language Learner* (pp. 47–65). Basingstoke: Palgrave Macmillan.

Falout, J. and Falout, M. (2005) The other side of motivation: Learner demotivation. In K. Bradford-Watts, C. Ikeguchi and M. Swanson (eds) *JALT 2004 Conference Proceedings* (pp. 280–289). Tokyo: JALT.

Falout, J. and Maruyama, M. (2004) A comparative study of proficiency and learner demotivation. *The Language Teacher* 28 (8), 3–9.

Falout, J., Elwood, J. and Hood, M. (2009) Demotivation: Affective states and learning outcomes. *System* 37 (3), 403–417.

Falout, J., Murphey, T., Fukuda, T. and Fukada, Y. (2016) Whole-class self-referential feedback from university EFL contexts to the world: Extending the social life of information by looping it forward. *The Asia-Pacific Education Researcher* 25 (1), 1–10.

Falout, J., Murphey, T., Fukuda, T. and Trovela, M. (2013a) Japanese EFL learners' remotivation strategies. In M. Cortazzi and L. Jin (eds) *Researching Cultures of Learning: International Perspectives on Language Learning and Education* (pp. 328–349). Basingstoke: Palgrave Macmillan.

Falout, J., Fukada, Y., Murphey, T. and Fukuda, T. (2013b) What's working in Japan? Present communities of imagining. In M.T. Apple, D. Da Silva and T. Fellner (eds) *Language Learning Motivation in Japan* (pp. 245–267). Bristol: Multilingual Matters.

Francis, S.E. (1998) Chaos, complexity, and psychophysiology. In L.L. Chamberlain and M.R. Bütz (eds) *Clinical Chaos: A Therapist's Guide to Nonlinear Dynamic and Therapeutic Change* (pp. 147–161). Philadelphia, PA: Brunner/Mazel.

Fukuda, T., Fukada, Y., Falout, J. and Murphey, T. (2021) How ideal classmates priming increases EFL prosocial engagement. In P. Hiver, A. Al-Hoorie and S. Mercer (eds) *Student Engagement in the Language Classroom*. Bristol: Multilingual Matters.

Fukada, Y., Murphey, T., Falout, J. and Fukuda, T. (2017) Essential motivational group dynamics: A 3-year panel study. In R. Breeze and C.S. Guinda (eds) *Essential Competencies for English-medium University Teaching* (pp. 249–266). Switzerland: Springer.

King, J. (2013) Silence in the second language classrooms of Japanese universities. *Applied Linguistics* 34 (3), 325–343.

King, J. (2016) Classroom silence and the dynamic interplay between context and the language learner. In J. King (ed.) *The Dynamic Interplay Between Context and the Language Learner* (pp. 127–150). Basingstoke: Palgrave Macmillan.

Larsen-Freeman, D. and Cameron, L. (2008) *Complex Systems and Applied Linguistics*. Oxford: Oxford University Press.

Markus, H. and Nurius, P. (1986) Possible selves. *American Psychologist* 41 (9), 954–969.

Murphey, T. and Falout, J. (2010) Critical participatory looping: Dialogic member checking with whole classes. *TESOL Quarterly* 44 (4), 811–821.

Murphey, T., Falout, J., Elwood, J. and Hood, M. (2009) Inviting student voice. In R. Nunn and J. Adamson (eds) *Accepting Alternative Voices in EFL Journal Articles* (pp. 211–235). Busan, Korea: Asian EFL Journal Press.

Murphey, T., Falout, J., Fukuda, T. and Fukada, Y. (2014) Socio-dynamic motivating through idealizing classmates. *System* 45, 242–253.

Pinner, R. (2019) *Authenticity and Teacher-Student Motivational Synergy: A Narrative of Language Teaching*. New York, NY: Routledge.

Rose, T. (2015) *The End of Average: How We Succeed in a World that Values Sameness*. New York, NY: HarperOne.

Sampson, R.J. (2016) *Complexity in Classroom Foreign Language Learning Motivation: A Practitioner Perspective from Japan*. Bristol: Multilingual Matters.

Sampson, R.J. (2018) Complexity in acting on images of ideal classmates in the L2 classroom. *Konin Language Studies* 6 (4), 387–410.

Strogatz, S. (2003) *Sync: How Order Emerges from Chaos in the Universe, Nature, and Daily Life*. New York, NY: Hyperion.

Thelen, E. and Smith, L.B. (1994) *A Dynamic Systems Approach to the Development of Cognition and Action*. Cambridge, MA: The MIT Press.

8 Understanding Motivation through Ecological Research: The Case of Exploratory Practice

Sal Consoli

In this day and age, we are increasingly confident that reality is not as simple as it may often appear, and that focusing on one phenomenon in isolation means losing sight of parts of that very phenomenon. For example, as a practitioner-researcher, I know that my students are not solely educational minds ready to receive knowledge. Rather, they are human beings with lives outside the classroom, and what they may say, do or experience in the classroom is often interconnected, influenced by or a reflection of their own lives which are enriched with emotions, social values, beliefs and much more that a teacher might actually struggle to see in a lesson.

In this chapter, I would like to share the experience of investigating second language (L2) motivation from an ecological perspective through exploratory practice (EP), a form of practitioner research. I will begin by briefly discussing the concept of motivation as a complex and dynamic social phenomenon and will steer this discussion towards the context and participants of my study. I shall continue by unpacking the term *ecological* with reference to EP and will offer a detailed account illustrating how this methodological approach worked in practice. Finally, I will offer recommendations for teachers, researchers or teacher-researchers in a cognate context who may wish to follow a similar approach to researching a complex-dynamic construct such as motivation.

From L2 Motivation to Life Capital

Motivation is one of the most prolific areas of L2 research (Ortega, 2009). However, despite this sustained research interest (roughly since the mid-1950s), it has become apparent that conceptualisations have been unable to theorise and account in full for the complex nature of this construct (Dörnyei & Ushioda, 2011). The challenge remains that motivation, like any other complex-dynamic phenomenon, not only fluctuates in nature, quality and form over-time, but also shifts in relation to a myriad of other factors and variables which may be relatively internal or external to a human being, such as identity, emotions, sociocultural norms, duties and social responsibilities to name but a few. Thus, motivation exists in relation to several *other* phenomena which interact with each other.

In order to make sense of this complex reality, Ushioda (2009) proposes a 'Person-in-Context Relational View', which encourages us to regard the participants of a study as 'real persons' as opposed to 'theoretical abstractions.' Such a stance echoes Kramsch's (2002) invitation to no longer view learners as 'computers' but 'apprentices' within a community of practice. In this vein, Ushioda (2009: 220) suggests a focus on 'the agency of the individual person as a thinking, feeling human being, with an identity, a personality, a unique history and background, a person with goals, motives and intentions'. This framework highlights the interaction between self-reflective intentional agents (e.g. learners and teachers), and 'the fluid and complex system of social relations, activities, experiences and multiple micro- and macro-contexts in which the person is embedded, moves, and is inherently part of' (Ushioda, 2009: 220).

In order to operationalise Ushioda's theory within the realm of educational psychology, I wish to draw on Bourdieu's sociological notions of *habitus*, *capital* and *field*. Each person builds, throughout their life, a *habitus*, a kind of 'socialised subjectivity' (Bourdieu & Wacquant, 1992: 126) predicated upon their experiences. Day by day, people collect and build resources which allow them to live and interact with society and its social actors. These resources are what Bourdieu refers to as *economic capital* (e.g. money), *social capital* (e.g. friends and social network) and *cultural capital* (e.g. educational background, hobbies). Another important form of capital is called *symbolic* and represents the prestige or respect the individual enjoys depending on their social class.

In my view, habitus is close to the notion of identity, which is shaped and constantly reshaped by one's own *life story* as it continually evolves from the moment a person is born and throughout their life affairs. Each person's story is unique and rich, but such richness is not solely measurable through the above notions of capital. Rather, one's life story is rich with idiosyncratic memories, emotions, dispositions, needs and desires, to name but a few factors which constitute the complex essence of a human being. These factors or traits can carry both positive and negative connotations depending on the individual. It is this richness within everyone's life story that allows them to become social actors within society, or what Bourdieu calls *field of play* (i.e. the space where human affairs occur). Bourdieu maintains that a person's ability to navigate, negotiate and live through experiences in society is directly influenced by their own habitus. This interaction is also contingent upon the specific context (or field) in which they act because each field (or context) is characterised by societal, institutional and political structures to which an individual is able to respond in light of what they already know or have experienced during their own *life story*.

Therefore, if we move beyond Bourdieu's sociological project about social classes and look at human beings more holistically with their own idiosyncrasies, we could argue that people have more than just economic, social, cultural or symbolic capital. In my view, everyone is equipped with what I would call *life capital*. Life capital could be described as a wealth which every person possesses, a wealth which can be understood through the richness of one's life experiences. Life capital thus entails memories, desires, emotions, attitudes, opinions and these can be relatively positive or negative and explicit or concealed depending on how the individual manages, shares and employs their life capital. To illustrate this with one personal example, when I was studying French at university in the UK, I had the opportunity to go abroad and complete part of my master's at a French university. As a result, I lived, studied and acted (or perhaps learnt to act) in a similar way to the local French university students. This afforded me the opportunity to do academic work in a foreign academic context and in a foreign language.

If we analyse this experience, I was able to gain linguistic (or cultural) capital and, indirectly, economic capital, as this period of study abroad would contribute to obtaining a postgraduate degree which would then open more professional possibilities. This experience also allowed me to understand what it means to study and live in a foreign country on one's own, and to fulfil local responsibilities as a tenant, learner, new friend, and so on. In sum, this experience allowed me to develop a degree of awareness and knowledge, which may turn into empathy towards anyone who goes through a similar experience. As a result, as a teacher at university in the UK, I can now decide to draw on this area of my life capital to relate to my current international students who go through something similar. Life stories (or experiences) thus become life capital, which becomes a wealth of resources inherently attached to each person. People can decide to share (or not) these resources with the outer world and, depending on with whom and what one is interacting, may decide to conceal or allow elements of their life story (or capital) to freely emerge and influence their present experience.

Returning to the notion of motivation, according to Ushioda's (2009) Person-in-Context approach, an individual's motivation is to be understood in relation to this person's life story. This allows the individual to respond to, adapt to and interact with the context or field in which they find themselves, in connection with whom they interact, and in light of what the individual bears in their life capital. For instance, a student yawning, looking down and not participating in class may not be bored or demotivated; it could well be that this student did not sleep well because of a health-related or family issue. In other words, this student is in the physical context of the classroom but has a life story which influences their current social experience, in this case, the lesson. For example, Ahmad in Hanks (2015) was a student who clearly had a desire to study but could not do so in certain situations. That is, certain circumstances he was in interfered with his motivation to study. If we look at another scenario, where a student is talking to a classmate about revisions for a test, they may draw on the memory of a conversation they had with the tutor about the future test. By drawing on this memory stored in their *life capital* the student is, in turn, allowing this memory to affect, in one way or another, what is happening in the present moment in the context where they are situated. For instance, they might decide to focus their revisions on a particular area of the curriculum to which the tutor might have alluded. As such, the *life capital* humans carry, with all its idiosyncratic traits, has the ability to impact on and shape the individual's new experiences. This perspective on complex and dynamic systems falls within what has been termed an *ecological approach* to social research.

Towards Ecological Research

The concept of ecology is borrowed from the environmental sciences wherein researchers understand phenomena through the framework of ecosystems. Ecosystem, in this discussion, is a metaphor that illustrates the symbiotic and co-adaptive relationship between the individual and the life capital they carry, and the potential such capital has to shape the individual's present and future experience(s) in reaction or in line with the context in which they find themselves. In order to define ecology, van Lier (2010) utilises the example of utterance and argues that an utterance has several layers of meaning, as it may embed elements of the speaker's history and background, their way of looking towards the future, their interaction(s) with the outside world, and interactions with their inner world relating to identity, personal cognition and emotions. To build upon van Lier's example, an individual would therefore use certain words depending on what they have readily available in their own *life capital* in response to where they are and with whom or what they are interacting. According to Kramsch (2002: 22), ecology aims to 'encompass the totality of the relationships that a learner, as a living organism, entertains with all aspects of his/her environment. As such, it is a relational "way of seeing" that enables researchers and practitioners to account for phenomena that would otherwise go unnoticed or be unaccounted for.' Kramsch argues that an ecological research perspective 'opens up possibilities of embracing the paradoxes, contradictions, and conflicts inherent in any situation involving semiotic activity, rather than rushing to solve them' (Kramsch, 2002: 22).

In this light, a classroom-based or practitioner-led approach to research motivation (e.g. Sampson, 2016) appears suitable to shed some light on the complex and, somewhat obscure, interactions between human beings and their inner and outer worlds or, as I argue here, the power and influence of life capital over the individual. In particular, I am referring to an approach which deploys a 'small-lens' focus (Ushioda, 2016) in order to illuminate the dimensions of motivation which would be lost, if noticed at all, by doing a study that attempts to selectively separate this complex phenomenon from its natural fields (or contexts) such as the classroom, the learner's mind, the teacher's actions. In other words, an approach that can recognise and acknowledge the learner's life story whether this is relatively transparent or not, somewhat hidden away or explicitly manifest in the proximity of the individual's present experience. Thus, becoming aware of an individual's life story means being able to understand the actual nature, shape and quality of their motivation while this may be pulled, shaped and remodelled by various socio-cultural, emotional, historical and psychological forces embedded within the person's life capital and their field(s) of play (or contexts).

Whereas ecology may be a suitable approach to investigate a complex phenomenon such as motivation while acknowledging the life capital attached to our participants, researching from this perspective requires due considerations and pragmatic decisions. Ushioda (2015) raised the following questions: (a) if learners are 'persons-in-context', how can we meaningfully differentiate between the learner and the context?, (b) how do we deal with the psychological and historical elements of the evolving context which are internal to the learner (e.g. memories), (c) how do we define and circumscribe the external, internal and temporal boundaries of 'context' relevant to the specific learner? And given the multitude of 'nested' (Bronfenbrenner, 1979) contexts and subcontexts that we need to identify, how do we know which of these interact directly or not with the phenomenon under investigation, in this case motivation? Considering the life story metaphor proposed here alongside the notion of life capital, we could rephrase these questions into: how can the teacher or teacher-researcher identify and account for the symbolic presence of the learner's life capital (generated by their life story) and understand how this influence, unique to the individual, shapes their motivation?

In this chapter, I use my experience of adopting EP to illustrate how this research approach is fundamentally suited to offering ecologically-grounded insights to motivation.

Introducing Exploratory Practice

EP is an approach that integrates learning, teaching and researching. It was first developed in the early 1990s by Dick Allwright in Rio de

Janeiro where teachers and teacher educators began to devise new strategies to understand what was going on in the classroom (Allwright, 1993; Allwright & Bailey, 1991; Allwright & Lenzuen, 1997). Furthermore, at least partly in response to dissatisfaction with more traditional forms of classroom-based research, EP encourages the idea of teachers and learners 'puzzling' about their language learning and teaching experiences, using 'normal pedagogic practices as investigative tools' (Allwright, 2003: 127). Many varieties of EP have sprung up on the basis that there is no single approach to teaching and learning and that only teachers and learners can take ownership for *how* learning and teaching occur. These considerations thus empower teachers and learners by recognising them as 'best positioned to research, and report on their own teaching and learning experiences' (Hanks, 2017: 54).

EP may appear similar to other forms of practitioner research (e.g. Action Research and Reflective Practice). There are certainly similarities because practitioner research, in general, aims to empower practitioners, use reflection as part of the process, and claim the 'arena for research' should be the classroom. However, EP is not centred on solutions to problems but *understanding* classroom life and highlighting the *agency* of learners and teachers in the learning/teaching setting. Inspired by Allwright (2006: 15), proponents of EP expect 'teaching and learning [to be] done so that teachers and learners simultaneously develop their own understandings of what they are doing as learners and teachers.' Learners, teachers, as well as all the other social actors of the educational context (e.g. administrators) are defined as *practitioners* with equal degrees of agency.

Another concept connected with this notion of understanding is *puzzlement*, which is intended to develop more profound understandings. It rejects superficial changes for improvement and the burden on teachers to try new strategies to achieve targets; rather, users of EP focus on the 'interrogation of practice' (Hanks, 2017: 112). Hanks (2017) offers a nuanced discussion to differentiate a *puzzle* and a *problem*. A puzzled inquiry is one that is open-ended, welcomes reflections but more importantly does not exclusively focus on negatives (as problems do). Drawing on her own teacher experience, Hanks argues that *puzzling* is open to 'discussions of successes as well as failures'. Puzzling, thus, is the starting point of EP.

As guiding tenets, practitioners of EP strive to:

(1) Focus on *quality of life* as the fundamental issue.
(2) Work to *understand* this quality of life, before thinking about solving problems.
(3) Involve *everybody* as practitioners developing their own understandings.
(4) Work to bring people *together* in a common enterprise.

(5) Work cooperatively for *mutual* development.
(6) Make it a *continuous* enterprise.
(7) *Minimize the burden* by integrating the work for understanding into normal pedagogic practice.

(Allwright & Hanks, 2009: 260 – original emphases)

Exploratory Practice in My Context

Part of my teaching duties involves the running of pre-sessional programmes in English for academic purposes (EAP) with international students at a UK university. The pre-sessional equips international students with a foundation of academic skills to be able to integrate into the new English-speaking university and British society. Therefore, the pre-sessional represents a crucial transition period from the international home country, as well as educational home context, to the UK academic and sociocultural realities. Within the context of this study, I was the pre-sessional tutor delivering the EAP reading and writing module. However, at the same time, I had research interests at heart which consisted in understanding these students' life experiences with a focus on their motivation to study and live in the UK.

It is worth mentioning that, from the outset, it was clear to me that the L2 motivation literature would not be able to sufficiently support this study. As stated above, there is not one single theoretical approach that does justice to all the intricate facets of motivation as a construct. More crucially, based on my own life capital through experiences of studying abroad myself, I expected that motivation concerning international students completing a pre-sessional course and a postgraduate programme in a UK university would concern more than just learning or improving a foreign language (in this case English). I was aware that these students' motivation would be related to more than a language learning experience. It would rather concern their experience of living in a new sociocultural reality, facing the dissonance of cultural differences, adapting to and adopting new academic customs and practices. For these reasons, the guiding research question that I kept in mind was: *What are these students' motivations to study and live in the UK?* From the beginning of the research project it became clear that each student had carried with them very idiosyncratic motives which would then transform into specific motivational trajectories throughout their time in the UK.

By adopting EP's focus on *understanding*, I refrained from seeking problems and solutions (although at times this happened during the teaching programme). Rather, I wished to explore the EAP life world of which we (all practitioners) were part. Another advantage of drawing upon the EP framework is that data should come from pedagogic sources and fulfil pedagogic purposes (Allwright, 2003; Allwright & Hanks, 2009). This is achieved by using potentially exploitable pedagogic activities (PEPAs), which normally involve a certain degree of reflection and analysis in the classroom. On the grounds of my previous EAP teaching experience, I judged that several activities I normally use as part of my own EAP practice lent themselves well to becoming effective PEPAs. Among the PEPAs I used were *Day one short essay, Class reflective discussions* and *Weekly reflective reports* (further details below). Therefore, I adopted EP because this way I would not have to worry about creating extra burdens for my students. I also hoped that my research work may be manageable for other EAP teachers in similar contexts.

Despite my interest in EP and its principles, and despite all the reading I had done around this methodology, I had big concerns about how I would implement EP in my short and intensive pre-sessional (6 weeks – PS6 henceforth) context. I realised that not being a Listening and Speaking teacher compromised my case even more. As evidenced by Hanks (2015), a speaking and listening strand within a pre-sessional course offers a variety of opportunities to integrate EP. While some other EP experiences (e.g. Hanks, 2017) show that it is possible to incorporate EP within a writing module of a pre-sessional cohort (e.g. collaborative writing projects), in PS6 we worked under the strict guidelines that students would need to produce an individual written assignment - this was an essay (based on the reading of secondary sources) about a specific topic related to their future MSc programme. I do not wish to claim here that it is impossible to fully embrace EP within circumstances similar to PS6; however, at that time I was an enthusiastic proponent of EP, who had never actually *done EP* before. More critically, I was doing this as part of a wider project (my doctorate), which certainly compounded my apprehension and uncertainty.

Ecological Insights from Exploratory Practice

At the commencement of my teaching I did not reveal to my students that I would be doing research on their motivation. Although I was already collecting certain forms of data (e.g. post-class reflections on my teacher-researcher journal), I was determined to give priority to my students' needs as learners of EAP and new citizens of the UK – these were, after all, the core aims of completing the pre-sessional programme. After two weeks in the programme, I shared my research interests with the students and gave them relevant paperwork to decide if they wished to join as research participants. Waiting for two weeks gave me the opportunity to establish teacher–students rapport and gain a basic understanding of who they were and how they worked in the classroom. This allowed me to notice any potential differences between the first two weeks of PS6 and the following weeks with the students being aware of my research hat on. Again, this was to ensure that their educational needs came first and did not suffer because of my research intentions. Nevertheless, I began to implement the EP principle of turning pedagogical activities into PEPAs.

Here I offer some examples:

Sample PEPA 1
Out-of-class activity: Learning about students' writing skills

I always ask my new students (normally on day one) to write a few paragraphs about themselves to outline their interests and expectations of the course. While I would generally give them very broad guidelines to write freely; this time, and in the spirit of EP, I formulated the following instructions to ensure they wrote about their motivation or touch upon it even peripherally:

Write a paragraph for each question:

> (A) What are your reasons for choosing to study at [name of university]? Describe your personal motivation for coming here and what you hope to achieve.
> (B) Why are you doing the pre-sessional?
> (C) What are your expectations of the pre-sessional?
> (D) What are your expectations of the Text-based Studies module with me?

I will share here some sample answers to these questions from one student (Megan):

> **A: What are your reasons for choosing to study at this University? Describe your personal motivation for coming here and what you hope to achieve.**
>
> The reasons of me to choose to study at this university are quite simple. First of all, MSc is necessary for the future due to the fierce competition in the society. So the tertiary education is a plus for young person. Secondly, I will have more opportunity to get a higher position in a company after learning the methodologies of programme and project management, comparing to my past time. Last but not least, learning makes me happy. This means that studying at [name of the university] and making friends here are fabulous things in my life, and this would be a great memory in my life. In conclusion, I want to study here to get promotion and enjoy my life. I dream a lot about the life in [name of the university] and I do hope I can learn the practical knowledge here. Then, I want to know and analyze things in different ways and angles. Moreover, I hope I can find a good job after learning and acknowledging all the contents in this major.

This question was strategic in encouraging the student to explain the main reasons for coming to study in the UK for a year and at this institution. Here, we learn a lot about this student's motivation as well as her own story as a human being with her own understandings, needs and desires (or life capital). She begins by articulating the value of cultural capital in society and the relevance of this in a young person's life. She also taps into her inner motivation and joy for learning by stating that this contributes to her happiness; but this happiness is clearly linked to her wish of making friends in the new university context and desire to build good memories. She also highlights her intention to learn practical skills and become able to analyse and understand things from new perspectives thanks to her learning throughout her future master's programme. This PEPA question thus offers an initial picture of Megan's motivation and a glimpse of her own life story (e.g. expectations and hopes based on her past experiences) and how this intertwines with her motivation.

B: Why are you doing the pre-sessional?

There are two reasons why I attend the pre-sessional course. One is that I was not that confident to write a good PMA during the formal courses. The second one is that I am not good at exams. This also make me confused, because I do not know whether I am not skillful at 'exam' or I did not have the certain ability of English. Apart from these two, my parents want me here since I seldom leave home, and this would be a chance for me to make friends and become familiar with a new country in my life! Therefore, I come here and take the pre-sessional course.

I was aware that most students had a conditional offer from the university which relied upon successful completion of PS6. However, I decided to include this question in this PEPA because it would potentially yield information concerning the students' beliefs about PS6 which would, in turn, reveal dimensions of their attitudes and motivations in relation to this programme. As we can see, from the very beginning of this answer, Megan discloses her lack of confidence in writing her future assignments for the master's programme (PMA – Professional Master of Arts). She also shares her concern about sitting exams, which presumably stems from her previous experiences with exams. From this excerpt, it is clear that Megan's motivational drive to complete the pre-sessional is embedded within her perception of inadequate writing skills and her fear of a poor performance at exams. These sentiments of inadequacy and fear thus contribute to a greater understanding of Megan's motivation to either perform well in her assignments or potential lack of motivation, or even anxiety, in connection to completing assignments and sitting exams. Furthermore, when she mentions her parents encouraging her to take the pre-sessional course, she offers an extra layer of her own life story which suggests that her family has direct impact on her motivation to complete the pre-sessional, and possibly even her commitment to it.

C: What are your expectations of the pre-sessional?

To be honest, I did not think of this question before I came to [name of the University]. Today I saw the greatest teacher and my group mates, I felt happy about the course. If there would be some expectations, I think I hope every minute in pre-sessional is valuable.

While this question did not yield a lengthy or detailed answer, it was useful to confirm Megan's above-mentioned need for interaction and good rapport with the people around her in the new academic environment, thus fuelling her happiness. This text clearly shows that Megan's motivation is fundamentally dependent on her desire to be happy with the human relationships in the new UK reality. As such, her expectation and hope to enjoy the course acquire a whole new meaning and although there is no explicit mention of motivation one can gather that if these elements were missing from her academic experience then her happiness, and possibly her motivation to do well academically, would be compromised.

D: What are your expectations of the Text-based Studies module?

I am thirst for writing guidance. When I prepared the IELTS exam last year, my writing score was only five. Then I wrote a lot of things about IELTS writing, and things began changing. The final score of my IELTS writing part was six, which is not enough for academic writing I suppose. Therefore, I really want to improve writing ability and especially the correct expression of meaning. Under the suggestion of my friends, I need to write a lot to get familiar and collect the common expressions. However, revising essay is another important part of writing. Therefore, there is gratitude of you to help me with my text-based studies.

This answer illustrates the weight that Megan puts on other people's opinions and how these may affect her behaviour. Her friends have recommended that she work more on her writing which is directly connected to her motivation to practise her writing skills. She also shares part of her life story about the IELTS exam (a high-stakes English test for international study and work) which further promotes her motivation to work on her academic writing. This answer thus demonstrates that Megan's motivation to work on her writing skills does not exist in isolation but stems from her challenging experience with the IELTS test and her friends' suggestions that she practise more.

I would normally set this activity as homework after the first day of any programme I teach and would ask one generic question such as 'write a paragraph about yourself and why you are doing this course'; this would allow me to evaluate their writing competences. However, by turning this generic task into a PEPA to investigate motivation, I formulated each question with the aim of guiding the writing process and encouraging the students to write something about their motivation. More crucially, as we can see from the above example, Megan was able to express some critical thoughts about her own life story and how this connects with her motivation for being in the UK, doing a pre-sessional and her future master's programme. She outlined some clear desires, needs and expectations stemming from her life capital (e.g. her parents' influence, her wish to make good friends), which clearly interact with her motivation to live and study in the new UK reality. Thus, this activity allowed me, as a teacher-researcher, to gain an understanding of Megan's motives for choosing to embark upon this postgraduate experience and learn some critical knowledge about Megan as a human being with her idiosyncratic traits and story. Crucially, understanding the tapestry of her motivation and which exact pieces of her life capital this was made of (e.g. fear of poor writing performance, bad memories of the IELTS test) allowed me, the teacher, to behave more ecologically. By ecologically, I mean that the information I learnt about Megan's life story and how her life capital influenced her behaviour, in this case, her motivation, made me alert and sensitive to her specific needs.

Sample PEPA 2
Out-of-class activity: Learning about the student's weekly experiences

During a pre-sessional course, I normally ask my students to produce some weekly writing in order to reflect on their learning during each week and share what they have done during the weekend. I tell them that, when completing this activity, they do not need to worry about academic conventions and that they can relax. In other words, this is an opportunity to write in English and share their thoughts while not fretting about academic style, register and lexicon. I still find these activities conducive to useful feedback on grammar use and other aspects of their written expression. I can also understand and learn about how they are coping with the course. When I turned this activity into a PEPA to investigate their motivation to study and live in the UK, I gave them the following instructions:

Weekly writing task

Write about this past week. What did you like about your lessons? What did you dislike about your lessons? What did you like or dislike about your life outside the classroom? Share what you want and write as much as you want.

Here is a sample answer (from Xiaoxin) to the above instructions:

I felt upset because I realized how my poor oral English was. That's true, I know how smart I am in Chinese, but I am really stupid in English. I cannot adequately express myself well in English, therefore I can only choose very simple words and sentences to communicate, even though when I have complex emotion and deep thought.

Besides, I feel that my poor oral English make me become a rather boring and dull person. Although I can understand some jokes, I cannot find a right way to respond in English just choose to smile or don't say anything. I really don't want to be that! In addition, on Friday, a group of young people organised a party at the residence next door, they called me to join them when I passed by and glanced at them. I just refused them because I had no idea how to respond to them, at the same time I was afraid they would be unfriendly when they see me communicate with difficulty. Then

I heard someone called me 'CHING CHONG'. You know it sounded like a kind of prank, but for me, a Chinese, it sounded more like discrimination, which made me feel uncomfortable and angry. Nevertheless, I was disappointed soon when I found I didn't know how to fight back. That's why I felt depression this week.

However, my mood changed on the Saturday. We went to the Cambridge! An amazing place I really love there! We enjoyed punting in the River Cam and appreciated these fantastic buildings and bridges. More importantly, we met Steven Hawking! I have read his books before, but never imagined I'd meet him in reality. It definitely was a wonderful and unbelievable trip!

As for my pre-sessional classes, I find it is quite difficult for me to organize and conclude the information and resources of essay I collected, which took lots of my energy and time. Thus, for next four weeks, I am determined to improve my English as fast as I can, both in speaking and writing. I hope I can have a huge change after the pre-sessional courses!

This PEPA allowed me to learn plenty about this student both in terms of academic performance and her ability to cope with the pre-sessional programme. Crucially, I discovered how the student's life story was unfolding in the UK and which episodes of this student's life capital may have direct impact on her personal wellbeing and academic performance. This writing shows that Xiaoxin began the week with a low appreciation of her English-speaking skills which led to her saying that she felt stupid. She clearly recognised the struggle to operate fully as a social and academic being in another language thus highlighting her frustration for not being able to express herself as well and cleverly as she could in her mother tongue. This self-evaluation of her linguistic competence was exacerbated by the emotional impact it was having on her. She was sensitive to how other people in the UK may perceive her for her inability to communicate adequately, which clearly affected her adjustment to the new life in the UK. She was, however, able to see the positive in her experiences as evidenced by her review of the trip to Cambridge, but one cannot ignore that these negative feelings and perceptions about her language competences affected her so deeply that she even used the word 'depression' after describing herself as a dull person 'in English'.

Returning to the aim of identifying Xiaoxin's motivation to study and live in the UK, in this PEPA, we notice several factors that dented her enthusiasm to achieve her academic goals because she feared that her skills were not good enough. Also, her motivation to live well in the country was compromised by the perception she had of her interaction with other people in this new social context. This weekly strategy thus allowed the student to share with me, the teacher, some experiences which otherwise would have remained silenced and unnoticed and, more importantly, which may affect the student's performance. This activity thus helped me clearly see that her motivation to perform well was interconnected with her lack of faith in her skills which was compounded by her life story unfolding in the UK, i.e. the challenging interactions she had with other people in the new social and educational contexts.

Furthermore, as a teacher, when I read this PEPA, I immediately offered Xiaoxin advice about the law in the UK in relation to hate crime and sign-posted her to the people who may be able to assist. I do not claim that this kind of pastoral behaviour is a requirement for an EAP teacher as such, especially because contracts and institutions work in different ways, but I cannot ignore the ethical duty that we somehow fulfil by welcoming these high-fee-paying students to our country and universities. Thus, this PEPA, like many other weekly reflective texts from the same cohort, served multiple purposes to: (a) give the student an opportunity to write in English in a more relaxed manner which was not restricted by academic conventions while still receiving feedback on areas such as grammar and clarity of expression, (b) gain an understanding of the student's perception of the pre-sessional and her progress, (c) identify the student's motivation either in explicit statements or, more implicitly, in relation to the experiences and thoughts shared (i.e. life story and capital), (d) offer me the opportunity to provide signposting on issues that may go beyond the academic remit but which may easily affect her personal and academic wellbeing.

For the sake of brevity, I cannot share more sample PEPAs here, but I wish to add that during this pre-sessional experience I did not use EP just as methodology to learn more about these students' motivation. This is because although my learning about their motivation would allow me to inform my teaching, and therefore ensure the best possible experience for them, I felt that using EP to solely explore my interest in motivation was slightly selfish and would not necessarily allow the students to fully embrace EP to explore their *own* puzzles. Thus, when I realised that, as the Reading and Writing tutor, I was expected to devote a few hours a week to the teaching of British Culture, I formally introduced the students to EP as a research practice and showed some strategies to implement the approach within their pre-sessional context. I encouraged them to identify aspects of their new life in the UK that they may have found puzzling. This way, I ensured that these hours about British Culture would address specific topics which were relevant and meaningful to these specific students as opposed to making arbitrary choices just because I was the British teacher at a UK university. Some sample puzzles the students presented included:

Megan: Why do people in the UK like make appointment to do nearly everything?

Alita: Why don't Chinese students make new friends with the western students in the UK?

David: Why do we always write essays and papers instead of taking exams in UK Universities?

They used a variety of PEPAs to explore these such as interviews, Google searches, classroom discussions. Moreover, after gaining some practice exploring their puzzles about British culture, I encouraged them to identify academic puzzles. These are some examples:

Amber: why is critical thinking very important to write an essay?
May: why does academic writing need formal expressions?
David: Why are our own opinions required to be supported by references?

They explored these puzzles through web searches, interviewing students from other class groups, and doing mini debates in class with me.

I will not share the details of how the students explored their own puzzles because they do not pertain to my own investigation of motivation here described. However, I thought I would give the reader a flavour of the rich and diverse experiences that emerged by enabling these pre-sessional students to *do* EP. Also, I should point out that EP did have an impact on these students' motivation, which I was able to notice in their weekly reflective writing (PEPA described above) throughout the course. For instance, some of them claimed that this methodology gave them new tools they could use in the future master's programme; in other words, EP, as an experience, became part of their evolving life capital which, in this case, fuelled their motivation to study and perform well academically. The motivational impact that EP had on the students became clearer in my interviews post-pre-sessional which formed part of a second phase of data collection that went beyond the practitioner-research experience here described. Although sharing the details of this second phase here would mean going beyond the remit of this chapter, I would like to state that, as I argued in Consoli (2018), research that brings together the insights of practitioners (or teacher-researchers) and those gained through a more traditional (outside the classroom) research approach (e.g. interviews) can yield richer and more nuanced findings (or understandings) than those generated by practitioner research or more traditional (outsider) research alone.

Conclusion

An ecological approach to the study of motivation is suitable to understand the complex and dynamic nature of this construct more holistically. As shown in this chapter, motivation exists *in relation to* or *within the context of* what here I called *life story* (i.e. life as it unfolds for a human being) and *life capital* (i.e. the symbolic wealth resulting from the life story). The study reported here illustrates the interconnectedness between students' life capital, life story and motivation. This nuanced and insightful understanding of students' motivation was possible thanks to the ecological approach offered by EP. PEPAs thus generate practical research opportunities for overworked and busy teachers or teacher-researchers who may have a thirst for deeper understandings of their daily classroom life. Ultimately, I argue that teachers are well-placed to conduct sound ethical research with their own students, and EP promotes the ecological approach that helps detect and account for the symbolic presence of learners' life story and life capital and understand how these may affect complex constructs such as motivation.

References

Allwright, D. (1993) Integrating 'research' and 'pedagogy': Appropriate criteria and practical possibilities. In J. Edge and K. Richards (eds) *Teachers Develop Teachers Research* (pp. 125–135). Oxford: Heinemann.

Allwright, D. (2003) Exploratory practice: Rethinking practitioner research in language teaching. *Language Teaching Research* 7 (2), 113–141.

Allwright, D. (2006) Six promising directions in applied linguistics. In S. Gieve and I. Miller (eds) *Understanding the Language Classroom* (pp. 11–17). Basingstoke: Palgrave Macmillan UK.

Allwright, D. and Bailey, K.M. (1991) *Focus on the Language Classroom*. Cambridge: Cambridge University Press.

Allwright, D. and Hanks, J. (2009) *The Developing Language Learner: An Introduction to Exploratory Practice*. New York: Palgrave Macmillan.

Allwright, D. and Lenzuen, R. (1997) Exploratory practice: Work at the Cultura Inglesa, Rio de Janeiro, Brazil. *Language Teaching Research* 1 (1), 73–79 .

Bourdieu, P. and Wacquant, L.J. (1992) *An Invitation to Reflexive Sociology*. Chicago: University of Chicago Press.

Bronfenbrenner, U. (1979) *The Ecology of Human Development*. Cambridge, MA: Harvard University Press.

Burns, A. (2010) *Doing Action Research in English Language Teaching: A Guide for Practitioners*. Abingdon: Routledge.

Consoli, S. (2018) Understanding motivation through exploratory practice: Early musings Paper presented at the FOLLM research event, King's College London.

Dörnyei, Z. and Ushioda, E. (2011) *Teaching and Researching Motivation* (2nd edn). Harlow: Pearson Education Limited.

Hanks, J. (2015) 'Education is not just teaching': Learner thoughts on Exploratory Practice. *ELT Journal* 69 (2), 117–128.

Hanks, J. (2017) *Exploratory Practice in Language Teaching: Puzzling About Principles and Practices*. London: Palgrave Macmillan.

Kramsch, C. (2002) Introduction: 'How can we tell the dancer from the dance?' In C. Kramsch (ed.) *Language Acquisition and Language Socialization: Ecological Perspectives* (pp. 1–30). New York: Continuum.

Mann, S. (2016) *The Research Interview: Reflective Practice and Reflexivity in Research Processes*. London: Palgrave Macmillan.

Ortega, L. (2009) *Understanding Second Language Acquisition*. Abingdon: Routledge.

Sampson, R.J. (2016) *Complexity in Classroom Foreign Language Learning Motivation: A Practitioner Perspective from Japan*. Bristol: Multilingual Matters.

Ushioda, E. (2009) A person-in-context relational view of emergent motivation, self and identity. In Z. Dörnyei and E. Ushioda (eds) *Motivation, Language Identity and the L2 Self* (pp. 215–228). Bristol: Multilingual Matters.

Ushioda, E. (2015) Context and complex dynamic systems theory. In Z. Dörnyei, P.D. MacIntyre and A. Henry (eds) *Motivational Dynamics in Language Learning* (pp. 47–54). Bristol: Multilingual Matters.

Ushioda, E. (2016) Language learning motivation through a small lens: A research agenda. *Language Teaching* 49 (4), 564–577.

van Lier, L. (2010) The ecology of language learning: Practice to theory, theory to practice. *Procedia-Social and Behavioural Sciences* 3, 2–6.

9 Complexity as a Valid Approach in 'Messy' Classroom Contexts: Promoting More 'Ecologically Rich' Research on the Psychology of L2 Listening

Kedi Simpson and Heath Rose

Introduction: The Complexities of Classroom Research

It is widely regarded that real-world classroom research is indispensable in applied linguistics and educational research, as it is high in ecological validity. That is, the research findings from classroom-based research are by default highly contextualized, and therefore offer rich perspectives on similar learning and teaching environments. Yet, while there is a need for more practitioner-researchers to conduct high-quality research in the very contexts in which they work, such research tends to be lacking in our field. Part of this shortage is related to an observed disconnect between classroom practices and current research attention (see Marsden & Kasprowicz, 2018; McKinley, 2019; Rose, 2019), and often it stems from the fact that practitioner-led research usually involves research with intact classrooms, which is a 'particularly complex and multifaceted endeavour' (Mackey & Gass, 2005: 212).

In this chapter we argue that approaching classroom research from a complexity perspective allows us to better embrace the realities of classroom learning – allowing a researcher to explore not only the cognitive processes of learning, but also the psychology of the language learner, who is embedded within a complex and dynamic social context. Complex dynamic systems theory (CDST), thus, takes advantage of the contextualized and multifaceted nature of classroom research, building a wide lens within the research design, and thus enhancing a study's overall ecological validity. We make this argument by first justifying a need for more complex classroom research to take a more holistic exploration of learning. This is followed by an illustrative example in which we present the methodology of a study which uses CDST to investigate the complexities of L2 listening. In all, this chapter highlights how a complexity approach carries with it an ecological validity for classroom research that more reductionist approaches may lack. That is, CDST allows researchers to meld the psychological and individualistic aspects of learning with the cognitively oriented traditions of L2 listening development research.

Embracing the 'Mess' of Real Research Contexts

It has been noted that classroom research tends to be 'pretty messy' (McArthur, 2012: 428): that is, the learning is so psychologically complex that many confounding variables exist, which can be difficult to separate out, or control for, in traditional research designs. Moreover, unpredictable contextual elements can influence learning. As Rose and McKinley (2017: 6–7) note:

> A common cold can decimate student numbers on the day of important classroom-based research. An overly controlling and chatty group member can destroy a speech sample intended for discourse analysis. A gatekeeper to an important research site can simply decide to exercise his or her right to not take part in your study… There are an immeasurable number of ways in which a carefully planned research project can go awry in the real world.

As a result, many applied linguistics and educational researchers shy away from the messiness of conducting holistic classroom research due to a perceived lack of control over the multitude of variables that might affect a carefully designed study. Traditional approaches to research – especially those connected to applied psychology – tend to take a positivist stance to methodological planning. Positivism refers to an objective stance to research, where researchers aim to confirm or refute a hypothesis. This is often achieved by maintaining researcher control over all observed variables in order to isolate them and draw concrete conclusions of causality based on statistical probability. Due to the difficulties of this process, researchers tend to narrow their research focus and their constructs in order to be more certain of the conclusions drawn from the data. When psychological aspects are drawn into learning development research, they are often used to control for baseline measures of popular constructs such as motivation and aptitude rather than forming part of the core research design.

As a result of this narrowing, some second language learning research-ers ultimately simplify or compartmentalize their research in an effort to tame messiness in data and maintain (the illusion of) researcher control. For example, researchers may choose to focus only on a small number of research constructs to limit the number of data collection instruments needed; they may choose to limit the number of data collection points to ease data analysis; they may adopt linear assumptions about language development in order to fit the needs of statistical tests; they might remove outliers to meet the assumptions of certain statistical procedures. There are numerous ways applied linguistics and educational researchers end up narrowing their focus and their data when dealing with complexity, which creates 'cleaner' but not necessarily 'better' data.

Yet, 'applied linguists and educational researchers often deal with the "real world" rather than sanitized environments' (Rose & McKinley, 2017: 6), so we must question why this discipline values the sanitization and compartmentalization of the very research sites we investigate, which in turn destroys a study's ecological validity. Is simplicity reason enough to move away from the realities of the contexts within which we research, and to which we wish our findings to contribute? In answer to this, we offer a clear rationale for the adoption of holistic methods in classroom research, which a CDST approach is able to facilitate.

Adopting More Holistic Methodological Perspectives

If a biologist were aiming to understand how a certain type of plant grew simply by observing the plant, but failed to consider either the grow-ing medium, or nutrients, they would be neglecting a significant element of what fosters plant growth. This analogy can be easily transferred to research into developmental trajectories of language learning. In compart-mentalizing research, many conventional studies reduce observations of learning to a limited range of factors, only drawing conclusions about the relationships between them. In contrast, when we adopt a complexity per-spective for researching L2 development, we attempt to see the bigger picture: the growing medium might be seen as the teaching approach, the type of teacher and the curriculum and the light, water and other nutrients could be the learner's psychology – their self-efficacy, aptitude, strategies, motivation, or other external factors such as home life.

Approaching research from a complexity perspective allows us to embrace such messiness. One does not even need to dichotomize between psychological and cognitive approaches, or consider the extent to which the classroom environment creates confounding variables; instead adopt-ing a complexity perspective, we can embrace the chaotic system that is the classroom, and use its tenets to tease out the order which is hidden within (Larsen-Freeman, 2017). Indeed, given that a CDST ontology and meth-odology, with its multi-wave data collection and wide number of variables, permits us to begin to explore whether random, unpredictable events might influence the future (Larsen-Freeman & Cameron, 2008b), its departure from more traditional ways of research results in a more ecologically valid approach to the varied events that can take place in a classroom over time.

Most teachers know well that learners are complicated people, who bring their day-to-day experiences into the classroom, whether they are helpful to learning or not, and that therefore all manner of factors might influence the extent to which progress in learning is made. This inherent messiness can mean that traditional research, with its attempt to 'clean up' the learning experience by focussing on a small number of variables and attempting to remove confounds, can end up being hard to relate to the common classroom. By contrast, a CDST approach creates a 'shared space' between practitioner and researcher (de Bot *et al.*, 2007; Mercer, 2016). In other words, by dint of the fact that CDST does not decontextualize the learning, research undertaken in this vein has ecological validity, and sits comfortably with the teacher's acknowledgement of the myriad, complex processes and interactions that take place within the four walls of the classroom (Kostoulas *et al.*, 2017).

Detractors might claim that this means that any findings are too unique to be generalizable, but 'case-driven does not equate with "idiosyncratic" and "complexity" does not equate with "randomness"' (Sealey & Carter, 2004: 210). Instead of generalizing to populations, findings can be generalized to theories of learning (Lowie, 2017). Thus, we aim to illustrate this point with reference to a research case study carried out by one of the authors (Simpson's ongoing research project on the developmental trajectory of L2 listening). Drawing from the case study example, we aim to communicate an underlying message that, despite its complexity, holistic classroom-based research is needed and is valuable. We also aim to show that complexity research does not mean it is 'uncontrolled', but rather it aims to be inclusive of a wide range of factors – the cognitive, the social and the psychological. Further to this, adopting more holistic approaches to second language research need not mean researchers must abandon evidence-based positivist approaches to data collection and analysis, but rather more data from more constructs and time points need to be included.

Complexities Surrounding the Psychology of L2 Listening Development

The dominant methodology in applied linguistics research into second language listening aims to link L2 aural comprehension to one or two variables, be they psychological (metacognition, working memory, self-efficacy, motivation) or cognitive (vocabulary knowledge, grammatical knowledge, world knowledge), or a mixture of both, in order to provide a snapshot of 'how listening works' at a certain time-point, or possibly two.

Psychological elements of the study under discussion

Different models of how listening works give the psychological elements of listening different weighting, although it is clear that it is a process that straddles the cognitive and the psychological. In this section, we provide an overview of the three psychological constructs inherent in the listening process, which the methodology of our illustrative CDST case study incorporates: metacognitive strategies, which has been linked to learner psychology in the field of learner strategy research; working memory, which is positioned in learner psychology as a construct of aptitude (see Dörnyei & Ryan, 2015); and self-efficacy and the learning environment, which has been linked to L2 motivation. These three constructs are key elements of the research that underpins the case study presented in this chapter.

Metacognition and learning strategies

There is ample research into the role of metacognition in listening – that is, the extent to which the listener is aware of the cognitive processes which they are experiencing, and the extent to which they can regulate and direct them (Vandergrift & Goh, 2012). It might well be that strategy use is related to both the maturity and the skill level of the language user: Macaro (2006) points out that a learner needs skills before they can deploy strategies, and this could explain why Vandergrift and Baker (2015) found that among 13 year olds, metacognition was a strong predictor of L2 listening success, yet among 10 year olds, the link was weak and insignificant (Vandergrift & Baker, 2018). Strategy use has also been correlated simply with age or maturity (Dong, 2016; Schoonen *et al.*, 1998), although some success has been reported among younger children (Goh & Kaur, 2017).

A focus on metacognitive strategies is common in L2 listening research, yet is often measured in isolation of a range of other factors that may affect the processes of listening development. For example, listeners' strategy use can be limited by the type of task expected of them, or their knowledge of possible strategies (Macaro, 2006). This suggests that data on metacognition might be best supplemented with the testing of other psychological constructs (such as working memory or motivation), in order to create a fuller and more accurate picture of what is happening in the listener's mind as they listen, and as their listening skills progress.

Working memory

A language-user's working memory temporarily stores and manipulates information (Baddeley, 2012) in the phonological loop. Individual differences in working memory capacity are often invoked to explain differences in linguistic performance in adult learners more broadly (Juffs & Harrington, 2011), as well as in listening achievement specifically (Andringa *et al.*, 2012; Kormos & Sáfár, 2008; Miyake & Friedman, 1998). Unlike adults, the working memory of children and adolescents is still developing (Gathercole & Baddeley, 1989), which might explain why Vandergrift and Baker (2015, 2018) found an insignificant relationship between the two variables of working memory and L2 listening in their research involving 13 year olds and 10 year olds, respectively. An individual's working memory can fluctuate according to a range of factors – psychological (e.g. anxiety) or biological (e.g. hunger, time of day).

Tests of working memory have often been linked to measures of learning aptitude. For example, the 'High-Level Language Aptitude Battery' (Linck *et al.*, 2013) particularly targets working memory to measure language learning aptitude. Aptitude as a psychological measure has 'stood the test of time and remained a valid concept despite the big changes that have happened in classroom practice' (Wen *et al.*, 2017: 4). Thus, it stands to reason that students with more efficient working memory are likely to have higher aptitude, which is then highly related to language learning development.

Motivation and self-efficacy

Motivation research has a long tradition of showing the L2 learning environment and classroom experiences to be a predominant influence on a learner's language development. One of the key components of Gardner's (1985) conceptualization of the integrative motive included attitudes towards the learning situation (i.e. the teacher and the course) as one of its three core components. Likewise, in the more recent 'L2 motivational self-system' model of motivation, the 'L2 learning experience' is equally positioned as one component of the tripartite model (Dörnyei, 2009). Thus, in any study of foreign language learning in this context, it would seem that the role of the L2 learning context in promoting (or hindering) motivation is an important factor for a study to consider.

A key sub-theory of motivation is self-efficacy, where a learner has confidence in their ability to complete a task (Bandura, 1993). A learner's self-efficacy might well correlate with anxiety levels, flexibility in strategy use and their persistence (Mills *et al.*, 2006); indeed, a meta-analysis of self-efficacy in educational contexts found that it accounted for 14% of the variance in academic performance (Multon *et al.*, 1991).

The fundamental interconnectedness of many psychological constructs can be seen when second language listening is considered. Its inherent difficulties (ephemeral nature, the fact that listeners cannot control the input, and the product-oriented approach pursued in many classrooms) mean that it is a skill in which there can be particularly low levels of self-efficacy (Graham, 2006, 2011; Graham & Macaro, 2007, 2008). The consequence of this is anxiety (Xu, 2011), a compromised working memory and reduced use of strategy.

CDST: A Match with Theoretical Frameworks of Listening?

Despite the complexity of language learning in foreign language environments, there is a dearth of research which adopts a CDST approach to examine psychological elements in listening development. One exception is a study by Dong (2016), which explored the listening strategies deployed by one intermediate Chinese learner of English over a period of 42 weeks. The CDST approach with 21 data collection points adds to our understanding of the psychology of L2 listening, although the constructs measured were limited to strategies and self-reported development in listening skills. This can be contrasted with the study highlighted later in this chapter.

With the exception of the research undertaken by Dong (2016), it is rare for L2 listening researchers to take a CDST approach, which could provide a much more detailed picture of the learners' experience over time. Such an approach would provide an opportunity to explore the developmental trajectory and probe the crucial 'sliding doors moments' which, with hindsight, come to influence the classroom – moments which could be due to a huge range of factors.

Furthermore, it is an interesting idea to consider the extent to which the CDST framework fits neatly with theoretical models of listening. Models of listening such as those of Field (2013) and Anderson (1990) could be described as complex, dynamic systems: their ranges of subsystems (lexical and syntactic knowledge, world knowledge, strategy use and so on) interact constantly, and the balance between these subsystems changes as the input changes. How a listener comes to an understanding of the aural input is iterative and dynamic and depends on a range of external factors, such as prior knowledge of the topic, and the environment in which the listening is taking place. One could then argue that a CDST approach to researching the psychology of listening is more holistic and appropriate, as it offers the opportunity to learn more about the constantly changing relationship between the subsystems, including the psychology of the learner, their learning environment, and their progress (de Bot *et al.*, 2007).

Methodology of an Illustrative CDST Study of the Psychology of L2 Listening

This section outlines the methodology of a study that has built on listening research and adopted a CDST approach to understanding listening development. This research project aimed to discover more about the developmental trajectory of L2 French, within the setting of an English comprehensive school classroom in the UK. In keeping with the tenets of CDST, it took a longitudinal approach, collecting data over three academic years, from the beginning of secondary school (start of Year 7), until the end of compulsory modern languages education in the UK (end of Year 9). One hundred and five participants (four classes of 26 or 27 students each) participated in a battery of tests at the end of each half term, and additionally immediately after the school summer holidays in Years 8 and 9, meaning six data collection points throughout Year 7, and seven data collection points in Years 8 and 9.

Two students from each of the four classes were selected as case studies – four boys and four girls. They were selected to give as wide a range as possible of learning experiences from the cohort, and hence ranged in academic abilities, motivation and linguistic backgrounds within the educational cohort. The eight case studies were presented independently, with the whole-cohort quantitative data setting these eight learners into context. This approach is supported by recent CDST research, which encourages in-depth case studies of individuals within groups, as 'longitudinal case studies of L2 development are useful methods to provide complementary information about the process of development' (Lowie & Verspoor, 2018: 20). In their study, Lowie and Verspoor (2018) showed distinctly individual patterns of development of individuals within groups of highly similar learners, showing both sets of data to be necessary to understand the dynamic processes of language development over time.

The example study aimed to explore the relationship between the 'whole' of listening comprehension and a range of its contributory elements, as dictated by a selection of theories of listening. The CDST approach is illustrated in Figure 9.1.

Given that the study investigates how listening comprehension develops, or grows, the plant analogy is one to which we return again and again. Although the primary research interest is in the growth of the plant (listening comprehension) as a whole, the researcher also wanted to understand the complex, dynamic relationship between a range of elements, many of them psychological. The leaves represent the theoretical subsystems which make up L2 listening. However, just as the type of soil and size of pot plays a role in the plant's growth, other factors influence the growing medium within the classroom: these are illustrated on the plant pot. And as a plant will also not grow without light and water, so similar nutrients will influence the growth of learning. For these reasons, broader elements such as school life, home life and affect are included on the lamp to illustrate the wider learning environment, which may accelerate or decelerate development.

It is worth noting that each one of these factors (the growing medium, the interaction between food and water, even the number of leaves or the leaf size) could be seen as a complex dynamic system itself, and any complexity researcher needs to be cognisant of this fact (Larsen-Freeman & Cameron, 2008a). Equally, though, researchers need to define the complex dynamic system appropriate to their research based on the current literature. The model depicted in Figure 9.1 is the outcome of establishing such boundaries.

Figure 9.1 Growth in listening comprehension as conceptualized by a plant, its soil and its nutrients

As we have seen above, the current literature states many different influences on the psychology of listening comprehension. Furthermore, it suggests that different variables may have different levels of influence for different people or at different times (see Vandergrift & Baker, 2015, 2018). Bearing this in mind, when aiming to track the developmental trajectory, CDST becomes a natural fit: its basic requirements are explicitly to include time and change through many iterations of data collection, to capture continuously interacting variables over time, and to measure variability between individuals (Ortega & Han, 2017).

In addition to tests of listening development, vocabulary size and grammatical knowledge, of primary concern for the present chapter is a range of data collection tools that aimed to illuminate the impact of psychological elements on L2 listening development over time. These were, at each of 20 time points:

- the Metacognitive Awareness Listening Questionnaire (Vandergrift *et al.*, 2006), a well-established instrument with questions which probe problem-solving, planning and evaluation, mental translation, person knowledge and directed attention – given to all 105 participants;
- a self-report self-efficacy questionnaire, with a five-point Likert scale illustrated with emojis, exploring participants' feelings about school, French, French listening and the relationships between them – give to all 105 participants;
- a reverse digit span test delivered face to face to the eight interviewees.

Further to this, semi-structured interviews were also conducted as soon as possible after each test battery had been completed with the eight case study students in order to probe L2 listening experiences, and factors influencing both learning and performance during the tests. While traditional or reductionist approaches to research would prefer not to begin to probe the impact on second language acquisition (SLA) of, say, an argument with a best friend, worries about a maths test or problems at home, such elements are crucial from a CDST perspective. If we are aiming to look back with the benefit of hindsight, to pinpoint key turning points in a learner's journey, we need to collect these data; only at the end of the data collection period can we decide whether it is simply noise in the data, or more significant sound (Marin & Peltzer-Karpf, 2009). Herein lies a key element in which we embrace the messiness of classroom research in terms of the emotional lives of the learners – and given that CDST is a theory of process rather than product (Caspi & Lowie, 2013), it is important to accept that change in the global construct (in this case L2 listening development) is caused by how different subsystems interact.

Challenges Associated with a CDST Approach to Researching the Psychology of L2 Listening

Using the methodology of the above study as an illustration of a CDST approach to L2 listening research, we now turn to a discussion of the challenges associated with adopting a complexity methodology. A criticism frequently levelled at CDST research is where one draws boundaries around what to include in the research. If we draw a boundary, does this mean that we are no longer embracing our complex, dynamic system? Just as we note that Dong's (2016) study was limited in its boundaries around researching only strategies, is the above study equally limited in the constructs it has included, or more importantly not included? Have we simply tried to have our cake and eat it in terms of saying we have a complex system while following more reductionist models? Furthermore, when situating our research within the inevitably messy context of a classroom, it can be hard to know what data to collect and analyse, and what to leave behind.

One perspective which goes some way to solving this problem is to define a primary area of interest (in this case, L2 listening development), but accept that secondary areas of interest will intersect with these and influence them, possibly in unpredictable ways. The classroom is where the learning takes place, and so what is brought into the classroom – by the learners or the teachers – also needs to be investigated (Larsen-Freeman & Cameron, 2008b). One starts by referring to a range of psychological theories to anticipate what might influence classroom learning, and applying a pragmatic approach as to what kind of data are feasible to collect, cross-referencing this with theoretical models. Later on, at the data analysis stage, this should allow the researcher to look for explanations for unusual findings in the data. While it is impossible for CDST approaches to incorporate all possible elements that may influence the phenomena being researched, this should not prevent researchers from making research-informed decisions about what is essential to include within the methodological parameters of their study.

Researching L2 listening brings with it challenges of its own: listening is an inevitably psychological process, taking place as it does wholly within the mind. Any form of assessing what a listener (be it L1 or L2) has heard is reduced to a proxy – be it a dictation exercise, a comprehension test or a standardized psychometric measure. When taking a CDST approach one must take great care that tests of all subsystems (in this case psychological tests of working memory, metacognition and self-efficacy), as well as the tests of listening themselves, are as robust as possible, in order to ensure the rigour of the quantitative findings. During the data collection period of the present study, it became ever clearer that the qualitative data provided by the eight case studies were the backbone of the project: during the interviews the researcher was able to discuss what these eight learners had produced in online tests and probe the educational and emotional psychology of what the participants said, as well as referring back to what had been said in previous interviews. As a result, the qualitative data collection was able to capture additional psychological constructs such as personality, and affective factors such as anxiety.

With regard to the specific psychological tests, several challenges became apparent during data collection. Working memory tests (reverse digit span) were initially administered to the full cohort of 105 participants as part of the online tests: participants would hear a series of numbers, and then (on a new screen) be asked to input what they had heard via the computer. It became clear after four tests that an array of strategies was being used to boost results, necessitating a shift in the mode of delivery of the test. The MALQ has also presented an interesting psychological challenge in that sometimes the eight case study participants will contradict their MALQ statements in face-to-face interviews. Nevertheless, the CDST approach goes some way towards mitigating such contradictions by dint of the many time points, by which we can establish the extent to which a contradiction was indeed nothing more than noise in the system. In other words, this approach accepts the messiness in the system and works with it rather than against it.

A further psychological challenge associated with the CDST methodology is the effects of test fatigue by participants due to the high frequency of the tests, which may also result in a raised awareness of the research constructs. There may be an influence of the data collection procedure on the data itself – that is, the extent to which inclusion in the study will create a Hawthorne Effect, where the very act of observation changes behaviour. In our illustrative example, participants and class teachers could start to think more deeply about L2 listening and skills, and the repetition of the strategy questionnaire might have given participants ideas as to the kinds of strategies they could apply during listening. In CDST research, it is important to be aware of such issues, and unfortunately there is no way to avoid them. Instead a researcher should aim to collect data on their potential influence to shed some light on the extent to which the Hawthorne Effect impacted the data. Indeed, preliminary data analysis after the first year of data collection appears to suggest that most of the eight case-study participants are becoming more aware of their listening skills and progress than the rest of the cohort, but there is no suggestion that the repetition of the strategy questionnaire for the full cohort of 105 learners is influencing their strategy use in class.

A final challenge of CDST methodology is that complexities of data collection methods will inevitably be transferred to complexities in analysis of data. In studies that aim to explore case studies within the context of a whole-cohort dataset, such as our illustrative study and that of Lowie and Verspoor (2018), this can often require a mixed-methods analysis of the subsystems within the case studies and the group. Data from multiple constructs collected at multiple timepoints will often require advanced procedures to deal with the large volume. In our illustrative study, quantitative analysis on the whole-cohort data, focusing on variability, trends and interactions over time (Cross & Vandergrift, 2015; Lowie, 2017) of the most important subsystems, means that traditional methods of statistical analysis, which view learning as linear, become incompatible with the data. Other advanced techniques such as Generalized Additive Mixed Models analysis are more appropriate, coded through the use of the statistical package R (Lowie, 2017).

In the case studies of the illustrative research project it was also important to examine the extent to which the change in different subsystems was co-adaptive: this could be complementary (in which both grow), or competitive (in which one grows while the other shrinks. In research like this, there might also be situations in which two subsystems become uncoupled (Lowie, 2013; van Geert & van Dijk, 2002), that is to say, previous relationships between two subsystems might cease at a certain point in development. All of this complexity poses a challenge during data analysis, but if carried out well, can paint a more accurate and nuanced picture of L2 learning development over time, alongside the development of the psychological constructs measured at multiple time points.

Conclusions: CDST as Ecologically valid Research

It is expected that CDST approaches to language learning development within classroom settings will indeed be 'messy' – that is, different subsystems will flourish or recede, and progress is unlikely to be linear. It will also be expected that different individuals will go about learning in different ways, depending both on their learning environment and their own language learning psychology. In studies such as the one outlined in this chapter, the CDST approach might reveal that the learner's psychology becomes an increasingly important variable within learning as the highly motivated, and possibly also more able learner enters a virtuous circle in which their learning accelerates and boosts their motivation. This contrasts with the struggling learner, who loses motivation and experiences a vicious circle in which their lack of progress results in diminishing motivation, which in turn leads to further loss of progress. However, it might also become apparent that there are markedly different paths to success, some of which might depend upon other context-related variables, such as relationship with the teacher or other class members. By taking a case study within a whole-cohort approach, where many potentially influential constructs are measured over a long period of time, CDST research aims to achieve a more holistic understanding of this process.

CDST is gaining increasing interest in fields of language learner psychology at a conceptual level, but we need more examples of studies that put these ideas into methodological practice. In the field of language learning strategy research, for example, more researchers accept that learning cannot be isolated into discrete constructs, nor can individuals be isolated from their contexts and groups. Rose (2015: 424) argues that 'a researcher must embrace this complexity when setting up a study to ensure findings are situated in the context being studied'. This theoretical development is also supported by others in strategy research such as Oxford (2017) and Oxford et al. (2018), but we are yet to see the fruits of such research across diverse aspects of learning: the cognitive, the social and the psychological.

Perhaps researchers have shied away from CDST methods in classroom research due to their seeming messiness, especially when classroomresearch in itself is already perceived to be a messy endeavour (McArthur, 2012). However, we argue that CDST as methodological framework offers researchers a way to capture this messiness, rather than compound it. As CDST aims to explore the intricate relationships between learners and their environments, and the interplay of tangentially related constructs and their subsystems, it can offer a solution to tame this messiness for research purposes. To try to compartmentalize research could be said, in fact, to be a somewhat unreliable account of the complexities of the learning process itself. Thus, a CDST approach offers a truer account of the learning contexts we aim to investigate. Despite the inevitable complexity of CDST research methods, it is nonetheless worthwhile. The challenges surrounding a CDST research method are the very reasons that make it a more authentic and ecologically rich approach.

References

Anderson, J.R. (1990) *Cognitive Psychology and its Implications*. New York: WH Freeman.

Andringa, S., Olsthoorn, N., Van Beuningen, C.G., Schoonen, R. and Hulstijn, J. (2012) Determinants of success in native and non-native listening comprehension: An individual differences approach. *Language Learning* 62 (SUPPL. 2), 49–78. https://doi.org/10.1111/j.1467-9922.2012.00706.x

Baddeley, A. (2012) Working memory: Theories, models, and controversies. *Annual Review of Psychology* 63 (1), 1–29. https://doi.org/10.1146/annurev-psych-120710-100422

Bandura, A. (1993) Perceived self-efficacy in cognitive development and functioning. *Educational Psychologist* 28 (2), 117–148.

Caspi, T. and Lowie, W. (2013) The dynamics of L2 vocabulary development: A case study of receptive and productive knowledge A dinâmica do desenvolvimento do vocabulário L2: um. *Revista Brasileira de Linguística Aplicada*, 1–15. https://doi.org/10.1590/S1984-63982013005000002

Cross, J. and Vandergrift, L. (2015) Guidelines for designing and conducting L2 listening studies. *ELT Journal* 69 (1), 86–89. https://doi.org/10.1093/elt/ccu035

de Bot, K., Lowie, W. and Verspoor, M. (2007) A dynamic systems theory approach to second language acquisition. *Bilingualism: Language and Cognition* 10 (01), 7. https://doi.org/10.1017/S1366728906002732

Dong, J. (2016) A dynamic systems theory approach to development of listening strategy use and listening performance. *System* 63, 149–165. https://doi.org/10.1016/j.system.2016.10.004

Dörnyei, Z. (2009) The L2 motivational self system. In Z. Dörnyei and E. Ushioda (eds) *Motivation, Language Identity and the L2 Self* (pp. 9–42). Bristol: Multilingual Matters.

Dörnyei, Z. and Ryan, S. (2015) *The Psychology of the Language Learner Revisited*. Oxford: Oxford University Press.

Field, J. (2013) Cognitive validity. In A. Geranpayeh and L. Taylor (eds) *Examining Listening*. Cambridge: Cambridge University Press.

Gardner, R.C. (1985) *Social Psychology and Language Learning: The Role of Attitudes and Motivation*. London: Edward Arnold Publishers.

Gathercole, S. and Baddeley, A. (1989) Evaluation of the role of phonological STM in the development of vocabulary in children: A longitudinal study. *Journal of Memory and Language* 28 (2), 200–213. https://doi.org/10.1016/0749-596X(89)90044-2

Goh, C. and Kaur, K. (2017) Insights into young learners' metacognitive awareness about listening. *The European Journal of Applied Linguistics and TEFL* 2 (1), 5–26.

Graham, S. (2006) Listening comprehension: The learners' perspective. *System* 34 (2), 165–182. https://doi.org/10.1016/j.system.2005.11.001

Graham, S. (2011) Self-efficacy and academic listening. *Journal of English for Academic Purposes* 10 (2), 113–117. https://doi.org/10.1016/j.jeap.2011.04.001

Graham, S. and Macaro, E. (2007) Designing year 12 strategy training in listening and writing: From theory to practice. *Language Learning Journal* 35 (2), 153–173. https://doi.org/10.1080/09571730701599203

Graham, S. and Macaro, E. (2008) Strategy instruction in listening for low-intermediate learners of French. *Language Learning* 58 (4), 7470783.

Juffs, A. and Harrington, M. (2011) Aspects of working memory in L2 learning. *Language Teaching* 44 (02), 137–166. https://doi.org/10.1017/S0261444810000509

Kormos, J. and Sáfár, A. (2008) Phonological short-term memory, working memory and foreign language performance in intensive language learning. *Bilingualism: Language and Cognition* 11 (2), 261–271.

Kostoulas, A., Stelma, J., Mercer, S., Cameron, L. and Dawson, S. (2017) Complex systems theory as a shared discourse space for TESOL. *TESOL Journal*, 1–15. https://doi.org/10.1002/tesj.317

Larsen-Freeman, D. (2017) Complexity Theory: The lessons continue. In L. Ortega and Z. Han (eds) *Complexity Theory and Language Development* (pp. 11–50). Amsterdam: John Benjamins Publishing Company.

Larsen-Freeman, D. and Cameron, L. (2008a) *Complex Systems and Applied Linguistics*. Oxford: Oxford University Press.

Larsen-Freeman, D. and Cameron, L. (2008b) Research methodology on language development from a complex systems perspective. *The Modern Language Journal* 92, 200–213. https://doi.org/10.1111/j.1540-4781.2008.00714.x

Linck, J.A., Hughes, M.M., Campbell, S.G., Silbert, N.H., Tare, M., Jackson, S.R. and Doughty, C.J. (2013) Hi-LAB: A new measure of aptitude for high-level language proficiency. *Language Learning* 63 (3), 530–566.

Lowie, W. (2013) Dynamic systems theory approaches to second language acquisition. In C. Chappelle (ed.) *The Encyclopaedia of Applied Linguistics*. Chichester: Wiley.

Lowie, W. (2017) Lost in state space? Methodological considerations in Complex Dynamic Theory approaches to second language development research. In L. Ortega and Z. Han (eds) *Complexity Theory and Language Development* (pp. 123–141). Amsterdam: John Benjamins Publishing Company.

Lowie, W. and Verspoor, M. (2018) Individual differences and the ergodicity problem. *Language Learning* 69 (S1), 184–206.

Macaro, E. (2006) Strategies for language learning and for language use: Revising the theoretical framework. *The Modern Language Journal* 90 (3), 320–337. https://doi.org/10.1111/j.1540-4781.2006.00425.x

Mackey, A. and Gass, S. (2005) *Second Language Research Methodology and Design*. New York: Routledge.

Marin, M.M. and Peltzer-Karpf, A. (2009) Towards a dynamic systems approach to the development of language and music: Theoretical foundations and methodological issues. *Proceedings of the 7th Triennial Conference of European Society for the Cognitive Sciences of Music (ESCOM 2009) Jyväskylä, Finland* (Escom), pp. 284–292.

Marsden, E. and Kasprowicz, R. (2018) Foreign language educators' exposure to research: Reported experiences, exposure via citations, and a proposal for action. *The Modern Language Journal* 101 (4), 613–642.

McArthur, J. (2012) Virtuous mess and wicked clarity: Struggle in higher education research. *Higher Education Research & Development* 31 (3), 419–430.

McKinley, J. (2019) Evolving the TESOL teaching research nexus. *TESOL Quarterly* 53 (3), 875–884.

Mercer, S. (2016) Complexity and language teaching. In *The Routledge Handbook of English Language Teaching* (pp. 473–485). Abingdon: Routledge.

Mills, N., Pajares, F. and Herron, C.A. (2006) A reevaluation of the role of anxiety: Self-efficacy, anxiety, and their relation to reading and listening proficiency. *Foreign Language Annals* 39 (2), 276–295. https://doi.org/10.1111/j.1944-9720.2006.tb02266.x

Miyake, A. and Friedman, N. (1998) Individual differences in second language proficiency: Working memory as language aptitude. In A.F. Healy and L.E. Bourne (eds) *Foreign Language Learning: Psycholinguistic Studies on Training and Retention* (pp. 339–364). Mahwah, NJ: Lawrence Erlbaum Associates.

Multon, K.D., Brown, S.D. and Lent, R.W. (1991) The relation of self-efficacy beliefs to academic outcomes: A meta-analytic investigation. *Journal of Counselling Psychology* 38, 30–38.

Ortega, L. and Han, Z. (eds) (2017) Introduction. In L. Ortega and Z. Han (eds) *Complexity Theory and Language Development* (pp. 1–10). Amsterdam: John Benjamins Publishing Company.

Oxford, R. (2017) *Teaching and Researching Language Learning Strategies: Self-Regulation in Context*. New York: Routledge.

Oxford, R.L., Lavine, R.Z. and Amerstorfer, C. (2018) Understanding language learning strategies in context: An innovative, complexity-based approach. In R. Oxford and C.M. Amerstorfer (eds) *Language Learning Strategies and Individual Learner Characteristics: Situating Strategy use in Diverse Contexts*. London: Bloomsbury.

Rose, H. (2015) Researching language learner strategies. In B. Paltridge and A. Phakiti (eds) *Research Methods in Applied Linguistics: A Practical Resource* (pp. 421–437). New York: Bloomsbury.

Rose, H. (2019) Dismantling the ivory tower in TESOL: A renewed call for teaching-informed research. *TESOL Quarterly* 53 (3), 895–905.

Rose, H. and McKinley, J. (2017) The realities of doing research in applied linguistics. In J. McKinley and H. Rose (eds) *Doing Research in Applied Linguistics: Realities, Challenges and Solutions*. Abingdon: Routledge.

Schoonen, R., Hulstijn, J. and Bossers, B. (1998) Metacognitive and language-specific knowledge in native and foreign language reading comprehension: An empirical study among Dutch students in grades 6, 8 and 10. *Language Learning* 48 (1), 71–106.

Sealey, A. and Carter, B. (2004) *Applied Linguistics as Social Science*. London: Continuum.

van Geert, P. and van Dijk, M. (2002) Focus on variability: New tools to study intra-individual variability in developmental data. *Infant Behaviour and Development* 25 (25), 340–374. https://doi.org/10.1016/S0163-6383(02)00140-6

Vandergrift, L. and Baker, S. (2015) Learner variables in second language listening comprehension: An exploratory path analysis. *Language Learning* 65 (2), 390–416. https://doi.org/10.1111/lang.12105

Vandergrift, L. and Baker, S. (2018) Learner variables important for success in L2 listening comprehension in French immersion classrooms. *The Canadian Modern Language Review* 74 (1), 79–100.

Vandergrift, L., Goh, C.C.M., Mareschal, C. and Tafaghodtari, M.H. (2006) The metacognitive awareness listening questionnaire: Development and validation. *Language Learning* 56 (3), 431–462.

Vandergrift, L. and Goh, C.C.M. (2012) *Teaching and Learning Second Language Listening: Metacognition in Action*. New York: Routledge. Retrieved from http://ezproxy.msu.edu/login?url=http://search.proquest.com/docview/1315888878?accountid=12598 http://za2uf4ps7f.search.serialssolutions.com/?ctx_ver=Z39.88-2004&ctx_enc=info:ofi/enc:UTF-8&rfr_id=info:sid/ProQ%3Allbashell&rft_val_fmt=info:ofi/fmt:kev:mtx:

Wen, Z.E., Biedroń, A. and Skehan, P. (2017) Foreign language aptitude theory: Yesterday, today and tomorrow. *Language Teaching* 50 (1), 1–31.

Xu, F. (2011) Anxiety in EFL listening comprehension. *Theory and Practice in Language Studies* 12 (1), 1709–1717.

10 Equifinality Approach to Exploring the Learning Trajectories of Language Learners and Teachers

Takumi Aoyama and Takenori Yamamoto

In this chapter, we introduce an innovative approach to researching the complexity of language learner and teacher psychology. We outline a retrospective tool that adapts the Trajectory Equifinality Approach (Sato *et al.*, 2009 – hereafter TEA; see also glossary at the end of this chapter for a list of acronyms used in TEA), originally developed in the field of cultural psychology and applied to various disciplines. Although we describe the key concepts and theoretical underpinnings of TEA briefly, we put more emphasis on *how* we can profitably utilize TEA in studies on language learner and teacher psychology. Therefore, we will first review how TEA fits into current language learner and teacher psychology research and complexity theory (complex dynamic systems theory (CDST)), and then draw upon our own studies (Aoyama, 2016; Yamamoto, 2018) as examples of how we can apply TEA to a research project. Furthermore, for future applications of TEA in language learner and teacher psychology research, we reflect on and discuss our experience using TEA. Since TEA is a relatively new research methodology in language learning and teaching research and was originally developed by a group of researchers based in Japan, there are not many resources on TEA written in English in this field. As such, we aim to provide a comprehensive overview of TEA in light of the CDST paradigm. However, since space does not allow a comprehensive review of both CDST and TEA, we will briefly overview retrospective approaches to the psychology of language learning and teaching in CDST and their conceptual similarity to TEA.

Tracing Dynamics of Language Learner/Teacher Psychology

Ever since the introduction of CDST into applied linguistics by Larsen-Freeman (1997), there has been a great shift in the perspectives of research. Particularly, studies on language learner and teacher psychology have seen a steady development in approaches and perspectives, and there are growing numbers of studies applying CDST in the discipline (Dörnyei *et al.*, 2015). CDST has its origins in mathematical and physical sciences, and places emphasis on the interactions of multiple elements that are interconnected but acting independently, and the changes mediated by these interactions (Dörnyei, 2014). Compared to the conventional approaches used in past decades (e.g. the social-psychological and cognitive-situated periods in L2 motivation research) which looked at the generalizability and universality of language learner psychology, CDST focuses more on the individual and continuously changing nature of psychological elements in language learning and teaching.

However, while the idea of CDST has been broadly discussed by researchers in the field, concrete methods to investigate complex and dynamic aspects of language learner and teacher psychology still require further refinement. Researchers in the field are trying to develop and introduce many innovative research approaches suitable for the complexity paradigm. For instance, Larsen-Freeman and Cameron (2008) proposed an approach called Complexity Thought Modeling, which is formed of 16 steps. More concretely, some methods such as the idiodynamic method (MacIntyre, 2012; MacIntyre & Serroul, 2015) have been advanced to measure micro-level changes in psychological dimensions with the help of technology such as computer software specially designed for the investigation.

From a broader perspective, taking a longitudinal approach is one common way to capture the complexities in learner psychology (e.g. Lamb, 2009; Nitta, 2013). Longitudinal research designs have advantages when a researcher seeks 'satisfactory answers to questions concerning the dynamics and the determinants of individual behaviour' (Ruspini, 2002: 71). However, longitudinal studies require time and cost for data collection, particularly when the study focuses on phenomena which take place over a long period of time (e.g. psychological changes of a learner over 10 years). Also, researcher effects need to be considered when taking a longitudinal approach, especially in classroom settings. For instance, in Lamb's (2018) research, he reunited with a group of Indonesian people who participated in his PhD project for a follow-up study after 10 years. Although he was not aware of his own past impact on research participants while collecting data, the follow-up study found that some participants had been motivated by the presence of the researcher and interactions they had during interviews ten years prior. Thus, research activity itself could become a factor which mediates changes in a system, and we must carefully consider the effects of research on participants in longitudinal investigations.

Another approach to exploring complexity in language learner and teacher psychology, which we focus on in this chapter, is retrospective. In retrospective research designs, contrary to those conducted longitudinally, data collection relies on the participants' memories of past events experienced. As characterized in Dörnyei's (2014) retrodictive qualitative modelling (RQM), retrospective tracing of a complex and dynamic system is one approach that can successfully depict human development. Hiver (2017: 677) noted 'the ultimate goal of the RQM research design is to identify the complex causal mechanisms that led a system to produce a particular outcome (i.e. the signature dynamics)'. To give an example, we would use the well-known quote from the title of Edward Lorenz's talk:

'Does the flap of a butterfly's wings in Brazil set off a Tornado in Texas?'

(Title of a talk given by Edward Lorenz on December 29, 1972)

A complex dynamic system's behavior and outcomes are sensitive to its initial conditions; a slight difference in the system's initial conditions can lead to a huge difference in the final state of the system, as a result of the complex interactions among the system's elements (e.g. de Bot *et al.*, 2007). Then, drawing upon the viewpoint of retrospective research, what if we focus on the outcome of a system – 'a tornado in Texas' – first, and then trace phenomena back to 'the flap of a butterfly's wings in Brazil'? To put it differently, in the context of language learning, what if we observe a learner's current psychological profile (e.g. at the age of 20) first, and retrospectively review events back to the very first day of his or her language learning? What we address in this chapter is an approach which allows us to trace back the complex and dynamic process of psychological changes.

Trajectory Equifinality Approach

TEA aims to depict people's experience, focusing on the notion of 'equifinality' in a system. According to Sato *et al.* (2009: 228):

> Equifinality is the principle that in open systems a given end state can be reached by many potential means. It emphasizes that the same end state may be achieved through many different means, paths and trajectories. Variability of trajectories means richness of life.

A certain point of life which people equally reach is called the 'equifinal point' (EFP). With TEA, we focus on people's life course (i.e. trajectories) to such points, and attempt to figure out how people made decisions that evolved into such trajectories. Studies using TEA can describe the trajectories from different points of view, such as historical, cultural or social. The framework of TEA also gives clear directions for how to decide upon appropriate research participants, how to analyse verbal data and how to explore participants' behaviors and thoughts that are interconnected with each other. This approach focuses on common events and experiences through which the trajectories of people with the same or similar EFPs pass, and visualizes similarities in the human life course, as well as variabilities.

Thus, what TEA looks at is conceptually similar to some aspects of CDST, namely, attractor states and self-organization. In CDST, an attractor is an area of stability to which a dynamic system settles as a result of the components' interactions; self-organization is the process of interactions through which the components of a system gradually develop towards an attractor state (Valsiner, 2005; for more about self-organization and attractors, see Hiver, 2015). In other words, TEA traces the process of self-organization back from an attractor state by identifying signature dynamics at common passage points.

TEA is composed of three key components: Trajectory Equifinality Model (TEM); Historically Structured Sampling (HSS); and Three Layers Model of Genesis (TLMG). Each element has different roles in the scheme of the TEA, and different combinations of the components can expand the possibilities of analysis. We will discuss this point later by looking at two examples from our own studies that combine different components of TEA.

Trajectory equifinality model

TEM is the key component of TEA. Sato and Valsiner (2010) developed TEM in order to treat 'lived time' in developmental psychological research, in contrast to the 'clock time' which experimental psychologists use in their research. TEM is a methodology which 'emphasizes the multiplicity of human life course trajectories' (Kullasepp, 2011: 218). TEM visualizes the dynamics of human development by identifying commonalities in the varied emergent trajectories in different people's lives. It enables us to see people's developmental process in lived time and the diversity of life course. In the developmental models, TEM uses the following subconcepts: EFP, Obligatory Passage Point (OPP), Polarized Equifinality Point (P-EFP), Bifurcation Point (BFP), Social Direction (SD), Social Guidance (SG) and Irreversible Time (Figure 10.1).

Equifinality point and polarized EFP

EFP is a point at which individual trajectories of development may converge, and from which they diverge after passing (Kullasepp, 2011). The EFP may have important meanings for some people since their experiences are similar at this point, and since their trajectories to reach the EFP may differ from each other. We usually set the EFP based on our research focuses or research questions. For example, we may define an EFP as 'starting to learn a foreign language other than English' based on the research question 'what is a turning point for language learners to start learning a foreign language other than English?' We easily understand that many people might share this EFP, but that their pathways to the EFP will no doubt vary.

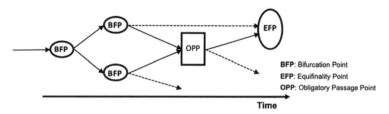

Figure 10.1 General idea of Trajectory Equifinality Model (adapted from Sato, Yasuda Kanzaki & Valsiner, 2014, with modifications)

P-EFP is a complementary set of EFP (Sato *et al.*, 2009). Psychology research tends to focus on something a person has done, and pays less attention to something a person has not done. TEM dares to put emphasis on both what people have and have not done. That is, it can work to make what people have done clearer by investigating what they have not done. One example of the relationship between EFP and P-EFP can be seen in Nishimura and Ito's (2017) study. They investigated how novice elementary school teachers overcome difficulties they face. They set an EFP as the desire to continue with confidence as a home economics teacher for a second year, and a P-EFP as the loss of confidence in continuing as a home economics teacher. Without P-EFP, they might not have thought about how the research participant behaved when they were trying to move away from the difficulties they face. A P-EFP gives us a sense of direction which shows how people behave when they do not successfully approach the EFP. In other words, we are able to identify the person's behavior in the trajectories toward the EFP as divergent behavior to reach the P-EFP. When building a TEM model, we put EFP and P-EFP on a vertical axis, and it helps to show that a research participant is approaching either EFP or P-EFP.

Obligatory passage point and bifurcation point

According to Sato *et al.* (2009), OPP is a concept originally developed in geopolitics. To give an example in the context of sailing, we can say that the Strait of Gibraltar is an OPP when we want to sail from the Atlantic Ocean to the Mediterranean Sea as fast as possible (Sato *et al.*, 2009). In regard to TEM, OPP is an event people obligatorily go through as part of their trajectories up to the EFP. However, it is important to be aware that the word 'obligatory' in OPP is understood as an adjective which indicates most people rather than all people. Another subconcept representing events in human life, BFP, is a point where people's trajectories diverge, and various or alternative pathways appear in their following trajectories. When people face multiple choices in their life course, they need to choose one of them, and the point at which they make such decisions is presented as a BFP in the TEM model. After a BFP (i.e. after making decisions), trajectories move closer to either the EFP or P-EFP, or perhaps stay in the middle of the EFP and P-EFP.

Social direction and guidance

EFP, BFP and OPP concern particular events which people experience in their developmental processes. Two more concepts, SD and SG, relate to the effects of social or cultural influences on one's decision-making processes or psychological changes, particularly the events identified as OPPs or BFPs. Sato *et al.* (2009: 230) explain that:

> [s]ocial direction derives the notion of directed social cultural power. It might be said that the 'common sense' provides tradition, social norm and social pressure. On the other hand, SG is the power of defence against the social direction. SG is the power supplied from the intimate persons such as a family, friends, teacher and others. Simply speaking, SD is defined as the power of inhibition to go to EFP, and SG is defined as the power of promotion to go to EFP.

Irreversible time

Last but not least, the idea of Irreversible Time is a particular concept of time underlying TEM which reflects 'lived time'. In TEM, we exclude the idea of 'length' in time (e.g. minute, hour, day, week ...) when considering people's life course. Although people may experience the same series of events and go through the events in the same order in their life trajectories, they do not necessarily experience the events simultaneously. We can understand this concept through an example of the process of departing from an airport. We usually go through check-in, security check and border control after arriving at the airport, and then go to the departure gates. This order is not changeable due to the manner of the airport, but the timing of each event may vary, depending on the individual. Some people go to the check-in counter earlier because they do not wish to queue for a long time; others do so much later perhaps because they do not care about such things. Similarly, after border control, some people may spend a longer time before proceeding to the departure gate since they like duty-free shopping, while others may pass through more quickly as they do not like shopping. This example illustrates that even though events at an airport emerge in the same order, despite people's intentions to arrive at the same goal these events come up at different times based on people's own decision-making processes. In the TEM model, Irreversible Time is represented as a horizontal arrow to show the flow of time without the idea of length.

Historically structured invitation (or sampling)

TEA adopts a unique sampling procedure, Historically Structured Invitation (HSI: Valsiner & Sato, 2006; or sometimes called Historically Structured Sampling). HSI is a type of theoretical sampling and is different from common sampling methods used for quantitative inquiries, such as random sampling, practice-based sampling and representative sampling. Valsiner and Sato (2006) contend that sampling in the context of human psychology does not have to represent a population, but it needs to reflect the cultural history of individuals. In TEA, cultural history has strong connections to EFP. Thus, researchers often choose participants based on the EFP they set. If there is someone who has experience of the EFP event, we can ask the person to join the study. Naturally, we understand that there may be concerns that this type of sampling is too subjective. In the norm of statistical sampling, researchers try to find a 'true value' that is common among people, and human variation is considered as 'error'. Therefore, in statistical approaches, one needs to decide samples randomly in order to keep the errors as small as possible. However, qualitative inquiries regard human variation as the result of human development or life course, and researchers work to describe variations in the context of individuals' lives. With HSI, we ask people with a certain experience to be research participants so that we are able to gain insights to life trajectories more effectively.

In addition, Arakawa *et al.* (2012) recommended, based on their experience of TEA research, the number of participants we should select in HSI. As a rule of thumb, they suggest one, four or nine participants: Data collected from one participant can reveal the deep background of his or her trajectory, data from four people can allow description of a diversity of trajectories and data from nine people can illustrate a pattern of trajectories among participants.

Three-layer model of genesis

The third concept of TEA, TLMG, is 'a framework for understanding the transactional nature of signs as they are organized into a working in dialogical system of self at the levels of microgenesis, mesogenesis and ontogenesis' (Sato *et al.*, 2014: 98). Sato *et al.* (2009: 236) explain:

> At the lowest level, micro genetic level, the process of Aktualgenese (this German word was translated into English 'microgenesis' by Heinz Werner) is constantly at work. But in macro genetic—that of ontogenetic—level nothing needs to change. It is in between the two levels—the mesogenetic level where changes are consolidated to be either taken as novelties to the macrogenetic level, or become regulators ('promoter signs') of the microgenetic processes.

TLMG encourages us to look at and understand activities more deeply, particularly the decision-making process at BFPs. When people face different options at a BFP and have to choose one of them (which is observed at the microgenetic level), signs emerge at the mesogenetic level. At the ontogenetic level, the signs are sometimes selected and become a part of the structures of this level. In other words, the values of the individual are formed. These values guide the person in his or her life course, which in turn appears as his or her behavior at the microgenetic level. Therefore, TLMG prompts us to figure out why individuals choose a certain pathway at BFP based on their values and signs in each level (for more on TLMG in language learner psychology research, see Yashima & Arano, 2015).

Doing TEM: Our Own Studies

In this section, we review the use of TEM in language learning research drawing on the data from two of our own studies, Aoyama (2016) and Yamamoto (2018), including re-analysed interpretation from the original reference. To familiarize readers with the procedure for doing TEA, we present some step-by-step graphical examples of how to build a TEM.

Aoyama[1] (2016)

The first study, Aoyama (2016), utilized TEM to understand Japanese returnees' adaptation processes when re-entering the Japanese educational setting, particularly from the viewpoint of psychological changes in their English learning. In the study, I adopted TEM and HSS for data collection and analysis to interpret the commonalities among returnees' experiences in their developmental processes. TLMG was not considered. In addition to TEM, in-depth qualitative analysis of narratives was performed, so that the data could be understood more deeply. However, the focus of this section is the part of the research project which utilized TEA.

The research questions emerged from my own experience as a returnee. Returnees are people who have lived outside Japan (usually because of their parents' jobs) and returned before the age of 20. They are now regarded as one social category in Japanese society. I was born and grew up in Japan but spent some period of time outside Japan (Canada and England) in my childhood due to my parents' work circumstances. Thus, my standpoint in the study was not only as a researcher, but also a person who shares the common experience of 'being a returnee' to Japan. For that reason, my reflexive background as a returnee played an important role during data collection and the analysis period. HSI was adapted to the selection of participants who had experience in facing problems and hardships while studying in Japan after moving back. Also, EFP was set at the point when 'participants with returnee experience had overcome difficulties and adapted themselves in the Japanese environment'. The study sought to explore how returnees' processes of adaptation after moving back to Japan are mediated by social and cultural factors to which they are exposed in their daily lives, particularly in relation to classroom language learning. To interpret the dynamic process of their psychological changes, an in-depth analysis of their stories, as well as modeling of their experience using TEA were combined.

The study was originally performed in 2016 as my MA dissertation project, inviting three Japanese returnees studying at a university in the

Tokyo metropolitan area as participants. As mentioned earlier, the number of participants recommended for TEM research is one, four or nine (Arakawa *et al.*, 2012). I originally planned to analyse the stories of four returnees, but one of the potential participants was not able to join the actual interview sessions and thus I decided to proceed with three participants. However, since the ideal number of participants are the rule of thumb, data from three participants can still present diversities in trajectories. Data were collected through sets of semi-structured interviews asking mainly about the participants' stories associated with their school experiences and experiences in studying English before and after returning to Japanese schools. Collected data were first qualitatively analysed in accordance with the framework of thematic coding proposed by Mann (2016). After this initial analysis, I developed a TEM, which visually represents the complex and dynamic aspects of psychological changes and interactions between participants' internal (i.e. psychological) factors and social forces (i.e. SG/SD).

In the analytical procedure, development of the final TEM model followed a five-step approach as proposed by Arakawa *et al.* (2012):

(1) Segment text data into meaningful topics by each participant.
(2) Place segmented text data of each participant chronologically (Figure 10.2).
(3) Align similar experience vertically, and place by each participant (Figure 10.3).
(4) Place SGs and SDs to each phenomenon.
(5) Put similar items together and add labels (Figure 10.4).

Firstly, data from the series of interviews were segmented and coded, and events each participant experienced were placed chronologically in a

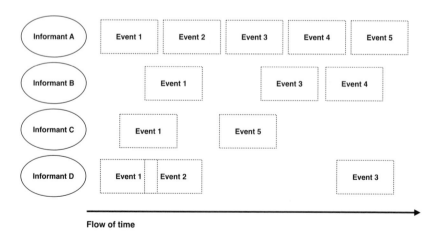

Figure 10.2 Place segmented text data of each participant chronologically

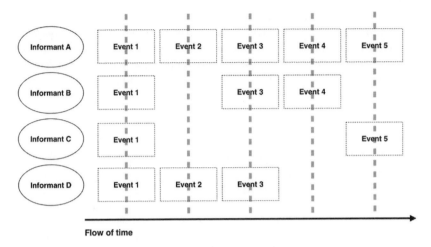

Figure 10.3 Align similar experiences vertically, and place by each participant

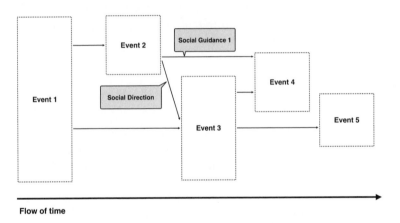

Figure 10.4 Put similar items together and add labels

matrix. Then, on the matrix, I moved each experience horizontally to see if there were any common experiences shared among the participants in the same chronological order. Subsequently, OPPs were selected by drawing upon the common experiences among participants, as well as the theoretical definition of 'returnee' which characterizes the common backgrounds among participants. In the study, the OPPs I selected were those three points at which participants: (1) moved to a foreign country; (2) moved back to Japan; and (3) started studying English in the Japanese educational system. Thus, the assumption was that all three participants would have common experiences related to the three OPPs and an EFP. Furthermore, I selected BFPs, drawing upon commonalities and variabilities observed from the participants' life histories. In addition, my reflexive viewpoints were also included in the identification process of BFPs. Although space is limited, let me show some extracts from the original interview data and their relationships with the BFPs I selected.

The first event related to BFP1 emerged when participants started studying at a school in the countries to which they had moved, and started using English at school. For instance, Maki mentioned:

> I didn't know anything until the first day of my school … plunged into a local school, and it was a survival. (Maki)

After the events related at BFP1, participants all started using English in their daily lives, particularly at school. Encouraging my decision in selecting BFP1, I myself also have the similar experience of encountering the 'all-English' environment on the first day of school outside Japan. The second BFP (BFP2) event was found to be the time when participants realized, after having moved back to Japan, that they are recognized as 'returnees'. For example, Aya apprehended this when she was introduced in front of all students at the 'shigyoushiki', an assembly which takes place at the beginning of every semester in Japanese schools. Typically, all students who have moved from different schools are introduced at such assemblies, but she felt that students' reactions were different when she was introduced:

> All other students who moved into my school with me were from the cities in Japan, for example, Hokkaido. So, I remember everyone started buzzing when I introduced myself that I am from Singapore. (Aya)

After the assembly, her new friends started asking her if she could speak 'Singaporean'. She realized, although not being called a 'returnee' at that point, that people who had lived abroad are treated differently. Similarly, Yui and Maki both expressed feelings of being treated as a returnee when their friends started asking them to translate what their English teachers said in the classroom or tried to make them speak in English. Thus, what we can see here is that all three participants became aware of being returnees (although not directly called returnees at that point) as the people around them reacted differently when they transferred back in to Japanese schools.

The third BFP (BFP3) was the time when participants formally started studying English at school. Participants had all studied English in English-speaking countries (the UK, USA and Singapore), and they already had basic English skills. However, since formal English lessons back in Japan started in junior high school, their levels of English proficiency were already higher than their peers:

> You know, English lessons in Japan start from the alphabet, like apple, ant, but I already knew these basic things, so I could answer all the questions my teacher asked. And my friends were surprised at it. (Aya)

At the same time, BFP3 was found to be interlinked with their confusion in studying English as a school subject, rather than a language. In the exam-oriented nature of the Japanese educational system, English lessons are sometimes criticized for not being communicative (e.g. Ryan & Mercer, 2012). Thus, participants mentioned that they struggled with the examination-oriented language lessons at school that are characterized by grammar-translation or repetitive memorization of vocabulary:

> I realized that studying English only for the entrance examination is meaningless to me, especially the study of kakomon (Note. kakomon is the collection of past test questions which is often used in the preparation for entrance examinations). But I had to study because I wanted to pass the entrance examination to enter university. (Aya)

> I believe that English is one of the languages, and I use languages to express my feelings. So, studying and using English in the same way as mathematics was awkward to me. (Maki)

My interpretations of these excerpts are that both Aya and Maki experienced conflicts between the beliefs toward learning English that were formed through their learning experiences abroad and social forces that were formed in the Japanese sociocultural and educational settings. In the face of conflict, they decided to follow what they were expected to do, while they maintained their own beliefs toward language learning.

The last BFP (BFP4) was the time when participants entered university and 'disentangled' from the Japanese-style English lessons with which they had once felt discomfort. At BFP4, although participants all had different career options, they found their own internalized values of learning and using English, and continued learning English at their own paces:

> Currently, I study English to become a good English teacher in my future career. (Aya)

> Since I want to work in a service industry, I know it should be better if I can speak English, but I don't think I want to use English actively, like going abroad to work. Of course, I would like to go abroad for a trip. (Yui)

Finally, Maki expressed her feelings of being called a returnee in her life, and here we can see the example of how a returnee reaches the EFP I set:

> Everyone is afraid of being regarded as different from other people, and we sometimes have negative feelings about it. But I think we (returnees) are lucky that we have experienced different lives from other people (non-returnees), and we can transform these experiences into a positive force. (Maki)

After identifying four BFPs from the interview data, social forces that affected participants' behavior or a change of mind were labelled as SGs and SDs, and I developed the final model (Figure 10.5), combining the components of TEM identified through the steps mentioned earlier.

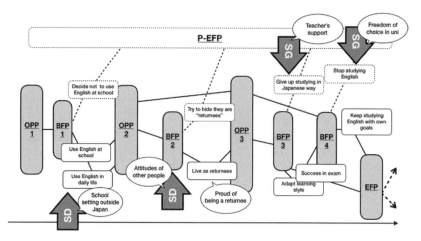

Figure 10.5 Final TEM model (simplified) generated from the data of Aoyama (2016)

As a result of analysis with TEM, my study revealed the process of adaptation among Japanese returnees in relation to English language learning. Each participant expressed different experiences they had in their life, but there were also common experiences shared among all three. All of them faced difficulties when moving back to Japan because they were labelled as 'returnees' by people around them, who regarded them as proficient users of English, even though they felt they were actually not. The way English was taught at their schools was also exam-oriented and conflicted with their beliefs about language learning. However, by the time they became university students, their learning behavior and psychological factors had settled, as a result of interactions between themselves and external social factors.

In alignment with the scope of TEA/TEM, as well as my own interpretations through the lens of someone who experienced similar life events, the key findings of the study fall into the following points. Japanese returnees' psychological adaptation process is mediated by the complex interaction between contextual factors and each person's internal values such as beliefs. Significant dynamics between person and context were found among what returnees developed while they were staying abroad, common social values and beliefs which many non-returnees possess, and ethos in the Japanese educational settings. Thus, although the findings of the study do not necessarily generalize the learning trajectories of returnees, the analysis using TEM highlights the commonalities of trajectories, together with the relationships with their background contextual factors.

From the viewpoint of the variation of learning trajectories, although there are variabilities in developmental trajectories, people may experience the same sets of key milestones as they move toward a state of interest (i.e. EFP/attractor state). To sum up, my example of TEA focused particularly on similarities in common passage points (e.g. BFP and OPP), and diversity in the pathways between common passage points. At the same time, this example suggests that TEA is suitable for studies that take researchers' reflexive perspectives into consideration, as researchers can select EFP, OPPs, BFPs and social forces more intuitively.

Yamamoto (2018)

In this section, 'I' refers to the second author, Takenori Yamamoto. In contrast to the first author's study, my study (Yamamoto, 2018) was driven by a practitioner-oriented research question involving classroom practice. The aim of the study was to investigate participants' learning history of learning English using e-learning system, which were assumed to be complex and dynamic in terms of the interactions between a learner and surrounding factors. In this study, I used TEA so that I might understand a teaching practice for English learning at the college at which I am employed. In this section, I put emphasis on why I implemented TEA for my research interest and how I carried out TEA in order to answer my research question.

I focused on my own first-year experience of implementing an English e-learning system. Due to a high demand for English proficiency at the institution, English teachers are under increasing pressure to foster students' English competence. My colleagues and I were struggling to provide students with opportunities to learn English, and we started an English e-learning system so that students could have more time to learn English outside lessons. The goal of the e-learning was to achieve a certain score in the Test of English for International Communication (TOEIC), a test of English for predominantly business purposes, as well as a designated amount of learning time with e-learning. We monitored students' learning processes and gave some feedback to them. Unfortunately, this practice did not reach our expectations, so we had questions as to why students in our classes did not reach the goal: Whether or not our support for them was sufficient; What environmental factors prevented them from focusing on the e-learning, and so on. We decided to reflect on this practice in order to encourage students who would take the same class the next year.

The other English teachers and I had interests in students' learning processes, learning situations and the effects of teacher support. As a result, we wanted to explore students' learning histories and to figure out the differences of learning between those students who reached the goal and those who did not. What I needed to do at the beginning of TEA was to make a decision on the EFP, select participants based on HSI, and consider OPPs. In line with the research purpose, EFP for a successful participant was 'reaching the goal with e-learning', and that for an unsuccessful participant was 'giving up learning with e-learning'. I also set P-EFPs to 'giving up studying with e-learning' and 'continuing studying with e-learning' respectively. I chose two participants: a male student who reached the goal, and a female student who did not reach the goal. At last, I defined an OPP as 'starting the English e-learning' since I was keen on investigating participants' procedures of e-learning.

The next step involved preparation for data collection and analysis. For the first interview, I prepared three interview items in order to encourage the participants to describe their process, choices, thoughts and backgrounds of their study with e-learning. The items were: 'When and what did you do on the e-learning?', 'What did you think about when using the e-learning?' and 'What happened to you before and during the e-learning?' I asked follow-up questions for further information.

After the first interview, I started building TEM models. In the first step, I divided the transcribed data into different categories such as actions, thoughts, or beliefs of the participants, environmental events around them, and so on. I sorted these pieces of information into chronological order. Following, I prepared the frames of TEM figures (Figure 10.6).

Subsequently, I set layers. I adopted the TLMG for the layers of 'actions and thoughts', 'signs' and 'values and beliefs'. In addition, I placed an additional layer, 'environmental factors', in order to illustrate SD and SG. Above Layer 1 'actions and thoughts', a long arrow was added to show the flow of Irreversible Time, and I arranged OPP, EFP and P-EFP in Layer 1 as shown in Figure 10.6. This arrangement was to demonstrate movement of participants' trajectories. Movement from left to right shows the flow of lived time, and movement from top to bottom describes moving

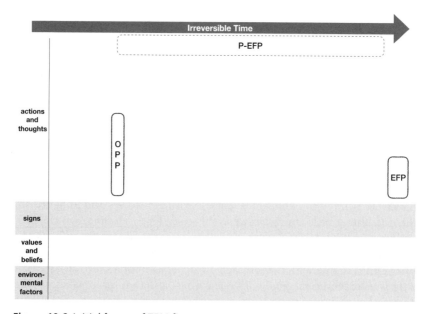

Figure 10.6 Initial frame of TEM figure

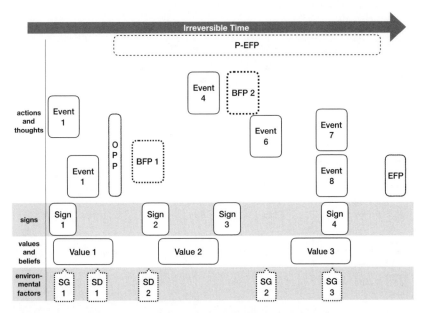

Figure 10.7 TEM figure with events, signs, values and social forces

toward EFP, and vice versa. I then placed additional pieces of information onto the frame of the TEM figure (Figure 10.7).

Drawing on the participants' stories, I identified information which would be placed in each layer (actions and thoughts, signs, and values and beliefs). SD and SG were added to the bottom layer. SD and SG indicate the social/environmental effects on the participants' stories. SD affects in a manner that participants move toward P-EFP. On the other hand, SG encourages participants to make steps forward toward EFP. While I plotted pieces of information on the TEM figures, I categorized some information as BFPs, and arrows showing connections among the three layers were added (Figure 10.8). For example, in Layer 1, I placed 'finding that other students haven't used the e-learning at all'. Also, in Layer 2, 'decreasing one's motivation toward the e-learning' was placed. Furthermore, in Layer 3, I put 'belief that intensive learning is more efficient for him/herself'. I analysed the action 'finding out that other students have not used e-learning system at all' as a BFP because his/her trajectory significantly moved toward P-EFP here. At this point, the belief seemed to have a significant impact on the action and the sign appeared clearly in the story.

After making the first version of the TEM figures, I conducted the second and third round of interviews which put emphasis on exploring the participant's trajectories more deeply, and fixing and confirming the figures. I asked the participants to give comments particularly on the connection between beliefs, signs and actions. At the end of the third interview, I made the final version of the TEM models.

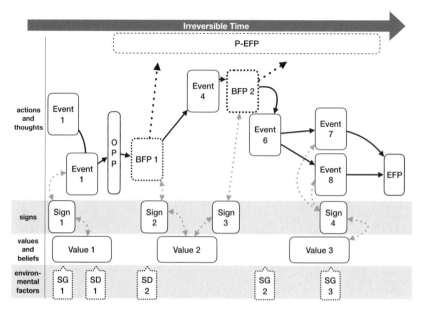

Figure 10.8 TEM figure with BFPs and paths

Figure 10.9 displays a simple version of the final TEM model generated as a result of this study. I extracted OPP, EFP, P-EFP, BFPs, signs, values and beliefs, SGs, and SD from the series of interviews, and all these components were added to the model. The model presented is the TEM from a participant who used e-learning but could not reach the goal: Hence, I set EFP as 'giving up learning with e-learning' and P-EFP as 'continuing studying with e-learning'. The participant presented a significant shift between EFP and P-EFP throughout the period of study with e-learning.

The framework of TEM and TLMG greatly helped me to dig out the background of the significant shift. Through the first interview, the participant talked only about her experience of using e-learning. Some examples of her experience are 'she believed in the quality of e-learning because her teacher recommended the learning material', 'she started to use e-learning to study for TOEIC test', and 'she received an unexpected result of TOEIC test'. Her responses seemed to strongly focus on one of my questions 'When and what did you do on the e-learning?', and this inclination prompted me to plot most data I collected in Layer 1 of the TEM figure.

In this research, I tried to understand not only the participant's learning history but also her thoughts which affected her learning. However, with the results of the TEM figure after the first interview, I found that I had not collected enough information to explore the participant's thoughts. Therefore, my second interview focused on another question,

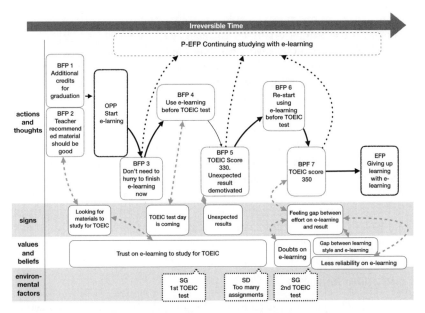

Figure 10.9 Final TEM figure (simplified)

'What did you think about when using the e-learning?' During the second interview, I showed the TEM figure which I had made based on the first interview, and shared what the TEM figure illustrated. We also checked whether each action was on the side of EFP or P-EFP, and I asked what she thought.

The second interview with the TEM figure revealed the participant's learning history focusing on dynamic changes and the roles of background contexts which make the process complex. She said that her actions had moved up and down for using e-learning. However, despite of great shift between EFP and P-EFP throughout the period of study with e-learning, she insisted that her thoughts had been rather stable towards using e-learning. She trusted the e-learning at the very early stages of the learning period, and she was able to maintain this trust even though she got an unpleasant score in her first TOEIC test. She asserted that this continuous trust in e-learning had enabled her to keep herself studying with e-learning. Then she pointed at one of her actions and described it as a critical point at which she lost trust in e-learning: when she got an unexpectedly low score in her second TOEIC test. In addition to the unpleasant score, she also referred to the environmental factor related to this point. She mentioned that the number of assignments overwhelmed her and did not let her have enough time to engage in e-learning. This factor is shown as one of the SDs in the TEM figure. Despite the fact she could spend a very limited amount of time to prepare for TOEIC test, she trusted that the e-learning might enable her to learn English effectively, and she tried to use e-learning as much as possible. However, she received the depressing result, and she said she started to feel a gap between her efforts with e-learning and her TOEIC test results. This perception led her to doubt the effectiveness of e-learning.

Through a series of interviews, the TEM figure supported the research process, and allowed me to understand the dynamics and complexity in the participant's learning history, particularly when I sorted the events apparent in data and planned follow-up interviews. In addition, the figure helped the participant to review what she did and what she thought. Especially, she seemed to feel comfortable in recollecting her beliefs. After the series of interviews, she remarked that because the TEM figure made her actions and movement between EFP and P-EFP visually clear, it was not so challenging to connect her actions and her thoughts, and to describe them. Thanks to these advantages, the participant's learning process and background to the process became clearer for both me and the participant.

Concluding Remarks

In this chapter, we introduced the TEA as a new approach which enables us to interpret complex and dynamic changes mediated by social and cultural factors in language learners' and teachers' psychology through a visualization of human life trajectory. Also, to familiarize researchers in the field with the conceptual idea of TEA we explained how TEA can be adapted to the psychology of language learning and teaching research by giving examples from our own research projects with different themes, target groups and approaches. Through the review of two studies performed originally by each of us, we hope to have highlighted some advantages of using TEA in the psychology of language learner and teacher research.

One of the advantages is that TEA has great flexibility in the number of participants, and combinations of components forming TEA. In the first example, Aoyama focused on the dynamics of psychological aspects among multiple learners and commonalities using HSI and TEM. On the other hand, Yamamoto's second example selected a single case to investigate the dynamics in-depth with HSI, TLMG and TEM. This means that, while TEA can observe both complexity and dynamics in language learner or teacher psychology, researchers can choose how much emphasis they place on complexity and how much on dynamics by choosing different combinations of TEA components, as well as the number of participants (i.e. the 1/4/9 rule).

Another advantage is the length of time we can explore with TEA. As mentioned earlier, retrospective approaches are suitable for a relatively longer period of time, compared to longitudinal approaches. TEA's timescale is even more flexible, thanks to the concept of irreversible time (i.e. it focuses on the flow of time and does not need to consider the length of time). Therefore, regardless of the length of time (e.g. one month, one semester, 20 years), what TEA looks at is the bifurcation process of life trajectories, social forces at bifurcation points and the paths toward an equifinality point. For instance, Aoyama's study focused on a much longer period of time (i.e. 10+ years) compared with Yamamoto's semester-long classroom investigation.

Although TEA was originally developed in the area of cultural psychology and not many studies have been done with TEA in the field of language learner and teacher psychology, the flexibility of TEA has advantages over approaches and methods that have been previously used in the field. Also, as we exemplified in our sample studies, TEA's research process is straightforward and clear with visual representation of data and findings. Thus, TEA's potential in language learner and teacher psychology research is inestimable. We hope that this chapter might encourage more researchers in the field to become interested in applying this approach to explore complex and dynamic phenomena.

Note

(1) Since we introduce studies carried out by each of us, we use 'I' in the upcoming sections. In this section, the first person 'I' refers to the first author, Takumi Aoyama.

Glossary

BFP: Bifurcation Point
CDST: (Complex and) Dynamic Systems Theory
EFP: Equifinality Point
HSI: Historically Structured Invitation
OPP: Obligatory Passage Point
P-EFP: Polarized Equifinality Point
SD: Social Direction
SG: Social Guidance
TEA: Trajectory Equifinality Approach
TEM: Trajectory Equifinality Model
TLMG: Three Layer Model of Genesis

References

Aoyama, T. (2016) Dynamics and complexity of the psychology of language learning in context: A case study of three returnees in Japan. Unpublished MA Dissertation, University of Warwick.

Arakawa, A., Yasuda, Y. and Sato, T. (2012) A method for analyzing with trajectory equifinality model. *Ritsumeikan Journal of Human Sciences* 25, 95–107. (in Japanese with English abstract)

Boo, Z., Dörnyei, Z. and Ryan, S. (2015) L2 motivation research 2005–2014: Understanding a publication surge and a changing landscape. *System* 55, 145–157. https://doi.org/10.1016/j.system.2015.10.006

de Bot, K., Lowie, W. and Verspoor, M. (2007) A dynamic systems theory approach to second language acquisition. *Bilingualism: Language and Cognition* 10, 7–21. https://doi.org/10.1017/S1366728906002732

Dörnyei, Z. (2014) Researching complex dynamic systems: 'Retrodictive qualitative modelling' in the language classroom. *Language Teaching* 47, 80–91. https://doi.org/10.1017/S0261444811000516

Haken, H. (2006) *Information and Self-organization: A Macroscopic Approach to Complex Systems* (3rd edn). New York: Springer.

Hiver, P. (2015) Attractor states. In Z. Dörnyei, P.D. MacIntyre and A. Henry (eds) *Motivational Dynamics in Language Learning* (pp. 20–28). Bristol: Multilingual Matters.

Hiver, P. (2017) Tracing the signature dynamics of language teacher immunity: A retrodictive qualitative modeling study. *The Modern Language Journal* 101, 669–690. https://doi.org/10.1111/modl.1243.

Kullasepp, K. (2011) Creating my own way of being a psychologist. *The Japanese Journal of Personality* 19, 217–232.

Lamb, M. (2009) Situating the L2 self: Two Indonesian school learners of English. In Z. Dörnyei and E. Ushioda (eds) *Motivation, Language Identity and the L2 Self* (pp. 229–247). Bristol: Multilingual Matters.

Lamb, M. (2018) When motivation research motivates: Issues in long-term empirical investigations. *Innovation in Language Learning and Teaching* 12, 357–370. https://doi.org/10.1080/17501229.2016.1251438

Larsen-Freeman, D. (1997) Chaos/complexity science and second language acquisition. *Applied Linguistics* 18.

Larsen-Freeman, D. and Cameron, L. (2008) *Complex Systems and Applied Linguistics*. Cambridge: Cambridge University Press.

MacIntyre, P. and Serroul, A. (2015) Motivation on a per-second timescale: Examining approach-avoidance motivation during L2 task performance. In Z. Dörnyei, P.D. MacIntyre and A. Henry (eds) *Motivational Dynamics in Language Learning* (pp. 109–138). Bristol: Multilingual Matters.

MacIntyre, P.D. (2012) The idiodynamic method: A closer look at the dynamics of communication traits. *Communication Research Reports* 29, 361–367. https://doi.org/10.1080/08824096.2012.723274

Mann, S. (2016) *The Research Interview: Reflective Practice and Reflexivity in Research Processes*. New York: Palgrave Macmillan.

Nishimura, Y. and Ito, K. (2017) The process of overcoming difficulties faced by novice home economics teachers in elementary schools. *Theory and Research for Developing Learning Systems* 3, 13–25.

Niita, R. (2013) Understanding motivational evolution in the EFL classroom: A longitudinal study from a dynamic systems perspective. In M.T. Apple, D. Da Silva and T. Fellner (eds) *Language Learning Motivation in Japan* (pp. 268–290). Bristol: Multilingual Matters.

Park, H. and Hiver, P. (2017) Profiling and tracing motivational change in project-based L2 learning. *System* 67, 50–64. https://doi.org/10.1016/j.system.2017.04.013

Ruspini, E. (2002) *Introduction to Longitudinal Research*. London: Routledge.

Ryan, S. and Mercer, S. (2012) Language learning mindsets across cultural settings: English learners in Japan. *OnCUE Journal* 6, 6–22.

Sato, T., Hidaka, T. and Fukuda, M. (2009) Depicting the dynamics of living the life: The Trajectory Equifinality Model. In J. Valsiner, P. Molenaar, M. Lyra and N. Chaudhary (eds) *Dynamic Process Methodology in the Social and Developmental Sciences* (pp. 217–240). New York: Springer.

Sato, T., Yasuda, Y., Kanzaki, M. and Valsiner, J. (2014) From describing to reconstructing life trajectories: How the TEA (Trajectory Equifinality Approach) explicates context-dependent human phenomena. In B. Wagoner, N. Chaudhary and P. Hviid (eds) *Culture Psychology and its Future: Complementarity in a New Key* (pp. 93–104). Scottsdale: Information Age Publishing.

Sato, T. and Valsiner, J. (2010) Time in life and life in time: Between experiencing and accounting. *Ritsumeikan Journal of Human Sciences* 20, 79–92.

Valsiner, J. (2005) Attractors, repulsors, and directors: Making dynamic systems theory developmental. *Research and Clinical Center for Child Development Annual Report* 27, 13–25.

Valsiner, J. and Sato, T. (2006) Historically structured sampling (HSS): How can psychology's methodology become tuned in to the reality of the historical nature of cultural psychology? In J. Straub, D. Weidemann, C. Kölbl and B. Zielke (eds) *Pursuit of Meaning: Advances in Cultural and Cross-cultural Psychology* (pp. 215–251). Bielefeld: Transcript Verlag.

Yamamoto, T. (2018) Case Study of Failed English e-learning: Analysed by Trajectory Equifinality Approach. Paper presented at the 16th Asia TEFL, 1st MAAL & 6th HAAL 2018 International Conference, 29 June 2018, University of Macau.

Yashima, T. and Arano, K. (2014) Understanding EFL learners' motivational dynamics: A three-level model from a dynamic systems and sociocultural perspective. In Z. Dörnyei, P.D. MacIntyre and A. Henry (eds) *Motivational Dynamics in Language Learning* (pp. 285–314). Bristol: Multilingual Matters.

11 Understanding Complexity in Language Classrooms: A Retrodictive Approach to Researching Class Climate

Ryo Nitta and Yoshiyuki Nakata

Introduction

Language classrooms are complex and dynamic spaces, where various agents and elements continuously interact with, and co-adapt to, one another. In this complex and dynamic environment, individual students interact to co-form the language-learning class group, and this co-formation between all members of the class group ultimately determines the direction and quality of learning (Sampson, 2016: 7). The direction and quality of learning in the classroom are likely to be reflected in a certain quality of *class climate*, which is tangible for language teachers. In a classroom with a positive climate, many students are actively engaged in activities, while those experiencing a negative climate are likely to show reluctant attitudes towards learning and often feel that they are forced to complete given tasks. More specifically, even in a positive classroom climate in which many students are most of the time working together with the shared classroom goal in mind ('convergent'), not all the students are always positively engaging in activities; some may occasionally be quite rebellious against the teacher or content ('partially divergent') (Pinner, 2019: 57).

Generating a positive class climate is important because its condition affects students' motivation to learn the language in the classroom. Dörnyei and Ushioda (2011: 110) observed that '[l]earner involvement will be highest in a psychologically safe classroom climate in which students are encouraged to express their opinions and in which they feel that they are protected from ridicule and embarrassment'. A class climate is a key concern of many language teachers, and experienced teachers are likely to notice 'intuitively when a class has reached a state of bonded equilibrium' (Senior, 1997: 10), but it is little understood how a class climate evolves.

Emergent Class Climate as a Complex Dynamic System

This chapter explains the methodology of understanding a class climate more fully by taking the perspective of complex dynamic systems (CDS). Class climate is regarded as one particular dimension of group dynamics where behavioral and psychological processes occur within a social group. Class climate is analogous to geographical climate; that is, a number of factors interact to create a group feeling and atmosphere, which affects people's desire to engage in certain activities (Beebe & Masterson, 2014: 141). In a word, a class climate can be defined as an emergent phenomenon involving various CDS characteristics in a language classroom.

From the perspective of CDS, any effort to advance a particular method of teaching, techniques and/or tasks would be futile because what is taking place differs significantly among language classrooms (Larsen-Freeman & Cameron, 2008: 198). For example, many researchers have attempted to find effective methods of corrective (oral or written) feedback. Findings of such studies show that a particular method significantly affected the learning of their learners, but it does not guarantee the effectiveness for other learners in other contexts. Although such studies try to control the *independent* variables, it would not be meaningful to isolate them from the class as a whole. This is primarily because the effectiveness of a particular method largely depends on the *interaction* of all the relationships in the classroom.

While various agents (e.g. teachers and students) and elements (e.g. tasks, materials, desks) are interconnected in the classroom, a particularly important interconnection responsible for class climate is that between all participating people, i.e. a teacher with students and students with each other. The significance of this dimension has been recognized as *group cohesiveness* in the field of group dynamics (see Dörnyei & Murphey, 2003, for its application to the language-classroom context). According to Beebe and Masterson (2014: 141), a cohesive group emerges from the interaction of a number of components such as group composition and learning tasks, but the first and foremost is communication: 'How group members communicate, with whom they communicate, and how often they communicate influence their satisfaction as well as their productivity'. From the CDS perspective, communication between class members can be characterized by *co-adaptation*, which refers to 'change in connected systems, where change in one system produces change in the other' (Larsen-Freeman & Cameron, 2008: 199). In the present context, change in one student produces change in the other students through communication.

Co-adaptation also emphasizes reciprocity (Larsen-Freeman, 2010). That is, in traditional language classrooms, communication flow is considered one-directional from teacher to students, but what reciprocity implies is that both the teacher and students are subsystems of the whole class system where each subsystem has equal significance. Because there is no centralized agent when we consider the classroom as a CDS, the teacher can neither directly produce a positive class climate nor control students' learning; rather, a certain quality of climate emerges as a consequence of dynamic co-adaptation between all class members, and the collective presence is likely to be co-adapted to individual students' minds and learning. In other words, a class climate is *emergent* – not a simple aggregation of its members but 'the arising of something new, often unanticipated, from the interaction of components which comprise it' (Larsen-Freeman, 2016: 378). In a word, a class climate is an emergent phenomenon arising from co-adaptive communicative behaviors between all class members from the perspective of CDS.

Retrodictive Approach to Researching Class Climate

Regarding class climate as an emergent phenomenon, how can this be meaningfully researched? Class climate and group cohesiveness have been mostly investigated using large-scale questionnaires. For example, Clement *et al.* (1994) surveyed the relationship between motivational factors and group cohesiveness in 11 schools in Hungary and found correlations between group cohesiveness and students' motivation and teachers' evaluation of students' L2 proficiency. In a similar vein, Joe *et al.* (2017) conducted a questionnaire for 381 students in Korean secondary schools and found that classroom social climate has an impact on several motivational factors and learning outcomes. Although such a survey method indicates correlations between students' motivation and a class climate, it seems to simplify the classroom phenomena and to 'reduce life's complexities to something knowable and controllable by tending to the smallest parts' (Stanley, 2009: 2). The results of questionnaire surveys suggest the resultant outcomes of complex co-adaptation in researching context, but the static snapshots presented as such quantitative outcomes neither tell how a certain climate emerges from the interaction between participating members nor reflect the complexity of real language classrooms.

From the CDS perspective, however, because students' learning as a class is non-linear and full of diversity, learning and teaching in the classroom need to be complexified rather than simplified (Stanley, 2009). Research based on CDS has attempted to preserve this complexity as it is occurring in the language classroom. This attitude, however, poses a real challenge to researchers; that is, 'if everything is connected with everything else, how can we adopt a perspective that does justice to the complex system that is the classroom in all its multiple embeddedness?' (Larsen-Freeman, 2016: 384). Because it is not practically possible to attend to every component and every interaction within and beyond the classroom, our realistic option is to select particular systems to focus on from all the embedded systems. In other words, what we can do is to draw 'conceptual boundaries' (Mercer, 2018: 515) around the complex systems while regarding the other components as 'the dynamic environment in which these focal systems operate,' but that are 'still connected to and able to influence them' (Larsen-Freeman & Cameron, 2008: 203).

To describe the classroom as a CDS without reducing the system to a simplistic one, we adopt *retrodiction*. With this approach, we start by identifying the outcomes or end states of a focal system and then retrospectively examine how the system evolved into these outcomes (Chan *et al.*, 2015). By reflecting on the trajectory or trace of the focal system, we identify salient *patterns* of behaviors or phenomena, which are likely to operate in significant ways and emerge within other contexts (Byrne, 2002). In other words, reversing the usual research direction from prediction (or forecasting) to retrodiction (or retrocasting) (Larsen-Freeman & Cameron, 2008), we aim to explore 'reasons why the system has ended up with a particular outcome option' (Dörnyei, 2014: 85).

This retrodictive approach to understanding classroom complexity is similar to that adopted by historians. According to Gaddis (2002), historians do not try to predict the future but assume what is likely to take place by representing the past; more precisely, they regard the past as a 'landscape' and history as the way the past is represented. In doing so, historians try to experience vicariously what they cannot directly experience and ultimately gain a 'world view'. In the present interest, what is particularly significant is Gaddis' (2002: 30) recognition of 'patterns' – recurrent phenomena – as a key to historical research; that is, historians use patterns as foundations for their attempt to generalize human experience, and by being armed with 'patterns that extend across time' they can prepare for what will happen in the future.

Identifying distinctive patterns that recur across time seems to offer one promising direction for researching classroom complexity from the perspective of CDS. This orientation is also emphasized by Burns and Knox (2011: 7):

> Taken as a complex dynamic system, a classroom cannot be meaningfully described by separating off individual agents and elements; rather the complexity of a classroom can be mapped by describing emergent *patterns* of behavior, which comes as a result of the interactions between different elements of the system. (emphasis added)

There have recently been several empirical attempts to identify patterns in language learning and teaching contexts by applying the retrodictive approach. For example, Chan *et al.* (2015) asked teachers to find salient learner archetypes in classrooms in a Hong Kong secondary school, then conducted in-depth interviews with one prototypical learner from each archetype to gain insights into their motivational trajectories. In an L2 classroom at a Korean university, Poupure (2018) identified emergent patterns of social climate in small groups by drawing on various data sources.

Looking at L2 writing development in an English class at a Japanese university from the end point of the observation period, Nitta and Baba (2018) selected average and unsuccessful L2 writers and retrodictively identified patterns of the self-regulatory process of each learner in their post-task reflections. All these retrodictive studies did not attempt to find simple causality but to identify patterns of change and understand how such patterns emerged from the system. In addition, these studies increasingly illuminated the potential of qualitative methods to describe the dynamics and complexity of language learning and identify emergent patterns of change in specific educational contexts. Following these attempts, we present how a combination of research methods, in particular using class observations, can be meaningfully adapted to analysing complex classroom phenomena and identifying patterns of emergent class climate.

Example Study

The example study we describe here is taken from our ongoing research into English classrooms in Japanese high schools (Nakata *et al.*, 2020). We briefly explain the research background and steps of researching the classroom complexity with some of our tentative findings. We present an example of how various research tools can be used in an integrative manner to develop understandings of classroom complexity.

Background

The research team consisted of two researchers (the authors of this chapter) and one teacher practitioner with the aim of exploring what components affect students' motivation and learning in the classroom. We investigated three classes in the original study, with this chapter focusing on the findings from two of these groups (Classes X and Y). Class X indicated higher English proficiency than Class Y based on a standardized English test. While English proficiency differed between the classes, students shared a number of similarities, such as speaking the same first language and preparing for university entrance exams for the following year.

A unique dimension of this study lies in the fact that the same teaching was offered to different classes in the school; that is, the same teacher (one of the members in this project) provided the same lesson content and tasks under the same curriculum by using the same method of teaching. The objective of this course was to develop students' capacity of critical thinking in English through theme-based instruction. Five different topics were used over the year, and students were engaged in various tasks in relation to one of the themes for about one month. In a typical teaching procedure, a reading text about a particular topic was presented, and students were instructed to work individually and discuss questions about the text in small groups. As a whole-class discussion, the teacher then encouraged students to share their answers and thoughts. Thus, the class frequently shifted between individual, small-group and whole-class modes of learning.

To understand the class from different angles, we used a variety of data sources. These tools can be divided into three questionnaires, which mainly consisted of closed questions with some follow-up open-ended questions, and other qualitative methods:

- Questionnaire 1 on students' motivation (provided two times);
- Questionnaire 2 on students' perceptions towards small-group work (provided two times);
- Questionnaire 3 on students' self-reflection about their learning (provided five times);
- Focus group interviews (conducted one time);
- Class observations (conducted five times).

After the completion of all data collection, the research team met several times in the following year and discussed what differences and similarities were revealed between the classes and what contributed to these outcomes in each class. In addition to the above data sources, the teacher's reflections on her own teaching and understanding of individual students within and beyond the classroom provided valuable information to our retrodiction. Through these processes, differences, rather than similarities, were more markedly pronounced between the classes, and class climate was identified as a key component to understanding the distinctive qualities of teaching and learning in each classroom.

Retrodictive steps for analysis

We attempted to understand classroom complexity in a retrodictive manner through a general three-step framework – examining the outcomes, identifying patterns of change in the system and exploring reasons for emergent patterns. We also present here tentative findings and interpretations. It should be emphasized that the following section gives more specific descriptions of class observations (Step 2), though all the applied research methods made a significant contribution to our understanding of the class as a whole.

Step 1: Examining the outcomes

In our retrodiction, we first looked at the results of the three questionnaires as a method of examining the outcomes of teaching. The first two questionnaires were provided twice – at the beginning and the end of the year – while the third questionnaire was provided five times during the year upon the completion of each topic. The results of questionnaires

1 and 2 suggested that, in spite of higher English proficiency in Class X, students' motivation and positive perceptions towards small-group work tended to increase more in Class Y. This trend was also consistent with the results of questionnaire 3, in which students were requested to self-evaluate their learning in terms of 'engagement', 'participation' and 'learning outside'. Although the results indicated some fluctuations, overall attitudes and behavior characterized from all three respects tended to be higher in Class Y than in Class X. Most strikingly, participation among Class Y students continued to increase and was persistently higher than that in the other class throughout the observation period. To put these findings together, we thought it conceivable that how students perceived group work in the class likely had some relationship with their motivation towards learning English.

Step 2: Identifying patterns of change in the system

To explore classroom events in the context of these emergent outcomes, we observed video-recorded lessons. The video recorder was set next to the teacher at the front of the classroom so as to observe the whole class atmosphere and students' behavior from the teacher's viewpoint. Following the findings from the questionnaires, we initially focused on how students collaborated in small-group activities but, through repeated observations, we noticed that certain distinctive qualities of class climate prevailed in each class. We also found that the quality of small-group work was not linearly linked to that of whole-class work. That is, students who actively participated in small-group work might not be actively engaged in whole-class discussion, which suggests that class climate is not a simple aggregation of each small-group activity.

We now present characteristic episodes identified from the video-recorded lessons, in particular those relating to interactions between the teacher and students in the whole-class session. First, students in Class X were talkative, which made the classroom rather noisy throughout lessons. The class atmosphere was too relaxed – when the teacher started the lesson, some students outwardly showed that they were sleepy and did not even hesitate to yawn. Despite this unpromising start, however, the overall lesson proceeded smoothly. All the students followed the teacher's instructions and appeared seriously engaged in individual and collaborative work.

As one characteristic moment, individual students were actively engaged in small-group work; thus, the class generally exhibited a noisy and vibrant atmosphere during this period. On the other hand, in the whole-class session, where individual students were asked to speak about their answers, the class became silent. In the following excerpt, the teacher directed students to summarize a part of the reading text. Students first prepared answers individually for 20 seconds and rehearsed their summaries in pairs, then several students were appointed to read out their answers one after another.

> Teacher: OK... ja... would you please... um... A-san, do? How did Urbani [the character in the text] deal with the patients? [**Initiation**]
>
> A: Urbani visited his patients and he sat by their beds and tried to give them hope. [**Response**]
>
> Teacher: OK, ... tried to give hope... Very good. [**Feedback**] OK... how about you... B-san? [**Initiation**]

As indicated within the excerpt, this part of the lesson follows a typical initiation–response–feedback (IRF) pattern of classroom discourse, which was recurrent throughout the observed lessons. It went smoothly probably because the students were familiar with this discourse pattern as a usual procedural framework of this class.

The above teacher–student exchange was conducted as a step in whole-class learning, but the other students were inattentive, which gives an impression that they lost interest in the whole-class learning; some were looking at the reading material, while others lowered their eyes to their desks or showed an absent look on their faces. That is, despite being intended for whole-class learning, such ritualized exchanges were done only between the teacher and the chosen student. This part of the recorded lesson revealed a low level of cohesiveness in the class group. Referring to Pinner (2019), the classroom climate appeared to be 'convergent' on the surface but a closer look at the video-recorded interactions revealed that it was in reality 'partially divergent'.

Like Class X, students in Class Y were also talkative during the same lesson content. In the beginning of the lesson, noise and a lack of order prevailed; students were engaged in their own acts – some were chatting with peers and others were preparing for the class. When the teacher started to talk, however, the class suddenly changed into an orderly state; they stopped doing their own diverse activities and quickly shifted attention to the teacher's instruction. Although the class members continued to be talkative throughout the lesson, this noisiness worked as 'a productive buzz' (Senior, 1997: 10) in this class, where students actively participated in both small-group and whole-class interactions. The class members seemed to have a very close relationship with one another; there was much laughter throughout the lesson, and every student showed that they were comfortable, which was also confirmed in the focus-group interviews.

One characteristic episode was identified at the end of a lesson when students were asked to translate English passages into Japanese; one student was chosen to read out his answer. (The following interaction took place in Japanese and is translated here into English. The original Japanese is given in parentheses.)

Teacher:	OK, C-kun. Go ahead. [Ja, C-kun. Dozo]
C:	Well… Because Urubani risked his life, what he continued to give became 'virus information'. [Etto…, Urubani ga… Kareno inochi-wo tsuiyashitanode… okuritsuzuketamonoga… uirusu (virus) no joho to natta.]
Teacher:	Not 'virus' but 'vital'. ['Virus' janakute, 'vital'.]
C:	Virus… Bacteria's? ['Virus'… saikin no?]
D:	'Vital'
E:	'Vital'
C:	Life's? [Seimei no… Inochi no…?]
D:	Vital![Judaina!]
C:	um… It became 'vital information'. [Aa… Judaina joho ni natta.]
Teacher:	Yes, yes, yes. [So so so.]

We evaluated this excerpt as an important characteristic because this reflects the responsive and cooperative attitudes of the class. What happened was that, responding to C's misunderstanding of *vital* as *virus*, other students (D, E) jumped in to offer their help. That is, these students were engaged even when they were not responsible for answering, and each turned towards and attentively listened to the chosen student, which contrasts with the detached manners observed in Class X. This collaborative interaction could be considered as motivational scaffolding, which seems to involve students' sense of belonging, or attachment, to the class – they were attentive to the progress of, and might even have felt responsible for, their classmates' learning (Ushioda, 2007). This sort of social support is likely 'to promote positive evaluations and enhance learners' feelings of competence and skill development, and thus reinforce their intrinsic motivation' (Ushioda, 2007: 11).

Step 3: Exploring the underlying reasons for emergent patterns

To understand what led to the emergence of the different patterns of class climate, we zoomed out from focusing on the class to the wider school system, as argued by Ushioda (2016) in her proposal for a 'small lens' approach – extending the analysis of specific events in the immediate context back to the shared history of previous experience among students. The focus-group interviews were conducted at the end of the observation period when four or five students from each class were invited to talk about their learning in and beyond the classroom. The interviews, together with the teacher's reflections, revealed the significant impact of the students' out-of-class experiences on their learning in the classroom. That is, the distinctive differences in class climate might be attributed to experiences they shared outside the English class. For example, Class Y happened to be a *homeroom* class, which was not the case for Class X. In a homeroom class, students spend time together for many different subject areas (including this English lesson) on a daily basis, and work together even in various extracurricular activities such as sports competitions and school festivals. Through such extended experiences, students are likely to become intimate with each other and develop mutual trust and understanding; thus, this group became cohesive. In other words, what made Class Y collaborative was, at least partly, their shared experience as members of their homeroom group, which was interconnected with the wider system outside the classroom.

Reflection on a Retrodictive Approach to Researching Class Climate

In this section, we reflect on what we found and interpreted from observing the two classes over one year and discuss methodological issues with the retrodictive approach to researching the language classroom.

Benefits of multiple data sources

We presented a three-step retrodictive approach to researching the complexity of language classrooms. We used a variety of data sources in a longitudinal manner. Our experience tells us that using multiple, rather than single, data sources is useful or even indispensable for CDS-oriented research because the analysis of each data source explains different facets of the researched system, and these multiple analyses collectively construct an overall picture of complex language classrooms. In the example study, the questionnaire results indicated the outcome of students' learning over one year (Step 1), the class observations suggest the traces of the system by understanding how students were engaged in learning and what class climate emerged (Step 2) and focal group interviews and teacher reflections suggested one component – students' out of class experiences – might affect the quality of class climate and their learning in the class (Step 3). In the present form of retrodiction, using multiple data sources would be paramount also because the significance of a particular event is not apparent at the time of data collection, and we do not know what aspects are keys to understanding the system. Only with retrodiction, by tracing back the trajectory from the end point, are we able to grasp the essential components of the system.

Identifying patterns through retrodiction

In the example study, because we retrodictively recognized students' communicative behaviors as a key to determining the quality of learning in the context, we explicated the second step – identifying patterns of class climate – through class observations in some detail. We illustrated only one characteristic episode from each class, but these distinctive patterns recurrently emerged in other video-recorded lessons throughout the year. Referring back to Burns and Knox (2011: 7), 'the complexity of a classroom can be mapped by describing emergent patterns of behavior, which comes as a result of the interactions between different elements of the system', and the patterns can only be described through retrodiction. Because of their recurrent emergence, the patterns are likely to involve essential elements of the observed system.

The contrastive patterns arose from the co-adaptation between group members in each class. Co-adaptation is inevitable but, as suggested from both positive and negative climates, 'not necessarily for the benefits of learning; all sorts of forces may push a system to stability' (Larsen-Freeman & Cameron, 2008: 199). In the case of Class X, the IRF pattern of class discourse stabilized through being repeatedly exercised in lessons throughout the year. On the other hand, the more open communication style was practiced in Class Y. Despite the same learning conditions, such different patterns emerged as a result of complex co-adaptive behaviors between the members of each class group, and as suggested from the analysis in Step 3, co-adaptation can be extended to the wider school system.

Can classroom-based research be generalizable?

As discussed thus far, we believe that the retrodictive approach offers a promising direction for understanding the complexity of language classrooms, but it is worth considering the issue of *generalizability* of retrodiction – how the findings drawn from a specific class situated in a particular local context can be generalizable to another class located in another context. This sort of *contextualized* research, typically using qualitative methods, is often criticized as *un*-generalizable. However, we should consider whether generalization is possible or even appropriate in a classroom-based study whose purpose is to explore the dynamic and complex classroom space in which a real person 'as a thinking, feeling human being, with an identity, a personality, a unique history and background ... with goals, motives and intentions' (Ushioda, 2009: 220) works with others for a lengthy period. As previously mentioned regarding corrective feedback, even when researchers attempt to generalize their findings by using experimental methods involving sophisticated statistical tools, what are claimed as effective approaches often fail to work in other contexts.

As pointed out by Gaddis (2002), generalization seems to be conflated with *universal* generalization, which hard science (e.g. chemistry, physics) usually aims to achieve. Instead, Gaddis (2002: 66) emphasizes the importance of *particular* generalizations – a type of generalization 'only from the knowledge of particular outcomes'. In a similar vein, Van Lier (2005: 198) argues that it is difficult to generalize from an individual (or group) to an entire population; but insights from a particular case 'can inform, be adapted to, and provide comparative information to a wide variety of other cases, so long as one is careful to take contextual differences into account'. The extent of what we as individuals can experience is limited, but by drawing on the experiences of others in comparable contexts in the past, we could be able to increase our *chances* of acting wisely' (Gaddis, 2002: 9). In a similar vein, in her discussion of a 'small lens' approach, Ushioda (2016: 573) suggests that accumulating a number of events, lessons, or classroom groups will yield significant insights into 'motivation-related patterns of classroom events that are generic across contexts of practice for a particular teacher, as well as insights into highly context-specific processes of motivation'. In other words, the present type of CDS-based study is beneficial for teachers as it has a 'metaphorical power as exemplary significances in particular settings capable of illuminating other [their own] settings' (Dunne, 2015; Macintyre Latta & Kim, 2010: 143). Learning from what retrodictive research reveals in a particular classroom can certainly widen our views as a teacher and/or researcher.

Conclusion: Towards Teacher – Researcher Collaboration

Researching the language classroom from the perspective of CDS can make us aware of the difficulty and the complexity of teaching: 'language teaching is an exceedingly complex undertaking which can be very personal, individual, highly varied, and often difficult to predict in its development' (Mercer, 2013: 376). As described in the example study, different groups of students in the same school respond differently to the same teaching. Teachers need to shift their attention between different system levels and identify what has a significant effect on the quality of teaching for a particular group or individuals in a particular classroom context. In a word, teaching is not a simple act based on linear causality but a creative artifact based on complexity.

Although the importance of classroom research has been much emphasized in the area of instructed second language acquisition (SLA) (Doughty & Williams, 1998; Long, 2017), Larsen-Freeman (2016: 378) claims that 'classroom-oriented research has not contributed towards this effectiveness to the extent that it might because our construction of the classroom has been too limited.' Similarly, in the area of language learning motivation, researchers have called for and attempted to conduct classroom-based research (Crookes & Schmidt, 1991; Dörnyei & Schmidt, 2001). However, significant roles of particular local contexts have not been sufficiently considered because the aim of many researchers is to continue to 'uncover rule-governed psychological laws that explain how context affects motivation, rather than to explore the dynamic complexity of personal meaning-making in social context' (Ushioda, 2009: 217). Presumably, one significant reason for the limited contributions of research to language teaching practice could be attributed to 'the general scarcity of published work reporting on classroom-based *practitioner-led* investigations' (Ushioda, 2016: 566; emphasis added).

In response to Ushioda's call, the research direction we need to take is clear – to collaborate with teachers who have 'huge funds of knowledge over their professional lifetime' (Lamb, 2017: 335). Via such means, we can develop our understanding of the realities of language classrooms, and based on this understanding, we can contribute to improving language teaching and language teaching research in a reciprocal manner. Towards this direction, Tudor (2003: 8) emphasizes the significance of understanding local meaningfulness for effective teaching, 'what language learning and teaching *mean* to local participants in the full context of their lives, within but also beyond the classroom'. With the same spirit, Ushioda (2016) argues that we should develop our understanding of how teachers actually work responsively and adaptively to shape students' day-to-day interactions and events in motivationally constructive ways. Therefore, locally situated understandings of teaching and learning in a particular environment 'can clearly have much wider resonance and contribute to informing theory and practice at a broader level' (Ushioda, 2016: 574). Such locally situated research would make us confront complex and often confusing realities in the classroom. Thanks to this very nature of complexity, however, we can delve deeper into the details of what is happening in real language classrooms, which we would otherwise tend to overlook.

It is probably right to say that the retrodictive approach presented in this chapter has much in common with an approach used by experienced or expert teachers who develop their own manner of teaching built on their reflections. As argued by Mercer (2013: 393), 'while recognizing the uniqueness and diversity of each learning-teaching encounter, expert teachers are also able to recognize patterns in the dynamics and emergent situations in classrooms and thus act accordingly'. Expert teachers attempt not only to understand what happens within the classroom but also recognize events and phenomena beyond the classroom. This understanding of a class as a nested system is significant because L2 learning is only part of learners' identities, and their learning is influenced by what they experience beyond the language classroom. With the recognition of students nested in a multi-class system within the school system (which is, of course, extended to the wider social system), teachers need to observe how students are engaged in the class and encourage their learning adaptively.

In conclusion, the CDS approach encourages us to reconsider the relationship between researchers and teachers. Researchers may assume that researching always precedes teaching – research findings orient and guide how teaching should be conducted. However, at least at present, research cannot fully represent the complex reality in a language classroom. Rather than being guided by researching, teaching practices used by teachers and their experiences are likely to offer directions that researchers need to pursue in exploring complexity. Because there are so many factors operating in the classroom, researching all of them simultaneously is far beyond our limitations. Experienced, expert teachers, on the other hand, can manage various operating factors simultaneously and adopt the optimal option in their local context. Such teachers can do this by accumulating all relevant information through careful observations of and close collaboration with students. In other words, teachers who understand the phenomenon of complexity in their teaching careers tend to be in far more advanced positions than researchers. We believe that the CDS approach will empower teachers and, in return, their awareness about the complexity of teaching will enlighten us about the realities of teaching in a classroom full of complexity.

References

Beebe, S.A. and Masterson, J.T. (2014) *Communicating in Small Groups: Principles and Practices* (10th edn). Harlow: Pearson Education.

Burns, A. and Knox, J.S. (2011) Classrooms as complex adaptive systems: A relational model. *TESL-EJ* 15 (1), 1–25.

Byrne, D. (2002) *Interpreting Quantitative Data*. London: Sage.

Chan, L., Dörnyei, Z. and Henry, A. (2015) Learner archetypes and signature dynamics in the language classroom: A retrodictive qualitative modelling approach to studying L2 motivation. In Z. Dörnyei, P.D. MacIntyre and A. Henry (eds) *Motivational Dynamics in Language Learning* (pp. 238–259). Bristol: Multilingual Matters.

Clément, R., Dörnyei, Z. and Noels, K. (1994) Motivation, self-confidence and group cohesion in the foreign language classroom. *Language Learning* 44 (3), 417–448.

Crookes, G. and Schmidt, R.W. (1991) Motivation: Reopening the research agenda. *Language Learning* 41 (4), 469–512.

Dörnyei, Z. (2014) Researching complex dynamic systems: 'Retrodictive qualitative modelling' in the language classroom. *Language Teaching* 47 (1), 80–91.

Dörnyei, Z. and Murphey, T. (2003) *Group Dynamics in the Language Classroom*. Cambridge: Cambridge University Press.

Dörnyei, Z. and Schmidt, R. (eds) (2001) *Motivation and Second Language Acquisition*. Hawaii: University of Hawaii Press.

Dörnyei, Z. and Ushioda, E. (2011) *Teaching and Researching Motivation* (2nd edn). Harlow: Pearson Education.

Doughty, C. and Williams, J. (eds) (1998) *Focus on Form in Classroom Second Language Acquisition*. Cambridge: Cambridge University Press.

Dunne, J. (2005) An intricate fabric: Understanding the rationality of practice. *Pedagogy, Culture and Society* 3, 367–390.

Gaddis, J.L. (2002) *The Landscape of History: How Historians Map the Past*. Oxford: Oxford University Press.

Joe, H-K., Hiver, P. and Al-Hoorie, A.H. (2017) Classroom social climate, self-determined motivation, willingness to communicate, and achievement: A study of structural relationships in instructed second language settings. *Learning and Individual Differences* 53, 133–144.

Lamb, M. (2017) The motivational dimension of language teaching. *Language Teaching* 50 (3), 301–346.

Larsen-Freeman, D. (2010) The dynamic co-adaptation of cognitive and social views: A complexity theory perspective. In R. Batstone (ed.) *Sociocognitive Perspectives on Language Use and Language Learning* (pp. 40–53). Oxford: Oxford University Press.

Larsen-Freeman, D. (2016) Classroom-oriented research from a complex systems perspective. *Studies in Second Language Learning and Teaching* 6 (3), 377–393.

Larsen-Freeman, D. and Cameron, L. (2008) *Complex Systems and Applied Linguistics.* Oxford: Oxford University Press.

Long, M.H. (2017) Instructed second language acquisition (ISLA): Geopolitics, methodological issues, and some major research questions. *Instructed Second Language Acquisition* 1 (1), 7–44.

Macintyre Latta, M. and Kim, J.-H. (2010) Narrative inquiry invites professional development: Educators claim the creative space of praxis. *The Journal of Educational Research* 103, 137–148.

Mercer, S. (2013) Towards a complexity-informed pedagogy for language learning. *Revista Brasileira de Linguística Aplicada, 13* (2), 375–398.

Mercer, S. (2018) Psychology for language learning: Spare a thought for the teacher. *Language Teaching* 51 (4), 504–525.

Nakata, Y., Nitta, R. and Tsuda, A. (2020) *Understanding Motivation and Classroom Modes of Regulation in Collaborative Learning: An Exploratory Study* [Manuscript submitted for publication]. Faculty of Global Communications, Doshisha University.

Nitta, R. and Baba, K. (2018) Understanding benefits of repetition from a complex dynamic systems perspective: The case of a writing task. In M. Bygate (ed.) *Language Learning through Task Repetition* (pp. 279–309). Amsterdam: John Benjamins.

Pinner, R. (2019) *Authenticity and Teacher–Student Motivational Synergy: A Narrative of Language Teaching.* Abingdon: Routledge.

Poupure, G. (2018) A complex systems investigation of group work dynamics in L2 interactive tasks. *The Modern Language Journal* 102 (2), 350–370.

Sampson, R. (2016) *Complexity in Classroom Foreign Language Learning Motivation.* Bristol: Multilingual Matters.

Senior, R. (1997) Transforming language classes into bonded groups. *ELT Journal* 51 (1), 3–11.

Stanley, D. (2009) What complexity science tells us about teaching and learning. *What Works? Research into Practice* (Research Monograph #17, pp. 1–4). Ontario Ministry of Education.

Tudor, I. (2003) Learning to live with complexity: Towards an ecological perspective on language teaching. *System* 31, 1–12.

Ushioda, E. (2007) Motivation, autonomy, and sociocultural theory. In P. Benson (ed.) *Learner Autonomy 8: Teacher and Learner Perspectives* (p. 5–24). Dublin: Authentik.

Ushioda, E. (2009) A person-in-context relational view of emergent motivation, self and identity. In Z. Dörnyei and E. Ushioda (eds) *Motivation, Language Identity and the L2 Self* (pp. 215–228). Bristol: Multilingual Matters.

Ushioda, E. (2016) Language learning motivation through a small lens: A research Agenda. *Language Teaching* 49 (4), 564–577.

van Lier, L. (2005) Case study. In E. Hinkel (ed.) *Handbook of Research in Second Language Teaching and Learning* (pp. 195–208). NJ: Erlbaum.

12 Investigating Group-DMCs and Complexity in the L2 Classroom

Christine Muir

Introduction

Over the last decade, complexity thinking and complexity-inspired approaches to research have become increasingly recognised throughout many disciplines in the field of second language acquisition (SLA), including second language (L2) motivation. This trend has pushed a re-evaluation of traditional research paradigms and notions of cause and effect, and in doing so has prompted re-thinking of models less able to realise the full complexity of instructed language learning environments. In essence, this has required us – and has concurrently provided a means by which to allow us – to approach and analyse the world by embracing it in *the way it really works* (Schumann, 2015).

A related development in L2 motivation research has been a shift from investigating more generalised groups of language learners – for example through wide-scale, quantitative research – to include a focus on the experience of individual learners situated in specific educational environments. This *person-in-context-relational-view* of motivation (Ushioda, 2009) also has its roots in the re-imagination of language learning motivation from the perspectives of self and identity (Dörnyei, 2005, 2009). As Ushioda (2009: 215) describes, such a perspective understands motivation as 'emergent from relations between real persons, with particular social identities, and the unfolding cultural context of activity'.

Although technological advances have led to an increasing amount of language learning occurring online, a significant proportion of learning still occurs among groups of learners in instructed contexts. Davis and Sumara (2006: 146) describe one vital facet of such settings thus: '[F]rom the first days of the term, the members of each new classroom grouping are engaged in the complex activity of negotiating social positionings, establishing group norms, and inscribing a collective identity'. The powerful influence of the motivational dynamics of groups on individual participants is well documented. After all, language learners' motivation is shaped not only by internal processes but also by the surrounding L2 learning environment (Dörnyei, 2005, 2009). A considerable proportion of motivational influence is rooted in the social context of the learner group, and it therefore follows that any complexity approach to researching motivation '*also* suggests a focus on what is emergent at the class group level' (Sampson, 2016: 169).

Whether at an individual or a group level, the adoption of a complexity approach to researching L2 motivation poses considerable challenges. If we accept that the motivation of any individual language learner is situated in a complex, ever-changing environment existing continually in flux, and that it cannot be predicted in advance nor generalised between contexts, it is not immediately clear what a principled approach to investigation might look like. As we pondered in 2015, 'what general principles can be deduced from an unpredictable situation?' (Dörnyei *et al.*, 2015: 96). In this chapter I highlight several key ideas from the complexity literature which have direct applications in developing our understanding of group-level motivational emergence. I root this discussion in the context of *directed motivational currents* (DMCs; cf. Dörnyei *et al.*, 2016), and focus on practical issues related to research design and data collection. In particular I argue for the potential of *formative experiments* (Reinking & Bradley, 2008). In doing so, through this chapter I hope to provide an entry point for interested practitioner-researchers who wish to employ complexity principles to investigate the emergence and management of group-level motivation – and of group-DMCs – in their own L2 teaching and learning contexts.

What is a Directed Motivational Current?

A DMC is a surge of highly focused motivation towards a clear and personally valued goal (Dörnyei *et al.*, 2016; Muir, 2020). Core DMC characteristics include an explicit starting point and defined end goal, set behavioural routines and an immersive and highly positive emotional tenor. Many DMCs are experienced individually. In the context of language learning, an example of an individual DMC might be a student focusing all their spare time and efforts in trying to improve their L2 competency before taking an upcoming high-stakes exam, or before embarking on a life-changing travel adventure from coast to coast across countries (or continents!). Throughout a DMC, individuals become entirely caught up in an outpouring of motivational energy, as though they are 'swept up' in the excitement and momentum carrying them forwards towards achieving a much-desired goal.

To date, empirical research investigating individual DMCs has primarily drawn on retrospective accounts in an endeavour to verify their initial conceptual presentation (e.g. Henry *et al.*, 2015; Ibrahim, 2016;

Zarrinabadi & Tavokoli, 2017). It has further begun to investigate their broader relevance and generalizability across contexts. In an initial study, around a third of participants reported having personally experienced DMCs to a *similarly high level* of motivational intensity, with this figure more than doubling when including participants who reported motivational experiences similar to that of a DMC, if 'not quite as intense' (Muir, 2020). From a pedagogical perspective, it is of note that this study did not identify material differences in individuals' propensity to experience a DMC across variables including participants' L1, sex and cultural/geographical context (although further investigation is certainly needed).

Group-DMCs

DMCs can also be experienced in groups (Dörnyei *et al.*, 2016; Sampson, 2016). In educational contexts, we have argued that we can best understand group-DMCs as emerging via *intensive group projects* (IGPs; Dörnyei *et al.*, 2016; Muir, 2020). For example, this might be a group of students working together to rehearse a performance, or collaborating to film and edit a short video segment to upload onto a school website. As a language teacher (even one that has not stood in front of a group of language learners for several years!), this is an area of DMC theory I find particularly enticing. When focusing on motivation at the group level, rather than talking about students' values, attitudes, goals and intentions – important characteristics of individual level motivation – we must *also* pay attention to their group-level counterparts, including group cohesiveness, group norms and leadership. That is, 'when we discuss the learning behavior of groups of learners, motivational psychology and group dynamics converge' (Dörnyei & Muir, 2019: 11).

Empirical research investigating group-DMCs remains sparse, and sparser still is research investigating possibilities relating to the *purposeful facilitation* of group-DMC experiences with classes of language learners. Initial research has provided encouraging results (Muir, 2020; Muir *et al.*, under review), yet conclusions remain tentative, rooted in a single educational environment, and this remains a ripe area for future research.

Complexity and DMCs

Let us first consider the arguments for adopting a complexity approach in this instance. That is, let us assess both the significance of DMCs from a complexity perspective, and also the significance of a complexity approach to researching group-DMCs.

In Dörnyei *et al.* (2015) we argued that DMCs offer a unique opportunity for research. We likened the motivational trajectory of a DMC to that of a rocket, in that after launching it 'will follow a set path as determined by the conditions surrounding its launch' (Dörnyei *et al.*, 2015: 103; I return to the notion of *initial conditions* later in the chapter). In this sense, we argued that DMCs function as a regulator of motivation and behaviour. This is significant because it opens up a 'window for systematic research' (Dörnyei *et al.*, 2015), aligning diverse factors in our chaotic world and overriding obstacles in order to regulate fluctuation. That is to say, once a DMC has begun, up until the point at which the current of motivation begins to wane, action within it becomes – to a large extent – predictable.

In addition to DMCs being able to provide this 'window of opportunity' for research, complexity approaches likewise also offer considerable practical inroads through which we might investigate the conditions underpinning group-level motivational emergence. As noted above, group-DMCs manifest in L2 classrooms through IGPs. It is unquestionable that projects have a long, varied history within education, and there is no shortage of anecdotal accounts of wholly *un*successful L2 projects (both with respect to motivational, L2 and other outcomes). Rigorous research into projects has been limited, variable in quality and has provided few concrete foundations from which teachers and other materials writers might develop resources or fully understand practical implications (see Muir, 2019). The lack of consistency in the implementation of L2 projects should therefore not be surprising: the complexity of interrelated factors contributing to the emergence of group-level motivation is – as yet – far from fully understood. In this respect, it is helpful to remember that even the most thoughtfully crafted project may only ever be considered as having '*DMC potential*' (Muir, 2020).

Formative Experiments: Investigating Group-DMCs in the L2 Classroom

Formative experiments – also known as design or teaching experiments (see Reinking & Bradley, 2007: 13–16)[1] – are a deeply pragmatic methodology which strives to test 'theory and empirical research in the real world of practice' (Reinking & Bradley, 2004: 155). As Reinking and Bradley (2007: 9) have argued, they resemble approaches comparable to those in engineering, acting as 'a testing ground for ideas and for the application and development of theory within a systematic attempt to accomplish specific ends in real classrooms'. With these arguments in mind, the question has even been asked as to whether educational research might be more at home within the field of engineering than the social sciences (Sloane & Gorard, 2003). Cobb *et al.* (2003) posit that formative experiments should put theory 'in harm's way' (2003: 10), and that a fundamental hallmark is the central relationship between theory and instructional practice: '"What works" is underpinned by a concern for "how, when, and why" it works, and by a detailed specification of what exactly, "it" is' (2003: 13). Further characteristics also include the highly iterative and interventionist nature of the approach (Cobb *et al.*, 2003; see also Reinking & Bradley, 2007).

Writing from a complexity perspective, Larsen-Freeman and Cameron (2008: 244) explain: 'Formative experiments investigate the potential of a system rather than its state … [and attempt] to describe the interconnected web of factors influencing change'. Formative experiments look to answer two questions typically omitted from 'conventional' experimental designs, both of which are fundamental to pedagogy: 'What factors add to or detract from an intervention's success in accomplishing a valued pedagogical goal?' And further, 'how might the intervention be adapted in response to those factors to better accomplish that goal?' (Reinking & Watkins, 2000: 384, 387). In this sense, we can understand formative experiments as being:

> … simply a more systematic, intense, and data-driven way of doing what they [experienced teachers] do every day: setting pedagogical goals, making instructional moves to accomplish those goals, determining what works or doesn't work in helping or hindering the achievement of those goals, making appropriate adjustments, and assessing and reflecting on what has been accomplished. (Reinking & Bradley, 2007: 3)

In fact, experienced teachers are often able to anticipate and make these 'tweaks' even *before* they enter the classroom.

Bradley and Reinking (2011: 161) offer the following set of six questions as a 'useful guide for others interested in conducting formative experiments'. By way of concluding this overview, from the perspective of the current chapter interested in investigating group-DMCs, I offer my own brief responses:

(1) *What is the pedagogical goal and what theory establishes its value?* The goal is the facilitation of a strong current of group-level motivation (i.e. facilitation of the emergence of a *group-DMC*). The specific L2 goal of any IGP will be dependent on the nature of the intervention (e.g. increasing spoken fluency or productive vocabulary knowledge).

(2) *What classroom intervention has the potential to achieve the pedagogical goal?* The introduction of a well-designed IGP (see Muir, 2019, for more detailed elaboration of 'well-designed' motivational projects than I am able to offer in this chapter, and Muir, 2020, for discussion more specifically of IGPs *'with DMC potential'*).

(3) *What factors enhance or inhibit the effectiveness of the intervention in achieving the pedagogical goal?* Factors influencing the effectiveness of an IGP will include the nature of the goal, project structure, personal relevance and feedback, among many others.

(4) *How can the intervention be modified to achieve the pedagogical goal more effectively?* 'More effectively' might be interpreted in different ways. For example, the *earlier* emergence of a group-DMC, more

reliable/consistent success in facilitating a group-DMC, or striving for all students to experience a group-DMC to *the same/similar levels of intensity.* Success will be affected by all factors offered in answer to the previous question.

(5) *What unanticipated positive or negative effects does the intervention produce?* Unanticipated positive effects may include e.g. the development of teamwork skills, critical thinking and problem-solving abilities. Unanticipated negative effects may include e.g. students feeling overwhelmed or tired, during/after the experience.

(6) *Has the instructional environment changed as a result of the intervention?* Positive changes may include a greater openness from others (teachers, students, parents, school management) to IGPs, and greater financial and/or time investment from relevant stakeholders. Researcher/practitioner collaborations may open up new appetite and opportunities for research and collaboration, for both teachers and researchers alike. Negative experiences may lead to no change at all (or, worse still, increased appetite *against* any of the above).

An Example Study

The example study that I will use as a basis for discussion in this chapter involves a collaboration that came about – as many do – unexpectedly. It began with an email sent to a colleague here at the University of Nottingham from an Australian teacher who wished to share her experience of running a project with a class, out of which a group-DMC emerged organically. Many interviews (see Dörnyei *et al.*, 2016, Chapter 8), many emails and several years later, Jessica Florent, her colleague David Leach and I began our collaboration. The primary question we were interested in was, at its heart, a very simple one: was it was possible to run an L2 project in such a way that it might *purposefully facilitate* a group-DMC?

The project

Owing to the fact that Jessica had already experienced success in her classroom – and because I had detailed knowledge of this from many years of interviews and discussion – we replicated this same basic project framework: students were challenged to design, organise and host a 'Biggest Morning Tea' for international students on campus to raise money for the Cancer Council.[2] The project was designed around an 'All Eyes on the Final Product' framework (Dörnyei *et al.*, 2016), the defining feature of which is a *clear end-goal.* We designed the project to include all features we knew to be important, including a clear end goal – both with regards the fundraising event itself and in terms of specific L2 outcomes – and a clear project timeline (with explicit, regular subgoals). Other important foci included developing a robust group dynamic in the first week of the five-week course, and conscious effort to help learners personalise the project (again, both with regards the fundraising event itself and specific areas of L2 development).

Participants

Jessica and David team-taught the project (Jessica two days, David three days each week). Both are highly experienced English language teachers with prior experience of project-based learning. The language school has upward of 700 students, and is attached to a prominent university on East coast Australia. The learner group comprised 16 Business English students of seven L1s (the largest groupings of each being Japanese $N = 8$ and Spanish $N = 4$). The male/female split was equal.

Data collection

Commensurate with the primary research objective, data was collected from a variety of perspectives. Students completed twice-weekly structured journal entries, and were invited to participate in interviews via Skype. Jessica and David completed individual, structured diary entries at the end of every teaching day, and likewise participated in Skype interviews. This resulted in a combined dataset of approximately 62,800 words (11,400 words from journals and 51,400 from Skype interviews).

Full details of the methodology, data analysis and results can be found in Muir (2020; see Muir *et al.*, under review, for a concise summary of key findings with a focus on pedagogical implications and a specific call for teacher-led research in this area). To spoil the conclusion for anyone wishing to read this original work, findings provided convincing evidence that a group-DMC *did* emerge.

It is important to note that this study was not initially conceived of as a formative experiment. However, there are compelling parallels between this study and the underpinning principles of formative experiments, and I am further encouraged in positioning it in this way following Reinking and Bradley's (2007) presentation of similarly disassociated studies as exemplary of the approach. In the remainder of this chapter I use this study as a basis to introduce key terms and ideas from the considerable body of complex dynamic systems theory (CDST) literature. In doing so I highlight potential variations to this study, and alternative possibilities which may capture additional insight and further develop our understanding of group-level motivational emergence.

A Complexity Approach to Investigating Group-level Motivational Emergence

In their 2006 book exploring complexity and education, Davis and Sumara (2006) highlight several conditions required for complex emergence, including *internal diversity and redundancy*, *neighbour interactions* and *distributed control*. After first introducing key terms and ideas related to CDST and the emergence of group-DMCs more broadly, I return to discuss each of these areas separately, concurrently highlighting ideas and opportunities for future research.

Triggers and 'motivational phase-shifts': The emergence of group-DMCs

The complexity literature describes a *phase shift* as a point at which a 'dramatic and sudden' change occurs, leaving a system (the entity under investigation; for example, a class group) materially different to the way in which it was before (Larsen-Freeman & Cameron, 2008: 45). A phase shift engenders a newly emerged whole 'that is more than the sum of its parts and that cannot be explained reductively through the activity of the component parts' (Larsen-Freeman & Cameron, 2008: 59). To draw on Larsen-Freeman and Cameron's (2008) metaphor, an easy way to imagine this shift occurring is to picture a grain of sand being dropped onto a pile below. However, unlike the single grain of sand added prior, this one leads to a dramatic collapse and significant change in the pile's overall topography. This approach to understanding has also been reflected in research in other disciplines; for example, history:

> The habit of historians has been to identify such moments as the *keys* when they may only be *triggers*. They do not *cause*, in the direct linear sense. Rather, the 'pile' of accumulated events determines the outcome. In other words, history is being rethought, not in terms of sudden monumental events and 'great men,' but in terms of slow accumulations and triggers. (Davis & Sumara, 2006: 54)

The notion of a 'trigger' has also been used to describe the final piece that falls into place marking the emergence of a DMC (Dörnyei *et al.*, 2016). Colloquially known as a 'butterfly effect', these sometimes seemingly insignificant acts can lead to disproportionately large effects (Gladwell, 2000). So, *phase shifts* occur when this 'tipping point' is reached, wherein a discrete action/event functions as a trigger for significant change.

In his 2016 book, Sampson describes a *phase shift* witnessed in his Japanese students during their L2 English classes. This occurred after the introduction of 'informative noise', designed to 'upset the status quo' (2016: 175). The informative noise in this instance was a series of self-reflective classroom activities, but might equally be the introduction of an IGP. Sampson argues that his conclusions not only found positive motivational outcomes occurring on an individual basis, but 'the potential for positive motivational outcomes through using activities that introduce "informative noise" *across* a class group' (2016: 174). As he posits, 'radical phase-shifts in the motivational trajectory of not only individuals but also a *class system* may be possible' (Sampson, 2016: 137). That is, to use Sampson's turn of phrase, a class group can collectively experience a *motivational phase-shift*. Sampson argues that the motivational phase-shift witnessed in these students fostered the emergence of a group-DMC.

While the introduction of a planned trigger or 'informative noise' (such as the introduction of an IGP) may bring about a response from a system (such as the emergence of a group-DMC), this is far from guaranteed. In Australia, the group-DMC ultimately emerged later than we anticipated. The fundraising event itself was scheduled for Thursday of week four (of the five-week course), and evidence of the emergence of a group-DMC was seen only mid-way through the third week. There was a clear point – identifiable in both teacher and student datasets – that marked the emergence of the group-DMC, when the project finally became 'real' to students (the point at which it dawned on them that it was not merely a theoretical exercise):

> I've got a funny feeling that between yesterday and today there was a bit of a handover. In that we – I definitely pushed yesterday, you [David] definitely pushed today, and I just saw them all hovering, they're downstairs now, there's like 8 of them hovering – you know this is half an hour after, now nearly an hour after class. Oh no longer, an hour and a half, and they're still down there ... they've got a real idea of what they're doing now I think, I think we'll see a difference now, I have a funny feeling. (*Week 3 Day 2, Jessica*)

It is difficult, however, to speak with certainty with regards what acted as the ultimate trigger that led to this 'tipping point' (richer data collected at *shorter timescales* would have been invaluable in this respect – I return to discuss this further in the following section). In later iterations of the project (Jessica and David have run this project every year since our collaboration began in 2015; see Muir *et al.*, under review), Jessica and David have proactively addressed this issue in the first week of the course, and have tasked students with running a pre-organised 'taster' mini-morning tea. This practical demonstration has provided a tangible example of what their own realisation of this goal might look like, and has made it easier for students to comprehend the nature of the challenge they were being tasked with. Although this does appear to have aided earlier emergence of a group-DMC, this event in and of itself has not necessarily functioned as the trigger on every (or indeed any) occasion.

A complexity perspective would imply that every time we have run this same project, taught by the same teachers and in this same Australian context, it is likely that different factors have functioned as the final trigger ultimately initiating the emergence of a group-DMC. No two class groups are the same, nor should we expect any two triggers to be. However, it is not necessarily imperative that we seek to pin down these specific triggers in each instance. In terms of future research questions, a key focus may be investigation into specific factors which can *hold back* the emergence of group-DMCs (i.e. things which might dampen the effectiveness of potential triggers), and of how these factors might be proactively managed (as in the example above of Jessica and David's 'mini-morning tea').

Initial conditions, attractors and classroom dynamics

In complexity research, the importance of a system's *initial conditions* on its subsequent behaviour is well established. Returning to the sandcastle analogy, it is not the final grain of sand added that dictates the way any collapse will occur, but the topography of the pile below. To be able to predict the effectiveness of any potential trigger, 'we would need to know absolutely every small detail of the starting state' (Larsen-Freeman & Cameron, 2008: 57). This being said, some basic initial conditions required for group-level motivational emergence may be more generalisable. These include the core set of basic motivational conditions required in any classroom, including *appropriate classroom roles and norms* and *appropriate teacher leadership styles* (see Dörnyei & Muir, 2019).

In the context of group-DMCs, initial conditions are important on two primary levels: at an individual level (i.e. each individual learner) and at a group level (i.e. considering the dynamic of the class as a whole). Let us begin by considering the former. Verspoor (2015: 40) depicts the notion of initial conditions particularly accessibly, reproduced in Figure 12.1. For the purposes of the current chapter, let us imagine that the ball represents a student's past experience with and attitude towards group projects in educational contexts. As Verspoor (2015: 41) describes: 'The flat line represents a rather neutral subsystem and with just the slightest force the ball could move either left (negative) or right (positive)'. A student with no experience of IGPs in education will likely be relatively easily influenced as to their preference or dislike towards them. Assuming the project is introduced in such a way as to encourage positive initial evaluations, we can imagine that '[t]he ball will be vacillating on the positive side of the line and start making an indentation there, resulting in a shallow basin' (2015: 40; see (b) in Figure 12.1). This basin represents something known as an *attractor*. However, attractors do not 'attract', in the traditional sense, rather, they 'are critical outcomes that a system evolves toward or approaches over time' (Hiver, 2015: 21).

Continuing Verspoor's (2015) example, '[t]he longer the ball remains in a particular attractor, the deeper the attractor state becomes and the more difficult it is to move it out of that particular attractor' (2015: 40; see (c) in Figure 12.1). In practical terms, this means that a student who

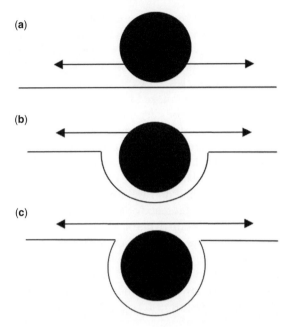

Figure 12.1 Examples of three different states a subsystem (the ball) can be in (adapted from Verspoor, 2015: 40)

has a very strong, long-standing negative attitude towards educational IGPs may find it considerably more difficult to become positively engaged. It therefore follows, too, that this student may be materially less likely to experience a group-DMC in this context. In Australia, a stipulation from the school was that we were only allowed to run the project with agreement from the class, and a small number of students opted instead to complete a parallel, non-project class (possibly indicating a view of projects which could be described in the manner of (c) in Figure 12.1).

Of course, attitudes towards group projects are only one dimension among a gamut of initial conditions learners will bring with them into a classroom: this will also include their L2 level, their overall motivation to study, their L2 goals, how busy they are in other aspects of their lives and an undocumentable number of other factors. Further, while each factor may experience periods of stability, it will nevertheless exist itself in a state of flux. This perspective is challenging to the study of individual motivation, and is compounded when considering the motivation of learner groups: group-level motivation is influenced on a moment-by-moment basis not only by all other systems with which it interacts (e.g. other class groups, the wider school community), but also by the continually evolving motivational subsystems of each individual learner.

Classroom dynamics (i.e. the initial conditions of the group as a whole) are a key contributing factor in the triggering of a *motivational phase-shift* and the emergence of a group-DMC. In Australia, the group met only at the start of the five-week course, and as such a prime focus for the first days and weeks was on building a strong, positive group dynamic. Appropriate classroom conditions can provide a core foundation (Dörnyei & Muir, 2019), and although such experiences as *motivational phase-shifts* 'cannot be scripted or managed into existence', Davis and Sumara postulate they 'can sometimes be occasioned' (2006: 152; indeed, this was the basic premise we worked from in approaching this study). Dedicated team building exercises were organised for the first week, and – as noted earlier in the chapter – both teachers and students were cognisant of the moment at which this translated into the emergence of a group-DMC.

In both teachers' individual diaries, immediately prior to this *motivational phase-shift* and the emergence of the group-DMC was evidence of the class 'storming'. In the group dynamics literature, it is understood that groups move through a series of stages before they reach a point at which they are able to work productively together: forming, storming, norming, performing and adjourning (Tuckman & Jensen, 1977, in the context of SLA see Dörnyei & Murphey, 2003). There is variation in the length and nature of each phase (owing to differing initial conditions), yet there is typically a period of friction and transition in which group norms and identities are collectively negotiated (storming) before this settles (norming) and students are ready to work productively together (performing; I return to the notion of adjourning later in the chapter). In Australia, the start of the performing stage emerged in tandem with evidence of the emerging group-DMC.

One approach to identifying periods of friction and transition may be through *critical incident technique* (CIT; see e.g. Butterfield *et al.*, 2005). While Ushioda (2016: 572) cautions that 'there are no straightforward criteria for determining what makes an incident "critical" or significant', she goes on to suggests that 'one relatively simple approach may be to consider an event as potentially interesting or significant if it causes us to wonder why a particular learner (or a group of learners) is behaving in a particular way.' If teachers are also involved in the research process, they are perfectly situated to be able to identify such incidences as they occur, yet, data collected throughout a project may also be supplemented or expanded upon through retrospective interviews. For example, after a project has ended students might be invited to plot their motivational trajectories throughout the project on a simple timeline. Exploring these trajectories in retrospective interviews may serve multiple goals. Firstly, this could offer greater elaboration and insight into critical incidents already emerged from analysis of other datasets. Secondly, it may highlight whether key critical incidents or turning points in a project are identified similarly by students as by teachers and/or researchers. Finally, if novel incidents are later identified by students, this would then allow for re-examination of other data collected pertaining to this time (this would therefore be able to mitigate unseen weaknesses or gaps across other areas of data collection). Periods of friction and transition might not be the only critical incidents worth of exploration via CIT. Other foci might include sudden or unexpected behaviours (for example students staying behind longer after a class ends) or abrupt changes in individual or group attitudes towards various aspects of the project or process.

From a data collection perspective, the teacher diaries yielded unexpectedly rich insights. Unexpected, simply because such diaries tend to be easily forgotten in the midst of practical classroom concerns, and especially considering the fact that Jessica and David also found themselves wrapped up in the emerging group-DMC (the quality of these daily diaries is entirely attributable to Jessica and David's immense commitment). Practically speaking, Verspoor (2015: 45) advises that one must 'consider the initial conditions of all the relevant sub-systems involved and measure them very frequently (probably daily) in the first few weeks, as the emotional sub-systems especially are likely to show considerable variability early on'. The implication is that to fully understand any instance of motivational emergence, thorough and deep data collection is required, at multiple different *timescales* (cf. de Bot, 2015).

In this study, data were collected daily (a teacher journal entry and two/three 10-minute student interviews), twice-weekly (student diaries) and – roughly – fortnightly (teacher interviews). This was very effective in providing data able to address the research objective, which required evidence capable of robustly capturing any emerging group-DMC. The focus was therefore on *longer* timescales (days, weeks), and on emergence at the *group-level*. Future research might focus on data collection at shorter timescales, and one practical way this could be achieved may be through classroom observations. The rich dataset this could yield would also be better able to investigate, for example, specific triggers or roadblocks to group-DMC emergence (as discussed earlier in the chapter).

Further to a focus on initial conditions, other contributing factors are also important for the emergence and maintenance of a group-DMC (i.e. to keep it within a stable *attractor state*). These include the notions of *redundancy and diversity*, and of *short-range relationships* and specific *network architectures*.

Redundancy and diversity in complex collectives

Davis and Sumara define *specialisation* as 'the dynamic combination of diversity and redundancy', and stress its importance with regards considering '*simultaneously* the individual agents and the collective system' (Davis & Sumara, 2006: 140, italics in original). *Redundancy* refers to attributes which are common among group members. For example, redundancies might include common L1s or similar educational or social backgrounds. Davis and Sumara (2006: 139) highlight two key roles for redundancy: 'it enables interactions among agents', and 'makes it possible for agents to compensate for others' failings'. *Diversity* describes those features and skills that are unique to individuals, and is equally vital. This is needed so that a group, or a *complex collective*, is able to respond positively to perturbations – 'informative noise', for example the introduction of an IGP – and so that it is able to work effectively.

From a pedagogical perspective, it is important to ensure that a group has sufficient opportunities to draw on both its redundancy and diversity. In Australia, positive elements of diversity that contributed to the project were clear in students' accounts, and for some areas of this project related particularly to students' past professional or life experience, for example expertise in marketing or accounting. Having highlighted the success of the teacher journals above, for students, it was interviews that provided a richer dataset over their diaries. The interviews proved very effective in encouraging students to open up and, had it been possible, it would have been valuable to increase the number of interviews conducted each day to further utilise this rich data source (it would not have been reasonable to request students to stay even later after school to speak with me). Future studies might arrange a research assistant to conduct parallel daily interviews with more students – the positive way in which the opportunity to converse one-on-one with a proficient speaker was perceived by students meant that there certainly may have been appetite for this. Such an approach in future studies would also lead to a more nuanced understanding of students' *individual* experiences of group-DMCs.

Key aspects of redundancy in the group included a shared academic context and environment, yet on occasion, in future iterations of this project it has been necessary to actively foster more. One example of this we have described as the 'Hisashi Principle' (see Muir *et al.*, under review). Hisashi was a Japanese student who struggled particularly in interaction and making himself heard among a group of classmates with varied cultural backgrounds. He suggested a task in which students observed their peers conducting a meeting in a manner typical of their context, followed by a Q&A focused on the differing conventions and communication styles observed. This newly gained common understanding of cultural and other differences in meeting styles immediately served to explain the frustrations the group had run up against in working collaboratively together, and this increased redundancy in knowledge among group members saw an immediate positive effect.

Questions of redundancy and diversity are particularly pertinent when considering the widely differing context in which IGPs might be introduced worldwide. Are different elements of diversity and redundancy important in environments where, for example, groups have the same versus different L1s, amounts/types of life experience, or with different project designs and goals?

Network architectures, short-range relationships and the importance of feedback

Further insights a complexity perspective can offer to understanding of the emergence of group-DMCs relate to the nature of students' interpersonal relationships: of different *network architectures*, and the importance of *short-range relationships.*

A centralised network architecture can be considered representative of a typical classroom environment, with the teacher at centre stage, managing and directing communication (see (a) in Figure 12.2). Information can travel very quickly in this formation as agents are 'separated at most by one intermediary' (Davis & Sumara, 2006: 53). However, such a formation is unlikely to lead to emergent outcomes (Davis & Sumara, 2006). The network architectures most relevant to our current discussion are therefore *decentralised* and *distributed* arrangements (see (b) and (c) in Figure 12.2). Distributed arrangements are immensely robust – 'many nodes could be removed before the system would begin to fail' (Davis & Sumara, 2006: 53) – however, this comes at the cost of laboriously slow information transfer from one side of the network to the other. Decentralised arrangements are less robust, but are able to facilitate a quicker exchange of information (as messages must pass through fewer individuals). Interaction between students is core to the functioning of a complex system: 'Clearly, neighbors that come together in a grander unity must communicate' (Davis & Sumara, 2006: 142). However, Davis and Sumara downplay the importance of interactions 'for their own sake', arguing instead that the 'neighbours' that must interact 'are ideas, hunches, queries, and other manners of representation' (Davis & Sumara, 2006). The 'right' type of student groupings and classroom arrangement at any point is, therefore, that which is best able to facilitate such interaction.

Without overt appreciation of this terminology or theoretical background, it is interesting to note that spontaneous discussion of these ideas is evident in data collected through the teacher journals (indeed, such considerations are likely to be a continual concern of all language teachers).

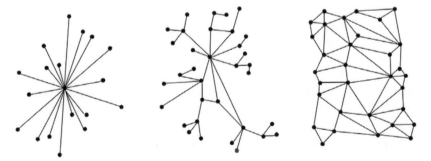

Figure 12.2 Types of network architectures: (a) centralised, (b) decentralised or scale-free and (c) distributed (adapted from Davis & Sumara, 2006: 52)

Although decentralised control, with its happy medium between efficiency and robustness has been argued to be superior in educational contexts (Davis & Sumara, 2006), this may be dependent on the size of the class group: if the group is small enough, the drawback of distributed architectures – the slower transfer of information – may not be prohibitive. Indeed, what can be seen in the teacher journals is the group moving from more of a decentralised architecture (with discrete subteams) to a distributed one (with students working as a single unit). It is further interesting to note that evidence of the emergence of a group-DMC came at around the time at which the group's way of working appears to have been successfully negotiated:

> *Week 2 Day 1, Jessica*: 'Lowlights: different groups not attempting to communication with other groups'
>
> *Week 2 Day 2, David*: 'Highlights: Discussion in random groups – so much more productive than their teams'
>
> *Week 2 Day 4, David*: 'one of the 2 students in control said 'we only need 2 for this, why don't you (meaning class and me) write letter of intro-duction?' Brilliant!! So, we started to brainstorm content on board. This class like it when we <u>all</u> work together on composing a text – especially as we encourage <u>everyone</u> to make a contribution. Working well with each other in pairs/small groups' [underlining in original]
>
> *Week 2 Day 5, David*: 'Lots of discussion in groups and more participa-tion by quiet students'

Short-range relationships allow for immediate *feedback* to be communi-cated and received among group members, a further element of critical importance in the context of group-DMCs. *Positive feedback mechanisms* facilitated by 'healthy local interactions … among near neighbours' can be considerably more important than feedback received from a 'top-down organisation' (Davis & Sumara, 2006: 104). Indeed, Lewis (2005) describes such 'positive feedback loops' as vital for processes of 'self-amplification' following a perturbation in a system, and this reflects exactly the same processes by which DMCs emerge and through which they gather increasing momentum (Dörnyei *et al.*, 2016). This feedback might be formal or informal, verbal or non-verbal. Once a DMC emerges, closely spaced (or observational) data would be able to offer valuable insight on the impact of various types of feedback (for example in the context of exploring triggers and initial emergence, re-triggering after dis-tractions/bumps in the road, or the final dissipation of motivation at the end of a DMC – for the latter see also the following section). Research investigating the impact of various network architectures and mapping of their influence would also be of immense practical value.

Other important factors for consideration

In this chapter I have focussed on a range of key, practical consider-ations related to the emergence of group-DMCs, yet it is far from comprehensive. Below I briefly highlight two final factors for consideration: *individual variation*, and issues relating to management of the *end of group-DMCs*.

Acknowledging individual variation

An important focus within all complexity approaches is that of individual variation, and as I have already intimated though this chapter this remains so even in the context of *group*-DMCs. In the same way that even a powerful group-DMC cannot offer perfect predictability, so too will it not guarantee that this is identically experienced by all group members. In Australia, two students were markedly less engaged than the group as a whole, manifesting in two different ways: one as increasing disengagement with the project element of the course, and the other through outwardly motivated engagement concealing personal reflections indicating concern with regards personal L2 development (for full discussion see Muir, 2020). A follow-up study using retrodictive qualitative modelling (Dörnyei, 2014), for example, would have been informative in tracing these different motivational trajectories and investigating the initial conditions of these two students, against those of other students more fully engaged in the group-DMC. This is a fascinating and highly important avenue for future research.

Transitioning out of group-DMCs

Group-DMCs are always finite, and upon completion students' motivation must transition from being governed primarily at the group-level to again being individually managed. The way a group adjourns can have a significant impact on the way an experience is remembered (Dörnyei & Murphey, 2003). In instructed environments, in order for any *ongoing* positive motivational impact to be realised, these final stages require careful teacher management. Investigation, for example through a detailed case study, might focus on how different individuals navigate this change, the ways in which this management is linked to the experiences and attitudes a learner brings with them into a classroom (i.e. as linked to *initial conditions*), and the factors most important in affecting and maintaining any positive or negative change.

Conclusion

In this chapter I have highlighted several ideas from the complexity literature which are particularly relevant to developing our understanding of the emergence of group-DMCs, and of group-level motivational emergence more broadly. I have highlighted the particular relevance of *formative experiments* and key areas of inquiry around which they might be centred, and have further highlighted other methodological approaches that might be employed, in addition to putting forward potential research questions. For practitioner-researchers interested in adopting a complexity approach to researching the emergence and management of group-DMCs – and of group-level motivation more broadly – I hope that this chapter may offer a tangible springboard.

Notes

(1) There is some overlap in the presentation of methodologies. Each have slightly different emphases, yet are rooted in the same tradition and share many key characteristics. I have opted for the term 'formative experiment' to mirror others in the field (e.g. Larsen-Freeman & Cameron, 2008).

(2) https://www.biggestmorningtea.com.au/

References

Butterfield, L.D., Borgen, W.A., Amundson, N.E. and Maglio, A-S.T. (2005) Fifty years of the critical incident technique: 1954–2004 and beyond. *Qualitative Research* 5 (4), 475–497.

Bradley, B.A. and Reinking, D. (2011) Revisiting the connection between research and practice using formative and design experiments. In N.K. Duke and M.H. Mallette (eds) *Literacy Research Methodologies* (pp. 188–212). New York: The Guildford Press.

Cobb, P., Confrey, J., diSessa, A., Lehrer, R. and Schauble, L. (2003) Design experiments in educational research. *Educational Researcher* 32 (1), 9–13.

Davis, B. and Sumara, D. (2006) *Complexity and Education: Enquiries into Learning, Teaching and Research*. Mahwah, NJ: Lawrence Erlbaum.

de Bot, K. (2015) Rates of change: Timescales in second language development. In Z. Dörnyei, P. MacIntyre and A. Henry (eds) *Motivational Dynamics in Language Learning* (pp. 29–37). Bristol: Multilingual Matters.

Dörnyei, Z. (2005) *The Psychology of the Language Learner: Individual Differences in Second Language Acquisition*. Mahwah, NJ: Lawrence Erlbaum.

Dörnyei, Z. (2009) The L2 motivational self system. In Z. Dörnyei and E. Ushioda (eds) *Motivation, Language Identity and the L2 Self* (pp. 9–42). Bristol: Multilingual Matters.

Dörnyei, Z. (2014) Researching complex dynamic systems: 'Retrodictive qualitative modelling' in the language classroom. *Language Teaching* 47 (1), 80–91.

Dörnyei, Z. and Muir, C. (2019) Creating a motivating classroom environment. In A. Gao, C. Davidson and C. Leung (eds) *International Handbook of English Language Teaching* (2nd edn). New York: Springer.

Dörnyei, Z. and Murphey, R. (2003) *Group Dynamics in the Language Classroom*. Cambridge: Cambridge University Press.

Dörnyei, Z., Henry, A. and Muir, C. (2016) *Motivational Currents in Language Learning: Frameworks for Focused Interventions*. New York: Routledge.

Dörnyei, Z., Ibrahim, Z. and Muir, C. (2015) 'Directed Motivational Currents': Regulating complex dynamic systems through motivational surges. In Z. Dörnyei, P. MacIntyre and A. Henry (eds) *Motivational Dynamics in Language Learning* (pp. 95–105). Bristol: Multilingual Matters

Gladwell, M. (2000) *The Tipping Point*. London: Abacus.

Henry, A., Davydenko, S. and Dörnyei, Z. (2015) The anatomy of directed motivational currents: Exploring intense and enduring periods of L2 motivation. *The Modern Language Journal* 99 (2), 329–345.

Hiver, P. (2015) Attractor States. In Z. Dörnyei, P.D. MacIntyre and A. Henry (eds) *Motivational Dynamics and Language Learning* (pp. 20–28). Bristol: Multilingual Matters.

Ibrahim, Z. (2016) Affect in directed motivational currents: Positive emotionality in long-term L2 engagement. In P.D. MacIntyre, T. Gregersen and S. Mercer (eds) *Positive Psychology in SLA* (pp. 258–281). Bristol: Multilingual Matters.

Larsen-Freeman, D. and Cameron, L. (2008) *Complex Systems and Applied Linguistics.* Oxford: Oxford University Press.

Lewis, M.D. (2005) Bridging emotion theory and neurobiology through dynamic systems modelling. *Behavioral and Brain Sciences* 28, 169–245.

Muir, C. (2020) *Directed Motivational Currents and Language Education: Exploring Implications for Pedagogy.* Bristol: Multilingual Matters.

Muir, C. (2019) Motivation and Projects. In M. Lamb, K. Csizér, A. Henry and S. Ryan (eds) *The Palgrave Handbook of Motivation for Language Learning* (pp. 327–346). Cham, Switzerland: Palgrave Macmillan.

Muir, C., Florent, J. and Leach, D. (under review) Designing and managing motivational group projects. *Journal of Languages, Texts and Society.*

Reinking, D. and Bradley, B.A. (2004) Connecting research and practice using formative and design experiments. In N.K. Duke and M.H. Mallette (eds) *Literacy Research Methodologies* (pp. 114–148). New York: The Guildford Press.

Reinking, D. and Bradley, B.A. (2007) *Formative and Design Experiments: Approaches to Language and Literacy Research.* New York: Teachers College Press.

Reinking, D. and Watkins, J. (2000) A formative experiment investigating the use of multimedia book reviews to increase elementary students' independent reading. *Reading Research Quarterly* 35 (3), 384–419.

Sampson, R.J. (2016) *Complexity in Classroom Foreign Language Learning Motivation: A Practitioner Perspective from Japan.* Bristol: Multilingual Matters.

Schumann, J.H. (2015) Foreword. In Z. Dörnyei, P.D. MacIntyre and A. Henry (eds) *Motivational Dynamics and Language Learning* (pp. xv–xix). Bristol: Multilingual Matters.

Sloane, F.C. and Gorard, S. (2003) Exploring modeling aspects of design experiments. *Educational Researcher* 32 (1), 29–31.

Tuckman, B.W. and Jensen, M.A. (1977) Stages in small group development revisited. *Group and Organisation Studies* 2 (4), 419–427.

Ushioda, E. (2009) A person-in-context relational view of emergent motivation, self and identity. In Z. Dörnyei and E. Ushioda (eds) *Motivation, Language Identity and the L2 Self* (pp. 215–228). Bristol: Multilingual Matters.

Ushioda, E. (2016) Language learning motivation through a small lens: A research agenda. *Language Teaching* 49 (4), 564–577.

Verspoor, M. (2015) Initial Conditions. In Z. Dörnyei, P.D. MacIntyre and A. Henry (eds) *Motivational Dynamics and Language Learning* (pp. 38–46). Bristol: Multilingual Matters.

Zarrinabadi, N. and Tavakoli, M. (2017) Exploring motivational surges among Iranian EFL teacher trainees: Directed motivational currents in focus. *TESOL Quarterly* 51 (1), 155–166.

13 The Complexity Lens: Autoethnography and Practitioner Research to Examine Group Dynamics

Richard S. Pinner

Introduction

The complexity paradigm in applied linguistics as a research approach is essentially grounded on incorporating more qualitative understandings, retrospection and reflection (Kramsch, 2011; Larsen-Freeman, 2011; Sampson, 2016a); all of which are gaining traction now due to their potential for bringing research and practice together (Barkhuizen, 2017; Walsh & Mann, 2015). My research used autoethnography to bolster practitioner research, by adding a more nuanced understanding of the various layers of context in which a course takes place. In particular, I wanted to include my own reflections on the various psychological states that I (as a teacher) went through as I taught a compulsory English course in a Japanese university over one academic year. Despite this personal focus, autoethnographies are not merely about one person, but draw on the interactions of the community to make observations, just as ethnography does (Chang, 2008; Denzin, 2014). This methodology places emphasis on context, making autoethnographies ideal for in-depth qualitative reviews in institutional, local and social settings (Canagarajah, 2012; Ellis *et al.*, 2011; Mirhosseini, 2018). In this way, I also attempted to gain richer insights into how the students experienced the course as well. The main focus of this inquiry became the synergistic link between teacher and student motivation (see Pinner, 2019), which was facilitated through creating a culture of authenticity (here meaning the congruence between activity and beliefs). However, this chapter will focus chiefly on the methodology itself and its fit within a complexity paradigm.

In this paper, I will reflect upon how autoethnography has enabled me to apply a complexity approach to my research as an analytical framework which harmonizes with the central methodology of practitioner research.

I will explain how a complexity lens helped me to recognize the gestalt nature of my class as its own 'small culture' (Holliday, 1999) developed. It also enabled me to understand the social dynamics between myself and learners, as our emotions and perceptions fluctuated throughout the study. I will discuss the fact that, although many of these insights came retrospectively, they have deeply informed my teaching and helped to crystallize my philosophy of practice. One of the most important tools for looking at group dynamics was the creation of sociograms of the class, which afforded me a different perspective from which to examine some of the relationships between students. The sample of data I present focuses on group dynamics, with particular emphasis on two very different students, Mr Charge and Mr Auxiliary, who actually had surprising similarities between them. To frame the narrative, I focus on seating positions, group work and the perception of introvert vs. extrovert features of these two particular students.

Autoethnography and Complexity Fit

One of the challenges posed by the complexity paradigm is that, as an actual research method it potentially poses a threat to dominant positivist approaches because it reduces the reliability of standardised, measurable research based on variables, although at the same time it increases the validity of second language acquisition (SLA) research by forcing us to acknowledge that we cannot simply isolate certain variables in order to understand the phenomena under investigation (Kramsch, 2011: 21). In other words, traditional approaches to SLA research which focus 'on averages and aggregates that lump together people who share certain characteristics' (Ushioda, 2011: 12) are insufficient, to say the least, and research methods that seek to gain contextualised understandings become paramount (see Ushioda, 2015, 2016 for further expansion on this issue). Autoethnography is one research method which has the potential to answer this call because it combines ethnography with the tradition of narrative inquiry (NI), which is an ontologically different approach to positivist methods because NI acknowledges that there is no fixed, singular truth and places context at the centre of any attempt to gain a deeper understanding into complex phenomena (Barkhuizen *et al.*, 2014; Polkinghorne, 2007).

The key aspects of autoethnography and its complexity fit are outlined as follows (see Figure 13.1). Firstly, autoethnographies seek for validity as opposed to reliability, in other words the believability of the story rather than its relation to some abstract notion of truth or a singular version of reality; Secondly, as mentioned previously, the 'auto' in autoethnography does not mean that it focuses purely on the self, but on the self in relation to others, thereby highlighting the wider social ecology and context of the inquiry; Finally, with central emphasis on context, autoethnographies are

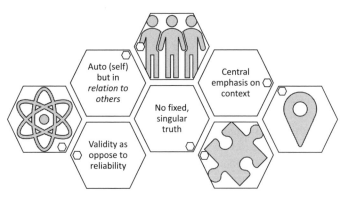

Figure 13.1 Autoethnography and complexity fit

useful for examining unfurling relationships, something which Ushioda in particular has long been advocating in the study of motivation (Ushioda, 1994, 1996, 2009, 2015, 2016). In this way, autoethnographies incorporate multiple lenses and gather various perspectives around one central lived experience, making this methodology a good way to harmonise complexity theory with practitioner research.

This is the theoretical basis for autoethnography, but how would a study like this look in practice? As a teacher, I wanted to collect data which were part of my everyday teaching activities. I did not want to particularly alter my actions, but simply to understand what was going on, and why, in more detail. For this reason, Exploratory Practice (EP) was the guiding methodology which I took with the class. Although entire books are written on this method which describe it in detail (Hanks, 2017), the basic premises which I took were the ideas that research should not be a 'third-party' endeavour (Allwright & Hanks, 2009), that the students were to be involved in the process as a much as possible and the aim of the research was to improve the 'quality of classroom life' (Gieve & Miller, 2006; see Consoli, this volume, for further expansion upon the method and principles of EP). In particular, what I took from EP was the fact that any research should contribute to the students' learning (an approach which I liked because it seemed highly ethical), and that most of the data should come from pedagogical sources, i.e. generated through the natural course of teaching, such as students' essays, comments, classroom discourse and so on, rather than using questionnaires which are designed purely for the purpose of research. All the data are in the target language (English), which may limit the depth of the data in some ways but ensures that the research is part of the learning process (see Sampson, this volume for further justification). Figure 13.2 and Table 13.1 list the types of data I collected. Essentially, I strapped a microphone to myself, went and taught the class, kept everything that any of the students did in class or said or wrote to me, made extremely

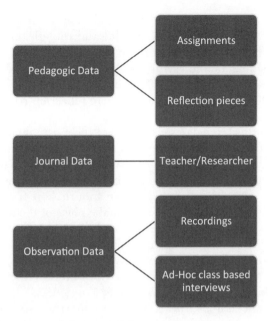

Figure 13.2 Three types of classroom data

Table 13.1 Summary of data types

Chronology	Data type	Data description
	Pedagogic data	Work done by students as part of the course, also includes my own teaching materials
	Field notes (as opposed to journal entries)	Logs, observations and notes made during the course
	Trace data	Includes emails and online interactions as part of the course Virtual Learning Environment
Data collected during the course	Audio/Audio-visual data	Recordings of every class Audio Teacher/Researcher journal Recordings made by students as part of coursework Recordings of students on-task ad-hoc interviews conducted while monitoring the students
	Institutional end of course (EOC) evaluation questionnaire	End-of-course evaluation done by the students anonymously when the teacher/researcher was not present and conducted by the institution
	Academic writing	My own published or in-progress academic writing that mentions the course or reflects on the themes being investigated (authenticity and motivation)
Data collected after the course	Journal reflections and narrative (as opposed to field notes)	Notes and observations made subsequently and transcribed as teacher/researcher journal entries, many of which use stimulated recall
	Student follow-up emails/meetings	Includes both coincidental and solicited reflections from students after the course. Meetings were only conducted with one participant (Mr Charge)

detailed notes (Emerson *et al.*, 2011) and kept an almost obsessively reflexive journal about everything I did and thought and felt for the whole year. The resultant dataset had over half a million words on word-processed documents and recorded 227 hours of audio data. My field journal alone runs to over 80,000 words, with students' essays adding a further 50,000 words, many of which were reflection papers and other such assignments.

Managing this large dataset was one of the most unwieldly tasks. As I collected data, I improved my system for taking notes, for filing things and staying organised. I found NVivo software very useful for this. I also would recommend anyone new to autoethnography to always start every entry with the date, as undated entries in a journal are frustrating to the later self who attempts to analyse and make sense of the narrative. Even something as simple as reconstructing the chronology of events was a serious process with so much detail and so much complexity.

Another tool available within NVivo is the ability to create a sociogram, which 'is a sociometric tool used to build a record of relations among members of a group' (Degenne & Forsé, 1999: 23). Sociograms were first pioneered by the Romanian-American sociologist Jacob Moreno (1934). Moreno's first sociograms still resemble those most widely used by teachers today in that they simply ask students to name two other students that they would like to work with on a task or project (Leung & Silberling, 2006). The resulting sociogram can be extremely useful for teachers to identify 'isolates'; students who may be excluded by the group, and also understanding the general dynamics of the class. They can be drawn with a pencil, although more complex sociograms plotted by computers are used for social network analysis, often looking at online interactions as well as relations between people in different communities.

Since the application of sociograms to classrooms, teachers have been administering questionnaires to students about their relationships to others in the class. I did not do such a questionnaire with my class, as I did not learn about sociograms until after I had collected the data. However, I still felt that creating a sociogram would be a useful way to visualise the group dynamics and understand some of the complexity of the class. Specifically I wanted to see if plotting a sociogram could help me to further recognise 'individuals as fundamentally social and relational beings' (Mercer, 2015: 74). I created a sociogram based on three relationships between students which were known and easily available to me: (1) members of the same department, (2) students who regularly sat together and (3) students who were in the same group when working on the two assessed group projects. The network sociogram represents visually some of the relationships between the students in the class. I will present examples later as they become relevant to the central narrative.

Fisheye Lens: Challenging Assumptions

The notion of different lenses is a useful metaphor for me in both my research and teaching. When I teach literature majors about various critical theories, I describe each theory (feminist theory, Marxist theory, reader response) as a different lens to help us focus on certain aspects of a text (following Tyson, 2011). Ema Ushioda (2016) advocates a 'small lens approach' to studying motivation, which I think can be broadened to apply to studying all aspects of classroom interactions at a more personal, contextually embedded and nuanced level. This approach involves zooming in to the classroom as a situated context, placing the interactions within a context-dependent frame of reference rather than attempting to extrapolate data as if they would be applicable to a sandbox of similar variables. Complexity perspectives are also a lens, a wide-focus lens which has a powerful zoom. The main difference about the complexity lens is that it tries to capture moving images, or dynamic interactions with a focus on change. As Larsen-Freeman and Cameron (2008: 25) observe about the language class, 'in all sorts of ways, the group is never the same two days running, or even from one minute to the next'. Another lens metaphor is the idea of the fisheye syndrome, which Gonzalez (2013) explains is when our perception of a class's participation gets distorted as if looking through a fisheye lens. Fisheye lenses are wide-angle lenses designed to capture 180-degree angles. The security camera or peephole on a door's intercom will generally have one. Now, if we imagine looking through such a lens at a group of people, only the ones nearest the lens will be clear and enlarged, whilst the people further away from the lens seem smaller. Gonzalez uses this analogy to highlight the fact that in a classroom, we might feel everyone is participating well, when in fact there may only be a small number of students participating, but they dominate the class and hence our perception of it through the distorted lens. Due to the nature of this inquiry, I avoided doing this right from the first class, as the narrative will show. However, by adding a complexity perspective to the fisheye lens, I came to see that there was more to learn about those students who appeared small or distant in terms of their participation and motivational orientation towards the class.

As a teacher who has utilised reflection as an approach to both teaching and researching, I have found that reflection, if done badly, can potentially lead to a process of 'mythologising' certain aspects of a class or certain critical incidents (Pinner, 2018). As we re-tell the story and it becomes a tighter and tighter narrative for making sense of phenomena, if we move away from the original source data it is possible that the narrative becomes simplified in the telling, or changes in some way in order to highlight the punchline or the end-point. In writing this chapter, I wanted to re-visit one of my own well-trodden narratives and bring something new to it. The renewed focus on the complexity perspective enabled me to notice one particular issue involving how I see students and their personalities in relation to motivation, and to bring it more sharply to consciousness. I decided to focus in particular on the autoethnographic aspect of this research and how I utilised sociograms as an analytical tool as I was reflecting on my own practice. The following narrative presents the story of how I built up an understanding of two very different students, one who was enlarged by the fisheye lens due to his active participation and overtly positive orientation to the class, and one who would appear diminished through the fisheye lens.

The Narrative of Mr Auxiliary and Mr Charge

The study I would like to revisit was conducted at a Japanese university in Tokyo, where I taught a year-long compulsory course to non-English mixed-majors who met twice a week for 90-minutes per session. The course was called Academic Communication, and there were 25 students in the class. When I first met the class, I made a note of where people were sitting, making a seating map which reflected the students' own choices about where to sit and with whom. At the time, this was simply a technique to help me learn the students' names. It was not until after all the classes had finished over a year later that I realised these seating charts could be used as data to help draw a sociogram. Initially, my desire to make a sociogram was purely out of interest, based on having read a fascinating paper by Mercer (2015) on social network theory. By this stage, group dynamics had become an important focus in the study, so I wanted to see if I could zoom my lens in further, and the sociogram appealed to me as a visual form of analysis.

After introducing myself and going over the syllabus, I asked people to draw a picture which represented their relationship to English as a diagram (RED). This is what is known as a Pedagogically Exploitable Material (PEPA) in EP, as it functions both as a learning material and as research data (Hanks, 2017). As I went through the class, I spoke with various students. The two main protagonists of this narrative are Mr Charge and Mr Auxiliary.

First impressions

Initial conditions are important as they represent the start of measuring for a complex system (Finch, 2010; Verspoor, 2015). Right from the first class, it was really quite obvious to me that Mr Charge was going to be one of the more 'motivated' students in the group. Although there is no space to discuss them here, one of the main things to arrive from this study was my taxonomy of indicators of teacher–student motivational synergy (Pinner, 2017, 2019). Without having yet brought my taxonomy of indicators to consciousness, I was already applying them to Mr Charge and Mr Auxiliary the moment I walked into the classroom that day in April when our one-year compulsory course began. Here is Mr Charge, bright eyed, sitting at the front, keenly watching me and looking interested. There is Mr Auxiliary, sat at the back as far away as possible. This was further compounded when I actually talked to the two students in question on the first day of class.

As they were doing the communicative part of the RED task, I went around and spoke to different groups in turn. As I was wearing a microphone, I was also collecting audio data which I later transcribed.

Here is my first talk with Mr Charge, who was sitting with his friend Mr Fly[1]:

1	RICHARD:	What's your relationship to English like.
2	MR.CHRG:	Ah. English is the tool that I can connect with foreign people
3	RICHARD:	Ah okay. Yeah that's interesting that you use the word tool. Yea:h I think I think that's a good explanation. So do you like English?
4	MR.CHRG:	Yes Very
5	RICHARD:	Oh good good. Yeah @ that's good. Why do you- Why do you like English?
6	MR.CHRG:	By using English... I can... I can connect many people

Of course, Mr Charge confirmed what I had already presumed based on easily observable indicators; here was a man who came with motivation pre-installed. As long as I kept him happy and encouraged him, I knew we would be able to energise one another through the course. I came away from the discussion feeling good about myself and the work I do.... Feeling energised. In his RED, Mr Charge wrote 'I think English is very important and I will study English hard'. He also drew a portrait of me and made a reference to one of the jokes I made in the class to build rapport. I think this emphasis on me personally shows that his orientation to English was in part based on his having taken a liking to me personally. My initial impression of Mr Charge was that he was quite extroverted and outgoing, clearly with a positive orientation towards English. I will return later to this issue of extroversion or introversion as a personality trait.

After this pleasant exchange, I began making my way towards the back of the class, discussing the REDs with other students. Finally, when I arrived at the very back of the class, I met Mr Auxiliary and some of the other quieter students who were working there. I was tempted to write that they had finished the discussion task and were sitting together in silence, neither using L1 or L2. However, this would be a case of mythologising and the reality is that such an observation is now lost due to the limits of my data and notes, as when I actually re-listened to the audio I could not tell if they were sitting in silence or not. This is due to the excessive background noise from other students who were speaking mainly in Japanese and a little English, but by this stage most of the students were doubtlessly chatting off-task and getting to know one another. As they were all first-years in the first semester, many from different departments, many of the students were meeting for the first time, although Mr Charge sat with Mr Fly, and they already knew each other from being in the same department. However, Mr Auxiliary was sitting with one person from his department (Mr Nintendo) and one person from another department (Mr Dawn), and none of them seemed to know each other, and indeed over the year they never seemed to form much of a bond, as evidenced by certain observations I made and to which I shall return shortly.

The discussion with Mr Auxiliary is markedly different from that with Mr Charge:

1 **RICHARD:** And I have to ask you guys about yours huh. You've drawn a… is this a snake?

2 **MR.AUX:** Snake

3 **RICHARD:** So, why did you draw a snake…… Ah, why did you draw a snake

4 **MR.AUX:** English attack me

5 **RICHARD:** Really. And you're a frog? A:w…. Why do you feel English attacks you ((…..5))

6 **RICHARD:** Why does English attack you

7 **MR.AUX:** I can't understand English

8 **RICHARD:** A:h, right. Yeah. Eng-…So English is scary?

9 **MR.AUX:** Scary? (?Scared), yes.

Mr Auxiliary's RED of course reveals a great deal about his orientation towards English (see Figure 13.3).

Ordinarily, one might assume then from these initial conditions that Mr Charge is 'motivated' to study English and Mr Auxiliary is either 'not motivated' or certainly much less so than someone like Mr Charge. However, this is the beginning of an assumption, and one which will be compounded through the course if left unchecked. This is an example of the fisheye lens applying to a teachers' perception of motivation, as the seemingly more outward or extroverted student might all too easily be seen as the more motivated one. These initial conditions are the most important for both students and the teacher in forming an overall impression and in setting up what will later become the attractor states of the psychological landscape within the class (Dörnyei & Murphey, 2003; Hiver, 2015). However, this assumption about Mr Auxiliary's low motivation is based on incomplete data. Mr Auxiliary did not say that he was un-motivated, he simply said he was scared of English. Mr Charge is

Draw a diagram that shows how you see your relationship to English. Use words and pictures to explain it.

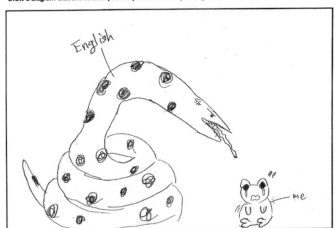

Figure 13.3 Mr Auxiliary's RED

clearly a more confident person and not scared of English but keen to learn. Mr Auxiliary did not say yet how he feels about English, other than voicing his trepidation. He has not yet revealed much about his motivation. His choice to sit at the back could be due more to social anxiety than his orientation towards the class. However, in this first class I made my assumptions that Mr Auxiliary was not particularly motivated. It was only thanks to the complexity lens, my careful approach to autoethnography and the use of analytical tools such as sociograms and PEPAs that helped me to form a more complete picture of these two students.

Returning to the seating arrangements, despite my attempts to help the class gel and get to know each other, I never allocated seats and, as the sociogram in Figure 13.4 shows, very few students bridged a link between students in other departments by sitting with students from departments other than their own. One of the students who did sit with other departments' students was Mr Auxiliary, who sat with Mr Dawn. Conversely, the seemingly more extroverted Mr Charge sat exclusively with Mr Fly for the whole year, and even indicated a strong preference to either work alone or with Mr Fly when it came to choosing groups for the end of Spring semester video project. Mr Auxiliary, on the other hand, did not choose to work alone (although this was an option) and preferred to form a group with Ms Chennai who was in the same department as him, although he never normally sat with her. What is further odd about this is that Mr Dawn, with whom Mr Auxiliary tended to sit, indicated he would like to do a project on football, and I know that Mr Auxiliary's main goal for studying English was to learn enough to go to visit Arsenal's stadium in London. However, these two who always sat together did not form a group despite having an interest in the same topic.

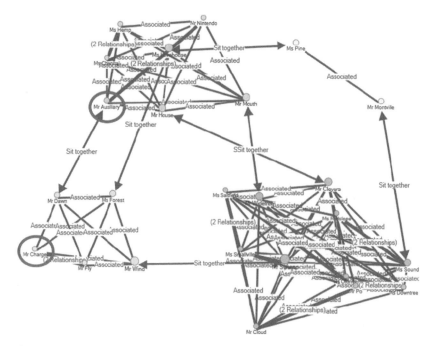

Figure 13.4 Seating and department membership

From this diagram we can see that my assumption that the enthusiastic and seemingly outgoing Mr Charge is more extroverted and socialised than the quiet and scared-of-English Mr Auxiliary is inaccurate and could lead towards further misconceptions regarding my perception of the two students' motivational profiles if left unchecked.

Revising assumptions

After the initial conditions were established, I reflected on the lesson in my teaching journal and much later on (after the entire year had finished) I transcribed some of the classroom discourse and began experimenting with sociograms. At the time of teaching, my initial hypothesis would have been quite simply that Mr Charge was 'motivated', Mr Auxiliary was either 'not motivated' or 'not very motived' to study English, and indeed by lesson three in my journal I had already labelled Mr Auxiliary as 'amotivated'. Simple, but as I will show shortly, rather incomplete and certainly not something which fits the complexity approach.

Another assumption that I had fallen into was the belief that Mr Charge was more extroverted, and Mr Auxiliary was introverted. Although these personality traits are potentially reductive labels, they still have much bearing on classroom interactions and group dynamics. Although I never used the data in my original study, during one make-up lesson in the computer room (which was not part of the syllabus but due to a cancelled class as a result of a back injury I sustained falling off my bicycle), I had students complete an online Myers–Brigg personality test.[2] This was not really a PEPA as it was originally designed purely as a way to get data (and fill time in a class I had not really prepared for). I did not want to use the data in the original study as I find personality tests, even well-established ones such as the Myers–Brigg test, to be quite reductive. However, the results are interesting here as they show that even after the study is over, I can still find new discoveries by revisiting the data, especially the large amount of unused data which tends to amass when doing a large longitudinal qualitative study such as this. Mr Charge's personality type was INFJ, which means he was an introverted person with strong intuitive and interpersonal skills. However, it is also notable that of the 13 people who were identified as Extroverts from the class of 25, Mr Charge was not one of them, despite the fact that he sat at the front and spoke to me with confidence and interest and showed a willingness to communicate which instantly singled him out to me. As I have mentioned, although he worked fine in groups, given the choice Mr Charge would always choose to work with his one other friend, Mr Fly, who was from the same department and with whom he did all his project work except for one in the second semester.

Realising personality

An additional data type which shed light on Mr Charge and Mr Auxiliary's motivation were the Self-Assessments for Classroom Participation (SACP). This is an exercise I have been doing for several years, based partly on Hattie's (2008, 2012) findings from the Visible Learning project, which highlighted the value of self-report grades and reflection in the class, and also matches well with Ushioda's (2014) discussion of the importance of metacognition and reflection for helping students to monitor and understand their own motivation. The class is given 30% of their grade for class participation, but this is done as a self-assessment with students awarding themselves their own grade based on a negotiated criteria of what they thought made a 'good participator', see Pinner

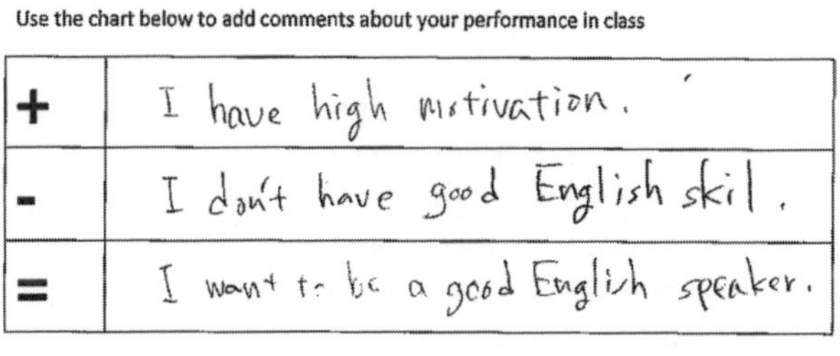

Use the chart below to add comments about your performance in class

+	I have high motivation.
-	I don't have good English skil.
=	I want to be a good English speaker.

Figure 13.5 Mr Auxiliary's self-assessment reflection

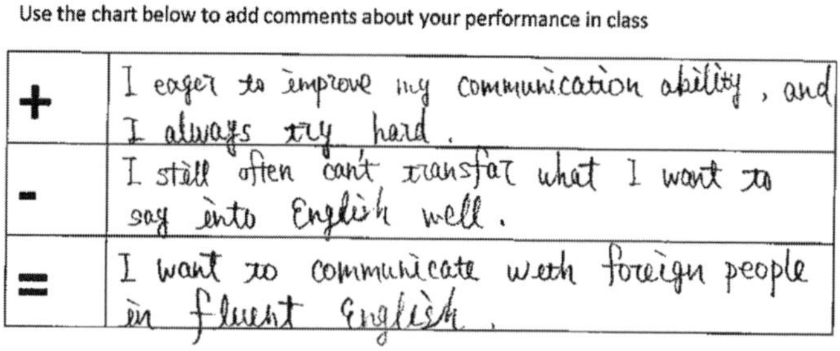

Use the chart below to add comments about your performance in class

+	I eager to improve my communication ability, and I always try hard.
-	I still often can't transfer what I want to say into English well.
=	I want to communicate with foreign people in fluent English.

Figure 13.6 Mr Charge's self-assessment reflection

(2016a, 2016b, 2019). We conducted this as a reflective task three times per semester, using the criteria the students developed as a questionnaire on which they scored themselves.

As part of the SACP students need to reflect on their strengths, weaknesses and goals for learning. Mr Auxiliary wrote in his strengths column 'I have high motivation'. This would be a recurring theme in all his self-assessments (see Figure 13.5).

In contrast to Mr Auxiliary's reflection, Mr Charge did not specifically mention motivation as an abstract concept, instead his reflection is slightly more fine-grained and shows that, although he and Mr Auxiliary share similar aims, Mr Charge has a more developed version of his future self in that his goals are more specific and focused (see Figure 13.6).

Unlike Mr Auxiliary who said, 'I want to be a good English speaker', which was rather vague and unfocused, Mr Charge had an image of himself 'communicat[ing] with foreign people in fluent English', a more specific vision involving how he would use English and showed a more social orientation.

Another similarity came in the form of the graphs that I asked students to make after the second self-assessment in spring, which showed how their motivation fluctuated. This makes more sense in the wider narrative of the study, but naturally both the students' and my own motivation fluctuated due to several events changing both in and outside of the classroom. One such event occurred after I fell off my bicycle and had to cancel class due to having a herniated spinal disc, which I have already alluded to when discussing the make-up lesson in which we conducted the Myers–Brigg test.

Interestingly, the graphs by most students showed a definite dip in motivation, and then going back up after I gave a motivational 'pep talk', which was based on feedback I had received from the class as part of an institutional questionnaire. By this stage both they and I had each exchanged several forms of feedback in this way, and doing the self-assessment was another way of creating a reciprocal feedback loop which helps maintain positive teacher–student motivational synergy.

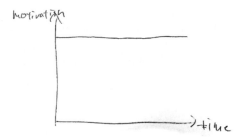

Figure 13.7 Mr Auxiliary's self-report on motivation (SA102)

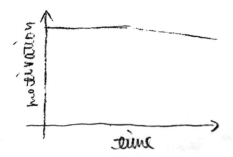

Figure 13.8 Mr Charge's self-report on motivation (SA102)

Although their personalities were very different, there are again similarities between Mr Charge and Mr Auxiliary in this way, see Figure 13.7 and Figure 13.8.

Despite the marked differences in their behaviour and the way their motivation manifested itself, at least from their self-reports they seem to

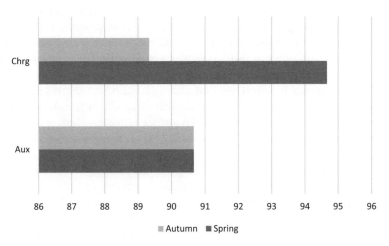

Figure 13.9 Mr Auxiliary and Mr Charge overall self-assessment score

have much in common in that they both perceived their own motivation as being relatively high and stable. Out of 25 students, only four had graphs which were straight lines like this.

If we look at the overall score for classroom participation (Figure 13.9) that Mr Charge and Mr Auxiliary awarded themselves, we can see that Mr Auxiliary's self-assessment of his own participation remained exactly the same in both Spring and Autumn. The average score for self-assessments in both semesters was around 91/100, and so Mr Auxiliary's score of 90.6 puts him very near the average, an indication that he was not aware that his participation was generally weak as he was not very communicative with other people in the class, or that he was not willing to score himself lowly for this assessment. Interestingly, Mr Charge actually scores himself lower than Mr Auxiliary in Autumn, giving himself 89.3 which is much lower than his Spring score.

As the class progressed, although I still found it quite painful or hard work to talk to Mr Auxiliary, I began to blame this not on his motivation or attitude to English or to me, but to recognise this for what it was as a personality trait.

In this way, although the goal was different in its scope, both students actually shared a lot in common with regards to the motivational profile they reported of themselves. I found this particularly surprising, having at the beginning of the class made the quite understandable assumption that these two students were very different in the motivational orientation.

Sociograms

Because of the complexity of the classroom as a context for group dynamics, I have chosen to present several different sociograms because I feel as a single visual these sociograms are not only illegible as the output from NVivo is far from optimal, but also these should not represent static relationships. The way I used the sociograms was by plotting various different ones and observing how the network diagrams changed depending on the relationships being shown, thus when analysing them on my computer screen they were dynamic representations rather than static images.

Finally, I would like to stress that although these sociograms may look complicated, and although I am presenting them here in a book about complexity research, these are actually rather reductive illustrations that focus on only three types of relationship. They only go some small way to describe the much more complex nature of group dynamics in the language classroom (for further discussion, see Sampson, 2015, 2016a, 2016b, 2018, 2019a, 2019b).

As I have already established in this paper, one way of 'disentangling complex and interwoven systems' (Caldarelli & Catanzaro, 2012: 41) is to examine the relationships between members of a network. In this case, these would be participants in the class, and the relationships could be

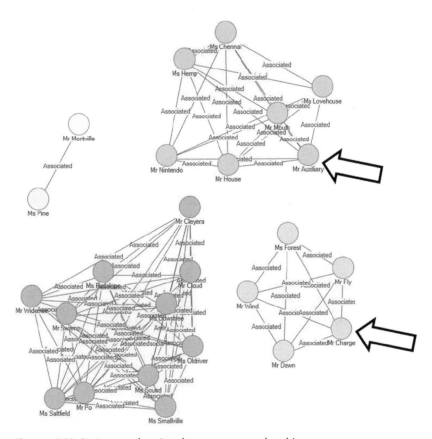

Figure 13.10 Sociogram showing department membership

almost anything that connects the participants to one-another. Each student is represented as a node (a circle) and their relationships are plotted as edges (a line).

The sociogram shown in Figure 13.10 represents only the members of each department, the relationships between each node are associative, meaning they are neither unidirectional nor bidirectional but simply established through membership of the same department, a relationship not built on personal factors. Node colour also indicates the degree of inness, meaning that a darker node shows that the student was generally more connected to the group. For this reason, Ms Pine and Mr Montville, the only two class members from the department of economics, are coloured more lightly than those in the department of materials and life sciences, which is the largest group. The other second largest group, containing Mr Auxiliary, is the department of information and communication sciences, while the second smallest group is the department of engineering and applied sciences, to which Mr Charge belongs.

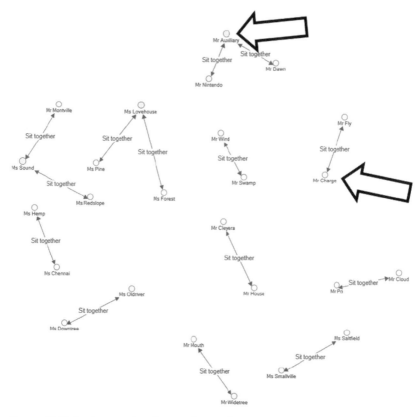

Figure 13.11 Sociogram showing seating preference

The next sociogram (Figure 13.11) shows only the seating preferences for each student. These are the default seating patterns that the students chose when they took their seats at the start of class, so these pairings remained fairly consistent throughout the academic year. I saw this as a bidirectional relationship, although it may be that the proximity of the seating was not evenly reciprocal, as perhaps was the case with Mr Auxiliary, Mr Dawn and Mr Nintendo.

This sociogram shows how the class breaks into much smaller groups when looking at seating, and most students sat in groups of only two or three. This is likely to be a result of my teaching style, as I generally have students discuss topics in pairs. Students did change seats whilst working in different discussion groups or whilst working on projects, which is shown by the third relationship I plotted as a sociogram. Figure 13.12 shows which students collaborated in assessed group work, on the group video project in the Spring semester. As students themselves formed these groups based on preference, this is also seen as a bidirectional relation. Note, some students chose to do this project by themselves. Again, it is notable that Mr Charge clearly told me

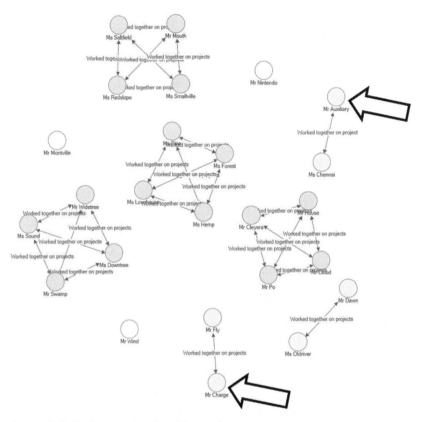

Figure 13.12 Sociogram showing video project groups

he would either work with Mr Fly or alone, whereas Mr Auxiliary chose to work in a group, despite his generally uncommunicative nature.

Figure 13.13 shows the session groups for the assessed group projects, known as output sessions, in autumn, while Figure 13.14 displays the combination of both assessments.

Finally, Figure 13.15 represents all these relationships and is a full network sociogram for these three relationships in class. In this diagram, the nodes are represented by the degree of centrality, a calculation based on the number of edges and the direction of the relationship. Nodes are also sized and coloured according to the same category, meaning that a larger node suggests that this student was more active within the group, and a smaller node represents a tendency toward being an isolate. The thickness of the edge represents the number of relationships between nodes, so a thicker line means that there are more relationships between the connected students.

The sociogram presented in Figure 13.15 is barely legible due to the number of relationships it presents, and yet it does not do justice to the real complexity of the actual classroom as uncovered in the narrative. For

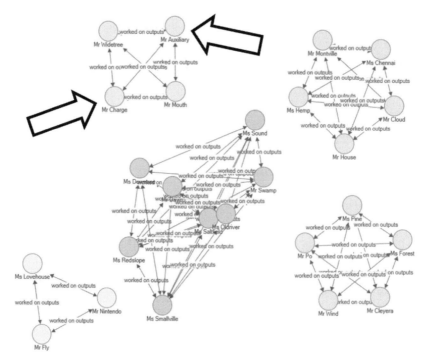

Figure 13.13 Sociogram showing session groups in autumn

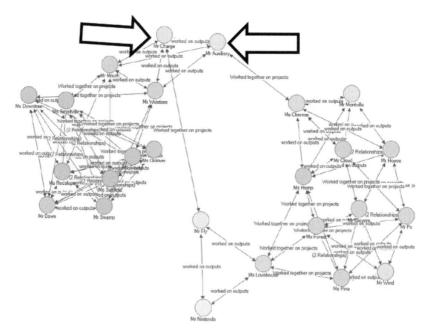

Figure 13.14 Sociogram showing both assessment groups

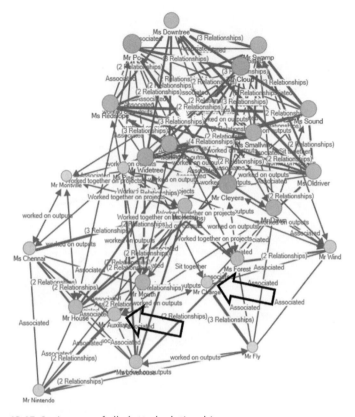

Figure 13.15 Sociogram of all plotted relationships

example, the picture of Mr Auxiliary from the sociograms does not show much of his uncommunicative nature. He was most certainly an isolate in almost every class, and furthermore in the main study I uncovered evidence that he seemed to lack the ability to read other people's feelings, based on comments he wrote reflecting on group assessments which were in stark contrast to other members of his group. Surprisingly, Mr Charge, despite his very strong motivational orientation to succeed in English, was also an isolate of sorts, because he was not keen to mix with other students and expressed a clear preference to either work alone or with his one friend from the class, Mr Fly. From the sociogram we can see that Mr Charge is represented by an even smaller, lighter coloured node than Mr Auxiliary. This observation of Mr Charge's slightly isolate quality is an observation that was facilitated by the social network analysis.

It is also possible to create egocentric sociograms, which take one group member as the central focus. Figures 13.16 and 13.17 show Mr Charge's and Mr Auxiliary's egocentric sociograms respectively.

Mr Charge's sociogram shows the relatively small number of people with whom he had a direct connection in the class. His strongest ties were

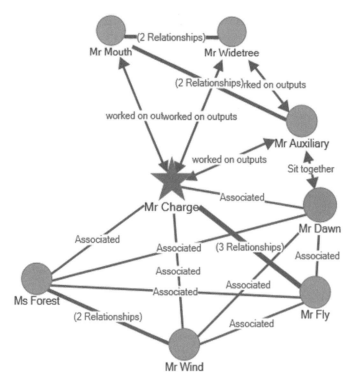

Figure 13.16 Mr Charge's egocentric sociogram

to Mr Fly, with whom he has remained very close friends over the years up until he graduated in 2018. The rest of the sociogram is made up of relatively uncommunicative students, such as Mr Auxiliary and Mr Dawn, and two students who were on the low end of the spectrum in terms of my overall estimation of their level of engagement.

Despite sitting close together in almost every class, Mr Auxiliary does not seem to have a strong relationship with Mr Dawn as they have only one relationship. This suggests that they sat close together only as a result of both wanting to sit at the back, perhaps because this was far from the teacher. They also shared similar traits in terms of the communicative ability and slight social awkwardness. It is also notable that the two both liked football, but did not work together on video projects although Mr Dawn had specifically indicated that he wanted to do a project about football. Also, regarding Mr Nintendo, neither Mr Auxiliary nor Mr Dawn seemed to know much about him and expressed indifference when Mr Nintendo dropped out of the class in Autumn.

In this way, the sociograms afforded me another way of seeing and visualising the relationships between people in the class. They allowed me to look at connections which were normally invisible to me, such as department

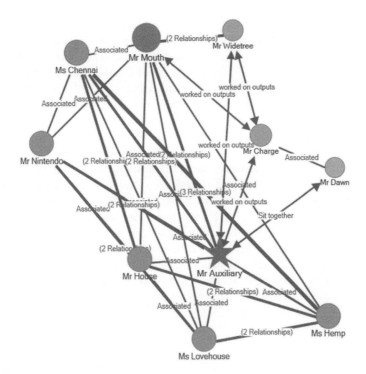

Figure 13.17 Mr Auxiliary's egocentric sociogram

membership, for example, which is information I have on the class list but do not keep close to mind during teaching. I strongly believe that if I were able to plot other relationships into the sociograms, I could build an even more finely nuanced profile of the class's group dynamics and understand certain interaction from the light of these relationships. Thus, sociograms help to add a layer of complexity to the analysis of classroom dynamics and situate relationships in context of the social network of the classroom.

Conclusion

Since teaching the course I have learned more about group dynamics and encountered the idea that forcing students to move seats regularly and work with different members of the group is a good way of avoiding cliques within the class and fostering better dynamics (Dörnyei & Murphey, 2003; Murphey et al., 2012). During the course of teaching this class, I did several mingling exercises and these were especially done when students found groups to work together during assessments (videos and outputs). However, in the ordinary course of teaching I rarely forced the students to change seats and generally let them choose where to sit. I preferred not to dictate where they would sit, particularly because having a map of where each person sat initially helped me to learn all their names. In hindsight, this might have led to the solidification of isolate type behaviour in learners such as Mr Auxiliary, Mr Dawn and Mr Nintendo, as well as Mr Charge and Mr Fly to some extent. This would certainly be something that warrants deeper inquiry in the future.

One finding from the analysis of the narrative is that my increased reflection on the class is what led me to seek a deeper understanding of group dynamics. In particular, I questioned my initial assumption that Mr Auxiliary was 'demotivated' or 'an English Hater' (Erikawa, 2009; Kikuchi, 2013) and came to a deeper understanding of him as a person-in-context (Ushioda, 2009, 2011). This is related to the 'Pygmalion effect', which refers to the fact that higher teacher expectations lead to greater performance. This effect is named after the Greek myth from a study conducted in 1965 (Rosenthal & Jacobson, 1992), which has relevance for L2 motivation (Dörnyei & Ushioda, 2011) and language classroom dynamics (Dörnyei & Murphey, 2003). Of course the effects can be reversed, which is often referred to as the 'Golem effect' (Babad *et al.*, 1982). As mentioned in the narrative, this is something I was aware of and tried to avoid as I taught the course, which led to my questioning my assumptions about students through deeper reflection. Rather counter-intuitively, by being more subjective about my learners as people, I believe I was actually better able to evaluate their work in class more objectively, or at least in a fairer way, which is how a rather uncommunicative student like Mr Auxiliary was still able to get a high score for the class and to be recognised as someone who was not simply lacking in motivation towards English. I believe a more thorough case-study of learners such as Mr Auxiliary who fit the profile of 'uncommunicative' would be a helpful area for future research. There are students like this in almost every class.

In this chapter, I have attempted to show how building a profile of the class from various perspectives using a complexity lens helped me to build up a more nuanced and contextually embedded view of my learners and their orientations towards the class. In presenting the narrative of Mr Charge and Mr Auxiliary, with their very different and yet at times surprisingly similar characteristics, I have tried to show how learners are indeed people-in-context (Ushioda, 2009), and that any view of their motivation should take this complexity into account if it is to attempt to capture a clearer picture of who they are as learners in the classroom.

Notes

(1) For transcription conventions, see Appendix.
(2) The Myers–Brigg Type Indicator is a general-purpose self-report questionnaire. We used an online version of this test from the following link https://www.16personalities.

com/free-personality-test. Although the Myers–Brigg test is known to be very unreliable and generally regarded as a purely superficial measure of personality, it is still used in some peer-reviewed papers. However, due to its unreliability it was not used in the original study and only mentioned here as an incidental reference. However, I would stress that all personality tests are likely to be over-general and inaccurate, so with this proviso I chose to present the test in this chapter.

References

Allwright, D. and Hanks, J. (2009) *The Developing Language Learner: An Introduction to Exploratory Practice*. Basingstoke: Palgrave Macmillan.

Babad, E.Y., Inbar, J. and Rosenthal, R. (1982) Pygmalion, Galatea, and the Golem: Investigations of biased and unbiased teachers. *Journal of Educational Psychology* 74 (4), 459–474.

Barkhuizen, G. (ed.) (2017) *Reflections on Language Teacher Identity Research*. London: Routledge.

Barkhuizen, G., Benson, P. and Chik, A. (2014) *Narrative Inquiry in Language Teaching and Research*. New York: Routledge.

Caldarelli, G. and Catanzaro, M. (2012) *Networks: A Very Short Introduction* (Vol. 335). Oxford: Oxford University Press.

Canagarajah, A.S. (2012) Teacher development in a global profession: An autoethnography. *TESOL Quarterly* 46 (2), 258–279. doi:10.1002/tesq.18

Chang, H. (2008) *Autoethnography as Method*. London: Routledge.

Degenne, A. and Forsé, M. (1999) *Introducing Social Networks* (A. Borges, Trans.). London: Sage.

Denzin, N.K. (2014) *Interpretive Autoethnography* (2nd edn, Vol. 17). London: Sage.

Dörnyei, Z. and Murphey, T. (2003) *Group Dynamics in the Language Classroom*. Cambridge: Cambridge University Press.

Dörnyei, Z. and Ushioda, E. (2011) *Teaching and Researching: Motivation* (2nd edn). Harlow: Longman Pearson.

Ellis, C., Adams, T.E. and Bochner, A.P. (2011) Autoethnography: An overview. *Historical Social Research/Historische Sozialforschung* 36 (4), 273–290.

Emerson, R.M., Fretz, R.I. and Shaw, L.L. (2011) *Writing Ethnographic Fieldnotes* (2nd edn). Chicago, IL: University of Chicago Press.

Erikawa, H. (2009) *Eigo kyoiku no politics [Politics in English Education]*. Tokyo: Sanyusha Shuppan.

Finch, A. (2010) Critical incidents and language learning: Sensitivity to initial conditions. *System* 38 (3), 422–431. doi:http://dx.doi.org/10.1016/j.system.2010.05.004

Gieve, S. and Miller, I.K. (2006) What do we mean by 'quality of classroom life'? In S. Gieve and I.K. Miller (eds) *Understanding the Language Classroom* (pp. 18–46). Basingstoke: Palgrave Macmillan.

Gonzalez, J. (2013) *The Fisheye Syndrome: Is Every Student Really Participating?* See https://www.cultofpedagogy.com/fisheye/

Hanks, J. (2017) *Exploratory Practice in Language Teaching: Puzzling About Principles and Practices*. London: Palgrave Macmillan.

Hattie, J. (2008) *Visible Learning: A Synthesis of Over 800 Meta-analyses Relating to Achievement*. London: Routledge.

Hattie, J. (2012) *Visible Learning for Teachers: Maximizing Impact on Learning*. London: Routledge.

Hiver, P. (2015) Attractor states. In Z. Dörnyei, P.D. MacIntyre and A. Henry (eds) *Motivational Dynamics in Language Learning* (pp. 20–28). Bristol: Multilingual Matters.

Holliday, A. (1999) Small cultures. *Applied Linguistics* 20 (2), 237–264.

Kikuchi, K. (2013) Demotivators in the Japanese EFL Context. In M.T. Apple, D. Da Silva and T. Fellner (eds) *Language Learning Motivation in Japan* (pp. 206–224). Bristol: Multilingual Matters.

Kramsch, C. (2011) Why is everyone so excited about complexity theory in applied linguistics? *Melanges CRAPEL* 2 (33), 9–24.

Larsen-Freeman, D. (2011) A complexity theory approach to second language development/acquisition. In D. Atkinson (ed.) *Alternative Approaches to Second Language Acquisition* (pp. 48–72). London: Routledge.

Larsen-Freeman, D. and Cameron, L. (2008) *Complex Systems and Applied Linguistics*. Oxford: Oxford University Press.

Leung, B.P. and Silberling, J. (2006) Using sociograms to identify social status in the classroom. *The California School Psychologist* 11 (1), 57–61.

Mercer, S. (2015) Social network analysis and complex dynamic systems. In Z. Dörnyei, P.D. MacIntyre and A. Henry (eds) *Motivational Dynamics in Language Learning* (pp. 73–82). Bristol: Multilingual Matters.

Mirhosseini, S.-A. (2018) An invitation to the less-treaded path of autoethnography in TESOL research. *TESOL Journal* 9 (1), 76–92. doi:10.1002/tesj.305

Moreno, J.L. (1934) *Who Shall Survive* (digital, available from archive.org ed.). Washington, D.C: Nervous and Mental Disease Publishing Co.

Murphey, T., Falout, J., Fukada, Y. and Fukuda, T. (2012) Group dynamics: Collaborative agency in present communities of imagination. In S. Mercer, S. Ryan and M. Williams (eds) *Psychology for Language Learning: Insights from Research, Theory and Practice* (pp. 220–238). London: Palgrave Macmillan.

Pinner, R.S. (2016a) Trouble in paradise: Self-assessment and the Tao. *Language Teaching Research* 20 (2), 181–195. doi:10.1177/1362168814562015

Pinner, R.S. (2016b) Using self-assessment to maintain motivation in a dynamic classroom environment: An exploratory practice inquiry of one Japanese university speaking course. *Asian Journal of Applied Linguistics* 3 (1), 27–40.

Pinner, R.S. (2017) Social Authentication and the synergies between teacher and student motivation: An Autoethnographic inquiry into the interaction between authenticity and motivation in English language teaching at a Japanese university. PhD Doctoral Thesis, University of Warwick, Coventry, UK.

Pinner, R.S. (2018) Re-learning from experience: Using autoethnography for teacher development. *Educational Action Research* 26 (1), 91–105. doi:10.1080/09650792.2017.1310665

Pinner, R.S. (2019) *Social Authentication and Teacher–Student Motivational Synergy: A Narrative of Language Teaching*. London: Routledge.

Polkinghorne, D.E. (2007) Validity issues in narrative research. *Qualitative Inquiry* 13 (4), 471–486. doi:10.1177/1077800406297670

Rosenthal, R. and Jacobson, L. (1992) *Pygmalion in the Classroom: Teacher Expectation and Pupils' Intellectual Development* (2nd edn). Berkley: Irvington and Crown House.

Sampson, R.J. (2015) Tracing motivational emergence in a classroom language learning project. *System* 50, 10–20.

Sampson, R.J. (2016a) *Complexity in Classroom Foreign Language Learning Motivation: A Practitioner Perspective from Japan*. Bristol: Multilingual Matters.

Sampson, R.J. (2016b) EFL teacher motivation in-situ: Co-adaptive processes, openness and relational motivation over interacting timescales. *Studies in Second Language Learning and Teaching* 6 (2), 293–318.

Sampson, R.J. (2018) The feeling classroom: Diversity of feelings in instructed L2 learning. *Innovation in Language Learning and Teaching*, 1–15. doi:10.1080/17501229.2018.1553178

Sampson, R.J. (2019a) Openness to messages about English as a foreign language: Working with learners to uncover purpose to study. *Language Teaching Research* 23 (1), 126–142. doi:10.1177/1362168817712074

Sampson, R.J. (2019b) Real people with real experiences: The emergence of classroom L2 study feelings over interacting timescales. *System* 84, 14–23. doi:https://doi.org/10.1016/j.system.2019.05.001

Tyson, L. (2011) *Using Critical Theory: How to Read and Write About Literature* (Second ed.). London: Routledge.

Ushioda, E. (1994) L2 motivation as a qualitative construct. *Teanga* 14, 76–84.

Ushioda, E. (1996) Developing a dynamic concept of L2 motivation. In T. Hickey and J. Williams (eds) *Language, Education and Society in a Changing World* (pp. 239–245). Clevedon: Multilingual Matters.

Ushioda, E. (2009) A person-in-context relational view of emergent motivation, self and identity. In Z. Dörnyei and E. Ushioda (eds) *Motivation, Language Identity and the L2 Self* (pp. 215–228). Bristol: Multilingual Matters.

Ushioda, E. (2011) Motivating learners to speak as themselves. In G. Murray, X. Gao and T.E. Lamb (eds) *Identity, Motivation and Autonomy in Language Learning* (pp. 11–25). Bristol: Multilingual Matters.

Ushioda, E. (2014) Motivation, autonomy and metacognition: Exploring their interactions. In D. Lasagabaster, A. Doiz and J.M. Sierra (eds) *Motivation and Foreign Language Learning: From Theory to Practice* (pp. 31–49). Amsterdam: John Benjamins.

Ushioda, E. (2015) Context and complex dynamic systems theory. In Z. Dörnyei, P.D. MacIntyre and A. Henry (eds) *Motivational Dynamics in Language Learning* (pp. 47–54). Bristol: Multilingual Matters.

Ushioda, E. (2016) Language learning motivation through a small lens: A research agenda. *Language Teaching* 49 (4), 564–577. doi:10.1017/S0261444816000173

Verspoor, M. (2015) Initial conditions. In Z. Dörnyei, P.D. MacIntyre and A. Henry (eds) *Motivational Dynamics in Language Learning* (pp. 38–46). Bristol: Multilingual Matters.

Walsh, S. and Mann, S. (2015) Doing reflective practice: A data-led way forward. *ELT Journal* 69 (4), 351–362. doi:10.1093/elt/ccv018

Appendix: Transcription Conventions

Based on Walsh and Mann (2015)

RICHARD: MR.CHRG:	Speaker attribution. Pseudonyms are used for all students, the teacher researcher is referred to as RICHARD. Names are abbreviated.
@	indicates laughter. Sometimes a further description of the type of laughter is explained in square brackets.
…	shows a short, untimed pause of less than three seconds.
((……6))	shows a longer, timed pause. The number of dots indicates one second of a pause, the duration is then given in seconds. The example shows a six second pause.
,	shows a continuation of tone
.	shows naturally falling intonation
?	shows naturally rising intonation
::	shows extended vowel. The number of colons roughly represents the length of the extension.
(?actually)	uncertain words or unclear words
Eng-	a word started but not completed
Er, um, ah, oh	onomatopoeic representation of exclamation sounds

14 A Collection of Contradictory Selves: The Dialogical Self and the Dynamics of Teacher Identity Transformation

Alastair Henry

> One of the odd things about being himself, Ferguson had
> discovered, was that there seemed to be several of him, that he
> wasn't just one person but a collection of contradictory selves, and
> each time he was with a different person, he himself was different as
> well. With an outspoken extrovert like Noah, he felt quiet and
> closed in on himself. With a shy and guarded person like Ann
> Brodsky, he felt loud and crude, always talking too much in order to
> overcome the awkwardness of her long silences. Humorless people
> tended to transform him into a jokester. Quick-witted clowns made
> him feel dull and slow. Still other people seemed to possess the
> power to draw him into their orbit and make him act in the same
> way as they did. Pugnacious Mark Dubinsky, with his endless
> opinions about politics and sports, would bring out the verbal
> battler in Ferguson. Dreamy Bob Kramer would make him feel
> fragile and unsure of himself. Artie Federman, on the other hand,
> made him feel calm, calm in a way no other person had ever made
> him feel, for being with the new boy brought home the same sense
> of selfhood he felt when he was alone.
> (Paul Auster, *4 3 2 1*, 2017: 300)

Introduction

For Archibald Ferguson, the protagonist in Paul Auster's disjunctive and labyrinthine novel that weaves together four intertwining narratives of a young American life, the appearance of a potential rival in his social scene causes him to contemplate the multifacetedness of selfhood. Having to relate to another boy (Federman) pushes Ferguson to consider who he himself is, and prompts him to reflect on the varying aspects of his self that are brought out in social interaction. In his seminal work on the continuity and discontinuity of the self, George Herbert Mead (1913) argued that when faced with dilemmas of a psychological nature, people engage in self-reflection, and that this takes place in a dialogical form. We have conversations with ourselves, Mead (1913: 378) argues, where 'different tendencies appear in reflective thought as different voices in conflict with each other'. In pondering the sudden changes in the social environment caused by a newcomer, and reflecting on his relationship to a peer remarkably similar to himself, Ferguson's different selves become characters in a story *of* himself that he tells *to* himself. Self-reflection of the type that Auster's protagonist engages in reveals how identity is dialogically constructed (Hermans, 1999). It enables us to understand how, in reflective thought, we are able 'to confront ourselves with the difference and alterity of self-positionings that voice different perspectives from our usual one, and [how] these can be contradictory and tensional' (Cunha & Gonçalves, 2009: 127).

Following a line of theorists who have explored the unity and diversity of the self (Allport, 1955; James, 1890; Mead, 1913), Hermans (1996, 1999) conceptualizes the self as a dialogical entity. Rooted in Bakhtin's dialogical approach, and his work on the polyphonic novel (Bakhtin, 1973, 1981), Hermans' (1999) argument is that in any particular act of speech or inner dialogue there is a reflection of the presence (real or imagined) of another person. It is on this interface between self and other, where opposing voices are differently positioned in a dialogical landscape, that innovation in the self takes place. For Auster's protagonist, the arrival of an alter-ego forces the question, 'Who am I in relation to him?'. Contemplating this question, Ferguson becomes engaged in a process of mapping the different identities that comprise his self. This enables him to understand how, when social experiences shift, different versions of his self are brought to the fore, and that being in the presence of different others means that he too becomes a different person.

Focusing on Hermans' (1996, 1999) theory of the dialogical self, and his conceptualization of the ways in which identities emerge through social interaction, in this chapter I describe a method for exploring the dynamics of identity innovation in the context of being 'someone learning to become a language teacher'. Because dialogical self theory is not well-known in applied linguistics, I first outline its basic tenets, focusing in particular on the ways in which innovation takes place. I then explain how the dialogical self can be understood as a complex dynamic system, and how complexity principles can be used to map innovation dynamics. I look at studies in which the dialogical self has been used to explore teacher identities, and describe a method I have used to examine identity development in the context of practicum learning. Here I show how complexity principles can cast light on mechanisms of innovation operating across varying timescales, and evaluate the contribution that complex dynamic systems theory (CDST) can make in understanding the nature of identity innovation. Finally, I consider the importance that insights rendered in this way can have for research into language teacher identities, and for mentoring in teacher education.

The Dialogical Self

In Hermans' (1996, 1999) theory of the dialogical self, the self is conceptualized as a complex holistic entity that is divided into functional subparts. In this way, it provides a structural and dynamic perspective on identity (Valsiner, 2004). Following Bakhtin (1981), the central idea in Hermans' theory is the existence of mutually related components of identity – I-positions – each of which is endowed with a voice:

> The dialogical self can be described in terms of a dynamic multiplicity of relatively autonomous I positions. In this conception, the I has the ability to move spatially from one position to the other in accordance with changes in situation and time. The I fluctuates among different and even opposed positions. For example, in actual or imaginal conversations I can move back and forth between my own position and the position of my actual or imaginal interlocutor. The I has the capacity to imaginatively endow each position with a voice so that dialogical relations between positions can be established (e.g. I converse with my image in the mirror, with the photograph of somebody I miss, with my conscience, with a character from a book, or with myself who is currently writing this article). The voices function like interacting characters in a story, involved in a process of question and answer, agreement and disagreement. Each of them has a story to tell about his or her own experiences from his or her own standpoint. As different voices, these characters exchange information about their respective Me's, resulting in a complex, narratively structured self. (Hermans, 1999: 72)

The complexity of the dialogical self is not limited to the number of voices that the self may contain, each with its own particular perspective, but relates also to the manner in which the self is structured. In addition to a temporal dimension, which is constituent within narratives told about the present, the past and the future, the dialogical self also has a spatial dimension. This too is a direct influence of Bakhtin's theorizing. As Hermans (1999: 73) explains, 'when there is a storyteller, there is always an actual or imaginal relationship supposed between a spatially located teller and listener'. Storytelling is thus a dialogical process where stories and viewpoints are exchanged. Consequently, any narrative has a spatial as well as a temporal dimension. This spatial dimension is reflected in the notion of an I-*position*, and in dynamical processes of *positioning* and *repositioning*, where the relative prominence of different voices (I-positions) changes in relation to shifts in the social environment (Hermans, 1999).

The dialogical self and the social environment

There is another very important respect in which the dialogical self can be understood as a complex dynamic system, namely its 'openness'. A characteristic of complex systems, and which distinguishes them from 'closed' or 'isolated' systems, involves the relationship of the system to the environment in which it is embedded. Unlike isolated systems, in which no exchange of matter or energy takes place, or closed systems in which only energy is exchanged, a complex system exchanges both energy and matter with the environment (Byrne & Callaghan, 2014). A complex system interacts constantly with its environment in rich are varied ways (Cilliers, 2008). As Larsen-Freeman and Cameron (2008) explain, whereas a closed system will reduce to a state of equilibrium or stability when fed by an energy source coming into the system, an open system will continue to maintain a dynamically ordered state. That is, an open system is able to maintain a state that falls short of total or permanent equilibrium, meaning that it is constantly able to adapt to input and stimulation from outside.

The dialogical self is a quintessentially open system. Dialogue is a fundamentally open process. Each articulation of consciousness is formulated in relation to preceding formulations. In describing the openness of dialogue, Hermans and Hermans-Jansen (2003: 537) refer to Bakhtin's (1929/1973: 26) ideas about its contingent nature:

> Consciousness is never self-sufficient; it always finds itself in an intense relationship with another consciousness. The hero's every experience and his every thought is internally dialogical, polemically colored and filled with opposing forces. ... open to inspiration from outside itself.

Because a dialogical relation is always unfinalized, permanently open to the influence of others in and outside of itself, the dialogical self can be understood as a system that has an 'episodic openness' to transformations to new states (Hermans & Hermans-Jansen, 2003: 537; see also Valsiner, 1997). Innovation is brought about dialogically, each new state that the system occupies being a dialogical construction that arises through the interactions of other voices in the system.

The Dynamics of Innovation

In dialogical self theory, the self has a 'dialogical disposition', and interchange and intersubjectivity are intrinsic properties (Hermans, 2008: 187). It is a space where the 'I' observes the 'Me' and, in a story-like manner, relates what the 'Me' does and thinks in an internal narrative. Through acts of imagining, the I is able to move around, carrying out things that do not actually take place. It is in this way that, as an active agent, a person can transcend the confines of a particular context and is able to 'act as if he or she were the other' (Hermans *et al.*, 1992: 29).

Innovation as emergence

In the dialogical self, innovation can take place in a number of ways (Hermans, 2008). One type of development is when a new I-position is introduced. In conditions involving uncertainty, and situations where there is low resistance to new perspectives, a new voiced position can emerge within the self. For a child beginning school, for a student starting a programme of higher education, or for a university academic who receives a promotion, a new position in the self is created. The emergence of a new position can bring about changes in other voiced positions, and can lead to processes where repositioning takes place. A newly introduced voice will influence the other voices in ways that change the overall constellation (Hermans, 2008).

As well as through gaining novel information about the self (for example conceptualizing oneself for the first time as a pupil, an undergraduate student, or an associate professor), a new position can also come from the outside. Real others with whom the person interacts can be reflected dialogically as external positions within the self. These external positions are not simply replicas of other individuals, but the imagined voices of these others. An external position indexes a person in the individual's social or cultural environment, and can be relevant in relation to the perspective of one or a number of internal positions (Hermans, 2019; Valsiner, 2004).

When an external position is created, it will impact on the dynamics of the self. It affects the self's internal positions, and functions to shift the balance within the constellation. Returning to Auster's protagonist, this is what happens when Ferguson finds himself in the company of different others. The imagined voices of these others influence the I-position that currently speaks, the effect being that Ferguson experiences himself as different each time he is with a different person. It is because the voice of an internalized other is at odds with other voiced positions that the self can be plagued by contradictions. This explains how Ferguson can experience himself as an 'outspoken extrovert' when in the company of or thinking about one person, 'quiet and closed in on himself' in relation to another, a 'verbal battler' with yet another, and 'fragile and unsure of himself' with someone else.

The idea that innovation is a consequence of dialogical interchange between imagined voices, each with its own perspective, means that shifts in social situations prompt corresponding shifts in the self. The self has a capacity for multiple positioning. Thus when we find ourselves in different situations, and with different social others, we also change. Further, because innovation is in part a consequence of the influence of external voices in dialogical interchange, a new voice (or a new perspective articulated by an existing voice) can disrupt routine dialogues and can bring about changes to existing positions (Hermans, 2008). This is what happens to Ferguson when the new boy arrives on the scene.

Innovation and self-organization

To explain how these shifts take place, Hermans (2003, 2004) draws attention to self-organization. Self-organization is a characteristic of complex systems and involves the sense in which the reconfiguration of elements in a system occurs from within, and independently of any external force (Byrne & Callaghan, 2014; Larsen-Freeman & Cameron, 2008). In the dialogical landscape of the self, positions are not static, and repositioning constantly takes place. Changes in situational parameters affect the influence of particular voices in the system. Innovation occurs as a consequence of the movement of I-positions from a peripheral or background part of the self into the foreground, and vice-versa. In this mode of innovation a pre-existing, but perhaps dormant or rarely activated aspect of the self, can once again become prominent (Hermans, 2008). A good example of this would be 'approach' and 'avoidance' motivational tendencies. While people tend to formulate goals in recognizable ways, focusing on either approach or avoidance, sometimes circumstances can trigger forms of self-regulation that are focused on the opposing tendency (Henry & Davydenko, 2020). As the self spontaneously reorganizes, an 'eager forward-thinking self' (an approach disposition) might be replaced by a 'vigilant, circumspect self' (an avoidance disposition). Over time, this new part of the self might become more familiar and more accessible (Hermans, 2003).

Innovation and co-adaptation

Another way in which innovation within the dialogical self takes place is when I-positions form a coalition. Through processes of co-adaptation – the manner in which change in one complex system is influenced by changes in a connected system (Byrne & Callaghan, 2014; Larsen-Freeman & Cameron, 2008) – new subsystems of the self can be formed, and existing I-positions can combine to create a new I-position. In forming a coalition, I-positions that have a common purpose or a similar orientation can function together in mutual collaboration (Hermans, 2003, 2008). Taking a case from his own clinical practice, Hermans (2003) explains how three prominent and competing positions in a client's self repertoire – a self-doubter, a perfectionist and an enjoyer of life – changed over time. When the 'perfectionist' and the 'enjoyer' formed a coalition, the 'self-doubter' became consigned to the system's background. In another study of identity dynamics, Bell and Das (2011) describe how, for a young pre-med student studying at the University of Texas and living at home with her Asian Indian family in Austin, I-positions indexing contrasting ethnic identities – 'I-as-Indian' and 'I-as-American' – could often be oppositional. However, over time, a new I-position – 'I-as-both' – was seen to emerge. This the authors attribute to the potential for variability within the two previously dominant I-positions.

To take an example from our own field, the identity system of a language teacher might be expected to contain a number of I-positions. These could be an 'I-as-a-lover-of-French', an 'I-as-a-person-who-connects-with-young-people' and an 'I-as-a-conscientious-professional'. While these I-positions can be mutually supportive, there is also the possibility that co-adaptation might at some point take place. Subsequent to an in-service training day on motivational strategies, the 'I-as-a-lover-of-French' and the 'I-as-a-person-who-connects-with-young-people' might combine to create a new position, the 'I-as-a-motivational-practitioner'. And, through further co-adaptation with the 'I-as-a-conscientious-professional', yet another novel coalition might arise.

Researching the Complexity of the Dialogical Self

If we return once more to the contemplations on selfhood that occupy the protagonist in Auster's novel, we can understand how thinking about, or being in the presence of a particular other can bring about (i) the activation of an external I-position, and (ii) the foregrounding of an I-position representing a particular dimension of the self. While in social interactions a person acts agentively, actively shaping the directions that discourse takes and the trajectories of interpersonal relationships, from a complex systems perspective the social environment is not simply the context within which an identity system independently operates. Rather, the environment is integral to the emergent behaviours of the system. The context can never be separated from the system, but is interconnected with it and a part of its complexity (Larsen-Freeman & Cameron, 2008). Changes that take place in the social environment affect the constellation of I-positions pertaining at a particular moment in time. It is in this way that we can understand how changes in the self can be rapidly brought about as a consequence of changes in the social environment, and how the presence of different others, real or imagined, can trigger a reconfiguration of I-positions.

For the researcher, the challenge in an empirical study involves tracing and describing the processes that are involved when changes occur, and when innovation takes place. This objective does not deny the operation of intentionality; rather it seeks to explain how, as a complex dynamic system, the self adjusts in response to changes in the environment, how variability within the self is systemic, and how stability is a contingent property that is neither fixed nor static (Larsen-Freeman, 2019; Larsen-Freeman & Cameron, 2008). Reflecting on this challenge, Cunha and Gonçalves (2009: 126) argue a conceptualization of the dialogical self as a self-organizing system nested in a sociocultural/relational background 'does not contradict notions like intentionality, agency or autonomy, but stresses the need to develop theoretical efforts to articulate these concepts'.

The Dialogical Self as a Lens for Exploring the Complexity of Teacher Identities

Although rarely encountered in applied linguistics, the theory of the dialogical self has generated a large and expanding body of empirical research, including studies examining teacher identity development (Meijers & Hermans, 2018). Interestingly, much of this work uses self-report and retrospective methodologies, and involves the generation of intra-personal data. For example, in a study of the dynamic construction of teacher identity, Vandamme (2018) used the Personal Position Repertoire (PPR) questionnaire (Hermans, 2001a, 2001b) together with semi-structured interviews to reveal varying compositional patterns. Another method drawing on intra-personal data involves the use of narrative accounts. In a study of preservice teachers' identity development, and the ways in which it can be supported, Leijen *et al.* (2018) describe how written assignments were used as a means of accessing tensions between conflicting I-positions. In studies such as these, innovation in the self is examined over longer timescales (a course, a semester, or a programme of study). Patterns of change are mapped in relation to regularly occurring, rather than disjunctive events. An additional way of investigating innovation in the dialogical self is to study dynamical changes that take place across shorter timescales, for example during a lesson, or from one day to the next. Research objectives of this sort require methodologies that can access shifts in constellations of I-positions close to the points in time when they occur. This can be facilitated through examinations of dialogical data. In the remaining part of the chapter, I describe a method I have worked with that involves mapping teacher identity development across varying timescales, and how complexity principles can be used to cast light on mechanisms of innovation at micro- as well as macro-levels.

Studies and participants

Both of the studies I focus on (Henry, 2016, 2019) draw on data gathered in a project exploring identity development during a practicum. While the practicum can be the most rewarding and influential part of a student teacher's education, it can also be one of the most challenging (Ferrier-Kerr, 2009; Trent, 2013). Leaving behind a campus environment with predictable routines and clearly assigned roles can be a destabilizing time for many preservice teachers (Beauchamp & Thomas, 2011). Not only might students feel unprepared to deal with the challenges of classroom experiences (Flores & Day, 2006), the negotiation of shifting relationships can be emotionally demanding. In the practicum, systems of relations co-exist in overlapping and frequently conflictive constellations. It is in the midst of relationships with pupils, classroom mentors, and university faculty that the preservice teacher first learns the work of teaching, and begins to develop a professional identity (Smagorinsky *et al.*, 2004). It is because these intersecting and often conflictive relations create tensions that the construction of a professional identity can be such a challenging process.

Against this background, the purpose of the studies was to examine and theoretically account for the mechanisms through which shifts in preservice teacher identities might take place, to consider how identity tensions could be understood systemically, and to discover whether a teacher identity system might have a recognizable 'signature' dynamic. The two participants were enrolled on a five-and-a-half year program at a Swedish university that provided a qualification to teach English in grades 7 to 12. Both were at the beginning of the second year of program, and about to begin a 4-week practicum. Both saw the practicum as providing an opportunity to gain indications as to whether teaching was the right career choice.

Data and timescales

Research into the dialogical self has tended to use self-report methods, the responses to questionnaires or interview questions being limited by the participants' own self-insight. In order to widen the window opening onto the dialogical self, and the processes in which innovation takes place, self-report data can be complemented with *dialogical data* (Jasper *et al.*, 2012). Dialogical data – data that is generated through interpersonal dialogue – has the advantage of being able to reveal narrative experiences through a participant's *automatic* engagement in processes of sense-making. Thus it has the potential to 'reveal the more subtle dynamics of implicit meanings and positionings' (Jasper *et al.*, 2012: 326). Insight into identity transformations can therefore be enhanced when *intra-personal data* (from interviews) is combined with *inter-personal data* (generated in naturalistic discourse) (van Rijswijk *et al.*, 2013). In studies where both intra- and inter-personal data is generated, access to a person's repertoire of I-positions gained in an interview can be combined with insights into situated processes of foregrounding and backgrounding that become accessible through analyses of discourse interactions.

In studies of teacher identity that embrace the full complexity and dynamics of development, and which seek to explore transformation and innovation from a dialogical self-perspective, Akkerman and Meijer (2011) argue that micro-analytical and macro-analytical approaches should be combined. At the micro-level, the objective is to describe the ways in which a participant 'takes on and shifts between I-positions in response to relevant others'. At the macro-level, self-narratives offer insights 'in terms of past, local and future stories, as well as the socio-cultural conditions of the teacher's environment' (Akkerman & Meijer, 2011: 316). Because the self can be understood as a dynamic and

Table 14.1   Data used in studies by Henry (2016; 2019)

Source of data	Type of data	Timescale and focus
Semi-structured Interviews	Intra-personal	Long-term focus: the practicum
Postings on an online discussion forum	Inter-personal	Medium-term focus: day-to-day
Stimulated recall dialogue	Inter-personal	Short-term focus: moment-to-moment

self-organizing system, a micro-level approach is valuable when investigating transformation processes. At the same time, these processes need to be related to macro-level processes and developmental patterns (Klimstra *et al.*, 2010; Lichtwarck-Aschoff *et al.*, 2008).

In the research I carried out, the aim was to collect data that would enable identity formation processes to be studied at both the micro-level and across the shortest timescale of classroom events, as well as at the macro-level and over longer timescales (evolutionary patterns observed over several days, or the practicum as a whole). To do this, the design incorporated the use of intra-personal and inter-personal data. While I used semi-structured interviews to generate intra-personal data (mapping the I-positions in the participants' teacher identity systems at the beginning and at the end of the practicum), to generate inter-personal data I asked participants to contribute postings on an online discussion forum, and to take part in stimulated recall dialogues. The source, the data type and the timescale in focus are set out in Table 14.1.

Engaging with the data – a complexity mindset

As previously mentioned, few studies in the dialogical self-paradigm have included dialogical data (Jasper *et al.*, 2012). Two noteworthy exceptions are those by Bell and Das (2011), and Duarte and Gonçalves (2007). Both studies focus on transitions. In the Bell and Das study, the transition is between differing spheres of cultural experience, while the study by Duarte and Gonçalves charts a woman's transition into motherhood. In an attempt to highlight the interplay between contradictory I-positions, both studies make use of microgenetic analyses of discourse data. These studies provided the basis of the method that I used in the studies investigating the identity development of the two preservice English teachers (Henry, 2016, 2019). Like these authors, I also used a discourse analytical approach (Coyle, 2006; Potter & Wetherell, 1995). In the first of these studies (Henry, 2016), I provide a detailed step-by-step description of the analytical process together with an illustration of the method using data from an online post.

In each study I began by carefully reading the transcripts from the interviews, the forum postings, and the transcript of the stimulated recall discussions. My aim was to gain an experience of these texts as a reader, and to develop an understanding of what the text was doing and how this was accomplished. In the next stage of the analysis, I coded the text. The coding focused on instances in the text where the articulation of an identity could be discerned. In this way I was able to identify different I-positions. On each occasion where an identity was articulated, I shaded the text segment. Using the comment function in Word, I copied the extract into an adjacent comment box. Here, I took an inclusive approach, and included even borderline instances of identity articulations.

Once the coding was completed, I examined the extracts in greater detail. Here, my aim was to try to understand the function of an utterance. This involved reading the text in a situated manner, and attempting to relate articulations of identity to discourses associated with practice learning and English language teaching in the Swedish context. This part of the analysis focused on the linguistic construction of the text. Using the same comment boxes, I added notes about the rhetorical function of discourse features, paying particular attention to features that might reveal an identity position that was currently foregrounded, and to variability within the discourse which might indicate that a shift in an identity position had taken place. Finally, and for each I-position identified in the text, I considered whether this was the same I-position as that narrated immediately previously, whether it might constitute an entirely new position, or whether it might be a position previously identified (and which was foregrounded anew). When a shift was identified, I made a note in a comment box. Working in this way, I was able to identify and plot movements between I-positions across each of the three data types.

The findings

In the first study (Henry, 2016), the participant (Lina) had mixed feelings about embarking on a programme of teacher education, and was ambivalent about a career as a teacher. Analyses of the interview data (one interview immediately prior to the practicum, and one immediately afterwards) revealed the existence of two contradictory I-positions: *'an extra person but not a teacher'*, and *'someone who wants to work with and help young people'*. These I-positions were also evident in her posts on the discussion forum, and in the stimulated recall discussion. These I-positions were conceptualized as representing two fixed-point attractors in Lina's teacher identity system. Shifts between the two attractors – the foregrounding and backgrounding of the contradictory I-positions – could be seen to coincide with changes in the social environment, and with the parameters controlling the system.

The presence in the classroom of Lina's mentor was a controlling influence, and an important initial condition. This meant that the *'an extra person but not a teacher*' I-position was most frequently fore-grounded, the system lodged in this governing attractor state. However, on some occasions, Lina described having opportunities to follow her own initiatives and to work beyond the circumspection and control of her mentor. In such situations the '*an extra person but not a teacher*' I-position moved to the background, and the '*someone who wants to work with and help young people*' I-position became foregrounded. Such movements were conceptualized as a shift to the system's counterpoint attractor. Thus the system had a signature dynamic of predictable instability.

In the second study (Henry, 2019), the participant (Sara) was much more confident about her choice, positioning herself at the beginning of the practicum as an '*emerging practitioner*'. However, during the practicum a contradictory I-position was seen to emerge, that of a '*student-apprentice*'. In a manner similar to the findings in the first study, shifts between the '*emerging practitioner*' and '*student-apprentice*' I-positions were brought about by changes in the social environment. This was specifically the case when perceptions of autonomy and scope to exercise initiative associated with the '*emerging practitioner*' I-position were perceived as being restricted by the mentor's approach and methods. As in the first study, shifts between these two I-positions regularly occurred, this pattern of foregrounding and backgrounding constituting the system's signature dynamic.

The self-narratives that create I-positions have a powerful imaginative dimension. While narratives about the future are constructed in the context of stories told about the present, the present is no more than an unstable moment in the process of the self's becoming (Akkerman & Meijer, 2011; Hermans, 2008). For Sara, a new I-position was identified towards the end of the period. In being future-focused, this differed from the '*emerging practitioner*' I-position. As could be seen in the inter-personal data (the forum posts and the stimulated recall discussion), Sara framed current problems as challenges to be addressed in the imaginal spaces of future practice. In formulating her concerns this way, and envisioning herself as a member of a broader community of teaching professionals, Sara could be understood as narrating a new identity. This identity – the '*challenged practitioner*' – emerges through the variability of the existing I-positions. Becoming increasingly acquainted with the constraints affecting classroom practice, the *challenged practitioner* I-position represents innovation through co-adaptation, not only between *internal* positions, but also *external* positions representing the 'voices' of her mentor and the other teachers at the school.

Insights obscured but for a complexity perspective?

In common with other theories of the self that view identities as narratively structured (MacAdams, 1985; Markus & Nurius, 1986), the dialogical self provides a conceptualization of identity that is inherently dynamic. Irrespective of the methodology, in research conducted within the dialogical self paradigm understanding of innovation is a primary objective. Largely overlooked by researchers in applied linguistics, the dialogical self offers a valuable construct when investigating the identity development of language teachers and language learners. This is because it divides the complex whole of the self into functional subparts that are located (and which can re-locate) within particular spatial confines, and because it embodies principles of self-organization (Valsiner, 2004). For researchers interested in gaining insights into the formation and transformations of identities, the mapping of I-positions, the plotting of shifts and the highlighting of changes in the social context coinciding with reconfigurations of the self, offer useful approaches. However, while the dialogical self provides a fully integrated model for empirical investigations, its value in offering a holistic account of identity dynamics can be further leveraged through use of a CDST design.

When studying developmental processes, CDST methods can be inherently rewarding; phenomena can be investigated as processes in motion, and events can be analysed in the contexts in which they occur (MacIntyre *et al.*, 2015). However, no matter how intrinsically satisfying this might be, the question remains as to the extent to which the insights and understandings that are generated would have been possible *but for* a CDST design, and *but for* the application of complexity principles when analysing the data. In assessing the contribution of a complexity informed study, the core objectives for CDST research listed by Hiver and Al-Hoorie (2016) provide a valuable evaluative framework: Does the study attempt to understand a specific system at varying scales of description? Does it attempt to identify and understand patterns of dynamical change and emergent outcomes? Does it model the mechanisms and processes through which dynamical patterns arise, and does it provide insight into the parameters influencing the system's behaviour? To these criteria, two additional questions could be asked; does it provide unique understandings of a language learning and/or language teaching phenomenon, and are these insights useful to practitioners? In relation to the work on language teacher identity development that I have described here, it becomes therefore necessary to consider whether any insights *over and above* those associated with the application of dialogical self-theory (Hermans, 1999) were gained through taking a CDST approach, and whether these insights might be *of value* to people engaged in learning or mentoring during practicum periods.

First and foremost, by working with different types of data, it became possible to account for variation at differing levels of situated experience. This enabled the identification and understanding of innovation characteristics, the mechanisms associated with patterns of variability, and the signature dynamics of particular identity systems. Further, because the data enabled light to be cast on identity development across different timescales, it became possible to identify patterns of self-similarity (Kaplan

& Garner, 2017). As could be seen in the first study (Henry, 2016), movements between the system's I-positions were replicated in a fractal manner, on each of the investigated scales (minute-by-minute, hour-by-hour and day-to-day). Equally, by making use of a dynamic systems topography and the notion of attractor and repeller states, situations when a participant experienced that an identity was challenged could be made sense of in a more holistic, systemic manner. Through an understanding of the effects that perturbations have on a dynamic system, it became possible to recognize how moments of worry and panic were not aberrations or idiosyncrasies in the data, but rather situations where the system momentarily lacked coherence (Henry, 2019).

A complexity conceptualization of the mechanisms, processes and parameters that influence the behaviour of a language teacher's self system are of value in two particular respects. In systematic research across a number of cases, and which is aimed at identifying the signature dynamics of individual systems, opportunities for generalization are provided (Byrne & Callaghan, 2014). Generalization, in this sense, does not relate to subjects; developmental trajectories will never be the same for any two systems. Rather, generalization concerns instances of observed process characteristics (van Geert & Lichtwarck-Aschoff, 2005). In systematic research, patterns of transformation dynamics characteristic for preservice teacher identity development, and the range of outcomes with which they are associated can be identified. Methods that enable the modelling of behaviour can be of particular value in identity-mapping interventions (Byrne, 2014). For example, as a part of their education, preservice teachers can make use of complexity principles in ways that enable them to become 'process researchers' of their own identity development (Steenbeek & van Geert, 2015; see also Henry, in preparation; Henry & Tynkkinen, 2017).

Future Research

In the examples discussed in this chapter (Henry, 2016, 2019), identity development was studied over a four-week practicum. Focus was directed to innovation in the participants' emerging professional identities, and the dynamical processes involved in shifts between contradictory I-positions. In this framing, the presence of a classroom mentor was conceptualized as a parameter controlling the system. Like Auster's protagonist – who realizes that 'each time he was with a different person, he himself was different as well' – the teaching identities of the participants changed in response to the presence (or absence) of other persons. However, as we have seen, the dialogical self is not only comprised of *internal* I-positions but also includes *external* positions. External positions refer to other people in the social environment made relevant from the perspective of a particular internal position. As Hermans (2001) explains, for a parent, the internal position 'I-as-mother' exists in relation to the external position of the child. Equally, for a child beginning a new school, the internal position 'I-as-pupil' exists in relation to the teacher. Therefore, an important direction for future research would be to investigate the 'voices' of important others that exist within a preservice teacher's identity system. In addition to classroom and faculty mentors, this could also include the pupils being taught. As Jasper and colleagues (2012: 320) make clear, for many people the presence in private thought of the perspectives of significant others is 'an everyday experience'. In this regard, it would be particularly interesting to examine dynamical relations between internal and external positions. Importantly, because dialogical self methodologies provide the means for studying the self 'in its social context' (Jasper *et al.*, 2012), it becomes possible to examine the broader *social* dialogues within which the self is embedded. Using designs drawing on dialogical data – for example where students engage in discussion with peers, teachers or practicum mentors – opportunities to develop understandings of the roles played by others in the development of teacher identities would become available.

Conclusion

Learning to become a teacher is often framed as a struggle. It involves a recognition that it is not a single, unified teacher identity that is under development, but rather a constellation of often varying identities. As Akkerman and Meijer (2011: 317) describe it, developing an identity as being someone who teaches can be understood 'as an ongoing process of negotiating and interrelating multiple I-positions in such a way that a more or less coherent and consistent sense of self is maintained'. Disambiguating these different selves, explaining how and why shifts take place, and identifying the dynamical characteristics for particular patterns of innovation, are all of importance in understanding the identity development of preservice teachers. With increased insight into these processes, teacher educators can become better equipped to guide students in the task of understanding identity tensions and disentangling collections of contradictory selves.

References

Akkerman, S.F. and Meijer, P.C. (2011) A dialogical approach to conceptualizing teacher identity. *Teaching and Teacher Education* 27, 308–319.
Allport, G.W. (1955) *Becoming: Basic Considerations for a Psychology of Personality.* New Haven, CT: Yale University Press.
Auster, P. (2017) *4321*. New York: Henry Holt & Co.
Bakhtin, M.M. (1973) *Problems of Dostoevsky's Poetics* (2nd edn). (R.W. Rotsel, Transl.) Ann Arbor, MI: Ardis.
Bakhtin, M.M. (1981) *The Dialogic Imagination: Four Essays by M. M. Bakhtin* (C. Emerson and M. Holquist, Trans.). Austin, TX: University of Texas Press.
Beauchamp, C. and Thomas, L. (2011) New teachers' identity shifts at the boundary of teacher education and initial practice. *International Journal of Educational Research* 50, 6–13.

Bell, N.J. and Das, A. (2011) Emergent organization in the dialogical self: Evolution of a 'both' ethnic identity position. *Culture & Psychology* 17 (2), 241–262.

Byrne, D. (2014) Thoughts on a pedagogy of complexity. *Complicity: An International Journal of Complexity and Education* 11 (2), 40–50.

Byrne, D. and Callaghan, G. (2014) *Complexity Theory and the Social Sciences: The State of the Art*. Abingdon: Routledge.

Cilliers, P. (2008) Responses. In C. Gershenson (ed.) *Complexity: 5 Questions* (pp. 27–32). Copenhagen: Automatic Press.

Coyle, A. (2006) Discourse analysis. In G.M. Breakwell, S. Hammond, C. Fife-Schaw and J.A. Smith (eds) *Research Methods in Psychology* (pp. 366–387). London: Sage Publications.

Cunha, C. and Gonçalves, M.M. (2009) Accessing the experience of a dialogical self: Some needs and concerns. *Culture & Psychology* 15 (1), 120–133.

Dörnyei, Z. (2014) Researching complex dynamic systems: 'Retrodictive qualitative modelling' in the language classroom. *Language Teaching* 47 (1), 80–91.

Duarte, F. and Gonçalves, M.M. (2007) Negotiating motherhood: A dialogical approach. *International Journal for Dialogical Science* 2, 249–275.

Flores, M.A. and Day, C. (2006) Contexts which shape and reshape new teachers' identities: A multi-perspective study. *Teaching and Teacher Education* 22, 219–232.

Ferrier-Kerr, J. (2009) Establishing professional relationships in practicum settings. *Teaching and Teacher Education* 25, 790–797.

Henry, A. (2016) Conceptualizing teacher identity as a complex dynamic system: Tensions during the practicum. *Journal of Teacher Education* 67 (4), 291–305.

Henry, A. (2019) A drama of selves: Investigating teacher identity development from dialogical and complexity perspectives. *Studies in Second Language Learning and Teaching* 9 (2), 263–285.

Henry, A. and Davydenko, S. (2020) Thriving? Or surviving? An approach–avoidance perspective on adult language learners' motivation. *The Modern Language Journal* 104 (2).

Henry, A. (in preparation) Working with identity work: Supporting the exploration of professional identity development in teacher education.

Henry, A. and Tynkkinen, M. (2017) Becoming a process researcher of one's own development: Using an identity mapping model to make sense of transformation dynamics during the practicum. In T. Gregersen and P.D. MacIntyre (eds) *Exploring Innovations in Language Teacher Education: Transformational Theory and Practice* (pp. 205–228). New York: Springer.

Hermans, H.J.M. (1996) Voicing the self: From information processing to dialogical interchange. *Psychological Bulletin* 119 (1), 31–50.

Hermans, H.J.M. (1999) Dialogical thinking and self-innovation. *Culture & Psychology* 5, 67–87.

Hermans, H.J.M. (2001a) The dialogical self: Toward a theory of personal and cultural positioning. *Culture & Psychology* 7 (3), 243–281.

Hermans, H.J.M. (2001b) The construction of a personal position repertoire: Method and practice. *Culture & Psychology* 7 (3), 323–365.

Hermans, H.J.M. (2003) The construction and reconstruction of a dialogical self. *Journal of Constructivist Psychology* 16 (2), 89–130.

Hermans, H.J.M. (2004) Introduction: The dialogical self in a global and digital age. *Identity: An International Journal of Theory and Research* 4, 297–320.

Hermans, H.J.M. (2008) How to perform research on the basis of dialogical self theory? Introduction to the special issue. *Journal of Constructivist Psychology* 21 (3), 185–199.

Hermans, H.J.M. (2019) Dialogical self theory in a boundary-crossing society. In H. Alma and I. ter Avest (eds) *Moral and Spiritual Leadership in an Age of Plural Moralities* (pp. 27–47). Abingdon: Routledge.

Hermans, H.J.M. and Hermans-Jansen, E. (2003) Dialogical processes and the development of the self. In J. Valsiner and K. Connolly (eds) *Handbook of Developmental Psychology* (pp. 534–559). London: Sage.

Hermans, H.J.M., Kempen, H.J.G. and Van Loon, R.J.P. (1992) The dialogical self: Beyond individualism and rationalism. *American Psychologist* 47, 23–33.

Hiver, P. and Al-Hoorie, A.H. (2016) A dynamic ensemble for second language research: Putting complexity theory into practice. *Modern Language Journal* 100 (4), 1–16.

James, W. (1890) *The Principles of Psychology* (Vol. 1). London: Macmillan.

Jasper, C., Moore, H., Whittaker, L. and Gillespie, A. (2012) Methodological approaches to studying the self in its social context. In H. Hermans and T. Gieser (eds) *Handbook of Dialogical Self Theory* (pp. 319–334). Cambridge: Cambridge University Press.

Kaplan, A. and Garner, J.K. (2017) A complex dynamic systems perspective on identity and its development: The dynamic systems model of role identity. *Developmental Psychology* 53 (11), 2036–2051.

Klimstra, T.A, Luyckx, K., Hale, W.W., Frijns, T., van Lier, P. and Meeus, W.H.J. (2010) Short-term fluctuations in identity: Introducing a micro-level approach to identity formation. *Journal of Personality and Social Psychology* 99 (1), 191–202.

Larsen-Freeman, D. (2019) On language learner agency: A complex dynamic systems theory perspective. *Modern Language Journal* 103 (S1), 61–79.

Larsen-Freeman, D. and Cameron, L. (2008) *Complex Systems and Applied Linguistics*. Oxford: Oxford University Press.

Leijen, Ä., Kullasepp, K. and Toompalu, A. (2018) Dialogue for bridging student teachers' personal and professional identity. In F. Meijers and H. Hermans (eds) *The Dialogical Self Theory in Education: A Multicultural Perspective* (pp. 97–110). Cham: Springer.

Lichtwarck-Aschoff, A., van Geert, P., Bosma, H. and Kunnen, S. (2008) Time and identity: A framework for research and theory formation. *Developmental Review* 28 (3), 370–400.

MacIntyre, P.D., Dörnyei, Z. and Henry, A. (2015) Conclusion: Hot enough to be cool – the promise of dynamic systems research. In Z. Dörnyei, P.D. MacIntyre and A. Henry (eds) *Motivational Dynamics in Language Learning* (pp. 419–429). Bristol: Multilingual Matters.

Markus, H.R. and Nurius, P. (1986) Possible selves. *American Psychologist* 41, 954–969.

McAdams, D.P. (1985) The 'imago': A key narrative component of identity. In P. Shaver (ed.) *Review of Personality and Social Psychology* (pp. 115–141). Beverly Hills: Sage.

Mead, G.H. (1913) The social self. *Journal of Philosophy* 10, 374–380.

Mead, G.H. (1934) *Mind, Self, and Society*. Chicago: University of Chicago Press.

Meijers, F. and Hermans, H.J.M. (2018) *Dialogical Self Theory in Education: An Introduction*. New York: Springer.

Potter, J. and Wetherell, M. (1995) Discourse analysis. In J. Smith, R. Harré and L. Van Langenhove (eds) *Rethinking Methods in Psychology* (pp. 80–92). London: Sage.

Smagorinsky, P., Cook, L.S., Moore, C., Jackson, A.Y. and Fry, P.G. (2004) Tensions in learning to teach: Accommodation and the development of a teaching identity. *Journal of Teacher Education* 55 (1), 8–24.

Steenbeek, H. and van Geert, P. (2015) A complexity approach toward mind–brain–education (MBE); Challenges and opportunities in educational intervention and research. *Mind, Brain, and Education* 9 (2), 81–86.

Trent, J. (2013) From learner to teacher: Practice, language, and identity in a teaching practicum. *Asia-Pacific Journal of Teacher Education* 41 (4), 426–440.

Valsiner, J. (1997) Dialogical models of psychological processes: Capturing dynamics of development. *Polish Quarterly of Developmental Psychology* 3, 155–160.

Valsiner, J. (2004) Temporal integration of structures within the dialogical self. Keynote lecture at the 3rd International Conference on Dialogical Self, Warsaw, Poland, August 28.

Vandamme, R. (2018) Teacher identity as a dialogical construction. In F. Meijers and H. Hermans (eds) *The Dialogical Self Theory in Education: A Multicultural Perspective* (pp. 111–128). Springer.

van Geert, P. and Lichtwarck-Aschoff, A. (2005) A dynamic systems approach to family assessment. *European Journal of Psychological Assessment* 21 (4), 240–248.

van Rijswijk, M.M., Akkerman, S. and Koster, B. (2013) Student teachers' internally persuasive borderland discourse and teacher identity. *International Journal for Dialogical Science* 7 (1), 43–60.

15 Using Microgenetic and Frame Analysis in Language Teacher Cognition Research

Anne Feryok

Introduction

Most of my research has been about specific language teacher beliefs or about 'how teachers' mental processes are conceived' (Freeman, 2002: 2); Borg (2006) uses 'cognition' to include both. Many language teacher cognition studies examine the specific beliefs of teachers as they are declaratively expressed, usually in research interviews, and tacitly practiced, usually in classroom teaching observations. Declarative and tacit beliefs are often found to differ; these differences are often described as inconsistencies; and these inconsistences are often evaluated negatively.

However, these alleged inconsistences can be explained. They may be evidence of teachers learning and developing (Freeman, 1993); being sensitive to contexts such as institutions, learners and instruction (Burns, 1996); making multiple connections between ideas and practices (Breen *et al.*, 2001); or having their own practical conceptualizations of theory (Mangubhai *et al.*, 2004, 2005).

Although I first read about the complex and interconnected networks of teacher beliefs at different contextual levels in Burns (1996), Larsen-Freeman and Cameron's (2008) book on complex systems and applied linguistics pushed me to consider whether teacher cognition was a complex system. One feature discussed in the book is heterogeneity, leading to the question of how cognition is heterogenous. Besides the different content of cognition, cognition is also psychologically heterogenous. In language teacher cognition research, it is often used inclusively to refer to multiple psychological states (Kubanyiova & Feryok, 2015) as well as the dual memory system already mentioned, declarative (e.g. stated beliefs) and procedural (e.g. tacit beliefs inferred from practices) (Feryok, 2010, 2018).

Another issue is that research methods may affect which beliefs become available to researchers. Nishino (2012) used both statistical path analysis (based on a survey) and qualitative analysis (based on observations and follow-up interviews) of influences on language teacher cognitions and practices. Some factors that were not statistically significant enough to be included in the path analysis were emphasized by teachers in the qualitative data.

I explored these issues with my co-author in a study, Feryok and Oranje (2015), which used dynamic systems theory to examine the emergence and development of language teacher cognition about an idea that was used to resolve a problem, which was then compared to stated beliefs on the same topic. I first present the study, then the three research methods I used, and briefly discuss their significance.

The Study

My co-author, Jo Oranje, designed a research project for her PhD on intercultural communicative language teaching (ICLT) in New Zealand secondary schools. This topic is important because language and culture are inseparable (Agar, 1994), but as is discussed in greater detail in Feryok and Oranje (2015), many studies in different contexts have reported that even though teachers have positive beliefs about the role of culture in language teaching, they spend little time teaching it because of a perceived lack of time in the curriculum for non-required, non-assessed topics. New Zealand presented the perfect context for the study, since ICLT is recommended but is not required in the curriculum and is not assessed on national exams. The research project first identified the ICLT cognitions and practices of teachers in a survey, and then implemented a cultural portfolio project to address the challenges of ICLT. Cultural portfolio projects involve teachers and students hypothesizing about an aspect of the target and home cultures, which they then research, reflect on (which can involve comparing home and target cultures), and report to their class. Ada, the teacher participant, became involved in the project when she heard Jo do a presentation about her survey results to a language teacher organization and asked if she could participate in the cultural portfolio project. She was a native speaker of German who emigrated to New Zealand as an adult. She had been teaching German in New Zealand for seven years at the time of the study. Although she was unfamiliar with ICLT, she said German culture was important in her teaching and so she was interested in learning about ICLT. She therefore seemed to be the ideal participant for a study aimed at discovering the dynamic interactions among teacher beliefs when a teacher is exposed to new ideas. I proposed this study as an addition to Jo's study; we planned, conducted, and wrote Feryok and Oranje (2015) together, but I performed the data analysis, and Jo read the data analysis memos, which we discussed. I am therefore using first person in this account of the data analysis.

Since the study involved introducing the participant to a new project, it was expected that the participant would develop beliefs about ICLT aims, the project and its implementation, and that some of these beliefs might change. In particular, it was expected that discussing the aims of the project might change the participant's understanding of ICLT.

The study took place in the first meeting held for planning how Jo's project could be incorporated into the usual curriculum and class schedule of Ada's Year 12 German class. Two data sets were collected back to back in the same session: the primary data set, which was an introductory session in which Jo explained the cultural portfolio project and then discussed it with Ada, and the secondary data set, a semi-structured interview which I conducted in order to collect background information about Ada and her beliefs about language and culture teaching.

Despite the planning, one significant change occurred when the project was being conducted. It was obvious that Ada was focusing on assessment in the introductory session, so I made a note to add it to the interview topics, even though I expected Ada to raise it herself, probably in response to a planned open-ended question on the curriculum. In the interview, however, Ada did not raise assessment. I therefore directly asked the question I had noted: How did assessments fit into her class?

The data analysis involved three methods: coding and two types of genetic analysis, microgenetic analysis and frame analysis. I first analysed both data sets thematically through coding in order to be able to make direct comparisons between them. This was the only analysis used on the interview data, and the process enabled me to recognize that additional analyses were needed for the introductory session because the participant performed different functions in the data sets. In the introductory session, Ada used language to examine the implications of this new project on her students and curriculum goals, so her ideas were being formed as she spoke; in the interview, Ada used language to describe her beliefs in response to interview questions, so her ideas were being recalled as she spoke (Wagoner, 2009).

The initial analysis of the introductory session showed that Ada spoke little while Jo explained the project, and then took the floor at line 102, where she asked if she could use part of the project as an assessment, even though assessment was not a part of Jo's project and was not mentioned by her. Ada maintained an active role until the end of the introductory session at line 399. She also maintained a strong focus on assessment, mentioning it in 22 of 43 turns, but mentioned the expected topic of culture in only four turns. Assessment therefore seemed significant because it was the first and most frequent topic in Ada's turns.

The initial analysis of the interview showed that Ada had fairly consistent beliefs, and that she mentioned assessment only when I directly asked her. Ada made a short comment that she 'made them fit.' She then explained that she did not teach to assessments because teaching language skills was more important, and students who were taught well engaged in learning and so automatically did well on assessments. Although these comments were consistent with other beliefs that Ada articulated in the interview, it seemed significant that Ada had not raised assessment herself and had so little to say about it, given its role in the introductory session.

Assessment, therefore, became the priority in a study that I had expected to be about culture and intercultural teaching. The way Ada mentioned it at line 102 made me think it had emerged, which led me to think of both complex and dynamic systems and microgenesis. In the following sections I briefly explain coding; then I address the microgenetic analysis and frame analysis in more detail by explaining what each method is and how they were used.

Coding

I am not going to explain coding in detail because it has been so frequently and extensively treated elsewhere (e.g. Saldaña, 2016), but simply describe the procedures and provide the reasons I used it. I began by listening to the recordings of each session while reading the transcripts, which were professionally transcribed broadly for content and a limited number of interactional features. This initial engagement suggested that Ada introduced a new idea, here named 'project-as-assessment.' As I read and reread the introductory session transcripts, I noticed that assessment repeatedly came up, often in relation to other ideas, but only after Ada had introduced her new idea. I also confirmed that in the interview data, assessment only came up when I directly asked about it. I therefore decided that I should begin by coding the data for assessment in order to systematically confirm what I had noticed.

I marked every instance where 'assessment' appeared by underlining the word and indicating in the margin where talk about assessment began and ended. I noticed and then listed the different topics within the assessment passages. I repeated the coding process for each of them. I then reread all of the data and carefully examined the codes in both the lists and interactional contexts and noted where I could collapse specific codes into more general categories (e.g. students). I then re-examined all of the data, looking for any other places where codes and categories could be applied to see if they added any new ideas to the assessment passages. Finally, I returned to the assessment passages and checked my work. I therefore used coding to facilitate the identification of frames.

I also coded the interview for assessment and other topics that appeared in it (such as culture). The interview included Ada's beliefs about her context, often related anecdotally: her school, the New Zealand school system and nation, and New Zealand's place in the world. Coding helped me identify where the content of Ada's beliefs was similar and different in the two data sets, which is analogous to comparing teacher practices (where beliefs are found in use) and stated beliefs (where beliefs are recalled). Coding facilitated direct comparisons; in particular the interview data provided contextual information for interpreting the significance of introductory session data.

Microgenetic Analysis

What is microgenetic analysis?

Feryok and Oranje (2015) is an example of a genetic analysis, which examines the origins and development of phenomena, especially percepts and thoughts, in order to understand the underlying systems of perception and cognition. One type is microgenetic analysis, 'any empirical strategy that triggers, records and analyses the immediate process of emergence of new phenomena' (Valsiner, 2000: 78). The Austrian psychologist, Heinz Werner, coined the term in German (*Aktualgenese*) in the 1920s and later translated it into English. The aim of microgenetic analysis is to examine change repeatedly over the period in which it occurs, so the scale on which change is observed is relatively smaller than the scale on which change occurs. For example, in visual perception, conscious percepts take tenths of seconds, so observations of unconscious processes that underlie them must be made on the scale of milliseconds (Herzog *et al.*, 2016). In child development, however, achieving success in reaching for objects occurs over a year, and monthly observations are the norm (Thelen & Smith, 2007).

Microgenetic analysis is historically associated with early psychological research in Europe in the 1920s, including Gestalt Theory and other organismic or holistic theories and the theories arising from Vygotsky's work (Wertsch, 1991), such as sociocultural theory, activity theory, and cultural-historical activity theory. These two groups of theories share two assumptions. According to Siegler (2006: 467), 'Theorists such as Werner (1948, 1957) and Vygotsky (1934/1962) viewed short-term change as a miniature version of long-term change, generated by similar underlying processes and characterized by identical sequences of qualitatively different stages.' Studying change as it occurred was considered important because Werner and Vygotsky believed that when a process concludes, only its product remains – the steps through which the process developed or was learned become abbreviated and obscured in the outcome. The other shared assumption is that parts of a whole should not be studied in isolation from the whole of which they are part, which implies that psychological processes should be studied with reference to the individuals experiencing those processes, and that individuals should be studied with reference to their context.

More recently, microgenetic analysis has been used with complex and dynamic systems theories, especially in child development research, in order to capture the emergence of new phenomena through the self-organization of systems. There are different systems theories, including the distinction between complex and dynamic, which are not relevant to this discussion, so here I refer to complex dynamic systems theory. A more relevant distinction is between self-organization and emergence, as described by van Geert and Steenbeck (2005) and Witherington (2007). One approach focuses on the human being as an embodied agent acting in their environment, whose development arises from the self-organization of moment-to-moment interactions in real-time. In this perspective, higher level psychological processes, from concepts to theory of mind, do not exist; they are mere epiphenomena that can be reduced to the lower-level moment-to-moment interactions.

The alternative approach also includes self-organized moment-to-moment interactions, but is not reductionist. When self-organization leads to higher-level phenomena that have causal power to act on their lower-level systems, they are emergent rather than epiphenomenal. This difference does not mean, according to van Geert and Steenbeck (2005), that any special ontological claims about the nature of higher-level phenomena can be made; for example, that they are mental rather than physical. Emergence is more compatible with Werner's and Vygotsky's ideas than epiphenomenalism. It should be noted that Vygotsky did make an ontological claim about psychological processes – he said they were physical rather than mental processes, but he also emphasized that reductionism did not explain higher-level psychological phenomena. His point is therefore a variation on the point van Geert and Steenbeck make.

Dynamic systems have multiple components that interact and change (Richardson *et al.*, 2014), creating variability. Variability self-organizes from multiple quantitative changes in different aspects of the system (Spencer *et al.*, 2011), creating a transition from an old pattern to a new pattern (Granott *et al.*, 2002). The new pattern is an attractor and constitutes an emergent qualitative change, that is, change or development (van Geert, 1998). Attractors stabilize a system, but they also constrain its flexibility, which is not necessarily negative. Attention is an example of an attractor (de Bot *et al.*, 2007); if a specific task attracts attention, it stabilizes performance on that task and constrains flexibility – in other words, it prevents distraction.

Microgenetic analysis can be used with different research designs, including natural, intervention and experimental conditions; everyday, classroom and laboratory settings; actional, behavioural and verbal data; and different skills, concepts and domains (Siegler, 2006). Siegler also notes that controls are unusual since microgenetic analysis is aimed at discovering the way change occurs, not whether one kind of experience is more effective than another at producing change. Generally speaking, studies are longitudinal, but this is relative to the nature of the change, so data may be collected over periods from seconds to years. Designs may vary from a single participant in single or multiple sessions to multiple participants in single or multiple sessions.

How did I use microgenetic analysis?

Microgenetic analysis typically involves the detailed examination of how an instance of a process develops, such as a problem that requires a particular strategy or concept to be used to solve it (Granott *et al.*, 2002). That instance is in an individual in a context, so the individual is the usual unit of analysis, not the change itself or the relevant parts of the individual (Lavelli *et al.*, 2005). In this study, once it became apparent that Ada thought that one part of Jo's research project could be done as an assessment, the problem was reconceptualizing the project to fit into Ada's class planning to cover the curriculum and meet New Zealand national assessment standards. Ada was the unit of analysis, and her context included her interactions with Jo and me during the data collection, and the environment in which Ada worked: her classes of German language learners, their school, the school system, and even New Zealand and its place in the world.

Microgenetic analysis has the following features, which I use to explain my analytic process:

(1) Observations span the period of rapidly changing competence.
(2) Within this period, the density of observations is high, relative to the rate of change.
(3) Observations are analysed intensively, with the goal of inferring the representations and processes that give rise to them. (Siegler, 2006: 469)

First, the data spanned the period of change. The introductory session began without Ada having heard about the specific stages of the cultural portfolio project, so it is clear that data was collected prior to the formation of the new idea; the idea began developing during her interactions with Jo, possibly initiated by a question Ada asked at line 63, and certainly by Ada's comment at line 102–103, and continued developing in relation to other ideas until the end of the session at line 399. It was not a direct topic of the interview that followed, where Ada's answer to a question about assessment bore little relation to her focus on the project-as-assessment, so there is also data from after the formation of the new idea.

Second, the idea emerged in ongoing real-time interaction, rather than dense but discrete observations. It is typical for microgenetic research using interactional data to use selected extracts of data from a single bounded speech event (Bamberg, 2012). The introductory session was a single bounded speech event, as marked by Jo's participation.

Third, the data were analysed intensively through repeated engagements. Bamberg (2012), who has used the microanalysis of interactions to identify the microgenesis of identity and self, argues that the third criteria is about the development of the real-world, real-time construction of rela-tions and dialogues, as opposed to intrapsychological or individually internalized knowledge. Granott *et al.* (2002) similarly point out that focusing on development allows psychological processes to be studied *before* they become automatized. Neither explanation asserts that psycho-logical processes do not exist; rather, as they are formed, they exist as a process; otherwise, they exist as a memory of the outcome – as an idea or a procedure. Herzog *et al.* (2016) make a similar argument about percepts, which are the outcome of multiple unconscious processes integrating *before* a conscious percept occurs. The developmental process is presented in detail in the frame analysis; here I present the first clear indication of its microgenesis.

As mentioned, while coding, I noticed the way Ada interacted in gen-eral with Jo during the introductory session. Although I did not know Ada, I had met her on several occasions, when she always presented as a well-educated, articulate, confident and engaging conversationalist. While Jo briefly summarized the project, Ada regularly backchanneled and made one- and two-word utterances. She only made three comments in the first 101 lines. One was about the ethics documents, one was a humorous com-ment, and one was at line 63, when Ada asked whether one part of the project, when students present the results of their research, involved com-paring cultures. However, Ada's interaction pattern changed at line 102, when Ada took the floor and initiated a topic for the first time, and con-tinued actively participating until the session ended (line 399). However, Ada's utterance at line 102–103 was quite disfluent compared to her other utterances during the session, in the interview session, and in my previous interactions with her. Taking control of the floor through an uncharacter-istically disfluent utterance convinced me that this line was significant.

The first three disfluencies appear as soon as she begins her utterance and then abandons it as a false start ('No, I'm kinda s-') and follows it with two fillers ('um, um'). She then makes an atypical utterance, 'I have a ques-tion in my head,' followed by an embedded question, 'if I can make that part of the assessment.' A reason follows, which begins with a filler ('um') followed by 'because' and then another filler ('um') and another false start ('we, they're'). There are six disfluent syllables out of 36 syllables.

> 102: Ada [[...]] No, I'm kinda s-, um, um, I have the question in my head if I can make
> 103: that part of an assessment. Um, because, um, we, they're doing a speech.

This passage does not resemble the disfluency of a non-native speaker struggling with the right forms for expressing ideas. There are no errors. What was so difficult? As I thought about it, I decided to interpret the atypical utterance 'I have a question in my head' literally: Ada was trying to get the question out of her head, and into her words. The problem was not about making language choices; it was about making an idea complete, much as Vygotsky (1986) describes.

Since Ada's new idea was simultaneously for her assessment and for Jo's project, it suggests that there were two attractors, with the new idea emerging as a result of their competition. The idea appears to have arisen from bottom-up processes over which Ada did not have agentive control. She did not know what she was going to say when she started speaking; she was constructing her utterance on the fly because she was formulating the new idea at the very same time. It is not until Ada actually connects 'that' (when students present their research) with 'an assessment' as she utters it that the new idea of 'project-as-assessment' emerges. The struggle may have been compounded by Ada simultaneously proposing a new idea while requesting Jo's agreement to it.

The originally published study did not include this lengthy account because the frame analysis stands on its own as a microgenetic analysis. Here I have been able to fully explain how lines 102–103 inspired the use of frame analysis.

Frame Analysis

What is frame analysis?

Frame analysis, as used in this study, is a type of microgenetic analysis (Lavelli *et al.*, 2005) of frames, which are 'stable attractors in a dynamic relationship system' (Fogel *et al.*, 2006: 21). Fogel (1993) cites Bateson (1955) for the concept of frames, as well as Goffman's (1974) frame analysis. Using a 'play frame' for an example, Bateson presents frames as analogous to picture frames and sets (from set theory): frames and sets determine what is included and excluded and how it is meaningfully interpreted. Whether it refers to a child's game or a theatre production, the interpretations of events in the play frame differ from their interpretation in an everyday work routine frame. Goffmann detailed the frames of everyday life and pointed to the linguistic and other interactional cues that made frames apparent to interactants.

Fogel (1993: 3–4) originally used frames in order to understand how relationships among individuals develop, based on the assumptions that 'individuals and relationships … are always dynamically constituted as part of a process', and that 'cognition and the sense of self are fundamentally and originally *relational*' (original italics). Fogel (1993: 77) emphasizes that this does not mean that internal states do not exist; rather, 'cognitions and emotions are created as part of the communication and are not fixed in advance'. Frame analysis is mainly used in child development research, although Fogel (1993) envisioned it as more generally relevant to relationships, and there have been calls for it to be used in clinical psychology, education and public policy (Lavelli *et al.*, 2005).

According to Fogel (1993: 34), communication is based on co-regulation, defined as 'a social process by which individuals dynamically alter their actions with respect to the ongoing and anticipated actions of their partners'. Co-regulation emerges from the constraint of anticipating an interactant's response and changing one's own actions to meet it. Fogel (1993: 6) stresses the continuous nature of co-regulation, which does not occur merely through discrete interactions based on the specific content of a specific verbal interaction, but through culture, 'the set of tools, media, communication conventions and beliefs that mediate all of our relational experiences.' Through co-regulation stability arises in the components, which contribute to recognizably repeatable patterns.

Fogel (1993: 51) suggests that in a systems perspective on communication, stability 'occurs by virtue of co-regulation'. This is apparent through the maintenance of a theme 'as a recognizable pattern with variations' (Fogel, 1993: 51), that is, frames: 'A frame is a *co-regulated consensual agreement* about the scope of the discourse: its location, its setting, the acts that are taken to be significant vs. those that are irrelevant, and the *main focus or topic*' (Fogel, 1993: 36; original italics and bolding).

How did I use frame analysis?

According to Fogel *et al.* (2006), there are three phases in frame analysis:

(1) identifying frequently occurring frames;
(2) identifying when the frames begin and end, and;
(3) observing changes in sequences of actions within frames and between frames.

Frames can be identified in interactants by the direction of attention, their location, their co-orientation through posture and the topic of communication. Fogel *et al* (2006: 77) indicate that the analysis 'should be tailored to the specific communicative situation'. (In fact, Fogel (1993) extensively uses examples of fictional adult dialogues from well-known novels to illustrate frames, which supports its use with adult interactional data.) I did not use location, since it did not change, and adapted the other features to the situation. In interactions between pre-verbal children, children's attention frequently shifts and must be inferred through eye gaze and movement. In this study I identified the object of attention as Ada and Jo picked up and repeated each other's themes and linked them to other themes. Although co-orientation was not determined through their physical posture, it was found in their communicative stances (Fogel *et al.*, 2006), which revealed underlying assumptions that led them to alter their mental and verbal actions (Fogel, 1993), such as converging on or diverging from a topic. I also used interactional features such as back-channelling, latching and overlapping utterances. Finally, I adapted frame analysis by focusing on the theme or topic of communication that had been identified through coding.

In order to identify when frames began and ended, I closely examined the thematic codes in the context of the transcript. Because it was interactional data, I then reread above and below each instance in order to confirm where topics shifted in order to identify boundaries. I also paid attention to interactional features, especially pauses, as well as functions, such as questions and evaluative comments, which can signal where topics begin and end.

I was able to identify changes in sequences within frames by examining codes that distinguished between major themes and minor themes, which created variations within major themes. However, there was no apparent significance to these variations within frames.

The extract below (chosen because it is the shortest) is from the published extract of lines 102–135 (Feryok & Oranje, 2015: 555–556). Assessment is mentioned at line 121 as a major theme that attracted variations on the minor theme of student self-regulation. Within the minor theme of student self-regulation, Ada mentions what she would let students do ('research') and not let them do ('write it in English') and why not in terms of student behaviour ('put it into Google Translate') and its outcome ('gobbledegook'), before returning to assessment, which is implied by the 'starting point' needing to be in German in line 127. In line 128 she then mentions Jo's research project, signalling the end of the frame.

121	**Ada:**	Cos if I did that as an assessment, I wouldn't – like I would let them research,
122		but I wouldn't let them write it in English. I wouldn't ask them to write it, because
123		otherwise what happens is they just put it into Google Translate/
124	**Jo:**	/oh right, yeah, yeah, yeah/
125	**Ada:**	/and I get a whole lot of/
126	**Jo:**	/Gobbledegook/
127	**Ada:**	/Gobbledegook. Um, but the starting point would have to be the language.
128		So you know – cos it needs to be valid and work for your, project, what we're doing.

I interpreted lines 121–127 in this extract as being an assessment frame. It is one of three assessment frames in lines 102–135, and this extract is the middle frame. It contributes to furthering the project-as-assessment by raising two issues, the students' limited ability to self-regulate and the language they will use.

In order to follow what happens in this frame, it is necessary to understand Ada was aware that Jo did not know German. Earlier in the session, from lines 14–46, Jo discussed steps for researching and comparing aspects of German culture and the students' home cultures, culminating at line 47, where Jo mentioned that work for the project could be done in either English or German. One way lines 121–127 express co-regulation is through convergence, as Ada focuses her attention on the alternative Jo had offered in line 47. In lines 121–127, Ada explored an aspect of setting assessments, the fact that her students did not self-regulate very well, something Jo could not have known. The latching between lines 123 and 124, the overlap at 125–126, and the latching of 126 and 127 show co-orientation. Despite Jo's lack of knowledge about the specific students, she appreciates the consequences and anticipates Ada's attitude, with both interactants taking a humorous stance towards it. (Ada and Jo have another humorous exchange a few lines later when Ada offers to translate the students' reports in German for Jo by using Google Translate). This co-orientation continues in the rest of line 127, when Ada makes an important point indirectly. She allows Jo to infer an assumption that Ada is working with, that the assessments must focus on language. This has two possible implications: assessments being written in German rather than in English or assessments having to be about language rather than culture. Ada assumes that Jo will make an appropriate inference, which is reinforced by 'so you know' in line 128, again showing co-orientation.

Without directly discussing it, Ada and Jo have negotiated a potential conflict in the project-as-assessment, since as an assessment, the focus must be on the German language, whereas as a project, the focus must be on culture (more specifically, intercultural comparison). The negotiation turns on two distinctions, between the language(s) used for conducting research and writing the report (which could differ) and between language and culture as the aim of the assessment (which must be simultaneously addressed). Ada then continues by attending to Jo's project by mentioning that 'it needs to be valid.' Line 128, therefore, links the assessment frame to the project-as-assessment macroframe. This pattern, in which Ada links her requirements for the assessment to Jo's requirements for the projects, also occurs with the assessment frames that precede and follow this extract and two other assessment frames that occur later in the session.

Both Jo and Ada purposefully set out to negotiate how Jo's research project could be conducted in Ada's classroom. Although both came with the conscious intention of discussing the project, neither had a specific conceptualization of how the project would be planned for the class, since Ada did not know the project requirements and conditions yet, and Jo did not know the class requirements and conditions yet. In particular, neither set out to reconceptualize part of the cultural portfolio project as an assessment. Nor did they set out to make particular interactional choices and take particular communicative stances. The project-as-assessment emerged from the new idea that Ada struggled to initially communicate, but that by the end of the session had become an agreed plan with a general framework and timeframe. This process occurred through co-regulation when Ada took a more active and equal role as a speaker, which involved attention and orientation self-organizing through interaction.

From line 102 onwards, assessment became an attractor for Ada as much as the project was an attractor for Jo. Co-regulation occurred as Jo and Ada jointly attended to topics and took up communicative stances. In particular, Ada mentioned earlier topics (in this example, the language of the project) that Jo had presented from her project perspective, which Ada related to new topics (in this example, student self-regulation) from her assessment perspective. Much of the negotiation of issues involved co-orienting to each other's perspectives by taking the same communicative stance (in this example, humour). By working through practical issues and maintaining a cooperative attitude, Ada and Jo uncovered and addressed the assumptions they made, which enabled the emergent idea of the project-as-assessment to develop.

Ada's concerns were largely practical, and this example shows how these practical concerns (preventing misuse of Google Translate) were closely related to pedagogical issues (student self-regulation) and, of course, were relevant to the ecological validity of the project as well as its concrete implementation. As more complex relationships developed between Jo's idea of the research project and Ada's idea of German language assessments, the project-as-assessment emerged as its own attractor that developed, frame by frame, through their interactions.

Discussion and Conclusion

What is the contribution of Feryok and Oranje (2015)? The study showed how a new teaching idea developed by being repeatedly related to other ideas in different ways, but that the idea was remembered as the outcome of a process of integrating those different ideas. Once Ada had sorted out what the project-as-assessment was, a few minutes later Ada could unhesitatingly and confidently state that she just 'fit' assessments into her teaching. If questioned right away, although Ada would almost certainly have recalled the issues she and Jo had worked through, she would not have experienced them in the same way, delving into one detail, and then another, and then repeating the process from another perspective.

How are the findings relevant to the issue of differences between beliefs and practices? There are two related reasons. One reason is that in the two data sets, Ada performed different actions with different goals that were related to different beliefs. The other is that the data sets were collected successively, and thus at different times. In the introductory session Ada and Jo shared the goal of developing a way of implementing Jo's research project in Ada's classroom; for Ada, it was a part of her presessional class curriculum planning in her job as a teacher. Ada was fitting the project-as-assessment into her mental model of teaching her Year 12

German class by considering aspects relevant to teaching that group of students. In the interview Ada and myself shared the goal of co-constructing Ada's image of herself as a teacher; for Ada, it was a part of her self-concept related to her identity as a teacher. The earlier process of fitting the project-as-assessment into Ada's mental model had been completed, and Ada was able to report her beliefs about assessments from the per-spective of having just successfully fit an assessment into her plans for covering the curriculum. Time is not merely a neutral metaphorical loca-tion; processes and events occur, and they may hold the key to under-standing data. Researchers need to consider the possible effects of time on different components in a study, not just as the means whereby change to a dependent variable is conveyed.

Interestingly, the results of Jo's complete project, which involved col-lecting additional data sets on the implementation of the cultural portfolio project, reinforce the value of a context-sensitive approach to data collec-tion. Teachers were free to negotiate their level of involvement in the proj-ect, with Ada leaving the implementation of the project to Jo until the part that used the project-as-assessment. When the time neared for that part, Ada again took on an active role, renegotiating an aspect of the project-as-assessment (students orally presenting their reports in German to the class and then discussing them in English, with both Ada and Jo present) so that it would instead be conducted as a traditional assessment (students orally presenting in German to Ada alone). Ada regarded this change as necessary to ensure the fairness of the assessment, especially for anxious or weak students who might be affected by having to present to the class. Assessment in school systems has been described as a powerful attractor (Larsen-Freeman & Cameron, 2008); it is a high stakes practice for mul-tiple interrelated systems – students, teachers, parents, schools, school sys-tems and even nations. Given that assessment had already appeared as a powerful attractor for Ada in the introductory session, it is interesting but not surprising that it re-emerged in her class and involved a similar pattern of activity, with Ada's active involvement again attracted by assessment, this time in competition with the project-as-assessment. Although research-ers need to define the parameters of the system they are examining, they cannot ignore that the system interacts with other systems.

This change Ada made to the project as it played out in her classroom is ontologically similar to the change I made to the project when I observed Ada nominating assessment as a topic for discussion. Ada intervened in how Jo was conducting the project, and I intervened in how I was con-ducting my research. These incidents express the idea in complexity thinking that the observer is not separate from what they observe. They are united in a system, whether the observer and the observed are different people or are one person, and whether the system exists on a long-term or short-term scale relative to the participants. By narrating the processes I undertook, I have come to see my own role in my research more clearly, in particular, how by following up on a few lines of talk, I set it in an entirely new and fruitful direction. Researchers need to consider how they contribute to the construction of the data.

Respecting contextual differences by carefully examining what was different in the data was not done in order to attribute differences to the context *per se*, but to see what was different about the individual in those contexts. In one context Ada (and Jo) wanted to solve a problem involving competing attractors, which was resolved at the time of the interaction with the emergence of a new attractor. The problem and attractors did not exist in the second data set. Directly comparing stated beliefs and inferred beliefs from practices does decontextualize the data, but more to the point, it fails to consider the participant as an active interactant in whatever activity she is performing (negotiating, teaching, being interviewed) for whatever goals she has (solving a problem, meeting a curriculum aim, projecting her identity). Researchers need to consider how participants contribute to the construction of the data.

Microgenetic analysis and frame analysis, augmented with content analysis, enabled a context-sensitive analysis of a teacher's tacit and declared beliefs. The sensitivity of the analysis turned on interactional features, particularly for identifying the onset of microgenesis and the onset and offset of frames. More formalized analyses, such as interactional sociolinguistics and conversation analysis, could further contribute to microgenesis in future studies using interactional data. Sociocultural theory could offer a more nuanced perspective by examining what mediated Ada's beliefs and attitudes about assessment and culture. Unlike complex dynamic systems theory, it is specifically aimed at understanding human consciousness – but that would be another study.

References

Agar, M. (1994) *Language Shock: Understanding the Culture of Conversation.* New York: William Morrow.

Bamberg, M. (2012) Selves and identities in the making: The study of microgenetic processes in interactive practices. In U. Miller, J.I.M. Carpendale, N. Budwig and B. Sokol (eds) *Social Life and Social Knowledge* (pp. 212–231). New York: Lawrence Erlbaum Associates.

Bateson, G. (1955) The message: "This is play". In B. Schaffner (ed.) *Group Processes* (Vol. 2). Madison, NJ: Madison Printing Co..

Borg, S. (2006) *Teacher Cognition and Language Education: Research and Practice.* London: Continuum.

Breen, M.P., Hird, B., Milton, M., Oliver, R. and Thwaite, A. (2001) Making sense of language teaching: Teachers' principles and classroom practices. *Applied Linguistics* 22, 470–501.

Burns, A. (1996) Starting all over again: From teaching adults to teaching beginners. *Teacher Learning in Language Teaching* (pp. 154–177). Cambridge: Cambridge University Press.

de Bot, K., Lowie, W. and Verspoor, M. (2007) A dynamic systems theory approach to second language acquisition. *Bilingualism: Language and Cognition* 10, 7–21.

Feryok, A. (2010) Language teacher cognitions: Complex dynamic systems? *System* 38, 272–279.

Feryok, A. (2018) Language teacher cognition: An emergent phenomenon in an emergent field. In S. Mercer and A. Kostoulas (eds) *Language Teacher Psychology* (pp. 105–121). Bristol: Multilingual Matters.

Feryok, A. and Oranje, J. (2015) Adopting a cultural portfolio project in teaching German as a foreign language: Language teacher cognition as a dynamic system. *The Modern Language Journal* 99 (3), 546–564.

Fogel, A. (1993) *Developing Through Relationships: Origins of Communication, Self, and Culture*. New York: Harvester Wheatsheaf.

Fogel, A., Garvey, A., Hsu, H.–C. and West–Stroming, D. (2006) *Change Processes in Relationships: A Relational Historical Approach*. Cambridge: Cambridge University Press.

Freeman, D. (1993) Renaming experience/reconstructing practice: Developing new understandings of teaching. *Teaching and Teacher Education* 9, 485–497.

Freeman, D. (2002) The hidden side of work: Teacher knowledge and learning to teach. *Language Teaching* 35, 1–13.

Goffman, E. (1974) *Frame Analysis: An Essay on the Organization of Experience*. Cambridge, MA: Harvard University Press.

Granott, N., Fischer, K.W. and Parziale, J. (2002) Bridging to the unknown: A transition mechanism in learning and development. In N. Granott and J. Parziale (eds) *Microdevelopment: Transition Processes in Development and Learning* (pp. 1–28). New York, NY: Cambridge University Press.

Herzog, M.H., Kammer, T. and Scharnowski, F. (2016) Time slices: What is the duration of a percept? *PLoS Biology* 14 (4), 1–12.

Kubanyiova, M. and Feryok, A. (2015) Language teacher cognition in applied linguistics research: Revisiting the territory, redrawing the boundaries, reclaiming the relevance. *The Modern Language Journal* 99 (3), 435–449.

Larsen-Freeman, D. and Cameron, L. (2008) *Complex Systems and Applied Linguistics*. Oxford: Oxford University Press.

Lavelli, M., Pantoja, A.P.F., Hsu, H.–C., Messinger, D. and Fogel, A. (2005) Using microgenetic designs to study change processes. In D.M. Teti (ed.) *Handbook of Research Methods in Developmental Science* (p. 40–65). Malden, MA: John Wiley & Sons.

Mangubhai, F., Marland, P., Dashwood, A. and Son, J.-B. (2004) Teaching a foreign language: One teacher's practical theory. *Teaching and Teacher Education* 20, 291–311.

Mangubhai, F., Marland, P., Dashwood, A. and Son, J.-B. (2005) Similarities and differences in teachers' and researchers' conceptions of communicative language teaching: Does the use of an educational model cast a better light? *Language Teaching Research* 9, 31–66.

Nishino, T. (2012) Modeling teacher beliefs and practices in context: A multimethods approach. *Modern Language Journal* 96, 380–399.

Richardson, M.J., Dale, R. and Marsh, K.L. (2014) Complex dynamical systems in social and personality psychology. In H.R. Reis and C.M. Judd (eds) *Handbook of Research Methods in Social and Personality Psychology* (pp. 253–282). New York, NY: Cambridge University Press.

Saldaña, J. (2016) *The Coding Manual for Qualitative Researchers*. Thousand Oaks, CA: SAGE Publications.

Siegler, R.S. (2006) Microgenetic analyses of learning. In D. Kuhn and R. Siegler (eds) *Handbook of Child Psychology* (6th edn, pp. 464–510). Malden, MA: John Wiley & Sons.

Spencer J.P., Perone S. and Buss A.T. (2011) Twenty years and going strong: A dynamic systems revolution in motor and cognitive development. *Child Development Perspectives* 5 (4), 260–266.

Thelen, E. and Smith, L.B. (2007) Dynamic systems theories. In W. Damon and R.M. Lerner (eds) *Handbook of Child Psychology* (pp. 258–312). Malden, MA: John Wiley & Sons.

Valsiner, J. (2000) *Culture and Human Development*. London: Sage.

van Geert, P. (1998) A dynamic systems model of basic developmental mechanisms: Piaget, Vygotsky and beyond. *Psychological Review* 105, 634–677.

van Geert, P. and Steenbeck, H. (2005) Explaining after by before: Basic aspects of a dynamic systems approach to the study of development. *Developmental Review* 25, 408–442.

Vygotsky, L.S. (1986) *Thought and Language*. Cambridge MA: MIT Press.

Wagoner, B. (2009) The experimental methodology of constructive microgenesis. In J. Valsiner *et al.* (eds) *Dynamic Process Methodology in the Social and Developmental Sciences* (p. 99–121). New York: Springer Science-Business.

Wertsch J.V. (1991) *Voices of the Mind: A Sociocultural Approach to Mediated Action*. Cambridge MA: Harvard University Press.

Witherington, D.C. (2007) The dynamic systems approach as metatheory for developmental psychology. *Human Development* 50, 127–153.

16 Doing Complexity Research in the Language Classroom: A Commentary

Ema Ushioda

Making Complexity Research Doable and Meaningful

In their introductory chapter to this fascinating volume, the editors express their motto that *complexity should be simple* and highlight their aim of making complexity research accessible and doable for language teaching practitioners like themselves who also engage in research. Importantly too, they explain that they have brought together this collection of chapters not only to illustrate a variety of complexity perspectives on researching language learner and teacher psychology, but also to show why taking a complexity perspective is useful in illuminating our understandings of these psychological areas, and in helping us to make sense of the lived realities of our classrooms. In short, making complexity research *doable and accessible* and making it *meaningful and relevant* for practitioner-researchers (the target readership) are the key underpinning principles of this volume. Another way of putting this can be to say that the book seeks to illustrate *how* we can do complexity research in our language classrooms as well as *why* we might do it, where *why* refers not just to goals and purposes but also to our experiences and starting points as practitioners from which complexity thinking and complexity research may emerge.

With this in mind, I would therefore like to focus my commentary on these twin principles and offer my own take on making complexity research meaningful and doable for practitioner-researchers, in the light of, and as a counterpoint to, the diverse perspectives offered in this volume. As a preamble to my commentary, and in keeping with the personal narrative approach modelled and encouraged by Richard Sampson and Richard Pinner as the book's editors, I will begin by briefly recounting the story of my own relationship with complexity thinking.

The Story of my Relationship with Complexity Thinking

As readers may be aware, my own interests in language learner and teacher psychology have focused primarily on motivation, and particularly its interface with theories of autonomy in language learning (e.g. Ushioda, 2007a, 2011). This engagement with perspectives from the autonomy literature in language education has strongly influenced my approach to motivation. While L2 motivation research has been traditionally concerned with developing generalizable models of motivation that have explanatory power across learning contexts, research on autonomy in language education has traditionally focused on the needs and concerns of specific groups of teachers and learners situated in specific contexts of practice. As Riley (2003: 239) has commented, a key characteristic of writing on language learner autonomy is its view of the language learner as a fully rounded person, with a social identity, situated in a particular sociocultural environment, rather than a view of the language learner as a theoretical abstraction. In the last ten years or so, influenced in part by this person-focused perspective from autonomy research, I have developed and advocated a *person-in-context relational view* of motivation (Ushioda, 2009). Core to this view is a holistic focus on 'real persons', rather than 'L2 learners' as theoretical abstractions – i.e. a focus on people who are engaging in language learning and use in particular social and relational contexts that dynamically evolve in interaction with their engagement. I came to develop this person-in-context relational view through a sense of dissatisfaction with the reductionist approach of stripping away the rich messiness of real life in order to distil abstract theoretical principles. Such abstract principles describe 'in theory' how motivation relates to language learning, as articulated in linear causal models that predict how certain 'types' of learner with certain 'types' of motivation are likely to perform, given certain 'types' of input conditions or contextual factors. But, as we know, language classrooms are not filled with idealized types of learners or teachers but with uniquely individual complex people, who have the capacity to exercise intentionality and reflexivity in how they respond to events and influences. Moreover, the evolving relationality among these people as well as their lives, experiences and social realities beyond the classroom will all contribute to constituting the 'context' of the learning and teaching taking place. In my view, this 'context' cannot simply be reduced to an abstract set of factors or background variables, such as cultural setting or type of educational institution, as if to imply that language learners, their motivations and their behaviours are determined by their context (in an essentializing sense). Rather, contexts are dynamically evolving ecologies that people are an integral part of, act upon and contribute to shaping and changing with varying degrees of agency, and this agency is itself socially constituted – i.e. supported, enabled or constrained through one's relationality with other people. As I wrote some years ago before articulating my person-in-context perspective on motivation, this means that we need to expand the unit of analysis beyond the individual to embrace the organic interaction between the individual and the social learning environment (Ushioda, 2003).

In broadening the unit of analysis to embrace this co-adaptive inter-connectedness between person and context, I offer a perspective that clearly has a great deal of affinity with complexity thinking. From a complex dynamic systems perspective, as Larsen-Freeman (2015: 16) has described, individual and context are 'coupled' with one another and are evolving together, and 'neither the learner nor the environment is seen as independent' but they are viewed as constituting, metaphorically speaking, an ecosystem. It is perhaps no accident that I formed my ideas about a person-in-context relational view of motivation during a period of growing interest in complexity thinking, emergentism and dynamic systems theory in the applied linguistics field (e.g. de Bot *et al.*, 2007; Ellis & Larsen-Freeman, 2006; Larsen-Freeman & Cameron, 2008). Indeed, in my 2009 chapter where I first wrote about my person-in-context relational view of motivation as an emergent process, I referenced the work on emergentism that was happening at the time. Moreover, that chapter was itself based on a colloquium paper I had presented at the American Association for Applied Linguistics conference two years previously (Ushioda, 2007b), which Larsen-Freeman and Cameron subsequently happened to cite (pp. 152–153) in their 2008 seminal volume on complex systems and applied linguistics. In short, the close affinity between my way of thinking and complexity thinking is unquestionable.

Despite this close affinity, nevertheless, I have preferred to keep to a perspective (and to a language) relating to *persons-in-contexts*, rather than to *complex dynamic systems*. This is not because of an obstinate desire to promote my own work but rather because of a fundamental concern (as a language teacher educator) to maintain a concrete holistic focus on language learners and teachers as *people* situated in specific social realities, as opposed to an abstract theoretical focus on self-organizing complex systems, processes, states or variables. In this respect, I draw inspiration not only from the writing on language learner autonomy but also from Lantolf and Pavlenko's (2001) longstanding arguments for understanding second language learners as 'people' rather than as language processing devices or decontextualized bundles of variables. According to Benson's (2019) recent historical analysis of how language learners have been viewed in applied linguistics research, it seems that what he calls this holistic and socially situated *person-centred* view of the language learner is now becoming increasingly prominent in our field, especially with the growth of more qualitative, ethnographic and narrative approaches to research inquiry. As I will discuss in my commentary in relation to the complexity research perspectives in this book, such a person-centred view has important implications for how we make complexity research both meaningful and doable for language practitioner-researchers, as well as implications for the discourse we use to articulate this research. I will begin my commentary by considering the question of making complexity research meaningful and will discuss why we, as practitioner-researchers, might want to pursue such research.

Making Complexity Research Meaningful for Practitioner–Researchers

Across all the contributions to this volume, there is a strong consensus that complexity thinking can help to capture and to illuminate the workings of various processes in language learner and language teacher psychology and classroom life. Such processes include the emergence of feelings (Sampson) and the regulation of emotions (Oxford & Gkonou); the dynamics of willingness to communicate (Yashima), alongside the complexity of silence in language classrooms (Smith & King); the evolution of motivation in relation to individual experiences and histories, self-concepts, or classroom and educational cultures (Aoyama & Yamamoto; Consoli; Falout); the psychology of L2 listening processes (Simpson & Rose); classroom and group dynamics and relationality (Nitta & Nakata; Muir; Pinner); or the complex dynamics of teacher cognition (Feryok) and of teacher identity (Henry).

Moreover, in their overview chapter, Peter MacIntyre, Sarah Mercer and Tammy Gregersen provide examples of further areas within language learner and teacher psychology that have been usefully informed by complexity research, such as language learner anxiety, teacher stress, or the dynamics of the self. As they argue, the work that has been done so far to apply complexity research perspectives to the psychology of language learning and teaching shows that such perspectives can lead to generating new understandings of familiar processes or to challenging traditional conceptualizations of these processes. As they add, adopting a complexity perspective can also lead to developing new approaches to analysis and representation, which make the possibilities for future research exciting. Illustrated within this volume are some of these interesting analytical and representational developments. These include, for example, Richard Sampson's representation of the 'multiple threading' of students' references to different feelings lesson by lesson; the Trajectory Equifinality Models of students' language learning or motivational journeys featured in Takumi Aoyama and Takenori Yamamoto's chapter; or Richard Pinner's use of sociograms to capture the relational connections and groupings among students in a classroom. Complexity research can thus be meaningful for practitioner-researchers in enhancing understanding of certain psychological and social processes that interact with learning and teaching, and in offering illuminating ways of analysing and representing these processes.

Furthermore, complexity approaches can be meaningful for class-room-based research because such approaches encourage a richer and more holistic perspective than traditional hypothesis-testing approaches that focus on a select number of dependent and independent variables and that seek to control for other factors. As Kedi Simpson and Heath Rose discuss in their chapter, this does not mean that complexity research is somehow 'uncontrolled' in its orientation, but rather that it adopts a holistic perspective on a wide range of cognitive, social and psychological factors that interplay with one another in the situated dynamics of classroom life. Compared to experimental research, as they note, complexity research thus offers much stronger ecological validity for practitioners dealing with the day-to-day complex social realities of their classrooms. Indeed, this holistic perspective may extend beyond what happens in a specific classroom to the social ecology of students' membership of other classroom groups, as illustrated in Ryo Nitta and Yoshiyuki Nakata's chapter. It may also extend to the wider ecology of the educational culture in which students have been socialized, as described by Joseph Falout in his analysis of Japanese students' perceptions of their English learning experiences. Importantly too, as illustrated in Sal Consoli's chapter, the ecological approach afforded by complexity research can enable insight into the social realities of students' worlds and experiences beyond class-room life that may impinge on their engagement with learning.

However, while complexity approaches may thus offer rich ecological validity for classroom research, they also raise issues of transparency and accessibility for those unfamiliar with such approaches, which may lead some to question their relevance and meaningfulness for practitioner-researchers. As Richard Pinner reflects in the introductory chapter, this was clearly a question he found himself having to confront during his doctoral viva, when his examiners challenged him on the technical complexity of some of his data and analysis. The editors of this collection acknowledge that complexity thinking can seem somewhat abstruse and off-putting for the uninitiated, not least because it comes with a specialized technical vocabulary (see MacIntyre *et al.*, this volume) and a high level of rather abstract theorizing using this technical vocabulary. The editors' mission of making complexity simple and accessible is thus a valuable one, if complexity research is to become truly meaningful and relevant for practitioner-researchers.

A focus on people and classrooms rather than on abstract systems

To this end, it seems important to try to keep the abstract theorizing and discourse to a minimum, and to focus instead on the people, events, behaviours or phenomena of interest to us as practitioner-researchers, so that complexity thinking is explicitly grounded in our own local classroom realities and pedagogic concerns. As I commented in my opening preamble outlining my relationship with complexity thinking, this holistic focus on teachers and learners as people situated in specific social realities reflects my own research orientation. This is in preference to the tendency in complexity thinking to move to a rather abstract theoretical and discursive plane where the focus is on self-organizing systems and their interacting components and processes. In a sense, as acknowledged in this volume (e.g. MacIntyre *et al.*; Simpson & Rose), discussions in complexity research can sometimes become rather opaque and difficult to interpret if the 'system' or complex reality under focus is not clearly specified and if its boundaries are not clearly described. To this I would add that such discussions of human behaviour can create, as Larsen-Freeman and Cameron (2008: 74) openly admit, something of a 'distancing' effect, where individual intentionality, reflexivity and decision-making become transmuted into mathematical models representing abstract systems above the level of the individual person. In a sense, it is as if the abstract self-organizing system has a theoretical life of its own, and we lose sight of the people themselves and their lived experiences and local realities. I argue here that, if we are to make complexity research meaningful and relevant for practitioners, we need to keep it firmly grounded in the social realities of the classroom and minimize the 'distancing' effect of theoretical abstraction. We should take care that the discourse of complexity thinking does not lead us to over-theorize and to make the simple and concrete unnecessarily abstruse or abstract. We should also take care that the discourse of complexity thinking does not lead us to forget that L2 learners are uniquely individual people and not complex systems nested within larger complex systems.

In other words, complexity research is likely to be more meaningful for practitioner-researchers (and for fellow-practitioners who choose to engage with this research) if its starting point emerges from a specific pedagogic question, need or concern that we face in our classrooms, rather than if the research is undertaken with the aim of theorizing abstract processes such as group dynamics or motivation as complex dynamic systems. In effect, the latter aim is the kind generally pursued by third-party researchers who are external to the classrooms under focus, and who seek to develop or refine our theoretical understandings of psychological and social processes in the language classroom. While such third-party research may have rigour and significance and contribute to the body of academic knowledge in our field, its relevance and meaningfulness for teachers and learners may not be immediately clear and direct. As Alastair Henry comments rather pointedly in light of his third-party research into teacher identity development, taking a complexity perspective in this context is meaningful only if it yields new and additional insights that could not have been gained otherwise and, importantly, that are of actual value for teachers themselves. In much third-party research, however, such relevance and meaningfulness for teachers and learners may (possibly) not be prioritized as of primary importance in shaping the inquiry. Instead, it is often the academic interests of the third-party researcher that determine what gets researched and why (Ushioda, 2020). Characterizing this tendency in a more critical vein, we could say that such forms of classroom research can often constitute (to borrow a turn of phrase from Allwright, 2005: 358) a 'parasitic activity', in the sense that such research is parasitic on the normal working lives of teachers and learners who accommodate the data-gathering needs of the researcher.

A pedagogic motivation for complexity research

In order to minimize the sense that complexity research is 'parasitic' on classroom life and maximize its meaningfulness for teachers (and their learners), it seems helpful for such research to be explicitly shaped by pedagogically motivated questions and concerns as the starting point for the inquiry. This is a principle that is clearly illustrated in several contributions to this volume. For example, Tomoko Yashima describes a concern with student silence or reticence in Japanese English as a Foreign Language (EFL) classrooms as the point of departure for her research into the phenomenon of willingness to communicate (WTC) in a second language, leading to the collaborative intervention study she describes in her chapter. As she writes, citing Larsen-Freeman and Cameron (2008), complexity research offers an approach and set of tools for closely examining a specific pedagogic issue we face in our classrooms, with a view to understanding this issue better (in all its dynamic complexity) and thus understanding how it may be possible to address it. This pedagogic interest in understanding the complexity of student silence in Japanese EFL classrooms similarly shaped the programme of research reported by Lesley Smith and Jim King in their chapter. Likewise, a local pedagogic issue provided the point of departure for Takenori Yamamoto's research inquiry. As he explains in his co-authored chapter, the starting point for his practitioner research was a practical concern that a new e-learning system designed to increase students' opportunities for learning English outside class was not achieving the desired results. Reviewing its first year of implementation and using the retrospective tools of inquiry afforded by the Trajectory Equifinality Approach, Takenori illustrates how he was able to trace the complex dynamic processes of students' learning journeys as they persisted with or gave up e-learning.

In discussing his pedagogic motivation for engaging with complexity thinking, Richard Pinner explains how it encourages him to view each student through a wide-angle 'fisheye' complexity lens – i.e. a lens that focuses on the individuality of each person while also taking into account the person's complex and dynamic relationality with others in the classroom. Adopting a wide-angle complexity lens can thus facilitate deeper and more nuanced local understandings of certain students and their orientations towards the class. In a similar vein, Richard Sampson explains how using multiple threading from a complexity perspective to explore the emergence of feelings in the classroom enables him to see how individual students' narrative strands contribute to the 'feeling narrative' of the class as a whole over a semester. As he explains, for a teacher, this kind of complexity perspective facilitates a simultaneously integrated and differentiated focus on the whole and its parts – i.e. on the classroom group and individual students, or on students' emotional journey through the whole semester and their experiences in a particular lesson. This value of complexity research in illuminating the dynamic relationality between the classroom group and its individual members is similarly reflected in Lesley Smith and Jim King's analysis of how individual silent behaviours in a classroom coalesce to push classroom discourse as a whole toward an attractor state of non-responsiveness, discouraging spontaneous contributions from students. Other chapters written by practitioner-researchers (Consoli; Falout) similarly report on the pedagogic value of adopting a complexity perspective to gain clearer insights into their own students' learning and psychological processes in relation to the wider social ecology of these processes.

Sustaining this explicitly pedagogic orientation to doing complexity research in the classroom, the volume also includes accounts written by 'third-party' researchers who have specifically collaborated with teachers on pedagogically focused research inquiry. For example, Christine Muir reports on her collaborative research with two teachers to explore whether it is possible to generate directed motivational currents (DMCs) through project work in their classroom, drawing on complexity principles to analyse the emergence of group-level motivation among their students. Similarly, Ryo Nitta and Yoshiyuki Nakata report on their collaboration with a teacher in a Japanese high school to explore factors influencing motivation and learning among different classroom groups, with a view to understanding the processes through which a positive classroom climate can emerge. They show how adopting a retrodictive complexity approach offers a useful methodology for investigating such processes.

In short, while the wider academic value of taking a complexity approach to language learner and language teacher psychology may lie in contributing to new theoretical understandings and insights, its meaningfulness for teachers and for researcher-practitioners lies in facilitating situated and nuanced insights into local pedagogic issues and classroom realities that can, in turn, inform local practice. As the studies illustrated in this volume show, complexity research with a pedagogic orientation can take different methodological and analytical approaches and generate a rich variety of data to yield these situated and nuanced insights. Having explored the 'why' of complexity approaches for classroom research and practice, in the next part of my commentary I will turn to focus on the 'how' of complexity approaches for practitioner-researchers and consider some interesting challenges and questions in this regard.

Making Complexity Research Doable for Practitioner-Researchers

A common theme running through the contributions to this volume is that doing complexity research generally entails compiling and working with rich, dense and complex datasets, often using innovative tools and methods of analysis. As noted already with reference to Richard Pinner's account of his doctoral viva, the 'technical complexity' of complexity research may be perceived by some to make it rather challenging for practitioners to engage with. In particular, complexity research that works with quantitative data may present significant analytical challenges. This is because it is not possible to apply familiar methods of statistical analysis based on linear modelling principles, and we may need to engage instead with rather more advanced analytical and technical procedures (for discussion, see MacIntyre *et al.*, and Simpson & Rose, this volume). However, while it is important to acknowledge the technical challenges of data analysis as potential obstacles to making complexity research doable for practitioner-researchers, I would like to focus my commentary on a few other perspectives concerning the actual doing of complexity research itself, and how doing complexity research interacts with the teaching and learning that is happening in the classroom. As Anne Feryok comments in her chapter focusing on teacher cognition research, complexity thinking entails the view that the researcher or observer is not separate from what they observe, and that researcher and researched are united in a complex system and are evolving together. For complexity research to be doable and practical for teachers-as-researchers, it thus seems important to take account of this dynamic inter-relationality between researcher and researched, or between researching and teaching.

The need for rich dense datasets

I will begin my commentary by considering the general requirement in complexity research to collect rich dense datasets comprising various forms of data accumulated over multiple time points from multiple sources. As illustrated in several studies reported in this volume, for classroom-based research this can often entail collecting data not only at the beginning and end of a period of learning (such as a semester) and at a few timepoints in between. It may also entail collecting data every week, or in every lesson, or even at multiple intervals during a single lesson, depending on the timescales under focus in the research (e.g. Muir; Sampson; Smith & King; Yashima). This cumulative, recursive and process-oriented approach to collecting data intensively or extensively through the course of teaching and learning raises some interesting questions about impact of the research procedures on the researched (i.e. teacher and learners), and on what is being researched (i.e. the psychological processes under focus).

In their chapter focusing on the psychology of L2 listening processes, for example, Kedi Simpson and Heath Rose acknowledge the risk of 'test fatigue' in their study where student participants repeatedly completed a battery of tests administered at 20 time points over three years. They also acknowledge the possibility of a Hawthorne Effect whereby teachers' and students' understanding that they were being researched may have influenced their behaviours and thinking about L2 listening skills, or whereby students' repeated exposure to a listening strategy questionnaire may have influenced their strategy awareness and use. In these authors' view, test fatigue and the Hawthorne Effect are risks that are difficult to avoid in complexity research, given the recursive and often intensive or extensive nature of the data collection process. They consequently advise researcher reflexivity in relation to such potential threats to data validity and reliability when conducting complexity research in classrooms.

The value of integrating teaching and researching processes

I certainly agree that researcher reflexivity is critically important during the processes of collecting and analysing data, so that we are aware of potential subjectivity and bias in these processes, and of the effect that our research may have on the people and the phenomena we are researching. At the same time, however, my own perspective on these issues is that, to make complexity research doable and practical for teacher-researchers, we might actually wish to encourage *integration* rather than *separation* of research processes (i.e. data collecting) and pedagogic processes (e.g. learner awareness-raising). In other words, instead of worrying about the possible impact that our data collection tools (and their intensive, extensive or repeated use) might have on the quality and reliability of the data elicited, we might wish to highlight the pedagogic value and potential of these tools for raising learners' metacognitive awareness of the processes under focus. This is a point underlined by Rebecca Oxford and Christina Gkonou in their account of their Managing Your Emotions (MYE) questionnaire. As they explain, they developed the MYE as an innovative data collection tool that serves also as a pedagogic tool for raising learners' awareness about emotions in L2 learning. Furthermore, they suggest that the MYE itself can provide a potential basis for promoting students' use of affective strategies to regulate their emotions during the language learning process.

Across other chapters too, the reflexive pedagogic influence of the complexity research process on student participants' learning and awareness-raising is similarly highlighted. For example, in his co-authored chapter, Takenori Yamamoto describes how a student's engagement in a series of research interviews with him (as teacher-researcher) and in the opportunity to comment on his analysis of her data contributed to clarifying for herself (as well as for him) her own learning process and the factors that had affected this process. For Joseph Falout, this reflexive interaction between research and pedagogy is core to his use of 'critical participatory looping' (CPL; Murphey & Falout, 2010), which he characterizes as a way of researching complexity with complexity by involving a whole classroom group in researching itself as a group in interaction with the teacher-researcher. As he describes it, CPL entails collecting data from a classroom group and looping back to them summaries of their data for critical analysis and feedback, thus not only generating further research data but also fostering metacognitive reflection and discussion among students. Elsewhere, we can also see this integration of research and pedagogic processes embodied in how language learner journals are used to generate self-report data and to promote learner reflection, as illustrated in the studies described by Richard Sampson, and by Christine Muir.

This principle of integrating research and pedagogy is of course fundamental to Exploratory Practice (EP; Allwright, 2005; Hanks, 2017), as discussed and illustrated in the chapters by Sal Consoli and by Richard Pinner. Interestingly, what underlies this principle in EP is not so much the importance of valuing the pedagogic or awareness-raising potential of our research tools, as I have highlighted in response to the concerns raised about the Hawthorne Effect and the impact of complexity research procedures on the people and processes researched. Instead, the emphasis in EP is the view that doing classroom research should not impose any additional burdens on teachers' workload or students' time. Importantly, it should not interfere with normal teaching and learning processes in the classroom or become (citing Allwright, 2005, again) an extra 'parasitic' activity that teachers and students have to accommodate. In other words, underlying the principle of integrating research and pedagogy in EP is a clear ethical concern about what role research activity should or should not play in classroom life (Hanks, 2019). In essence, from an EP perspective, any research activity we undertake needs to be seamlessly woven into our normal classroom practices. This means that any research data we collect from our classrooms should stem from normal pedagogic activity, while any research tools (e.g. language learner journals, questionnaires) we use should have a clear pedagogic purpose and should function as part of the teaching and learning process rather than as something extra that we ask students to do for data collection purposes.

This EP principle of integrating teaching and researching is embodied in what Hanks (2017) calls PEPAs (potentially exploitable pedagogic activities) – i.e. teaching and learning activities or materials that can serve as a focus for analysis and reflection (by teachers and by students), and that can generate research insights. In their respective chapters, Richard Pinner and Sal Consoli illustrate how they derived potentially exploitable pedagogic activities and materials from language-focused work or learning tasks that students engaged in as part of normal classroom life, and that provided the basis for generating research data. Their accounts show how such data generated through pedagogic activities can provide richly valuable insights for the teacher-researcher. At the same time, their accounts also demonstrate the fundamental importance that EP places on ethical principles in navigating the balance between researching and teaching. As Richard Pinner observes, the research undertaken should always contribute to students' learning, while as Sal Consoli highlights, students' own needs must always take priority over research objectives.

Ethical perspectives on doing complexity research in the classroom

In my view, this ethical question of balancing our roles as teachers and as researchers when undertaking practitioner research is an important one (see Li, 2006, for an insightful discussion), especially when this research adopts a complexity perspective. Of course, practitioner research is very likely to be pedagogically motivated and undertaken with a view to addressing problems and issues in one's practice or to enhancing the quality of students' learning and classroom experience. In this respect, following the principle that the ends usually justify the means, we might wish to argue that it is acceptable for us as teachers to collect various kinds of research data from our students since, ultimately, we are doing this to serve their interests or possibly the interests of subsequent student groups that we teach. As noted earlier, however, doing complexity research generally involves accumulating rich dense datasets comprising various forms of data collected over multiple time points from multiple sources. The recursive, intensive or extensive nature of the data collection process means that doing complexity research may impose a significant burden of time and effort on participants, and a significant intrusion into the teaching and learning process if conducted during normal class hours. While the scope and extent of the commitment required of participants will undoubtedly be made clear to them when negotiating informed consent, I believe it is important to reflect critically on the power relations shaping these negotiations when we as teacher-researchers wish to collect data from our own students. After all, these underlying power relations may well influence students' decision to participate. As Comstock (2012: 172) has commented rather pointedly: 'If subjects "agree" to participate in an experiment simply because they think an authoritative figure wants them to do it, have they really consented?'

In view of these ethical concerns, I would like to argue that making complexity research doable for practitioner-researchers should entail careful consideration of how we can make the research procedures themselves as pedagogically meaningful as possible for the learners who 'agree' to participate in our research inquiry, given the intensive or extensive nature of these research procedures. Returning to the earlier commentary around researcher reflexivity, I think it is important to add here that the focus of our reflexivity should be not only on potential threats to data quality and research rigour. Our reflexivity as researchers needs to extend also to the management of our relational processes with our research participants and the various data-collecting demands we make on them, especially when our research participants are our own students (Guillemin & Gillam, 2004; Ushioda, 2020). As several contributors to this volume have commented in one way or another, doing complexity research entails research complexity. Hence, we need to ensure that, as teachers, we are comfortable engaging our students in this research complexity, and that, as far as possible, this engagement can have meaning and value for them.

In this regard, the strength of EP as an approach to complexity research lies not only in offering a coherent framework for integrating pedagogic and research activity in a meaningful way. Its strength lies also in its collegial and inclusive approach to classroom inquiry (Hanks, 2019), since it highlights the shared agency of teacher and students exploring together with a view to understanding and enhancing classroom life in a collaborative way (Allwright, 2005). In more recent accounts of EP (e.g. Allwright & Hanks, 2009; Hanks, 2017, 2019), this sense of shared agency is reflected in the emphasis given to involving students as co-researchers and co-practitioners in pursuing their own explorations as an integral part of their learning process. Some examples of this are illustrated towards the end of Sal Consoli's chapter in this volume. In other words, teacher and students work together as co-researchers and co-practitioners, collectively researching and developing their practice in teaching and in learning, respectively.

Conclusion: Making Complexity Research Doable and Meaningful for Everyone Involved

Clearly, the inclusive ethical framework of EP thus makes it especially suitable for a complexity-oriented approach to practitioner research that is built on the synergistic relationship among teacher and students (Pinner, 2019). Nevertheless, the process of embedding complexity research and data collection in pedagogic activity is eminently feasible in other practitioner research approaches too. These may include, for example, action research approaches as illustrated in this volume by Richard Sampson (see also Sampson, 2016), or critical participatory looping as illustrated by Joseph Falout. At a fundamental level, it is perhaps not the choice of approach in itself that is important but rather the axiological principles shaping this choice. By this I mean that it is important for us to reflect on the values and meanings underlying what we do and what we ask our students to do and why, since complexity research may clearly involve us and involve them in doing quite a lot of things that might not have been originally planned or expected. Ultimately, and returning to my starting point in this commentary, making complexity research doable and meaningful for practitioner-researchers entails making it doable and meaningful for everyone involved in the complex social reality of the classroom, and in the day-to-day situated dynamics of the teaching and learning process.

References

Allwright, D. (2005) Developing principles for practitioner research: The case of exploratory practice. *Modern Language Journal* 89 (3), 353–366.

Allwright, D. and Hanks, J. (2009) *The Developing Language Learner: An Introduction to Exploratory Practice*. Basingstoke: Palgrave Macmillan.

Benson, P. (2019) Ways of seeing: The individual and the social in applied linguistics research methodologies. *Language Teaching* 52 (1), 60–70.

Comstock, G. (2012) *Research Ethics: A Philosophical Guide to the Responsible Conduct of Research*. Cambridge: Cambridge University Press.

de Bot, K., Lowrie, W. and Verspoor, M. (2007) A dynamic systems theory approach to second language acquisition. *Bilingualism: Language and Cognition* 10 (1), 7–21.

Ellis, N. and Larsen-Freeman, D. (2006) Language emergence: Implications for applied linguistics – Introduction to the Special Issue. *Applied Linguistics* 27 (4), 558–589.

Guillemin, M. and Gillam, L. (2004) Ethics, reflexivity, and 'ethically important moments' in research. *Qualitative Inquiry* 10 (2), 261–280.

Hanks, J. (2017) *Exploratory Practice in Language Teaching: Puzzling about Principles and Practices*. Basingstoke: Palgrave Macmillan.

Hanks, J. (2019) From research-as-practice to exploratory practice-as-research in language teaching and beyond. *Language Teaching* 52 (2), 143–187.

Lantolf, J.P. and Pavlenko, A. (2001) (S)econd (L)anguage (A)ctivity theory: Understanding second language learners as people. In M.P. Breen (ed.) *Learner Contributions to Language Learning: New Directions in Research* (pp. 141–158). Harlow: Longman.

Larsen-Freeman, D. (2015) Ten 'lessons' from complex dynamic systems theory: What is on offer. In Z. Dörnyei, P.D. MacIntyre and A. Henry (eds) *Motivational Dynamics in Language Learning* (pp. 11–19). Bristol: Multilingual Matters.

Larsen-Freeman, D. and Cameron, L. (2008) *Complex Systems and Applied Linguistics*. Oxford: Oxford University Press.

Li, N. (2006) Researching and experiencing motivation: A plea for 'balanced research'. *Language Teaching Research* 10 (4), 437–456.

Murphey, T. and Falout, J. (2010) Critical participatory looping: Dialogic member checking with whole classes. *TESOL Quarterly* 44 (4), 811–821.

Pinner, R.S. (2019) *Social Authentication and Teacher-Student Motivational Synergy: A Narrative of Language Teaching*. London: Routledge.

Riley, P. (2003) Drawing the threads together. In D. Little, J. Ridley and E. Ushioda (eds) *Learner Autonomy in the Foreign Language Classroom: Teacher, Learner, Curriculum and Assessment* (pp. 237–252). Dublin: Authentik.

Sampson, R.J. (2016) *Complexity in Classroom Foreign Language Learning Motivation: A Practitioner Perspective from Japan*. Bristol: Multilingual Matters.

Ushioda, E. (2003) Motivation as a socially mediated process. In D. Little, J. Ridley and E. Ushioda (eds) *Learner Autonomy in the Foreign Language Classroom: Teacher, Learner, Curriculum and Assessment* (pp. 90–102). Dublin: Authentik.

Ushioda, E. (2007a) Motivation, autonomy and sociocultural theory. In P. Benson (ed.) *Learner Autonomy 8: Teacher and Learner Perspectives* (pp. 5–24). Dublin: Authentik.

Ushioda, E. (2007b) A person-in-context relational view of emergent motivation, self and identity. Paper presented at the American Association for Applied Linguistics Conference, 21–24 April 2007, Costa Mesa, California.

Ushioda, E. (2009) A person-in-context relational view of emergent motivation, self and identity. In Z. Dörnyei and E. Ushioda (eds) *Motivation, Language Identity and the L2 Self* (pp. 215–228). Bristol: Multilingual Matters.

Ushioda, E. (2011) Why autonomy? Insights from motivation theory and research. *Innovation in Language Learning and Teaching* 5 (2), 221–232.

Ushioda, E. (2020) *Language Learning Motivation: An Ethical Agenda for Research.* Oxford: Oxford University Press.

Glossary

Attractor (state): Dynamic states can become stable over time by converging on a narrow range of 'preferred' states (a fixed-point attractor, Hiver, 2015). The attractor can develop in two ways: (a) internal states can synchronize through social interaction, or (b) internal states can self-organize with reference to a higher-order property (Nowak *et al.*, 2005). In state space landscapes, attractors are visualized as basins in which a system settles.

Autoethnography: A form of inquiry in which a researcher focuses on their own experiences. Critically, researchers do not focus purely on the self, but on the self in relation to others, thereby highlighting the wider social ecology and context of the inquiry. With central emphasis on context, autoethnographies are useful for examining unfurling relationships, incorporating multiple lenses and gathering various perspectives around one central lived experience. Autoethnographies seek for believability of the story rather than an abstract notion of truth or a singular version of reality.

Boundaries: In complex systems, boundaries are considered to be permeable and shifting, and might better be considered as interfaces defined by the observer. As Cilliers (2001: 141) remarks, 'we frame the system by describing it in a certain way (for a certain reason), but we are constrained in where the frame can be drawn. The boundary of the system is therefore neither purely a function of our description, nor is it a purely natural thing.'

Class Oral Participation Scheme (COPS): A systematic approach to observation used to obtain reliable quantitative data about the extent of silence in a classroom setting. This tool uses a one-minute time sampling method. Observers are able to measure who is speaking during a lesson and how interaction is organized, as well as gather more in-depth data by focusing on up to three individual students in each class, allowing students' modality (i.e. in terms of speaking, listening, reading and writing) to be tracked throughout a lesson.

Co-adaptation: A process of mutual causality through which two or more interconnected systems influence each other over time. Change in one system fosters change in other, connected systems, which also feeds back to co-influence the focal system.

Complexity: Runs in opposition to 'the principle of simplicity [which] either separates that which is linked (disjunction), or unifies that which is diverse (reduction)' (Morin, 2008: 39). It is 'a fabric (complexus: that which is woven together) of heterogeneous constituents that are inseparably associated: complexity poses the paradox of the one and the many. … Complexity is in fact the fabric of events, actions, interactions, retroactions, determinations, and chance that constitute our phenomenal world' (Morin, 2008: 5).

Context: The 'here-and-now in which a system is active' (Larsen-Freeman & Cameron, 2008: 34). In terms of language learners and teachers, context might involve such elements as the psychological (as in the ongoing personality processes forming the background context to experience of an emotion), historical (as in teacher experiences just before a lesson, during teacher training, or in the cultural world in the lead up to particular actions in the classroom), linguistic (as in utterances from an interlocutor), material (as in learning activities or textbooks), physical (as in the physical space of a classroom setting or classroom-external language use experience), and so on.

Critical participatory looping (CPL): A classroom research approach whereby a classroom-group researches about the group together with the group. CPL involves gathering data individually from students, compiling it anonymously and looping back the compilations to participants with invitations to reflect on and respond to the data further. Looping data could potentially go beyond a single class-group to multiple class-groups, and even data from previous classes can be looped to subsequent generations of classes.

Design-based study: A research approach effective when the focus of investigation is not the outcome of learning but learning processes. It deals with complexity by 'iteratively changing the learning environment over time – collecting evidence of the effect of these variations and feeding it recursively into future design' (Barab, 2006: 155).

Dynamism: Changeability or fluctuation within a complex system. The present or future state of a complex system depends on its history of interactions – its dynamics over time. As Larsen-Freeman and Cameron (2008: 29) remind, in complex systems 'everything is dynamic: not only do the component elements and agents change with time, giving rise to changing states of the system, but the ways in which components interact with each other also change over time'.

Ecological social research: A research approach in which social phenomena are understood through the framework of ecosystems. The ecosystem is a metaphor that illustrates the symbiotic and co-adaptive relationship between individuals and the life capital they carry, and the potential such capital has to shape the individual's present and future experience(s) in reaction or in line with the context in which they find themselves.

Emergence: The gradual evolution of a complex system through its inter-actions to display a unique, novel pattern of behaviours or structure as a whole. The emergent, holistic pattern would have been difficult to predict, and cannot be reduced to the properties of the elements in the system. That is, the emergent outcome is not a simple aggregation of its members but 'the arising of something new, often unanticipated, from the interaction of components which comprise it' (Larsen-Freeman, 2016: 378).

Exploratory practice: A practitioner form of research which encourages the idea of teachers and learners 'puzzling' about their language learn-ing and teaching experiences, using 'normal pedagogic practices as investigative tools' (Allwright, 2003: 127). It recognizes teachers and learners as 'best positioned to research, and report on their own teach-ing and learning experiences' (Hanks, 2017: 54).

Formative experiments: An approach in which researchers 'investigate the potential of a system rather than its state … [and attempt] to describe the interconnected web of factors influencing change' (Larsen-Freeman & Cameron, 2008: 244). Formative experiments look to answer two questions typically omitted from 'conventional' experi-mental designs: 'What factors add to or detract from an intervention's success in accomplishing a valued pedagogical goal?' and, 'how might the intervention be adapted in response to those factors to better accomplish that goal?' (Reinking & Watkins, 2000: 384, 387).

Fractalization: Refers to the characteristic of systems to display self-simi-lar patterns across levels. This means that the behaviour of a system on one timescale or level can potentially predict similar behaviour on different levels. Similarly, if patterns are found across timescales or levels, this can serve as evidence for a complex dynamic system.

Frame analysis: A type of microgenetic analysis of frames. In a systems perspective on communication, 'a frame is a co-regulated consensual agreement about the scope of the discourse: its location, its setting, the acts that are taken to be significant vs. those that are irrelevant, and the main focus or topic' (Fogel, 1993: 36). Frames can be identified in interactants by the direction of attention, their location, their co-orientation through posture, and the topic of communication.

Generalization (in complexity research): In systematic research across a number of cases, and which is aimed at identifying the signature dynamics of individual systems, opportunities for generalization are provided (Byrne & Callaghan, 2014). Generalization in this sense does not relate to subjects, since developmental trajectories will never be the same for any two individuals. Rather, generalization concerns instances of observed process characteristics (van Geert & Lichtwarck-Aschoff, 2005).

Initial conditions: The state of a system or systems at the time that (research) observation commences. Initial conditions are important to consider in research because 'in a complex system, in which many kinds of subsystems interact over time, small differences in subsystems at one point in time may have an impact on the eventual outcome' (Verspoor, 2015: 38).

Interconnectedness: The interactivity among various components at multiple levels within a complex system. No part of the system is independent; all parts are interdependent.

Lock-in: While complex systems constantly change and adapt, they tend to become locked-in to trajectories of increasing returns on emergent states (Arthur, 1989). Simply put, the rich get richer, even when they may not be the most 'fit' in some senses or at different historical points in time. The classic example from the realm of technology is the QWERTY keyboard, the layout of which was developed to prevent typewriter keys jamming. Despite being highly inefficient in the current day and age, people have become so used to this layout that it would be extremely difficult to change – it has become locked-in.

Managing Your Emotions (MYE) questionnaire: A scenario-based questionnaire, in which the scenarios represent hypothetical but realistic and recognizable situations. Used to collect data about language learners' affective strategies for emotion regulation, their experiences and interpretations of their emotions and strategies, whether emotion regulation strategies are generated by learners themselves or taught by others, and reveal the complexity of emotions and L2 emotion regulation strategies.

Microgenetic analysis: An approach to analysis which involves the detailed examination of how an instance of a process develops, such as a problem that requires a particular strategy or concept to be used to solve it (Granott & Parziale, 2002). That instance is in an individual in a context, so the individual is the usual unit of analysis, not the change itself or the relevant parts of the individual (Lavelli *et al.*, 2005). The aim of microgenetic analysis is to examine change repeatedly over the period in which it occurs, so the scale on which change is observed is relatively smaller than the scale on which change occurs.

Min–max graph: Show a score range for individual data points. This range of scores is presented as a bandwidth of values over a period of time, i.e. five minutes, ten minutes, and so on. From a complexity perspective, min–max graphs are able to show change over time because they display a system's development beside the raw data, visualizing moment-to-moment variability.

Multiple threading: A diagrammatic representational tool proposed by Davis and Sumara (2006). In their original exposition, these researchers used this tool to illustrate how often and to what extent individual voices or ideas contribute to an overall text, such as a research paper or dramatic performance. Multiple threading 'involves the presentation of several narrative strands' in which 'some may be only brief phrases or single images that punctuate the text, and strands may overlap or interlink at times' (Davis & Sumara, 2006: 162). In terms of classroom language learning or teaching, multiple threading can foster understanding of the ways in which *individual* students or teachers all contribute to the *whole* of the experiential narrative of their class.

Multiplicity: Involving diversity and redundancy. Diversity of elements in a complex system may involve variations in some characteristic, difference in kinds of elements, or diversity in the composition of groups of elements. Diversity allows various forms of behaviour. Redundancy concerns similarities across elements of the system. Redundancy facilitates interactions among elements, and also allows one element to take the place of another.

Nestedness: Complex systems are nested in a hierarchical structure of levels. Any subsystem or sub-subsystem can be viewed as a complex system, depending on the observer's focus. However, it is important to consider hierarchies as not *neatly* nested and structured – there will always be multitudinous relationships that cut across nested hierarchies. As Cilliers (2001: 143) remarks, 'these interpenetrations may be fairly limited or so extensive that it becomes difficult to typify the hierarchy accurately in terms of prime and subordinate parts.'

Network: A structure of relationships between elements (actors or nodes). Research considering networks 'represents a key shift in focus away from focusing on individuals as a set of attributes and isolated, independent beings, towards looking at individuals as fundamentally social and relational beings' (Mercer, 2015: 74).

Non-linearity: Different to linear cause–effect relationships, non-linearity refers to change that is not proportional to input. In a non-linear system 'the elements or agents are not independent, and relations or interactions between elements are not fixed but may themselves change' (Larsen-Freeman & Cameron, 2008: 31). The same energy introduced to the system at different points in time or through a different area of the system may end up in very different outcomes.

Openness: A complex system exchanges both energy and matter with the environment in rich are varied ways (Cilliers, 2008). An open system continues to maintain a dynamically ordered state. That is, it is able to maintain a state that falls short of total or permanent equilibrium, meaning that it is constantly able to adapt to input and stimulation from outside. Open systems 'not only adapt to their contexts but also initiate change in those contexts; these systems are not just dependent on context but also influence context' (Larsen-Freeman & Cameron, 2008: 34).

Phase-shift (bifurcation): Sharp alterations in the state and future possibilities of a system as a whole due to the accretion of change at different levels.

Retrodiction: A research approach which starts by identifying outcomes or end states of interest in a focal system and then retrospectively examines how the system evolved into these outcomes (Chan *et al.*, 2015). By reflecting on the trajectory or trace of the focal system, researchers identify salient patterns of behaviours or phenomena, which are likely to operate in significant ways and emerge within other contexts.

Self-organization: The gradual evolution of a system through its interactions to form patterns that are more functionally capable of responding to the environment. These processes occur without any predetermined plan or central governing agent that controls behaviour.

Sociogram: A diagram of a network, a sociogram is 'a sociometric tool used to build a record of relations among members of a group' (Degenne & Forsé, 1999: 23). Sociograms can be extremely useful for teachers to identify 'isolates', students who may be excluded by a group, and to understand the general dynamics of a class. They can be drawn with a pencil, although more complex sociograms plotted by computers are used for social network analysis.

State space landscape: A spatial or topographical visualization of all of the possible states in which a system might find itself. Each point in the landscape represents a state of the system at a particular point in time. As Larsen-Freeman and Cameron (2008: 47–48) describe, 'as the system changes, it moves from one point in its state space to another, and the sequence of these states can be plotted as a path or "trajectory" in the state space'.

Timescales: A timescale appertains to the granularity of a developmental process (de Bot, 2015). Timescales are nested within each other, as seconds are nested in minutes, minutes within hours, hours within days, and so on. It may be that different dynamics are visible on different timescales, or possibly that patterns repeat across different timescales. As de Bot (2015: 36) remarks, 'we cannot undo the interaction between timescales and study phenomena on one timescale without taking into account other timescales'.

Timescales analysis: A research approach which explicitly works to uncover the interactions between different timescales of experience and psychology through plotting them onto an egocentric coding comparison table. The perspectives of others (such as partners in communicative events or language learning activities) can be added to provide further context to understanding the interactions of timescales in the evolution of emergent outcomes of interest.

Trajectory equifinality approach (**TEA**): A research approach that focuses on people's life course (i.e. trajectories) to equifinal points (similar outcomes). Sato *et al.* (2009: 228) describe that 'equifinality is the principle that in open systems a given end state can be reached by many potential means. It emphasizes that the same end state may be achieved through many different means, paths and trajectories.' TEA researchers thus attempt to figure out what events, experiences or decisions evolved into such trajectories for specific people. Studies using TEA can describe the trajectories from different points of view, such as historical, cultural, or social.

References

Allwright, D. (2003) Exploratory practice: Rethinking practitioner research in language teaching. *Language Teaching Research* 7 (2), 113–141.

Arthur, B. (1989) Competing technologies, increasing returns, and lock-in by historical events. *Economic Journal* 99, 116–131.

Barab, S. (2006) Design-based research: A methodological toolkit for the learning scientist. In R. Sawyer (ed.) *The Cambridge Handbook of the Learning Sciences*. Cambridge: Cambridge University Press.

Byrne, D. and Callaghan, G. (2014) *Complexity Theory and the Social Sciences: The State of the Art*. Abingdon: Routledge.

Chan, L., Dörnyei, Z. and Henry, A. (2015) Learner archetypes and signature dynamics in the language classroom: A retrodictive qualitative modelling approach to studying L2 motivation. In Z. Dörnyei, P.D. MacIntyre and A. Henry (eds) *Motivational Dynamics in Language Learning* (pp. 238–259). Bristol: Multilingual Matters.

Cilliers, P. (1998) *Complexity and Postmodernism: Understanding Complex Systems*. Abingdon: Routledge.

Cilliers, P. (2001) Boundaries, hierarchies and networks in complex systems. *International Journal of Innovation Management* 5 (2), 135–147.

Davis, B. and Sumara, D. (2006) *Complexity and Education: Inquiries Into Learning, Teaching, and Research*. Mahwah: Lawrence Erlbaum Associates.

de Bot, K. (2015) Rates of change: Timescales in second language development. In Z. Dörnyei, P.D. MacIntyre and A. Henry (eds) *Motivational Dynamics in Language Learning* (pp. 29–37). Bristol: Multilingual Matters.

Degenne, A. and Forsé, M. (1999) *Introducing Social Networks* (A. Borges, Trans.). London: Sage.

Fogel, A. (1993) *Developing Through Relationships: Origins of Communication, Self, and Culture*. New York: Harvester Wheatsheaf.

Granott, N., Fischer, K.W. and Parziale, J. (2002) Bridging to the unknown: A transition mechanism in learning and development. In N. Granott and J. Parziale (eds) *Microdevelopment: Transition Processes in Development and Learning* (pp. 1–28). New York, NY: Cambridge University Press.

Hanks, J. (2017) *Exploratory Practice in Language Teaching: Puzzling About Principles and Practices*. London: Palgrave Macmillan.

Hiver, P. (2015) Attractor states. In Z. Dörnyei, P.D. MacIntyre and A. Henry (eds) *Motivational Dynamics in Language Learning* (pp. 20–28). Bristol: Multilingual Matters.

Larsen-Freeman, D. (2016) Classroom-oriented research from a complex systems perspective. *Studies in Second Language Learning and Teaching* 6 (3), 377–393.

Larsen-Freeman, D. and Cameron, L. (2008) *Complex Systems and Applied Linguistics*. Oxford: Oxford University Press.

Lavelli, M., Pantoja, A.P.F., Hsu, H.-C., Messinger, D. and Fogel, A. (2005) Using microgenetic designs to study change processes. In D.M. Teti (ed.) *Handbook of Research Methods in Developmental Science* (p. 40–65). Malden, MA: John Wiley & Sons.

Mercer, S. (2015) Social network analysis and complex dynamic systems. In Z. Dörnyei, P.D. MacIntyre and A. Henry (eds) *Motivational Dynamics in Language Learning* (pp. 73–82). Bristol: Multilingual Matters.

Morin, E. (2008) *On Complexity*. Cresskill, N.J.: Hampton Press.

Nowak, A., Vallacher, R.R. and Zochowski, M. (2005) The emergence of personality: Dynamic foundations of individual variation. *Developmental Review* (25), 351–385.

Reinking, D. and Watkins, J. (2000) A formative experiment investigating the use of multimedia book reviews to increase elementary students' independent reading. *Reading Research Quarterly* 35 (3), 384–419.

Sato, T., Hidaka, T. and Fukuda, M. (2009) Depicting the dynamics of living the life: The Trajectory Equifinality Model. In J. Valsiner, P. Molenaar, M. Lyra and N. Chaudhary (eds) *Dynamic Process Methodology in the Social and Developmental Sciences* (pp. 217–240). New York: Springer.

van Geert, P. and Lichtwarck-Aschoff, A. (2005) A dynamic systems approach to family assessment. *European Journal of Psychological Assessment* 21 (4), 240–248.

Verspoor, M. (2015) Initial conditions. In Z. Dörnyei, P.D. MacIntyre and A. Henry (eds) *Motivational Dynamics in Language Learning* (pp. 38–46). Bristol: Multilingual Matters.

Subject Index

Author Index